FRONTIERSMEN *in the* WAR OF 1812

FRONTIERSMEN in the WAR OF 1812

GLEN CONNER

Acclaim Press
MORLEY, MISSOURI

Acclaim Press
— Your Next Great Book —
P.O. Box 238
Morley, MO 63767
(573) 472-9800
www.acclaimpress.com

Book Design: Devon Burroughs
Cover Design: M. Frene Melton

Library of Congress Control Number: 2014921890
ISBN-13: 978-1-938905-90-2
ISBN-10: 1-938905-90-3

First Printing 2015
Printed in the United States of America
10 9 8 7 6 5 4 3 2 1

Editor's Note: Pictured on the front is "The Battle of New Orleans, Jan. 8, 1815", a copy of an engraving by H.B. Hall (designed by W. Momberger), c. 1861, courtesy of the Library of Congress. The scene represents General Andrew Jackson, American soldiers and frontiersmen fighting behind bales of cotton beneath the American flag. The actual flag used during the war is pictured on the back cover.

CONTENTS

Preface

Some have called the War of 1812 a forgotten war but, in my case, it wasn't that I had forgotten it — it was that I had not learned about it. So I was surprised when I read the book written by Louise Horton in 1975. In her Hills of the Pennyroyal, she listed seventeen men from Allen County, Kentucky, who had served in the war of 1812. I thought it was remarkable that that number of men could have served without me knowing about them.

I had heard of an ancestor who was said to have served during that war, but he wasn't among those on the list included in that book. I began to read about the War of 1812 to see if my ancestor had actually served, and if there were other soldiers omitted from that list.

The task would be daunting. It was made difficult because the boundary lines of the county and the state underwent several changes. No compilations by the current county names had been prepared for soldiers who were listed as having served in that war. In effect, there were no answers at the back of the book.

The task was made much more difficult by a decision made shortly after the Civil War, a decision made by the Adjutant General of Kentucky himself. A very large number of pension applications and supporting documentation by veterans of the Civil War and their survivors were arriving. Available file space had been filled. To make room for these additional files, he authorized the destruction of all of the military records of Kentucky during the period 1794 to 1860. Those destroyed records included those of the famous Kentucky Cornstalk Militia, the Kentucky militia in the War of 1812, and the Mexican war. Very few of those records had duplicates that were stored elsewhere.

Unit histories, military correspondence, battle reports, rosters, rolls, and other unique Kentucky records are now nowhere to be found. The documents most valuable to this study were destroyed 150 years before this study began.

Of the sources remaining, the primary source of information about the soldiers who served during the War of 1812 was found during five visits to the National Archives and the Library of Congress in Washington, D.C. Each of those visits was for more than a week of work. The National Archives' War of 1812 service and pension records were the principal source of materials used in the study. The amount of material in those records was staggering. For example, pension files included correspondence exchanged between an applicant and the pension office in Washington. It was common for those file folders to contain scores of sheets of paper.

There were additional trips to the Kentucky Historical Society's library in Frankfort, and the Kentucky Library on the campus of Western Kentucky University. Most valuable were the files maintained in the Allen County Historical Society's library in Scottsville, Kentucky. The research materials on file that were particularly useful included accumulations by Erskine Garrison, Ray Garrison, and Arles Weaver.

The study area itself further complicated the research. It straddled the Kentucky and Tennessee border, and the frontiersmen who lived there frequently moved from state to state or county to county. Very few of them were born in Kentucky or Tennessee. Most had emigrated with their families from Virginia, North Carolina, or South Carolina to the frontier after the Revolutionary War had ended. Many moves were the result of land grants that were available. Some of the soldiers served in the War of 1812 in Virginia or North Carolina and afterward came to Kentucky. Some of the soldiers served from Kentucky or Tennessee, and subsequently moved westward to Illinois, Missouri, or other states. All such moves made research more difficult.

The first task in the research was to identify the men who served in the army or the militias. The research began at the Allen County Historical Society's library with a search through the vertical files and book collections relating to family histories. The objective of that research was to find mention of men who had served during the War of 1812. Those names were compared to the soldiers who were known to have served. The association of the name with the soldier was complicated, and very time consuming. Those efforts were sometimes frustrating because of the multiple spellings of surnames, usually caused by variant phonetic spellings made by scribes. The first names also induced frustration because of the repetition of a few common names such as William, John, and James. Frequently, first names were of little use for discerning which individual had been a soldier.

Each man who was identified as a veteran of the war was discovered only after many hours of search, one name at a time. Most of the discovery efforts failed, genealogical associations were tenuous, and only a few research efforts found or confirmed the service of a frontiersman. This book would not have been possible without the help of volunteers from the Allen County Historical Society. Among the researchers who contributed significantly to this study were Berta Sue Chambers, June Chandler, Ann Clark, Jolene Cooper, Mary Farley, Paula Goodridge, Sheila Kearney, Jewell Keen, Patty Miller, Sandy Morgan, Sharon Tabor, Joyce Walden, Arles Weaver, Joyce Weaver, Wayne Weaver, and Dixie Woodward. To them goes my thanks and deepest appreciation for their diligence in resurrecting the memory of the Kentuckians and Tennesseans who served our country so well.

The maps included in this study were produced by Kevin Cary, Director of the Geographic Information Systems (GIS) Laboratory in the Department of Geography and Geology at Western Kentucky University.

I am deeply indebted to him for his design of the maps, skillful use of the ESRI's source materials to create them, and infinite patience with my evolving requests. He developed a map layer showing creeks and rivers to form the background for most of the maps. That reminds the reader of the numerous stream crossings by troops on the move. The lack of bridges required that those soldiers wade across the streams when horses were not provided. I am proud to include his maps, each of which illustrates the places or circumstances described in the text.

Kevin Cary's GIS laboratory is the hands-on part of the B.Sc in the GIScience program at WKU where students apply what they learn. That program meets the education requirements for becoming a certified GIS professional. The maps done by Austin Boys, an undergraduate major in the Department of Geography and Geology, are examples of the skills developed by students in that program.

The frontiersmen whose stories are included in this book earned my admiration. They answered their country's call, endured continuing hardships, and earned my respect by their service. Perhaps this book will present them to readers unaware of their considerable contributions to our heritage.

FRONTIERSMEN *in the* WAR OF 1812

Chapter 1

Trouble Brewing

The Evolution of the War of 1812

Immigrants came to the frontier from Virginia and the Carolinas, and built log homes in south central Kentucky and north central Tennessee. In 1811, the area was still sparsely populated, and most days were quiet, not yet disturbed by the noise of civilization. The quiet was the result of the isolation of the new settlers in virtually every way: isolation from their neighbors, from the families they left behind, and from the activities of their government. The county seats in Bowling Green, Glasgow, and Gallatin were miles away from most citizens. There was no capability to learn in real-time what local government was doing or planning to do. The isolation of the people on the frontier precluded them from keeping abreast of the news about state and national activities that were the growing pains of a still new nation. National news, when it arrived, reported Great Britain's growing belligerence toward the United States.

The verbal conflict between the relatively new country of the United States and the old great world power of Britain was becoming more intense. At issue were actions of Britain that the Americans considered to be illegal, insulting, and intolerable. Britain was engaged in a war with France that began in 1803. Britain did not recognize the neutrality of the United States in their war, and it authorized the British navy to search and seize merchant ships that violated the blockade that it enforced. Tensions increased with the interception of American merchant ships, and anger was evident in American condemnations of those actions. The British navy captured American merchant seamen aboard those ships, and impressed them to work on British ships.[1]

The British actions occurred far away and presented no immediate threat to the settlers on the frontier in America's West, the term used for Kentucky, Tennessee, and Ohio. However, there was another concern closer to home. The British provided arms to the Shawnee leaders Tecumseh and his brother the Prophet in the Indiana Territory. Arms were also provided to other Indian tribes throughout all the Old Northwest. By extension, the British could be blamed for whatever actions that the Indians took with those arms. News of the British activities, and the potential for expanded action, roiled the belligerent stew that simmered in Kentucky and Tennessee.

Memories of the Revolutionary War were still fresh, and the notion of independence was still treasured. The soldiers of that war were attracted to the frontier by land grants awarded for their service. They brought their families and began subsistence farming. They also brought their memories of the Revolutionary War. They recounted their wartime experiences to others who were too young to remember the struggle for freedom. It seems certain that each settler had known, and had heard first hand, those stories from a friend or a relative.

The significance of the news of the British actions was amplified by the isolation of people on the frontier. It resonated in the hearts and minds of the settlers with each retelling. Frontiersmen reacted differently to incidents that were considered to be just an affront by our leaders in our nation's capital. The nuances of diplomacy were likely lost as those incidents were told and retold. The depth of the concern on the frontier would soon be evident when their states and country asked for their help. As people say, they were riled up.

Congressional View

The national leaders in Washington were, in comparative terms, much better informed than the frontiersmen. Written accounts of national and international events, and the opinions of others, were readily accessible to the citizens there. The congressmen exchanged information with their states, and with each other. They heard and read reports about international incidents in their original form. The issues were discussed and debated at length. Within Congress, the string of tolerance was being increasingly shortened. The congressmen too were getting riled up.

Henry Clay, congressman from Kentucky and speaker of the U.S. House of Representatives, was one of those who demanded action. He, and other congressmen who voiced the same demands, were known as the War Hawks. They were the ones who insisted that our new country should assert its rights as an independent nation. They were not naïve about how the British would respond, and did not expect the British to quietly accede to our desire for national equality. The War Hawks advocated war if that became necessary, and they expected that it would become so. Clay's fervor fueled the demands by Kentuckians for American military action.

Felix Grundy was another of the War Hawks. He had served as Chief Justice of the Kentucky Supreme Court before moving to Tennessee. In 1811, he was elected as a Tennessee representative to the U.S. House of Representatives, and was appointed to the Foreign Affairs committee. It was said that he loved freedom more than peace, a view no doubt shared by the other War Hawks. He had no qualms about advocating military action, and was inspirational in that regard.[2]

The President's View

President James Madison was well prepared to address the threats to the United States and the actions advocated by the War Hawks. He had gained firsthand experience while he served as secretary of state under President Thomas Jefferson. They agreed that a standing army was neither desirable nor needed to counter the minimal degree of threat of invasion posed by a foreign country. There were no perceived threats from the British Territory of Canada to the north, the Spanish territory to the west, or from the Atlantic Ocean or the Gulf of Mexico. Indeed, Madison thought that a large standing army could itself be a serious threat to our freedom. He believed that the larger the standing army, the greater their threat to an elected government. He saw less fearful power in the militias of each state because their combined strength would be greater than that of a small standing army. Thus, they would be a deterrent to a standing army if it sought to overthrow the government. He wrote his view in 1788.

"Let a regular army, fully equal to the resources of the country, be formed; and let it be entirely at the devotion of the federal government; still it would not be going too far to say, that the State governments, with the people on their side, would be able to repel the danger. The highest number to which, according to the best computation, a standing army can be carried in any country, does not exceed one hundredth part of the whole number of souls; or one twenty-fifth part of the number able to bear arms. This proportion would not yield, in the United States, an

army of more than twenty-five or thirty thousand men. To these would be opposed a militia amounting to near half a million of citizens with arms in their hands, officered by men chosen from among themselves, fighting for their common liberties, and united and conducted by governments possessing their affections and confidence. It may well be doubted, whether a militia thus circumstanced could ever be conquered by such a proportion of regular troops." [3]

The second amendment to our constitution reflects the original intent to assure the capacity of state militias to protect our nation's freedom, from without or from within. That amendment reads:

"A well regulated militia, being necessary to the security of a free state, the right of the people to keep and bear arms, shall not be infringed."

The notion of citizen soldiers in the militias is preserved in our current system in the relationship between the governor of each state and its National Guard.

The armed state militias were expected to actively and effectively deal with whatever insurrection arose within their state. The anticipation was that the militia would quickly quell any disturbance, and that the militia would only see a relatively limited period of action. If needed, an adjacent state could be invited to help hasten the quietus of an uprising.

The threat posed by Britain was an altogether different matter. It was not just a threat to an individual state, but rather threatened the entire nation. The state militias had not been established to counter an international threat. For the scale of any adequately responsive action, the standing army would have to be used.

As President Madison weighed his options for the use of military force against Britain, he relied on Secretary of State James Monroe for advice. They shared common views on limiting the establishment of a large standing army and relying instead on the state militias for most of the force needed in any confrontation that might occur.[4]

For sure, the decision to go to war against Great Britain could not be made from a position of the military strength of our standing army. That was sufficient reason for the President to resist the War Hawk's call for immediate action. The British had a military force of 250,000 men and a navy of 600 war ships compared to the United States' authorized strength of sixteen ships and a standing army of about 6,000 men. The disparity between the British standing army and the meager Army we maintained was not something that could be disregarded, no matter how the philosophical views about our army's peacetime strength might be stretched.[5]

The United States Army

After the Revolutionary War ended, there had been a clamor to reduce spending on national defense. The budget of the new republic was strained, and there was a debate on the amount of funding for the Army that was prudent.

On one side of the debate were Thomas Jefferson and his Republicans, who held a belief that the size of the military was the result of the demands from special interest groups, not on the assessed threat of foreign countries. They believed that the Army was too large, its cost too high, and the threat from foreign powers was minimal. Another argument used was that the larger the army, the more probable that we would become involved in another war.

Alexander Hamilton and his Federalists held an opposing view. They believed that a strong national defense force was necessary because peace was best assured by being prepared for war. After the Revolutionary War, the number of navy ships had been reduced to zero. The congressional Federalists, led by President John Adams, rebuilt the fleet. They increased the Army strength from a grand total of 840 men in 1789, and authorized an army of 5,438 men in 1802.[6] That was still a pitifully small number that could not deter the British.

The constitution had given all executive power to the president thus placing the secretary of war under his control, not under congressional control. As commander in chief, the president could assume command of the army if he chose to do so. Secretary of War William Eustis was not a commander, but was an administrator without very much to administer. He exercised whatever other duties the president assigned. The Army was functionally leaderless in matters of training and combat readiness.

The congressional authorization for an increase in the standing army did not assure that the strength would be actually attained. It was still short about 1,400 men when Thomas Jefferson became president.

Even the 4,000 regular Army men then on duty were too many in his view.

Thomas Jefferson and his Republicans took office in 1801 just one hundred seven days after Congress held it first session in the new Capitol in Washington, D.C. They began to disassemble the Army and Navy. They reduced defense spending, and reduced the Army strength from 5,400 to 3,300 hundred in 1802. They stopped further construction of ships for the navy, and did not fund repair or maintain the existing ones. Only seven of the sixteen ships that formed the navy in 1801 remained by the time the winds of war began to blow. Secretary of the Navy Paul Hamilton was left with practically nothing and nobody to administer.

By the end of 1811, it became abundantly clear to President Madison and to his Jeffersonian Republicans that the standing Army and Navy were incapable of executing a contemplated war with Britain. The President and his Secretary of State James Monroe knew that the standing Army was underfunded, undermanned, and lacked sufficient armament. In November 1811, there were just 414 officers and 5,194 enlisted men in the entire United States Army. It had not yet regained the strength that it had before Jefferson had made the cuts.[7]

The 414 officers of that standing army had a normal pyramidal rank structure, the higher the rank the fewer the numbers. The number of officers with significant leadership experience followed a similar structure. The critically small number of officers had an unintended consequence. It severely constrained the maintenance of its institutional memory. The experiential lessons of leadership must be shared with fellow leaders as they are learned. Knowledge in any profession must be handed down through each generation of its leaders. The collective memory of a successful organization must be greater than the memory of any individual in it. Success depended on it. Without it, leaders were military novices, and grim results in battle were predictable. Years later, a similar situation produced an appalling number of casualties in the Civil War.

The standing army's capacity to respond to Britain was severely limited. The president submitted a request for expanding its strength by 10,000 men. Congress changed that number to 25,000, and the president signed it into law on 11 January 1812. The training and experience of our regular Army were not equal to that of the British army that was manned by regular soldiers who were trained for and tested in combat. The British units had more institutional memory at every level of command.

The Militias

With a small standing army, there was a recognized necessity for additional military assets to be available when needed. That need was filled by The Militia Act of 2 May 1792 that made the state militias subject to a call to active federal duty.

> *"That whenever the United States shall be invaded, or be in imminent danger of invasion from any foreign nation or Indian tribe, it shall be lawful for the President of the United States, to call forth such number of the militia of the state or states most convenient to the place of danger or scene of action as he may judge necessary to repel such invasion, and to issue his orders for that purpose, to such officer or officers of the militia as he shall think proper; and in case of an insurrection in any state, against the government thereof, it shall be lawful for the President of the United States, on application of the legislature of such state, or of the executive (when the legislature cannot be convened) to call forth such number of the militia of any other state or states, as may be applied for, or as he may judge sufficient to suppress such insurrection."*[8]

The first part of the Act was useful during the War of 1812 as the federal government called on states to provide troops for action against Indians or the British army. The second part seems quite prescient of the Civil War that would erupt about fifty years later.

In the War of 1812, there was neither capability for nor any interest in attacks against Britain directly. The only significant possibility was to attack the sparsely populated British territory called Canada. That possibility gave rise to a second issue. Was it constitutional for a state's militia to be sent by the federal government outside of its state or into a foreign territory like that of Canada? The U.S. Constitution, Article I, Section 8, Clause 15 provided for the "calling forth the Militia to execute the Laws of the Union, suppress Insurrection, and repel Invasions." The words used were specific. The purpose was to repel an invasion, not to initiate one. Even so, there was no alternative to the primary dependence on the state militias for success if war was to be waged. That choice was not obviated by the increase in the regular army, but it would be severely tested over the next few years.[9]

There was a need for state militias to be uniform if two or more of them were to be combined to defend the nation against attack. Congress provided the solution to the problem when they passed the Militia Act on 8 May 1792. The act established detailed requirements that became the framework for the states as they organized their militias. It prescribed requirements for organization and activities as a way to assure standardization of the state militias.

It directed that an adjutant general be appointed by each state to be responsible to the governor for all of the militia's activities. The very detailed law required that, within one year after its enactment, each state would have a militia organized into divisions, brigades, regiments, battalions, and companies. It specified how each of those militia units would be organized.

That Militia Act also established the eligibility requirements for becoming a militiaman in any state.

"...that each and every free able-bodied white male citizen of the respective States, resident therein, who is or shall be of age of eighteen years, and under the age of forty-five years (except as is herein after excepted) shall severally and respectively be enrolled in the militia, by the Captain or Commanding Officer of the company, within the bounds such citizen shall reside, and that within twelve months after the passing of this Act."[10]

By the words used, those infirm, non-whites, females, or non-citizens of the state were prohibited from service in the militia. For example, all African American men, whether free or enslaved, were excluded from service in the militia. Because the militia did not include the navy, that exclusion did not apply to sailors, and as many African Americans served in the United States Navy without segregation aboard ship.

Some automatic exemptions were listed, all of which were apparently considered to be indispensable: the vice president, members of congress, all post officers, those who deliver the mail, ferrymen on post roads, and those exempted by the state. The intent seemed to be that exemptions were not intended for ordinary inconveniences.

The Militia Act also laid out the responsibilities of enrolled militiaman in great detail. It required the company commander to notify the individual when he had been enrolled. Within six months of enrollment, each militiaman was required to equip himself.

"That every citizen so enrolled and notified, shall, within six months thereafter, provide himself with a good musket or firelock, a sufficient bayonet and belt, two spare flints, and a knapsack, a pouch with a box therein to contain not less than twenty-four cartridges, suited to the bore of his musket or firelock, each cartridge to contain a proper quantity of powder and ball: or with a good rifle, knapsack, shot-pouch and powder-horn, twenty balls suited to the bore of his rifle, and a quarter of a pound of powder; and shall appear, so armed, accourtred and provided, when called out to exercise, or into service, except, that when called out on company days to exercise only, he may appear without a knapsack."[11]

The responsibility for obtaining the equipment lay with the militiaman, not the state. In effect, it required each militiaman to possess a gun. That requirement was consistent with the Second Amendment: "A well regulated militia, being necessary to the security of a free state, the right of people to keep and bear arms shall not be infringed." It was also a requirement to bear arms if the individual was a militiaman. The arms that they were both required and free to bear were their personal rifle or musket. These they would keep at home and bring with them when they met for training or were called to duty. Their personal weapons were so important that their rifle, ammunition, and accouterments were exempted from all lawsuits to reclaim debts or pay taxes. It made clear that the Second Amendment gave the civilian militiamen the right to bear arms, and the militia act required them to provide those arms.

The act established the organizational hierarchy for the state militias, and required the companies to call out their men to exercise their military skills. Each state, including Kentucky and Tennessee, responded to the act by establishing its Militia.

Kentucky's militia was authorized by the Militia Act of 24 June 1792 to enroll free men between the ages of eighteen and forty-five years. Subsequently, exemptions within the limits imposed by the congressional act were made inter alia for ministers, judges, post office workers, and people who repaired or manufactured firearms. The governor determined the boundaries for the enrollment areas for each regiment.

The areas were changed as new counties were created. In Kentucky in 1804, the 45th Regiment's area encompassed Barren County, and the 25th Regiment was formed for Warren County. Company musters of each regiment were required four times between 31 May and 30 September of each year, and regimental musters were to be held each October. The fall regimental muster gave rise to the term "Corn Stalk Militia," a name descriptive of their drills using dead corn stalks instead of guns.[12]

Tennessee became a state in 1796, and its statehood came with the requirement for a militia. Its Militia had been formed even earlier when it was needed to react to the Shawnees when the area was still part of North Carolina. In 1801, Andrew Jackson was appointed as commander of the Tennessee Militia. The Tennessee Militia was already preparing for the eventuality of the war with Britain when hostilities resumed with the Creek Indians.[13]

Military Unit Designations

The variations in the titles of army units and the inconsistency in the use of those titles make war history confusing. Each was supposed to indicate the composition of the unit, and the term of commitment of its members. As a practical matter, the original meanings eroded somewhat over the years. There were four descriptors used in the titles given to the soldiers who fought in the war. Among the following four descriptors, the use of regular and militia were the most common.

Regular

Regular was the descriptor given to a soldier in the United States Army. Generally, the regulars enlisted for a period of from one to five years. Some enlisted for an indefinite period, such as for the duration of the war. These troops were professionals, to use that term loosely. They were uniformed, trained, and disciplined soldiers whose experience built with each passing month. For example, the 44th U.S. Infantry Regiment had two years of combat experience behind them by the time when they fought in the Battle of New Orleans. They had by then accumulated a considerably expansive institutional memory.

U.S. Volunteers

The U.S. Volunteers were soldiers who were not in the regular army but served in special units or augmented regular units. Those men enlisted at the beginning of the war and only a few such soldiers had that designation.

Militias

Each state had military units called militia that the state's governor could call upon to defend itself from attacks from either within or without. The Jeffersonian policy was still in effect that restricted the use of the militias by the federal government. Later, that clause was quoted when some Pennsylvania Militia units refused to cross over into Canada because such action did not fit under any of the three acceptable uses of the Militia. President Jefferson's idea of limiting the federal use of militias was being tested.

The militiamen were called to duty for short duration periods of service. Typically, they served for three or six months. The soldiers went home when that commitment was satisfied. Needless to say, the turnover of militiamen every three months allowed for little continuity of action. Commanders had to take care to assure that terms of enlistment did not expire in the middle of an expedition or battle. Looking back, we have difficulty understanding the rationale of self-imposed limitations like those.

With few exceptions, the men who joined the militia had recently walked to the frontier from Virginia, North Carolina, or South Carolina. Most of the younger men came with their parents and had families who depended on them to help carve a homestead out of the forest.

What motivated the frontiersmen to become militiamen? It would have been easy to think of reasons not to respond to the call to serve. There was no immediate threat from either the Indians or the British. The British were no closer than the Gulf Coast or the Great Lakes. Indian raids on new settlers were relatively far north and far south. The militia was for local eventualities for which preparations were made but real threats were neither immediate nor near. The militiamen seldom met, were untrained by today's standards, but their patriotism was never questioned.

Volunteer Militia

Some militia units were formed for a specific mission and the militiamen enlisted for a specific length of service. The specific mission assigned to them had to be completed within that enlistment time limit. For example, militiamen from our area rendezvoused with others to form the 11th Kentucky Volunteers, marched to and invaded Canada, fought the Battle of the Thames, completed their enlistment, were discharged, and were back home in just over ninety days (Chapter 6).

Military Strength During the War

The number of men who served in the War of 1812 was difficult to calculate. Soldiers might serve more than one stint, and thus be counted twice. It was common for the stint of service to be a month, three months, six months, or a year. Many soldiers served two or three stints and therefore may have been counted once for each stint. The totals could, as a result, be inflated over the number of actual individuals who served. One estimate of totals was made by the Third Auditor's Report to the Secretary of War in 1858. His estimate is shown in Table 1.[14]

Regular Army (includes about 5,000 sailors and marines)	56,032
Volunteers	10,110
Rangers	3,049
Militia	458,463
Total	527,463

Table 1. Number of soldiers who served in the army during the War of 1812.

The authorized number of regular army soldiers available in 1811 was roughly 6,000 men. By the end of the war, there would be ten times that many. But, in the beginning, the discussions about whether to declare war on Britain occurred with full knowledge that the outcome would depend mostly on the militias. That knowledge does not appear to have caused great concern among the legislators in Washington.

The frontier militiamen of the War of 1812 resembled the minutemen of the Revolutionary War in many ways. The soldiers in both were poorly trained, poorly equipped, and relatively undisciplined. On the other hand, they were similar in that the call for duty was answered with patriotism, allegiance, and honorable service. They were in demand for their unmatched skill with long rifles, and were welcomed into combat units.

Congress and the president continued to debate the advisability of a declaration of war against Britain. Meanwhile, the situation in the Indiana Territory continued to deteriorate as the Indians sought ways to stem the flow of settlers into their areas.

Dispossession of the Indians from the lands they had occupied for eons began with the first settlement in what whites called the "new world." To the Indians, the settlement at Jamestown must have been seen as a small and innocuous intrusion into a vast land. It would have been difficult for them to imagine the relatively rapid expansion that was about to occur, one that would threaten their very existence.

The settlers came from Europe with a different outlook. In their eyes, the virgin forest was an endless expanse of opportunities. The most important opportunity for them was to own land. Land ownership was the mark of economic success, and was rewarded with cultural prestige. Ownership was both the motivation for making the trip to the new world, and the objective that drove them to succeed.

With success came the acquisition of more land that in turn required more labor. Land became a commodity to be traded, sometimes in exchange for labor. Land speculation became an opportunity to expand one's holdings. As the settlements became more numerous, and the population rose, the need for land increased.

After the American Revolution, the United States awarded land grants on the frontier west of the Appalachians. The availability of that "free" land was irresistible, and the population on the frontier rose rapidly. Indians, who previously occupied the "free" land, were dispossessed to make it available for settlement. In general, the Indians were pushed farther and farther west, and the population pressure imposed by new settlements caused the process to be repeated. The quo in the Indian status quo was being inexorably erased.

By 1811, the Indians had gained renewed support from the British to help stem the tide of settlement. The resistance to the encroachment of white settlers was strengthening, and confrontations became increasingly frequent in the Old Northwest.

Chapter 2

The Tipping Point

The Battle of Tippecanoe

A portion of the Old Northwest Territory was renamed the Indiana Territory on 4 July 1800. William Henry Harrison was appointed by President John Adams to be governor of the new Territory, and moved to Vincennes, the territorial capital. He occupied Fort Knox that had been built there a short time before. Fort Knox was the most strategically important outpost because it was the westernmost army fort on the frontier. It was nearest to the threats to settlers who were immigrating into the area from the east. Captain Zackary Taylor, who like Governor Harrison, would become president in later years, commanded the army troops at the fort.

Many issues confronted Governor Harrison as he arrived to begin his duties as governor, but none were more vexing than the challenges presented by Tecumseh, the famous Shawnee leader. The Shawnee had supported the British during the Revolutionary War, and continued to receive support from them afterward. Tecumseh was already an accomplished leader and statesman with great powers of persuasion. He recognized that a confederation of the numerous tribes in the Indiana Territory would offer more concerted actions, and more success in slowing the incursion of settlers. He met with Governor Harrison in July 1811, and demanded that the land purchases by the U.S. Government from individual Indian Tribes should be rescinded because, in his view, they had been made under coercion. Harrison rejected his demands. Tecumseh issued a warning that he would ally with the British if his demands continued to be rejected. The die was cast, and both adversaries contemplated possible military actions.

The British had continued to support their Indian allies after the Revolutionary War ended. They provided food, guns, and ammunition as needed, and that obligated the Indians to continue to support them in return. Americans believed that the subsequent attacks against settlers who moved into the Territories of Indiana and Illinois had tacit approval by the British. More intolerable was that the British were supporting Indian action in territories of the United States, a separate and equal nation. They were interfering in internal matters of the United States. The national sovereignty of the relatively new nation was being threatened.

Tenskwatawa, more commonly known as the Prophet, increased his influence as the spiritual leader of the Shawnee. His brother, Tecumseh, was the military leader. Both were concerned about the increasing encroachment of white settlers into Shawnee land in the Indiana Territory. The Prophet was opposed to any and all assimilation into the white culture. He followed through on his denouncements, and initiated efforts to restore abandoned Shawnee customs that had been followed by their ancestors.[1]

Governor Harrison of the Indiana Territory became more demanding in negotiations with the Indians to obtain more land concessions. As the tensions rose, Tecumseh sought agreements among the Indians for them to act as a single Indian nation thereby strengthening their effectiveness. The Indians became more and more intolerant of the expanding areas of white settlements, and reacted with depredations that brought tensions to new levels.

Harrison asked for and received authority from Washington to gather troops sufficient to assert control over the deteriorating situation. He raised about one thousand troops in the fall of 1811. He developed a plan to go to Prophetstown, a village built by the Prophet at the confluence of the Wabash and Tippecanoe Rivers. There he would make demands that most assuredly would not be acceptable to the Shawnee spiritual leader. One of those demands was that all tribes had to be notified that any tribe that affiliated with the Shawnee would be considered to be hostile, as would any individual who participated with the Shawnee band.[2]

When Harrison received word that several disparate groups of Indians were gathering in Prophetstown, he decided to implement his plan. He knew that Tecumseh had gone south to gain support from the Creeks and Choctaws for his notion of an Indian nation, and would not be present to lead the Indians. Tecumseh's absence may have made Harrison less cautious about beginning his incursion into Indian dominated and controlled lands.[3]

The March North

Harrison's force consisted of about 910 men, a large number intended to assure success. The force consisted of about 250 regulars, about sixty Kentucky volunteers, and about 600 volunteers from the Indiana Territory. He departed Fort Knox at Vincennes on 26 September, and marched northward along the east side of the Wabash. Supply boats were being poled upstream on the Wabash River. Harrison adjusted his pace with that of the boats to assure protection of the supplies they carried.

Harrison halted the march at a point about two miles north of where the city of Terre Haute, Indiana now stands. As was the custom, he put the men to work building a fort to be used as a supply depot. It would become a forward outpost that could support his current and future plans to dominate the area. The new fort (Figure 1) could also be used as a refuge in case his operation met unexpectedly strong resistance that required withdrawal.

Figure 1. Fort Harrison in 1812.[4]

The fort was a square, 150 by 150 feet inside the walls. It had two-story corner blockhouses that provided an unobstructed view in all directions. There was room in the barracks for about 1,000 men. The construction was completed on 28 October, and the fort was christened Fort Harrison. More supplies arrived that day from Vincennes escorted by additional Kentucky volunteers. Harrison resumed his march northward after the construction of the fort was completed.

The army travelled through the forest until it reached the area where the Wabash River curved to a more westerly direction. At that point, there was a change to a dramatically different landscape from the forest through which they had been traversing. There was a transition area from the forest to a tall grass prairie. The prairie offered easier travel, and a reduced threat of ambush compared to continued travel through the woods. Some of the prairie had recently been burned.[5] Figure 2 shows the Indiana Territory as it was in 1812.

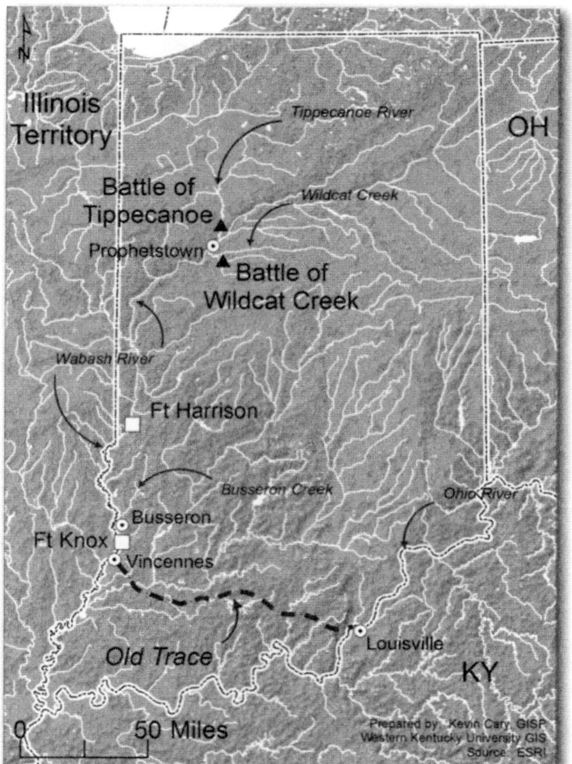

Figure 2. The Indiana Territory 1812.

On 31 October, Harrison crossed the river near where the current town of Montezuma, Indiana, is located. His force then moved along the west side of the Wabash, and reached a point about three miles south of the confluence of the Wabash and Vermillion Rivers. There he stopped on 2 November to build another fort. This one was smaller than that at Fort Harrison, only twenty-five by twenty-five feet square. It was named Fort Boyd after Colonel John Boyd, Harrison's second in command. The primary use of Fort Boyd was to store supply boats. The next day they crossed the Vermillion River, and continued toward Prophetstown.[6]

They reached a point occupied by the present day town of Montmorenci by nightfall on 5 November. They had covered about seventy miles during the previous six days, roughly eleven miles or so per day. For sure, they had not dawdled along the way.

When they resumed the march toward Prophetstown on 6 November, the infantrymen placed their backpacks on the supply wagons. They encountered three Indians as they moved along a relatively wide road. The Indians asked the purpose of the march toward their village, and declared that the Prophet wished to avoid hostilities. They suggested that a meeting be held with the Prophet on the following day in Prophetstown.[7]

Harrison's troops stopped about one and a half miles short of Prophetstown and prepared their camp where they would await the meeting scheduled for the next day. He chose to encamp on about ten acres of high ground, and deployed his men in a triangle with the apex pointing toward the southwest. That defensive posture indicated the level of Harrison's trepidation about the Prophet's intent, feelings no doubt shared by his troops. He ordered his men to sleep within a few feet of the anticipated battle lines along the sides of the triangle, with their weapons within reach. The regulars slept in uniform and in tents. The militiamen had no tents and slept fully clothed on the ground. The horses, wagons, and baggage were placed in the center of the triangle. The army also brought cattle with them as was customary, a kind of "meals on wheels" of that day one might say. The cattle were held in the center area of the triangle too (Figure 3).[8]

The Attack

As feared, the Prophet did not wait for next day's meeting. Instead, he sent a collection of Kickapoos, Winnebagoes, and Potawatomis to attack the encamped soldiers in the predawn hours of 7 November.[9] Private John Tipton of the Indiana Territory Militia wrote that the battle began "at precisely 15 minutes before 5 in the morning" and that the battle lasted "for two hours and 20 minutes."[10] The combat raged as the Indians fired their guns, and charged to engage hand to hand with war clubs, tomahawks, and knives.[11] The initial attack was against the 4th U.S. Infantry Regiment, a regular army unit. The line of regulars held. Other attacks engaged the Kentucky militiamen and they, too, held. However, they absorbed casualties perhaps because they had been silhouetted against the light from the campfires behind them.

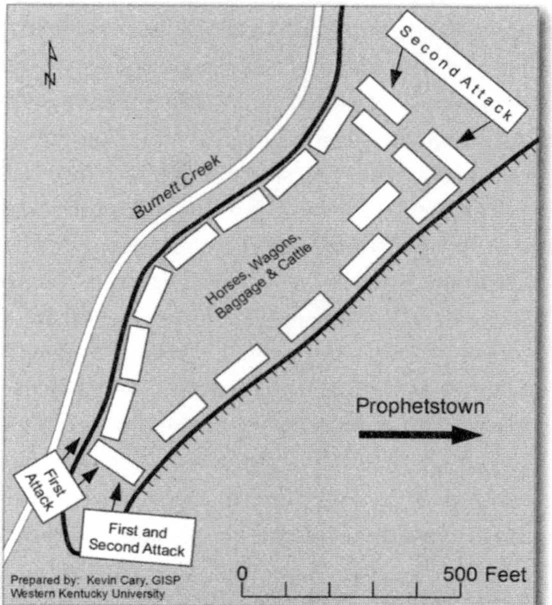

Figure 3. The battlefield on 7 November 1811.

When daylight came, six companies charged, and drove the Indians back toward a swampy area. The Indians withdrew from the battlefield, and the battle was over. Of the about 1,000 men in Harrison's army, thirty-seven were killed and 151 were wounded. Nine of those wounded men died before the return march began. An additional sixteen of the wounded would die with the next week and a half. They found the bodies of about forty Indians on the battlefield, and more may have been killed. During the following day, the troops buried their comrades, and tried to camouflage the burial site by burning logs over the graves.[12]

The Aftermath

A mounted force was sent to Prophetstown the day after the battle. The village was deserted, but they found that the Indians' food supply was still there. They took the beans, corn, hogs, and some chickens before they torched the village. They returned to camp with their booty, a welcomed sight to the hungry soldiers. The cattle that the army had brought with them had fled during the battle and the men had resorted to eating boiled horsemeat. One could safely assume that the choice arose from hunger rather than from preference.

Harrison's army left camp on 9 November, and headed back south retracing their approach route. The wounded were placed on the wagons, and the entire force made their way back to Fort Boyd. There they loaded the most severely wounded onto boats for the trip downstream on the Wabash River to Fort Harrison. The remaining troops marched overland, and arrived at Fort Harrison on 15 November. A company of regular troops was left there to guard and maintain the fort. The remainder of the troops continued the march back to Vincennes.[13]

They arrived at Fort Knox in Vincennes, tired and weary after having marched over 300 miles during their foray. The militia troops were discharged on the 17th and went home. The entire mission had taken just fifty-three days, but it resounded with the War Hawks and others who blamed the British for arming, and some thought inciting, the Indian resistance. The War of 1812 had not yet officially begun, and what lay ahead was unknown. Yet, all knew that nothing had been resolved, and that the future was not brightened by thoughts of peace.

Congressional Reaction

It was clear to everyone that Britain was fomenting violent actions by the Indians in the Old Northwest by providing them with arms and other support. The British were accused of using the Indians in the same way they had used the Hessians during the Revolutionary War, as mercenaries. That was a poor analogy because the Indians were not mercenary; they had real concerns and self interests in their desire to force an end to the loss of their lands to white settlements. Nevertheless, Britain's role was subversive, and they stood to gain by an Indian insurrection. Congress focused on that role, agreed that it was intolerable, but debated about the proper reaction.

In December, the House Foreign Relations committee recommended increasing the size of the regular army, arming our merchant ships, and repairing warships no longer in service. Resentment of congressional inaction rose higher in Kentucky during the following months.

In April, the House of Representatives passed a sixty-day embargo on American shipping as a prelude to a declaration of war. The Senate extended it to ninety days, and Kentuckians fumed.

Finally on 1 June, President Madison asked Congress to declare war on Britain. Congress was not of one mind about taking such an irrevocable step, and the vote showed its reluctance. The act passed seventy-nine to forty-nine in the House of Representatives on 4 June 1812. The vote revealed considerably regionalized differences among the congressmen. The Connecticut, Rhode Island, and Delaware representatives were unanimously opposed to going to war. A plurality of the Massachusetts, New York, and New Jersey delegations also voted against the declaration. The opposition was from a cluster of states in the northeast, and no doubt reflected the attitudes of their constituents.

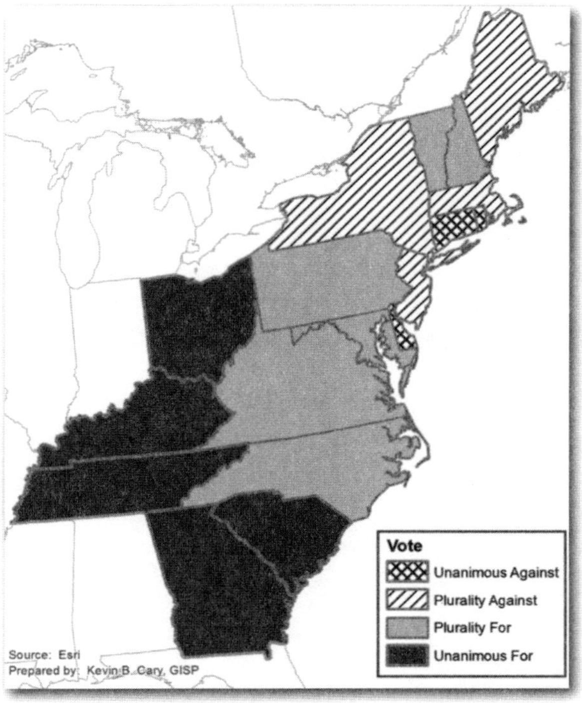

Figure 4. House of Representatives Vote on Declaration of War.

Support for the declaration was also clustered. In the far northeast, support came from Vermont and New Hampshire. A plurality of representatives in those states, and in Maryland, Pennsylvania, North

Carolina, and Virginia voted for it. The congressmen from Ohio, Kentucky, Tennessee, Georgia, and South Carolina voted unanimously in favor of the declaration. The unanimous support came from those contiguous states that were on the frontier where the threat of British supported Indian raids were most immediate and greatest. Kentucky and Tennessee had broad strong support for the war from their citizens (Figure 4).

On the 17th, the Senate voted nineteen to thirteen to concur. Henry Clay of Kentucky signed as speaker of the house and, on the following day, President James Madison signed the declaration (Figure 5). The persistence of the War Hawks, Henry Clay and Felix Grundy among others, had paid off. The United States was at war. The emphasis was about to shift from battles with the Indians to battles with the British.[14]

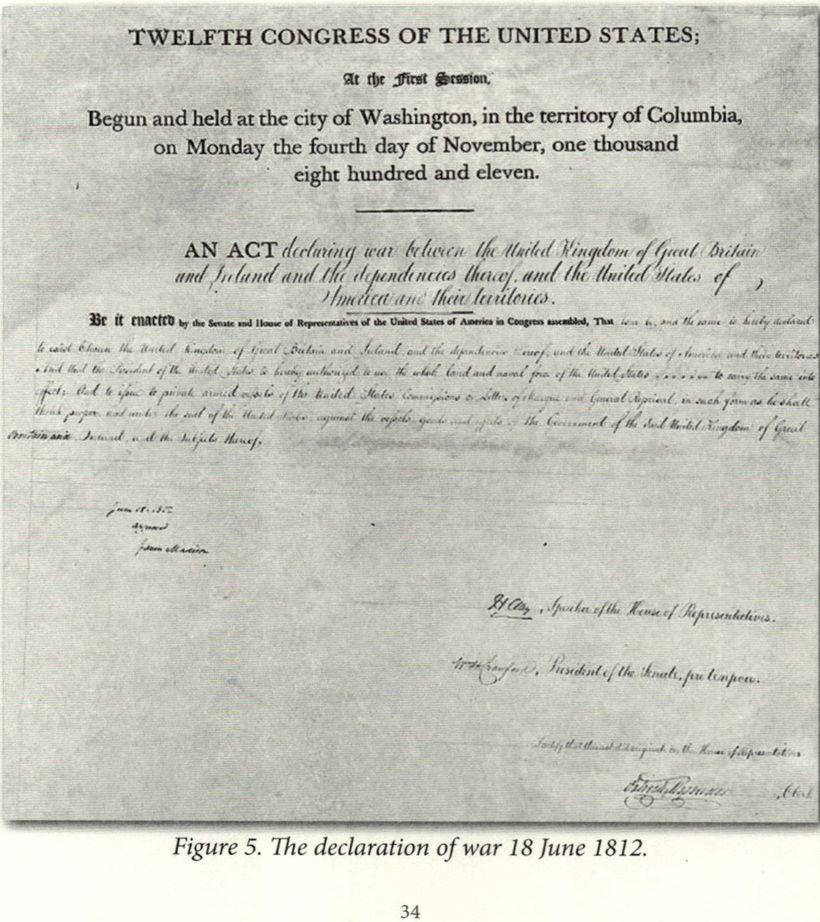

TWELFTH CONGRESS OF THE UNITED STATES;

At the First Session,

Begun and held at the city of Washington, in the territory of Columbia, on Monday the fourth day of November, one thousand eight hundred and eleven.

AN ACT declaring war between the United Kingdom of Great Britain and Ireland and the dependencies thereof, and the United States of America and their territories.

Be it enacted by the Senate and House of Representatives of the United States of America in Congress assembled, That

Speaker of the House of Representatives.

President of the Senate, pro tempore.

Figure 5. The declaration of war 18 June 1812.

The news was a surprise to some citizens who had expected some diplomatic success instead of the declaration of war. Kentuckians celebrated the decision with cheers and gunfire. On the other hand, some people were unhappy about the declaration. In New England, bells rang and flags were lowered to half-staff in protest.

Debate resumed in Congress but the Republican majority used parliamentary rules to thwart Federalist efforts by cutting off debate, using secret planning sessions, and not allowing proposals to come to a vote. Their view was that war had been declared and the time for debate was past. The Federalists believed that the declaration had been rushed and passed without sufficient consideration of the consequences. The Federalist view strengthened when the plans for invasion of Canada became known.[15] The word of the beginning of the War of 1812 arrived in the frontier and the following Fourth of July celebrations were more exuberant than ever before.

Meanwhile, it was clear that the British did not need nor want another war. They had been fully engaged in Europe against Napoleon. Napoleon had seized power in France in late 1799 and the war with Britain began in 1803. The United States had adopted a strategy of neutrality in the war between Britain and France.

The British did not understand the rationale for American neutrality in their war with Napoleon. After all, it was America that espoused freedom and deplored tyranny. Britain was committed to defeating Napoleon's effort to subjugate Europe. The British viewed as incongruous the United States' continued trade with a France that sought domination of Europe. It needed the United States to stop its trade with France and to continue its trade with Britain. They believed that it would stop.[16] The very last thing Britain needed was a war with the United States. They did not believe that a war would happen because it would, in effect, place the United States on the side of France.

No matter the beliefs, the war with Britain had officially begun, and those wishing for military action had little time to wait.

Chapter 3

Ignominious Beginning

Early Battles in the Old Northwest

President Madison had anticipated how the war would be fought once the official declaration was made. He had few options. There were far too few ships in the Navy that had virtually no capability to affect the outcome of the war. The president had only three viable options for invading the Canada Territory, his only choice for land action against the British. One prong of his plan was to strike from the Lake Champlain areas toward Montreal. The other two prongs offered what seemed to be better opportunities (Figure 6).

The second prong was to cross between Lake Erie and Ontario. The third was to cross between Lakes Huron and Erie. The latter area of Upper Canada, as it was called, was less well populated. It was defended by a small number of British regular army soldiers and militia supported by a large number of Indians under Tecumseh. It was the area that the president thought to be most promising of the three prongs of attack.

The president developed a plan for a decisive first action to be initiated immediately after war was declared. To be the first to attack, and to do it with overwhelming force, was President Madison's intent. Military planners still prefer that type of plan. The quaint statement, incorrectly attributed to the Confederate cavalry commander Nathan Bedford Forrest during the Civil War, was to get there "fustest with the mostest." The president's plan was an early, but extremely limited version of what would many years later be the World War II blitzkrieg and Iraq War's shock and awe. President Madison's plan had little chance to be as successful as he envisioned. The limited communication capability between the widely separated prongs made coordination of the efforts problematic at best. There was little hope that the prongs would work in concert.

It seems strange to us that the president, even as the commander in chief, was a military planner in this war. However, there was little precedent for who the planners of military actions should be, what actions should be planned, what those plans should contain, and how they should be implemented. There was no commanding general of the army during the War of 1812, but rather a weak facsimile of one. President Madison appointed Henry Dearborn on 27 January 1812, gave him the title of Senior Officer of the Army, and gave him the rank of Major General. He was a combat veteran of the Revolutionary War who fought at Bunker Hill, Valley Forge, and Yorktown. He left the army at the end of that conflict. Dearborn was the first of those appointed as Senior Officers of the Army to be provided with a General Staff. The General Staff would subsequently evolve to have the principal war planning responsibilities under a Commanding General of the Army. Those responsibilities would not be assigned until 1821. The evolution of a staff to do military planning was completed too late to have much impact on the strategies for the War of 1812.

Figure 6. Two possible avenues of attack into the Canada Territory.

Former President Thomas Jefferson had appointed William Hull as Governor of the Michigan Territory in 1805. President Madison met with Hull in Washington, and outlined his plan to invade Upper Canada as the third prong of attack. The president intended to obtain volunteers from the Ohio Militia to build the army needed to do it.

Hull was not very enthusiastic about the plan. He knew that Upper Canada was sparsely settled, and that local foraging for supplies in that area would not likely suffice. There would certainly not be enough contribution to obviate the need for supply lines that would stretch over hundreds of miles into Ohio. The British controlled Lake Erie, and water transport of supplies was not a possible option. Therefore, the supply line would have to be overland, and through the northern part of Ohio that was still populated by Indians. Many of them were considered to be hostile. The bigger problem was that the overland road capable of becoming such a supply route did not exist. It would have to be built.

The president offered Hull the rank of Brigadier General and command of the entire assault force, including one regiment of the regular army. One can imagine that it would be difficult to reject a request from any president, particularly one that involved military action within your own territory, and one that would directly affect your own citizens. Hull's skepticism about the odds of success remained. He was not persuaded, and he declined the offer.

A few days later, the president discussed the plan with Hull again, and renewed the offer. That time the governor accepted. He was by then fifty-nine years old, and would have been considered by most to be too old for military duty. Major General Hull departed for the Old Northwest with the understanding that, as soon as he had official notification of the declaration of war, he would invade Upper Canada.

On 5 April 1812, Ohio Governor Meigs ordered volunteers from his militia to rendezvous at Dayton to join Hull's army. About 1,200 Ohioans responded. They met their new commander at Urbana, and became part of his army that already had 300 regulars assigned. The first task for the new army was to build a 200-mile supply road through the forests and swamps of northern Ohio to Detroit in the Michigan Territory. The road was necessary because none of the concerns expressed by Hull to the president had been resolved. In particular, the British still controlled Lake Erie, and that precluded transport of supplies by boats.[1]

Whatever excitement the militiamen may have had when they volunteered soon dissipated when they learned that their task was road building. Most found that assignment to be particularly unexciting as the weeks of work continued. It was very hard work clearing a road through the forests, improving fords across streams, and laying puncheons across swampy land. They completed forty miles, and reached Kenton on 16 June. They continued the work, and arrived in what is now Toledo on 30 June. They continued working their way toward Detroit.[2]

The president had signed the declaration of war on 18 June 1812. The British in Upper Canada officially learned on 28 June that a state of war with the United States existed, and that they should expect the aggressors to attack. However, the official word did not reach Hull until 2 July as he was nearing Detroit. Three days later, his troops completed the extension of the road to Detroit, and preparations for the invasion began.

The British received intelligence that Hull's army was gathering in Detroit, and sent additional troops to Fort Malden to beef up their defense. Hull's army crossed the Detroit River that connects Lake St. Clair with Lake Erie into Upper Canada on 12 July (Figure 7).

Battle of Detroit

Hull sent scouts south to reconnoiter Fort Malden just eighteen miles away while his 1,200 men waited. He dallied by waiting for his heavy guns to be rafted across the river. Meanwhile, he tried to convince the Canadians to join the American effort. Although many of the Upper Canadians had migrated from what subsequently became the United States, it was a futile attempt at conversion. All Canadian men between eighteen and sixty were required to serve in their militia. The Upper Canada arm of that militia was the Incorporated Militia of Upper Canada. They would be defending their homeland from invasion by United States, and support of the Americans would be treasonous.[3]

Hull received two bits of alarming news: Fort Mackinac had been captured in northern part of the Michigan Territory on 17 July, and Fort Malden in Upper Canada was being reinforced with additional British troops. After a month of dithering and military inactivity, Hull made the decision to withdraw back across the river to Fort Detroit without having fought a battle. The third prong of President Madison's plan had not been successfully executed.

The withdrawal began on 8 August. Hull sent his regulars south to bring back supplies carried by seventy packhorses and a herd of 300 cattle that were at the River Raisin. Colonel Brock's British force from Fort Malden occupied the Sandwich area (now Windsor) across the river from Fort Detroit within the next week. During that time, the American regulars engaged a British force on the 9th, and returned having retrieved neither the supplies nor the cattle. To add to the dilemma, Brock allowed a fake document to fall into American hands that convinced Hull that he was facing thousands of Indians.[4]

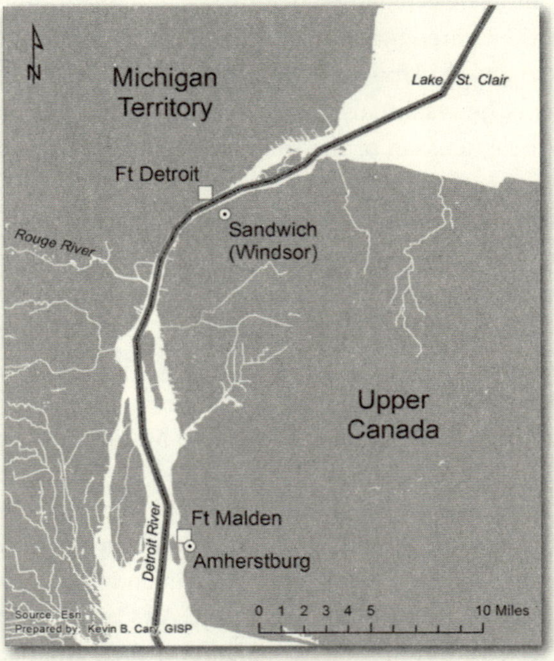

Figure 7. The area of Hull's invasion of Upper Canada.

Brock asked Hull to surrender on the 15th, but Hull immediately refused. The British artillery opened fire on the fort from across the river, and was joined by fire from two British ships on the river. The American shore battery returned fire. The next day, Brock's force of about 1,330 British troops and about 600 Indians crossed the river, and were positioned for an assault on the fort. On Sunday morning, the bombardment began again. The first shell exploded within the fort and killed two men. The second shell wounded a doctor and another killed two others. This time, Hull was decisive. He gave orders to his artillery to cease firing, and directed that a white tablecloth be raised on the flagpole as a sign of surrender.[5]

Surrender negotiations lasted less than two hours before Hull acquiesced to the surrender terms. Afterward, Brock and Tecumseh entered the fort, lowered the flag of the United States, and ran up the Union Jack. Everything and everyone was surrendered: the soldiers, including the ones not present at the fort; their equipment consisting of thirty cannons, 300 rifles, and 2,500 muskets; their supplies; and the some 800 citizens of Detroit, including Hull's wife and children.[6] The Americans lost seven men killed before Hull surrendered 2,423 men. The British casualties were just two men wounded.

The 1,600 Ohio militiamen were paroled to go home. The 582 American regulars were marched to Quebec City to prisoner of war camps. Major General William Hull was later paroled, and in 1814 faced a court martial. Hull had once led bayonet charges at Bunker Hill, survived Valley Forge, and led men into the Battle of Monmouth during the Revolutionary War. Now he faced charges of treason, cowardice, neglect of duty, and un-officer like conduct during a mission about which he had misgivings from the beginning. The presiding officer was his immediate superior officer, Major General Henry Dearborn who was the president's senior army officer. Hull was convicted of all charges except for treason, and sentenced to be shot. President Madison, who had given him the invasion plan, approved his conviction, but remitted the execution. Hull was dishonorably discharged the next day.[7] All army officers have the opportunity to perform well or poorly; commanders can only be right or wrong.

Charles Scott, the outgoing Governor of Kentucky, received word of Hull's precarious position and statements of need for additional troops in the Old Northwest. Scott was also dissatisfied with the federally appointed Major General James Winchester who was the overall commander of the Old Northwest army. He called a meeting for 25 August 1812 to address both issues.

The invitees were the incoming Governor Isaac Shelby, former Governor Christopher Greenup, Henry Clay, Supreme Court Justice Thomas Todd, General Samuel Hopkins, and U.S. Congressman Richard M. Johnson. All of them were already in Frankfort for the inauguration of Shelby. They reached an agreement that the Kentucky contribution should be increased from 2,000 to 3,400 militiamen, and that William Henry Harrison should be appointed to command them. His appointment presented a problem.

The state constitution required that only a citizen of the Kentucky could command the Kentucky militia. They circumvented that rule by giving Harrison a brevet (temporary) commission rather than a regular one. They agreed that Harrison should lead all the armed forces in the Old Northwest in place of Winchester who was in charge of them at that time. The incoming Governor Shelby lobbied President Madison and Secretary of State Monroe to concur.[8]

News of the humiliating defeat at Detroit and capture of most of the army in the Old Northwest reached the newly inaugurated Governor of Kentucky, Isaac Shelby. He recognized that Kentuckians were essentially the only militiamen available to repulse the British and regain military control over the Old Northwest. On 8 September, he announced that Harrison had been appointed to command Kentucky militiamen in the field. Eventually, the president agreed, and officially made Harrison the commander of all troops in the area. Winchester remained as a subordinate regimental commander.

Henry Clay had once said with pride that the Kentucky Militia alone could conquer Canada. Kentucky militiamen were not present at Fort Detroit when it fell, but Clay's confidence would soon be tested.

The Hopkins Foray

Action was underway to reinforce Harrison's army in the Indiana Territory. For that purpose, the 3rd Regiment Kentucky Detached Militia was formed on 1 September 1812 with Lieutenant Colonel Nicholas Miller as commander and Major Benjamin Shacklette as the ranking officer on his staff. The regiment had 714 officers and men. Local frontiersmen rendezvoused with them in Bowling Green on 24-25 August 1812, and went north to Louisville. From there they marched toward Fort Harrison in Vincennes to join the forces at the fort.

Indians attacked Fort Harrison on the night of 4 September while the Kentuckians were still en route. The fort's small contingent of the regular army's 7th Infantry under Captain Zackary Taylor fought all night and put out the fires the Indians set. The attack continued for ten more nights and eleven more days. When a relief force arrived on 16 September, they found that all the men were exhausted, and many were sick with fever. The Indians had taken the livestock from the Fort. Three of Captain Taylor's men had been killed, and three others wounded during the siege.[9] There were several thrusts and parries over the next month, all seemingly orchestrated by Tecumseh.

Governor Shelby asked for 2,000 volunteers to join Major General Samuel Hopkins with the objective of going into Indian Territory, and destroying the food supplies of those followers of Tecumseh. The Governor did not wait for federal authority to act, but rather acted in anticipation of approval. His decision had unintended consequences. First, without authority from the U.S. Army, he could not enlist the militiamen for longer than thirty days. Second, the soldiers would have to supply their own horse, arms, tomahawks, and blankets because the state had none to provide. Even so, Kentuckians responded to the call and the first of them began arriving at Vincennes (Figure 8) on 21 September.[10]

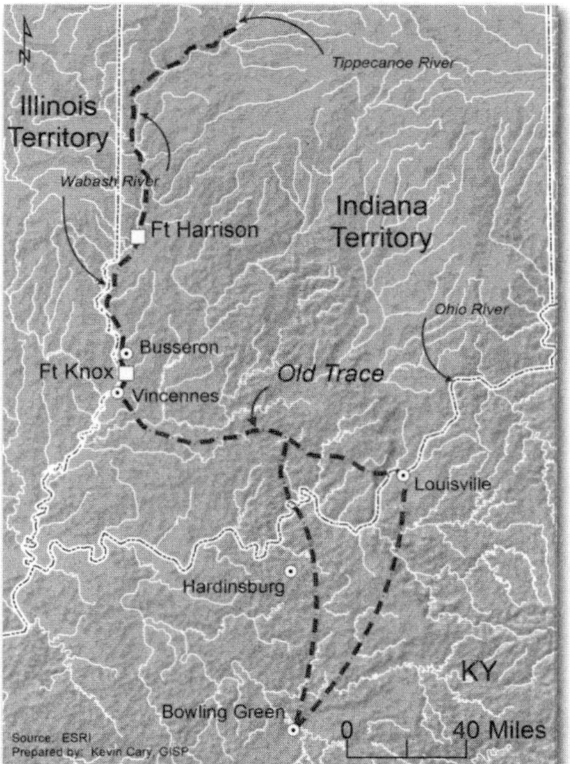

Figure 8. The route taken by Hopkins' troops.

The last of those militiamen arrived at Fort Harrison on 13 October without the fervor they had felt when they volunteered. The horseback ride of over 200 miles had left them weary, had dampened their spirits, and had buffed away their excited anticipation. A few days of rest would have been welcomed, but there was to be no respite. The very next morning, they mounted again, and rode out as part of a large force led by Major General Hopkins.[11]

They rode northward along the Wabash with the intent to destroy the Kickapoo and Peoria villages along the Illinois River. They rode about 120 miles during the next five days as they unsuccessfully searched for the villages. There were neither maps available nor specific directions of how to find the villages. There must have been a developing suspicion that the futility of their effort was the result of incompetence. The tired, demoralized, and recalcitrant troops demanded that they return to Vincennes. In an effort to compromise, Hopkins asked for 500 men to volunteer to continue the mission for another day. No one responded and the entire force returned to Vincennes.[12] A prairie fire, set by the Indians they could not find, hastened the pace of their withdrawal.[13] The mission ended with troop morale at its nadir.

The Kentucky militiamen in Hopkins' force were discharged when they arrived at Vincennes on 25 October. [14] Table 2 shows the names of the soldiers from our study area known to have participated in Hopkins' aborted campaign. Biographical sketches of these men are in Chapter 11.

Rank	Name
Capt	Hugh Brown
Ens	Andrew J. Walker
Trumpeter	Andrew J. Walker
Pvt	Larkin Garrett
Pvt	John Pullom
Pvt	Michael Hatler

Table 2. Some of the frontiersmen who were in Hopkins' force.

Second Battle of Tippecanoe (Battle of Wild Cat Creek)

At Vincennes, Hopkins organized another force of about 1,250 men from three regiments of newly arrived Kentucky militiamen. These were the regiments commanded by Lieutenant Colonels Barbour, Wilcox, and Miller. Lieutenant Colonel Miller's Regiment had several frontiersmen from the study area in it. One company of regulars from the 7th Infantry under Major Zachary Taylor and a troop of Indiana scouts were added to the militia regiments to form Hopkins' new army. This time the objective was to revisit Prophetstown and to destroy other Indian villages along the Wabash.

Hopkins led his force northward from Vincennes on 11 November 1812. They marched along the same route on the west side of the Wabash that General Harrison had used when he was on his way to the first Battle at Tippecanoe. They stopped at Fort Harrison on 5 November. They continued the march six days later, moving along the Wabash (Figure 9).

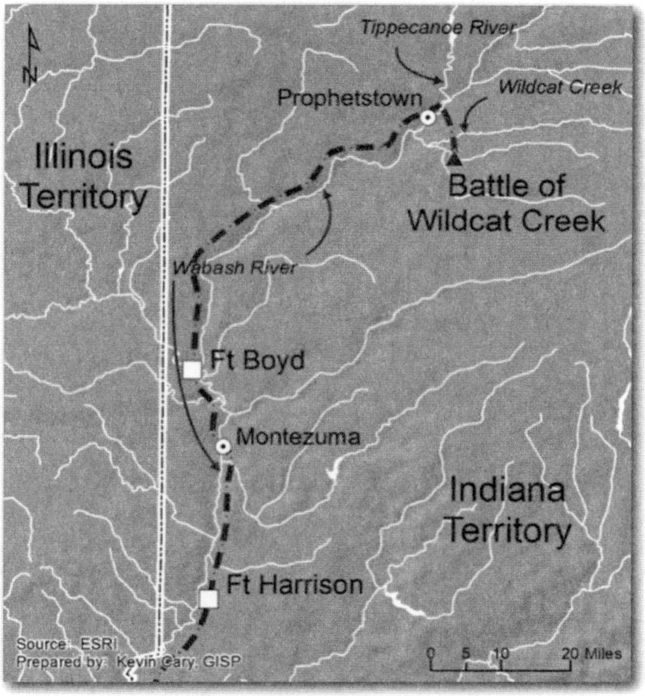

Figure 9. The route of Hopkins' second foray.

It was slow going. The streams were flush with runoff, the muddy lowlands and swamps made movement tiring. They arrived at the site of the first Battle of Tippecanoe to find that the graves of the soldiers who were killed in that battle had been exhumed. They reburied the remains before they continued on their way to Prophetstown. They found and burned a Winnebago village of about forty homes on Wild Cat Creek. They arrived at Prophetstown on the 19th to find that the village that had been partially rebuilt, and burned a nearby Kickapoo Village of about 160 huts. They encountered no Indians except for the one who killed one of the soldiers who was scouting the area ahead.[15]

On the 22nd, Lieutenant Colonel Miller and his 300 Kentuckians were sent to recover the body of the soldier who had been killed the day before. They found his head impaled on a stick, and nearby was a taunting warrior who fled. The Kentuckians chased him into what was an ambush.[16] The action that followed became known as the Second Battle of Tippecanoe, sometimes called the Battle of Wild Cat Creek.

Hopkins went to find what he believed to be a large force of Indians reported to have gathered for battle. They arrived on the 24th to find a deserted camp. A November snowstorm accompanied by frigid temperature delayed them. Many of the Kentuckians were barefoot, still wearing summer clothing with no winter coats. One observer was quoted as saying, "I pitied the poor Kentuckians. They were almost naked, and barefoot, only their linen hunting-shirts, the ground covered with snow, and the Wabash freezing up."[17] The next day, Hopkins gave up the chase, and returned to Fort Knox in Vincennes. It was a good decision in the eyes of the some 200 of his men who were either sick or frostbitten.

The Kentucky militiamen were discharged at Busseron on 17 November. Busseron was a village in what is now Knox County, Indiana. It was on the Wabash about thirteen miles north of present day downtown Vincennes. They returned home crossing the Ohio River near Hardinsburg. (Figure 8.)

Thirteen frontiersmen from the study area are known to have been members of Lieutenant Colonel Miller's Regiment. Of that regiment, slightly less than half participated in the Second Battle of Tippecanoe (Table 3). Biographical sketches of them are in Chapter 11.

Rank	Name
Pvt	Benjamin Shacklette*
Pvt	William Berry
Pvt	Sampson Cagle*
Pvt	John Dobbs
Pvt	John Gibson
Pvt	Frederick Graves*
Pvt	Henry Huntsman

Rank	Name
Pvt	Tarrance Kerby
Pvt	Samuel Merryfield
Pvt	Ephriam Spears
Pvt	William Sturdy
Pvt	George Waggle
Pvt	George C. Wilson

Table 3. The frontiersmen from the study area in Lieutenant Colonel Miller's 1st Regiment.

The other members stayed behind to protect the fort. Only three left specific records of how they participated. Major Shacklette and Private

Sampson Cagle stated that they were in the group that was in combat during the Second Battle of Tippecanoe. Private Frederick Graves stated that he was one of those who were ordered to remain behind to guard the fort. No records were found to specifically identity the contributions of the others but, for sure, they were doing whatever they were ordered to do.

The successful defense of Fort Harrison was good news to those whose spirits had been damped by the failures at Mackinac, Dearborn, and Detroit. Even with the setbacks of Hopkins, it was considered by them to be a victory. However, the worst was yet to come.

Battle of the Frenchtown

Actions were underway to build and position a force to eventually recapture Fort Detroit. The fall and early winter rains had made movement over muddy roads and trails very arduous for men, equipment, and supplies. The struggle sapped the men's energy as day after day they faced the same difficulties. The men under Winchester were finally stymied by the mud, and had to stop on the upper Maumee River. They remained there from October to January. While they waited, Winchester had sleds built, anticipating that the onset of winter would bring frozen soil and frozen rivers. His preparations facilitated the movement of his forces in early January over the frozen Maumee River to Fort Defiance at the rapids. He arrived there on 16 January 1813.

The plan was for Winchester to wait at Fort Defiance until Harrison and the remainder of the army arrived. However, when he arrived, Winchester received word that Frenchtown was under attack by the British and Indians. That town was located only thirty miles or so north. He made the decision to go to rescue the thirty-three American settler families who lived there.[18]

On 17 January, he sent 550 Kentuckians under Lieutenant Colonel Lewis to recapture Frenchtown. About two hours later, 110 Kentuckians under Lieutenant Colonel John Allen followed. Snowdrifts were as much as two feet deep, and the men walked on the ice along the shore of Lake Erie to avoid them.[19]

The ensuing battle on the 18th was furious with the Canadian militia charging several times supported by fire from the Indians. The Americans prevailed and the assault ended successfully, but at the cost of two American soldiers killed and forty-four wounded. Winchester ordered Lewis to hold Frenchtown until Winchester could arrive with 250 more men. He departed northward on the 19th with the reinforcements. Harrison arrived at Fort Defiance on 20 January and learned of Winchester's action. He immediately began moving his troops toward Frenchtown (Figure 10) as a precautionary reinforcement.[20]

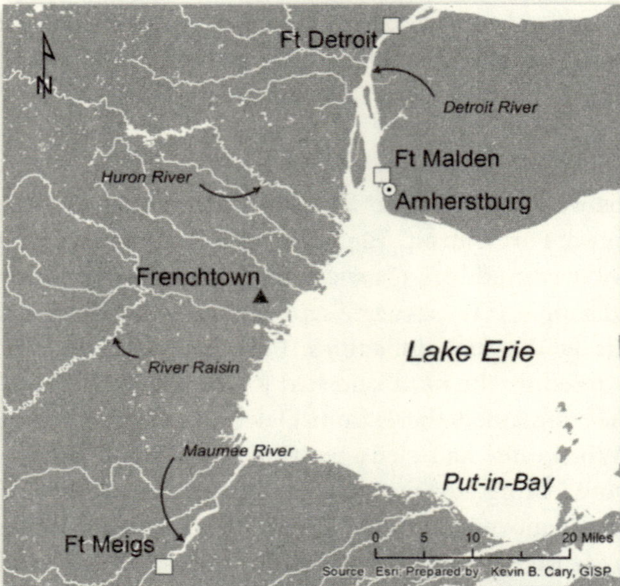

Figure 10. The area of the battles of Frenchtown and the River Raisin.

British Colonel Henry Proctor at Fort Malden was informed of the American movements and acted decisively. He led 597 soldiers and about 800 Indians across the frozen Lake Erie from Fort Walden in Upper Canada to Brownstown in the Michigan Territory. His artillery was mounted on sleighs, and was moved across the ice too. The artillery would not face opposing artillery because the Americans had none.

Proctor's army marched down the road along the shore of Lake Erie. His infantry and artillery deployed into combat positions under the cover of darkness. The Americans at Frenchtown were totally unaware that an opposing army was in position and ready to attack.[21]

Winchester was told about reports that the British were on the way but he discounted them. His troops were encamped on the north side of the frozen River Raisin. The Kentucky militia was placed behind a puncheon fence, but no special precautions were taken against an attack. The regulars were positioned to their right with only a rail fence in front of them. Winchester was in a home in Frenchtown while his men tried to sleep on the snow covered frozen ground.[22]

Before daybreak, the British artillery opened fire with devastating results. Their infantry advanced from the north, and the Indians opened fire from the west side. Winchester had encamped his regulars out in the open and they were especially hard hit. The Americans had no artillery with which to respond and they were cut to pieces. Both Lewis and Allen moved their militiamen in an attempt to support the regulars.[23]

They held their ground until after dawn. By then there were no alternative for the Militia and the regulars except to flee. The fire from the Indians on their flank was withering and inflicted heavy losses. Captain John Simpson who left his seat in congress to join Harrison's army was one of those killed. Simpson County was later named in his memory.

Lieutenant Colonel John Allen was wounded in the thigh, but he struggled along trying to rally his men to make a stand. Finally, exhausted from the effort and unable to continue, he sat on a log and waited. He killed one Indian with his sword before being killed by a bullet. His bravery was remembered by naming Allen County for him.[24]

Winchester was captured by the Indians early in the battle, and was turned over to Colonel Proctor. Proctor convinced him that further combat could only end in defeat, and that the cost in lives would be prohibitive. Winchester signed a paper ordering all of his men to surrender although, technically as a prisoner, he had no authority to do so. The order was delivered under a flag of truce. Surrender was not a palatable option to the Kentuckians.

Major Madison of the Kentucky militia knew that it was futile to continue fighting with only half of his men still surviving. The British and Indians had them surrounded and, even though the men were still behind the puncheon fence, they would not last long with no avenue of retreat and little ammunition remaining. However, he refused to surrender without assurance that his men would be protected. Colonel Proctor agreed to respect their private property, provide a guard to protect them from the Indians, and to send sleds the next morning to transport the American wounded to Amherstburg near Fort Malden. With those assurances, Major Madison surrendered his unit.[25]

About noon, the British marched away with about as many prisoners as they had soldiers. The Americans who were too wounded to move were left behind to an uncertain fate. Of Winchester's entire army, fewer than twenty escaped being killed, wounded, or surrendered.[26]

The Massacre at the River Raisin

The wounded were left under the care of American Surgeons Todd and Bowers, both Kentuckians. The British left behind a Major, three interpreters, and about fifty Indian guards.

Most of the Indians were about six miles away drinking to celebrate their victory. The next morning about 200 of those Indians came back to Frenchtown. They looted and plundered the town before turning their attention to the American prisoners lying wounded in some homes in the town. The Indians tomahawked and scalped the wounded, and set fire to the homes that they occupied.[27]

The precise number of men slaughtered during the massacre cannot be determined. One estimate was that about 100 wounded men were left behind when the other surviving Americans were marched away as prisoners. The Indians murdered and scalped between about sixty of the wounded where they lay. The Indians subsequently recaptured some of those who escaped without being killed.[28]

There was a massive monument (Figure 11) erected in 1904 in Monroe, Michigan to honor the Kentuckians who died at the River Raisin.

Kentuckians used the battle cry "Remember the Raisin" in subsequent battles, and that reflected a common sentiment on the frontier.

Proctor and his prisoners arrived at Amherstburg on the 23rd, and the

Figure 11. Memorial inscription to Kentuckians who died at the River Raisin.

Americans were crowded into a muddy area without tents or blankets. They endured a cold January rain throughout the night.

On the 23rd, Winchester wrote a letter to the Secretary of War from captivity. He explained that he ordered the surrender to "...preserve the lives of a number of our brave fellows who still held out..." He reported that there were thirty-five officers and 487 men being held as prisoners of war. He also said that the Indians held a few additional prisoners. He attempted to absolve himself when he wrote that, "...no material error is chargeable upon myself..." He ended his letter with a compliment for his men, "...no troops have ever behaved with more determined intrepidity."[29]

The prisoners were detained till the 26th when half of them began marching eastward toward Niagara. The other half left the following day. Some who were too weak from their wounds to make the trip were left behind. The militiamen were paroled after they arrived at Fort George on the strait between Lakes Erie and Ontario. The British had elicited promises that they would not rejoin the army. They traveled from Lake Erie to Pittsburgh and then down the Ohio River to Kentucky.[30]

Winchester began the battle at Frenchtown with 910 men. About 355 were killed and 522 were surrendered. Except for thirty-three who escaped capture, his entire army was gone. The word of the ignominious defeat, and the subsequent massacre reached Governor Shelby on 2 February. He said that the state was filled with mourning, and that hearts bled with anguish. The General Assembly prolonged its session another day, and voted to authorize another three thousand Kentuckians to rebuild Harrison's depleted army.

Harrison received word of the defeat, and recognized that the outcome was irreversible. He withdrew all the way back to Fort Meigs. There he waited out the winter, and the arrival of more Kentucky militiamen. The frontiersmen from the study areas were not part of the Hull and Winchester defeats but they would be part of the new army that Harrison would build.

The news about the River Raisin came to the quiet and peaceful frontier in south central Kentucky and northern middle Tennessee. News of the Massacre at the River Raisin reinforced the existing support by Kentuckians for action against the British. The news spread through the sparsely populated frontier, and stirred their patriotism.

While the action in the Old Northwest was continuing, action in the south was heating up. The threat there was not from the British directly, but from some of the Creek Indians they were encouraging. With that threat came calls for assistance. The frontiersmen from north central Tennessee responded to the call of Andrew Jackson for volunteers. Kentuckians from the border counties of the study area joined in the response. Both were responding to their country's call, not just in answer to their state's.

Chapter 4

A Dry Run

The Round Trip to Natchez

After the United States declared war on 1 June 1812, the activities of the British in the Gulf of Mexico caused new concerns about the potential for expanded conflict. The logical focus of British interest was the city of New Orleans because it controlled access to the Mississippi and, through it, to the vast interior of the United States' territory.

President Madison asked the Governor of Tennessee, Willie Blount, to provide 1,500 men to backup the American citizens at New Orleans in response to the perceived and expected threat of a British invasion. The plan was to dispatch troops to Natchez in the Mississippi Territory, and be staged there for redeployment as the need arose to New Orleans.

The Governor gave the task to Andrew Jackson to fully respond to the president's request. Jackson was a lawyer of some prominence who had been elected as the commander of the Tennessee Militia, and given the rank of Major General. He won that position by a margin of just one vote. He had military fervor, but lacked any actual military experience as a leader.

He did have military experience of another sort. He was a young boy in Camden, South Carolina during the Revolutionary War. When the British army came into his area on a recruiting trip, a British officer ordered him to brush his boots. The officer struck him when he refused, and took him and his brother as prisoners. Subsequently, during the time of that war, he lost both brothers and his mother. His father had died about the time Jackson was born. He grew up as an orphan who along his way developed a hatred of the British.[1]

He had business connections in Natchez, a city that was a significant port for Mississippi River traffic. Governor Blount instructed Jackson to solicit volunteers sufficient to form two regiments. Jackson ordered his militia to rendezvous in Nashville on 10 December 1812, and 2,500 volunteers showed up.

The volunteers brought their own rifles rather than using the less accurate muskets that the army might have provided. They were shivering from the bitter cold temperature when they arrived at Nashville, and found it covered by a foot of snow. They were saved by the foresight of the quartermaster who had laid-in a 1,000 cords of firewood. The temperature returned to a more normal level for wintertime after several days as the force of volunteers was readied, and the trip south was planned.[2]

Among those volunteers were four frontiersmen with ties to our study area (Table 4). Their biographical sketches are in chapter 11.

Rank	Name
Pvt	William H. Allen
Pvt	Thomas Caruth
Pvt	William House
Pvt	Hiram Richards

Table 4. Frontiersmen from the study area who went to Natchez.

Jackson's army would of necessity take two routes to Natchez. He led the first group of 1,830 infantrymen in two regiments to the Cumberland River where they loaded the men and supplies onto the awaiting flatboats. Their route would be a float trip down the Cumberland, Ohio, and Mississippi Rivers to Natchez in the Mississippi Territory.

Flatboat people routinely floated down the rivers from as far upstream as Pittsburgh to deliver trade goods to Natchez. Kentuckians loaded tobacco, hemp, whiskey, and other products onto a flatboat or raft for similar float trips. The river currents would move them at about five or six miles per hour, just a bit faster than walking. Upon arrival they would sell their load of goods, and also sell the flatboat or raft they had used to bring them there. They would then walk back to Kentucky. They took the return route over what was called the Natchez Trace. The original route was along connecting paths through the forest, but by 1795 it had become a well-worn road. After the acquisition of the Louisiana Purchase, the movement of goods was extended to New Orleans with the Natchez Trace still being used for the major portion of the return trip for the flatboat people from Kentucky and Tennessee.[3]

On 7 January 1813, the flatboats pushed off to begin the float down the Cumberland, Ohio, and Mississippi Rivers. It was about 2,000 miles by river from Nashville to Natchez and the float trip was expected to take about three weeks.

The second group of Jackson's men was Colonel John Coffee's regiment of 670 cavalrymen for a horse ride along an overland route down the Natchez Trace.[4] Movement of the horses by flatboat was far too challenging and never was considered as an option.

Neither of the two routes (Figure 12) would be enjoyable at any time, but even less so in winter. Both routes would be tiring for all the men.

The trips were not without problems. Jackson's river route was slowed by three days when the flatboats encountered ice on both the Cumberland and the Ohio Rivers. The flow of the Ohio River was as yet uncontrolled by all the present day system of locks and dams. Because it was still a wild river, it was not uncommon for it to freeze over for a short time during low flow periods. Three of his soldiers died while en route. Jackson and his men arrived in Natchez on 14 February.

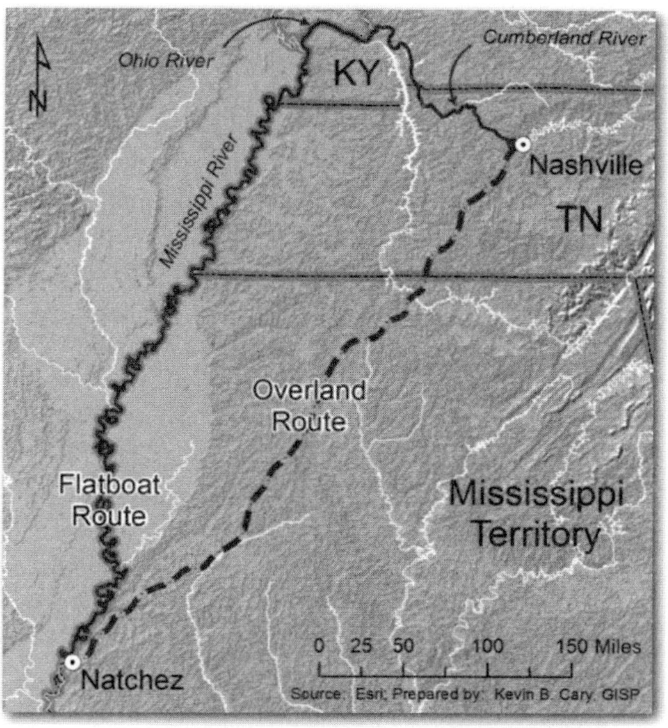

Figure 12. The routes to Natchez.

The overland route had severe problems too. Mud on the Natchez Trace complicated by freezing temperature slowed Coffee's trip. He also lost two days when they came to the Tennessee River. They had to pay the Chickasaws to ferry both the men and their horses across the Tennessee River.[5] Coffee's troops arrived in Natchez on 16 February after about twenty-eight days in the saddle.[6] The distance traveled over the two routes was vastly different, over 2,000 miles by river, and about 500 miles by the Natchez Trace. The two routes resulted in arrival dates about two days apart. However, the flatboat trip had taken thirty-eight days while the overland route had taken twenty-eight days.

Jackson was met with orders relayed to him from his superior, Major General James Wilkinson who was in New Orleans. The orders that he received were to stop, wait, and to take no further action until further advised. A month passed without further orders, and his men became impatient to either do something or go home. Soldiers are not good at waiting. Jackson himself was even more impatient. He fumed and fulminated over the delays, and the lack of action.[7]

Finally, the word came, and it wasn't satisfactory to either Jackson or his men. The Senate refused to support the administration's intent to invade Florida, and to rid the southeast of the Spanish and British. The Secretary of War John Armstrong directed that the plans be cancelled. He informed Jackson that the British were not approaching New Orleans, and there were no British forces for him to attack. Armstrong ordered him to disband the entire brigade, and discharge them at Natchez. The troops would then, as civilians, have to find their way back home at their own expense.[8]

Jackson was enraged by the cancellation of the expedition, but even more livid over the order to discharge his men in Natchez. He refused to obey that discharge order. In particular, he was concerned about the 150 men on sick call. Fifty-six of them were bedridden. He was appalled at the notion of all his men being discharged in Natchez. He wrote to Secretary of War Armstrong, "These brave men …deserve a better fate and return from their government." He added, "They followed me to the field; I shall carefully march them to their homes." He did not ask for permission, he told his superior in no uncertain terms what he was going to do.[9]

Jackson wrote to his wife Rachel about his close connection that he felt with his men.

Although their Patriotism has been but illy rewarded by an ungrateful officer, (not Country) it is therefore my duty to act as a father to the sick and to the well and stay with them until I march them into Nashville.[10]

His disobedience of the discharge order came at a cost though. Jackson's intense loyalty to his troops caused him to spend $3,000 of his own money to buy twenty days of rations, eleven wagons to transport the sick, and enough horses for those too weak to walk. He walked, rather than rode, at the lead for the trip up the Trace to share the hardships of the trips with his men. He directed his officers to give their horses to the sick who were still able to ride. His stand in defiance of orders, and his walk with them back home, gave rise to his nickname of "Old Hickory."[11]

Secretary of War Armstrong later explained that he had intended that the cancellation order be delivered in Nashville before Jackson embarked on the trip down to Natchez. Jackson did not accept that explanation, and found no solace in the Secretary's statement. He believed that the intent was to discharge his men who would have no funds for the travel home. Of necessity, their only option would then be to enlist into Wilkerson's regular army. To prevent that from happening, Jackson refused to discharge them there.[12]

After Jackson's troops reached Columbia, Tennessee, the brigade was disbanded, and the men discharged on 13 May 1813. Tennesseans William H. Allen and Henry House went home to Sumner County and Thomas Caruth went home to what is now Macon County. Kentuckian Hiram Richards went home to what is now Allen County where he stayed until he reenlisted in September to go with Old Hickory to fight the Red Sticks.

Jackson arrived in Nashville on 22 May and received a hero's welcome. His request for reimbursement of his expenses for the trip home was at first turned down. After further negotiation, he received approval.[13]

Jackson had not gotten his chance to prove his mettle in combat, but he had demonstrated his innate leadership abilities. His reputation as a leader would attract volunteers the next time he asked for them. That time would arrive sooner than expected.

Chapter 5

God Willing and the Creek Don't Rise

The Creek War

Tensions continued to build in the Mississippi Territory as they anticipated a British attack on New Orleans. However, a more immediate problem would have to be faced first. Before the New Orleans threat could be confronted, supply routes would have to be opened with assurance of staying opened. Those overland routes had to be through the Creek lands. Those lands were becoming increasingly dangerous because of the civil war between the two factions, the Upper and the Lower Creeks.

The residents of the homesteads in south central Kentucky and northern middle Tennessee knew of encounters with Indians during the earliest days of settlement of those areas. Such encounters were no longer common by 1811. Encounters still occurred in the Indiana Territory to the north and portions of the Mississippi Territory to the south. The Mississippi Territory included Indian lands of the Choctaw in the western side, the Chickasaw in the northern side, and the Creek in the central and southeastern side.

The white population in the area of the Mississippi Territory, the portion that is now Alabama, increased in the early 1800's in part as the result of the construction of the Federal Road, as it was called. The road was between the Chattahoochee River and Mim's Ferry on the Alabama River. It had been widened from a horse path to a wagon road, and the floodgate opened for an uninvited flow of settlers with their cattle, horses, and pigs into Creek lands.[1]

One area became increasingly dangerous because the dispossession of Creek land by white immigrants aggravated some of the Creeks. That area was in the Creek land in the area of the Mississippi Territory that would later become central and northern Alabama. The Upper Creeks in particular abhorred the subsequent modification of their customs and culture by the white influence (Figure 13).

The new white settlers showed little interest in being assimilated into the Creek Nation. The whites had little desire to learn the Creek language, and little interest in adopting the Creek customs and culture. Some of the Creeks wanted to keep their culture pure. Those Creeks had no capability of building a wall along the border of their land to stop the flow of unwanted immigrants. So tensions rose as some of them sought ways to oust the whites.

Into that scene came twenty Shawnees led by Tecumseh, a Shawnee whose mother was Creek. He had left his brother at Tippecanoe and gone south in 1811 to recruit the Choctaw, Chickasaw, and Creek, and to join the Shawnee and others from the Old Northwest to form an Indian Confederation. Collectively, that confederation would have potential forces capable of dispelling the intruders from their land, and stopping the inexorable expansion by the white settlers.

Tecumseh was a persuasive advocator of action, at least to some. His call to action caused a split in the Creeks that evolved into serious internal conflicts. The Lower Creeks, as they became known, were those who were not persuaded by the oratorical skills of Tecumseh.

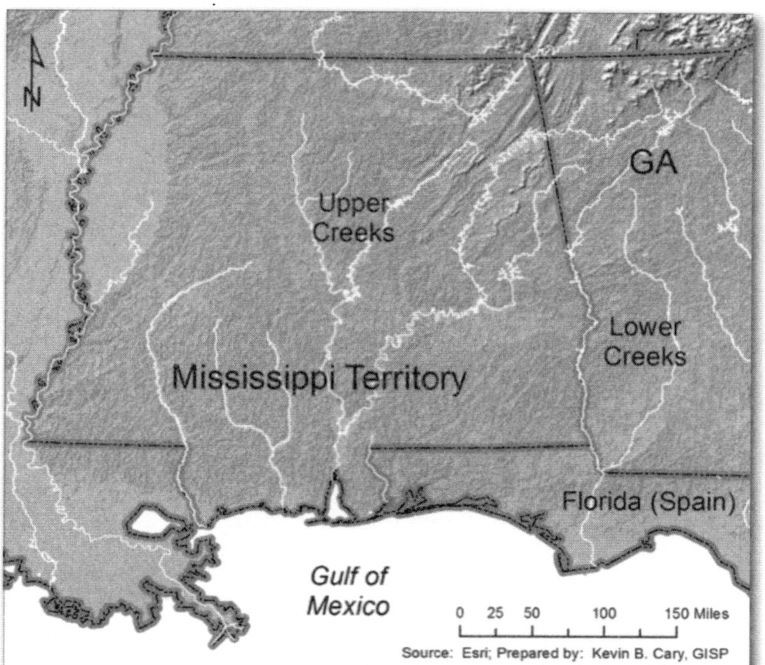

Figure 13. The Upper and Lower Creek lands.

Historians have called this group the friendly Creeks because they were not part of the assaults that were later made against the white settlers. They were farmers with livestock who had accepted several aspects of white culture including writing and education. The friendly Creeks had many mixed blood people whose heritage included both white and Indian ancestors.[2]

Tecumseh was more successful in igniting the Upper Creeks. They were the ones who were also known as the Red Sticks because they painted the heads of their war clubs red. Tecumseh also aroused those warriors to act against the white encroachment. A group of them, on a return trip from their visit with Tecumseh in the Indiana Territory, raided white settlements along the Duck River in middle Tennessee south of Nashville in May 1812. Even worse, they began an internecine war within their Creek Nation by attacking Lower Creek villages that had become allied with white settlers. The Red Sticks killed Lower Creek's livestock, burned their homes, and destroyed their crops. The result was a Creek civil war fought simultaneously with America's war against the British. The leader of the friendly Lower Creeks asked the United States for military assistance.[3]

It was advantageous for the British to provide arms and other supplies to the Indians. The threat of Indian attacks on white settlers would divert the attention and effort of the American Army away from their intrusion into the British Territory of Canada. So it was that the Indians of the Old Northwest were armed with British weapons, and participated with the British army in the battles with the Americans.[4] The Lower Creek in the south were not as well armed because they had to trade for weapons with the Spanish. The Spanish operated a trade center at Pensacola that catered to the Creeks' needs. The primary concern to the United States was that the British might find a way to provide arms to the Red Sticks.

The Creek War Beginning

A group of the Red Sticks went to Pensacola to obtain powder and lead. The Spanish traders there obliged, and the Red Sticks departed on 27 July 1813. A group of white militia and friendly Lower Creeks learned that the pack train was headed north. It was intercepted where the Pensacola road crossed the Burnt Corn Creek about ninety miles north of Pensacola. They attacked and, after a three-hour battle, captured the powder and lead. They moved what they considered to be contraband to Fort Mims for safekeeping (Figure 14).

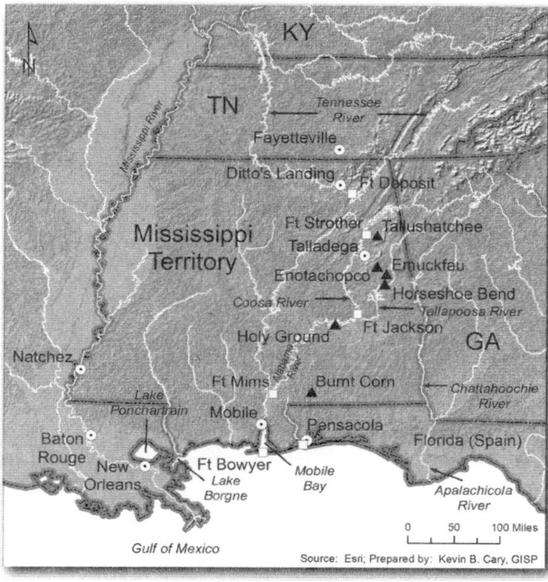

Figure 14. The Creek War arena.

The civil war between the factions of the Creek had begun in earnest, and the United States became involved. Retaliation for that involvement was inevitable.[5]

Fort Mims was a wooden stockade that surrounded an acre of land about thirty-five miles northeast of Mobile near the confluence of the Alabama and Tombigbee Rivers. The retaliatory response occurred on 30 August 1813 when the Red Sticks attacked the fort. The fort was overwhelmed, and the slaughter of over 250 men, women, and children began. Only twenty to forty people escaped. The attack became known as the Fort Mims Massacre. That retaliation prompted a series of retaliatory raids by the Georgia militia among others.

Governor Willie Blount of Tennessee responded to the Creek increased activity by asking for 3,500 volunteers to augment the force of 1,500 already assembled. Andrew Jackson was placed in charge, and plans were being made and implemented. Jackson was only thirty-five when he was first given command of the Tennessee Militia. Now he was leading another expedition at the age of forty-six, but this time he had experience in maneuvering large groups of men. His objectives were to destroy the Upper Creek warring parties, build a road to Mobile, force the Spanish out of Florida, and cut off the supply of arms to the Creek. That was quite an ambitious agenda to say the least.

The Supply Problem

The most formidable problem facing Jackson was how to supply and resupply his army as it advanced southward to engage the Creek enemy. He could not advance until that problem was solved. Flying flags, flashing sabers, and roaring guns come to mind when battles are remembered. However, none of that could occur until and unless supplies were available in sufficient quantity where and when they were needed. The success of attacks against the Creek would be determined by the dependable delivery of supplies as determined by the availability of roads. The needed supplies included ammunition, of course, but there were other critical needs as well. Each week, Jackson's 2,500 men would consume about 1,000 bushels of grain, twenty tons of meat, 1,000 gallons of whiskey, plus whatever food they could forage for themselves and 1,300 horses from the local areas.[6] If you imagine those numbers in terms of wagonloads per week, the magnitude of the recurring supply problem becomes apparent.

A supply road was needed because of the British blockade of the Gulf Coast. Sending supplies down the Mississippi to Natchez or to the Gulf and across to Mobile were not options. There was a plan for a road by widening the established, but little used Federal Postal Horse Path. That path connected Athens, Georgia, with Fort Stoddert near Mobile. The Creek War disrupted the schedule for its completion. Commercial shipments used the route from Nashville by way of Natchez to New Orleans. Three federal roads were planned: from the Tennessee River to Fort Stoddert, from the Flint River to Fort Stoddert, and from Mobile to New Orleans.[7]

Jackson could not wait to open the Creek campaign until a road from Nashville to New Orleans could be built. That planned road would run from Nashville through Columbia and Florence to Tupelo. There it would split from the Natchez trace and go south through the Noxubee swamp, Meridian, and Hattiesburg in the Mississippi Territory to Madisonville in St. Tammany Parish and New Orleans. Although the building of that road had begun, it would not be completed until after the war ended.[8] Jackson needed another more immediate solution.

No matter what route he chose, supplies would have to travel through hostile Upper Creek territory. There was no other option because supplies must go to where battles will be fought. To launch an attack required an assured supply route even if it was hazardous and slow. Jackson's decision was to deliver supplies before most of the army arrived. The placement of supplies in depots ahead of the arrival of the infantry and cavalry was a novel idea because it addressed the timing rather than the route of supplies. It did carry with it some danger of the supply depots being attacked and damaged or destroyed.

His solution did not obviate the need for a wagon road because the amount of supplies required wagons and wagons required roads. Jackson ordered that an overland road be cleared through the mountain forest. He ordered the construction of stockades as supply depots along the way. The militias of Georgia and North Carolina also got busy establishing a series of supply depots with a total of 50,000 rations to be ready when Jackson's forces arrived at the confluence of the Coosa and Tallapoosa Rivers.[9]

With his supply plan being implemented, Jackson ordered his men to rendezvous at Fayetteville, Tennessee, on 4 October 1813. Frontiersmen from the study area came to Fayetteville. Other notables who volunteered were Davy Crockett and Sam Houston from Tennessee.

Coincidentally, other frontiersmen from the study area were in Canada for the Battle of the Thames (Chapter 6) against British troops and the Indians led by Tecumseh. The war was still being fought on other fronts as Jackson's effort to subjugate the Creek began.

Colonel John Coffee's cavalry was the first to move out to prepare a camp at Huntsville, Alabama. A few days later, the rest of the army began the move to join them. Coffee's cavalry left Ditto's Landing on 15 October to search for corn to grind for food, and to destroy two Indian villages. The lack of maps required the use of guides, and that made reconnoiter uncertain and difficult. They found about 200 bushels of corn in one of the villages, a much-welcomed sight by the soldiers whose food supply was diminishing. Contractors had been hired to find food from local sources, but they too failed to find sufficient quantities of corn.[10]

Jackson went to Ditto's Landing on the Tennessee River near Huntsville. The supplies he expected to find were not there, the river flow was too low even for the flat-bottomed supply boats to float over the riffles.

It was 22 October before he could move about twenty-four miles upstream to begin cutting the road over the mountains to the confluence of the Thompson Creek and the Tennessee River. He built Fort Deposit there on the southernmost bend of the Tennessee River about eight miles north of present day Guntersville, Alabama. It was the first of several forts that would double as supply depots. Supplies could be transported by river to Fort Deposit. That would greatly reduce the time required to move supplies, and to increase the tonnage that could be moved. Nevertheless, the supply problem was intractable, and a constant concern to both Jackson and his troops.

Tallushatchee

Jackson waited for supplies to arrive, but was impatient to begin military action. On 3 November, he sent Colonel John Coffee to destroy the Creek village of Tallushatchee, now known as Tallasehatchee (Figure 14) that was about twelve miles away.[11] The village was near present day Wellington, Alabama. He thought that about 200 Red Sticks were in the village. The ensuing battle was the first in Andrew Jackson's military career.

Coffee encircled the village of Tallushatchee with his force of about 900 men. Among those soldiers were Ensign Samuel Ellis and Private John Conyers from the study area (Chapter 11). There were also some Cherokees and friendly Lower Creeks in Jackson's force. These Creeks and Cherokees were asked to wear white feathers or deer tails in their hair to identify them as friendly. The military knew that uniforms were necessary to identify friend from foe, but only the American regulars had them. Fortunately, in the encounters with the British army, their soldiers were uniformed, and that solved the identification problem.[12]

Upon Jackson's command, the attack was launched from all sides, and the slaughter began. When it was over, 186 Red Stick warriors were counted dead on the battlefield. Coffee had lost five killed and forty-one wounded in the battle.[13] Coffee's troops returned to the fort after the battle was over. Jackson had his baptism of fire, but there would be more severe tests of his abilities in future encounters with stronger opposition.

Jackson moved farther south later in October, and constructed Fort Strother on the banks of the Coosa River, about ten miles southwest of present day Gadsden, Alabama. It was another stockade structure that was to become a supply depot, and his primary base of operations. Again, he waited for resupply and reinforcement. Waiting was not something soldiers enjoyed, and the wait caused troop morale to wane.

Talladega

The waiting was soon over because word came four days later that the Red Sticks had attacked friendly Creeks in their village at Talladega. Jackson wanted to go to their aid, but to do so would incur several risks. One major risk was leaving Fort Strother unprotected while they were away in Talladega. He was expecting supplies and reinforcements to arrive very soon. He may have thought that the reinforcements would be able to provide adequate defense after they arrived. But, he did not know whether they would arrive in time to defend against an attack. The second concern was the availability of food before, during, and after the assault. Soldiers needed food, and should not be subjected to hunger when they should be concentrating on combat.

Jackson was decisive as usual even when faced with those challenges. On 7 November, he left behind about 200 sick and wounded men at Fort Strother, and headed south with about 1,200 infantrymen and Coffee's 800 cavalrymen. They would face about 1,100 Red Sticks who had Talladega under siege. Ensign Samuel Ellis from the study area was one of the sick soldiers who were left behind at the fort. He was given a disability discharge about a month later (Chapter 11).

On 9 November, Jackson's force encircled Talladega with the intent of trapping the Red Sticks in a manner that had been successful at Tallushatchee. During the ensuing battle, about 700 of the Red Sticks fought their way through the encirclement and escaped. However, about 290 of them were killed in the battle and that further depleted the Red Stick ranks. Jackson lost fifteen killed and eighty-five wounded.[14]

Jackson received word that the expected supplies and reinforcements had not arrived. His concern about the continued exposure of the fort prevailed, and he did not pursue the Red Sticks as he otherwise would have done. He hurried back to the fort. Privates John Conyers and Hiram Richards from the study area (Chapter 11) were among the soldiers in the battle who headed back to Fort Strother.

The Tennessee River was at low flow, and the flatboats bringing supplies and fresh soldiers were not able to complete the trip on schedule. Jackson arrived at Fort Strother on 11 November to find that food was not available, and they were facing famine. His men wanted to go back to Fort Deposit, a supply depot that would have food. He had to restrain his hungry men by force. The needed food had not arrived by 17 November, and he finally had to agree that going to Fort Deposit was the only option remaining. Fortuitously, after marching just twelve miles north, they met a supply train with nine wagons loaded with flour. It was followed by a herd of 150 beef cattle. Jackson ordered his troops back to Fort Strother where, without doubt, dinner was served. [15]

The hunger was sated, but another even greater problem arose to add to Jackson's woes. The end of the period of enlistment had arrived for many of his soldiers, and they should be discharged. Another confrontation occurred. Those tired and hungry militiamen wanted to go home, and he had no way to keep them beyond their obligated time. They had to be restrained from going back to Tennessee. Worse news was that the 1,450 reinforcement troops who finally arrived came with only ten days of service remaining before their enlistments were up. Even worse news was the order from Governor Blount of Tennessee to abandon Fort Strother, and return to Tennessee. Jackson was facing a repeat of his regretful experience at Natchez. He said that he would hold the fort even if only two men of his force agreed to stay with him. The rapid reduction in the size of his army was unimaginable, and he neared being a general without an army.[16]

On 29 December, he wrote to Governor Blount and demanded that he and the state legislature keep their pledge to maintain 3,500 men in the field so long as the Creek War continued. He was quoted as writing, "Let me tell you it imperiously lies on both you and me to do our duty regardless of consequences of the opinion of those fireside patriots, those fawning sycophants, or cowardly poltroons."[17] That was strong language from a subordinate to his superior.

Governor Blount answered Jackson's demands, and the first batch of replacement troops arrived just after New Year's Day 1814. Colonel William Carroll came with about 800 new militiamen. Jackson seized the moment with his 130 of Coffee's men and about 100 Cherokee and friendly Creek. The soldiers' work was cut out for them. They faced a cold January's weather, a continued shortage of rations, and the challenge of an encounter with a superior number of Indian warriors.

Another serious problem that Jackson faced was that the new militiamen were raw, untrained, and had enlisted for only sixty days. He did not see that as a reason to wait for the promised additional reinforcements to arrive. He saw it a reason to act sooner without wasting time. So, on 17 January, he sallied forth toward the large Creek village at Horseshoe Bend about seventy miles south.

Emuckfau and Enotochopo Creek

On 22 January, Jackson was camped about twelve miles from the Creek village of Emuckfau. The Red Sticks attacked Jackson's force and a battle raged for about thirty minutes. Coffee's cavalry was sent after the withdrawing Red Sticks. When he saw that his troops were outnumbered about three to one, Coffee gave up the chase and withdrew. The Red Sticks followed them, and attacked again. Coffee withdrew to Fort Strother.[18]

Jackson's army began the march back to Fort Strother taking a longer route this time because of the earlier difficulty in crossing the creek at Emuckfau on the trip south. On the morning of 24 January, Jackson's troops began going down the steep banks to cross through the cold water of the broad Enotochopo Creek. He knew that he would be most vulnerable at a time in the crossing when his troops were divided, half on one side and half on the other. As he expected, the Creek attacked the troops waiting to cross. He had prepared for that. The flanking men who had already crossed would diverge, some upstream, and some downstream. They would then re-cross the creek and encircle the attacking Creeks. The plan was good, but the inexperience of the troops waiting to cross caused their line to crumble as the Creek attacked from three sides. They struggled to flee across the creek, and even the personal presence and urgings of Jackson and Carroll could not rally them to stand and fight.[19]

The battles at Emuckfau and Enotochopo Creek were costly to Jackson. He lost twenty killed and seventy-five wounded. Of the wounded, twenty-three had to be carried away on litters. It was common for litters to be made from the skins of horses killed in battle if time and opportunity permitted. The battle was more costly to the Red Sticks who had 189 killed. The Red Stick loss would become critical in the coming battles.[20]

Jackson led his men back to Fort Strother to await resupply and the arrival of additional fresh troops. His army grew with new arrivals to about 4,000 men by February 1814. About 2,700 of them were green militiamen, about 500 were Cherokees, and about 100 were friendly Creek.[21]

Most welcomed were about 600 regular army men of the 39th Regiment of U.S. Infantry. For the first time, Jackson had a sizable number of trained and disciplined regular army soldiers in his command. He would use them wisely. He had finally assembled the overpowering force he needed for a decisive win against the Red Sticks.

Horseshoe Bend

He moved out again on 14 March with about 3,300 men toward Horseshoe Bend. To get there, he had to cut a fifty-two mile trail through the forest. Remarkably, he made camp on 26 March about six miles from the Creek village at Horseshoe Bend (Figure 15).

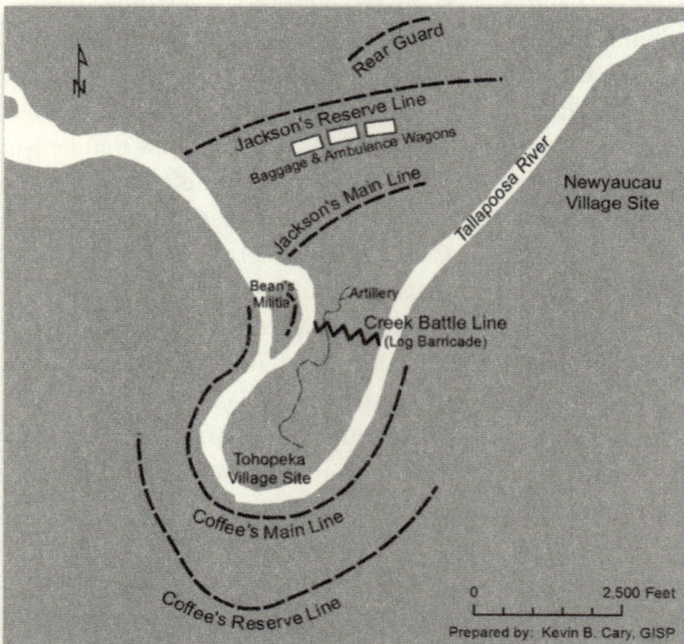

Figure 15. Horseshoe Bend battlefield.

Horseshoe Bend was a peninsula with the Tallapoosa River on three of its sides. The Red Sticks anticipated the attack. They had piled up tree trunks to a height over five feet in a zigzag pattern that stretched about two tenths of a mile across the narrow neck of the peninsula. The zigzag pattern assured that anyone approaching would encounter deadly enfilade from rifles.

Of the 1,000 warriors led by Chief Menawa, only a third had guns. Two thirds of them were armed with clubs, tomahawks, spears, and bows and arrows, hardly a match for rifles.[22] As a backup plan, Menawa had hundreds of canoes along the river in case they had to withdraw.

The next morning, Jackson sent Coffee with his 700 cavalrymen joined by 600 Cherokees and friendly Creeks to cross the river. They formed a line along the south side of the bend of the Tallapoosa River to seal possible canoe escape routes.[23]

About 10:30 a.m., Jackson's two small artillery pieces opened fire, one from eighty yards and one from about 250 yards away. The Red Sticks sent their women and children to cross the river, and Jackson held fire until they had crossed over.

A group of the friendly Creeks from Coffee's force crossed the river in canoes, and set fire to some buildings that were near the riverbank. Jackson ordered his infantry to attack at about 12:30 p.m. He placed the regulars of Colonel John Williams' 39th U.S. Infantry in the center. Among those regulars, who had enlisted for the duration of the war, were Privates James Durham and Peter Martin from the study area (Chapter 11). They, and their trained and disciplined comrades, would spearhead the attack.

Colonel Veneral Doherty's militia brigade was on their right, and General Thomas Johnson's militia brigade, with Private Eli Meadow from the study area, was on their left. They charged with fixed bayonets. The Red Sticks were badly outnumbered, and tomahawks were not much of a match with bayonets. The regulars were the first to breach the barricade, and Sam Houston received an arrow through his leg in that effort. The rest of the attacking infantry climbed over the barricade as the defense collapsed.

The Red Sticks were trapped and then killed as they attempted to escape. The slaughter continued until darkness came about five hours later. At the end of the battle, 557 warriors lay dead on the killing field and another 200 to 300 dead in the river. Only about 200 had escaped death. The full retribution for Fort Mims had been extracted. The cost to Jackson's army was forty-seven men killed and 159 wounded.[24] Included in that number were two comrades killed and ten others wounded from Privates Durham and Martin's company.

A North Carolina militia regiment arrived just after the Battle of Horseshoe Bend ended. Private Jonathan Davis (Chapter 11), who would later live in Allen County, was one of those militiamen present when his regiment accepted the surrender of 600 Creek at the confluence of the Alabama and Coosa Rivers in the Alabama Territory.

The Creek War, as a practical matter, was over and their ties to the British were severed. It came just in time, too, as the British landed troops on the Gulf Coast within the next two months. Jackson, Coffee, and Carroll had gained valuable experience that would favorably influence the Battle of New Orleans that lay ahead.

Another fort was built on the site of an old French Fort Toulouse at the confluence of the Coosa and Tallapoosa Rivers near the present day city of Wetumpka, Alabama. The new fort was named Fort Jackson (Figure 14). A peace treaty between the Creek and the United States was signed there on 9 August 1814. It assured safe passage though the Creek Territory. It also gave rights to carve out roads and to freely navigate streams. The Creek ceded over half of their land, 36,000 square miles of it, to the United States under the Treaty of Fort Jackson. White settlers subsequently flooded in to settle on the land the Creek gave up.[25]

The peace treaty came just in time to allow the focus of attention to shift south to concentrate on the British threat rather than being distracted by the Creek.

Mobile

The United States claimed Mobile and its bay as part of the Louisiana Purchase. Back in 1813, President Madison ordered that the point at the mouth of the bay be taken from the Spanish. That was done, and the Mississippi Territory was extended to encompass the bay. A wooden fort, Fort Bowyer, was built to guard the harbor.

Jackson moved his army to Mobile arriving there on 22 August. He covered about 185 miles is just eleven days. Among them was Private Tyre Adcock (Chapter 11) who was in a unit that was building supply roads along the route before arriving at Camp Mandeville near Mobile.

The arrival of Jackson's army was none too soon as it turned out. He would not learn until later that the British had captured and burned the public buildings in Washington on 24 August (Chapter 7). The American government was dispersed and incapable of providing guidance, orders, or permissions for a short time.[26]

Meanwhile, the British had developed a plan to invade and take Mobile, march westward to Baton Rouge, and turn south to take New Orleans. The Mississippi valley would then be opened all the way to Canada. The plan was based on the use of Indians, Spanish, and slaves who could be recruited to augment regular army British soldiers. It was assumed that the slaves would join in large numbers because of their hatred of their owners. They also assumed that the people in New Orleans would welcome their liberating force. The plan was approved on 30 July 1814, and the British army set sail for the Caribbean with sixty ships. Eventually, the size of the British force was raised to 14,000.[27]

The British landed arms and officers at Apalachicola in what is now Florida. They began recruiting in Florida and subsequently reported that over 3,000 Creek and Seminoles had joined. They asked the Creek to attack Fort Bowyer near Mobile.

The focus of the plan shifted to the Pensacola-Mobile area. Jackson learned of the plan, and asked the secretary of war to approve an invasion of the Spanish held Florida panhandle to take control of Pensacola. The United States was not at war with the Spanish, but Jackson was not deterred by that restriction. He wrote to the Spanish governor at Pensacola, "refugee banditti from the creek nation [are] swarming into Florida drawing rations from your government and under the drill of a British officer." He added that the United States would not tolerate Spanish protection of them.

Jackson immediately expedited work on the wooden and sand stockade at Fort Bowyer that was located on the tip of a spit that extended to the very mouth of Mobile Bay (Figure 16).

It had been built in June 1813, but was abandoned by American forces after about a year. A group of about 160 regulars were sent to repair and defend the fort. Two weeks later it was ready for action.[28]

They did not have long to wait. On the morning of 12 September, four British ships sailed to a point about six miles from the entrance to Mobile Bay. They were armed with seventy-eight guns. The 160 men at Fort Bowyer readied their twenty guns to engage them. About 4:20 p.m. in the afternoon of the 15th, the ships moved into position, and opened fire on the fort. The Americans returned fire and, after about an hour, damaged two of the ships. One limped away and another ran aground with shredded sails, and was burned to keep it from being captured.

From his location thirty miles away, Jackson heard the explosion of its magazine. It was a victory for the Americans.[29] The British attack was the trigger for Jackson to advance on Pensacola.

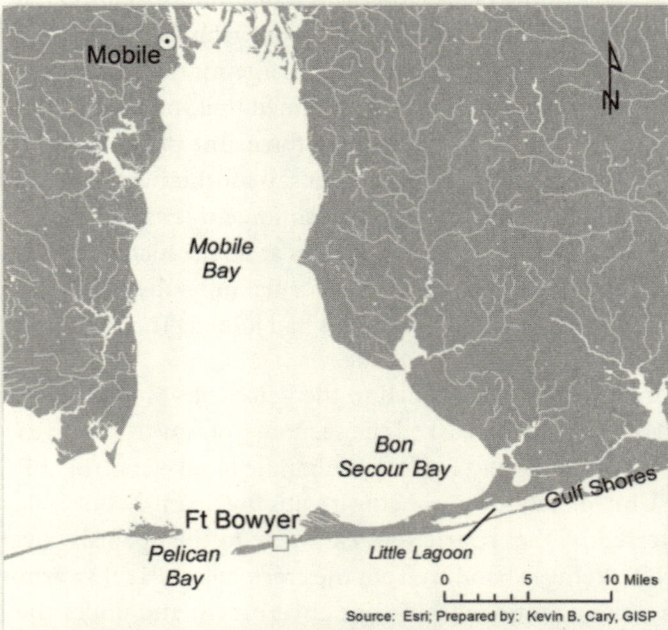

Figure 16. Fort Bowyer.

He had assembled an army of about 4,000 men at Fort Montgomery, Alabama Territory, a supply base on the east bank of the Tensaw River two miles north of Fort Mims. He had three regular army infantry regiments as his disposal: the 3rd, 39th, and 44th Infantries.

Privates Durham and Martin were still in the 39th, a unit that was by then filled with veterans of the Battle of Horseshoe Bend. The 44th had been recruited from the Nashville area, and had started south on 15 July. They passed through Huntsville on 26 July, through Talladega on 3 August, and arrived at Fort Jackson on 8 August. They continued on southward on 11 August. They made it downstream past Fort Mims by 19 August. Private Thomas Seagraves from the study area died that night, probably from disease (Chapter 11).[30]

Private Israel Anderson (Chapter 11) from the study area continued south with the 44th Regiment. There were militias in Jackson's army from Tennessee too. Privates John Conyers, Ephraim Claiborne, and John Dobbs (Chapter 11) from the study area were in those Tennessee regiments. A battalion of dragoons from the Mississippi Territory was there as well.

Private Peter Martin's one-year enlistment in the 39th Infantry Regiment was completed on 4 October 1813 (Chapter 11). He was discharged, but died from disease two days later, probably still at Fort Montgomery just north of Mobile.

Pensacola

About a month later, Jackson was ready to act against the festering situation with the Spanish and British in Florida. He sent an overwhelming force toward Pensacola. They reached within two miles of Pensacola on 6 November. On the 7th, 4,100 of Jackson's regulars, militia, and Indians marched to do battle.

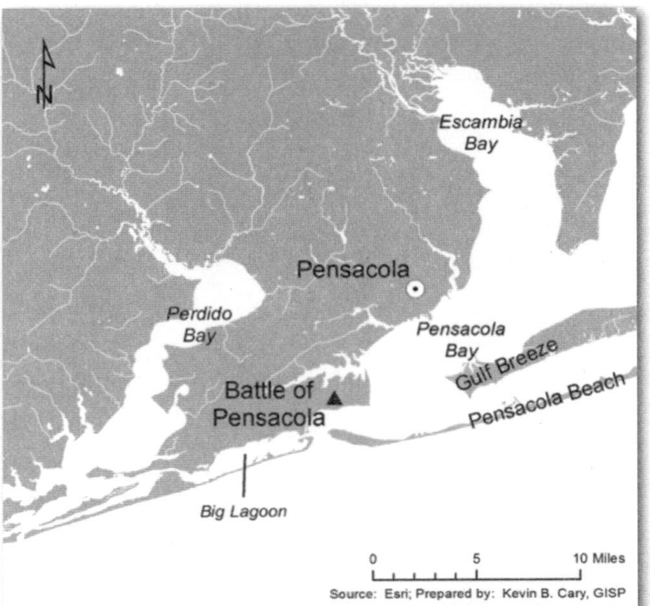

Figure 17. Battle at Pensacola.

They advanced along the beach aligned with the 3rd and 44th regular army regiments in the center. Tennessee's Drafted Militia and some

Choctaw Indians were on their left. Coffee's Tennessee Militia was on their right as they advanced along the beach (Figure 17). They came under artillery fire from the Spanish as they approached the town. The Americans made a bayonet charge that carried the day within a few minutes. The short battle produced eleven men killed or wounded. The Spanish governor, with only about 500 men, lost four killed and six wounded and did not resist further. He surrendered the facility that was soon occupied by the Americans.[31]

With Pensacola neutralized, Jackson turned his full attention to New Orleans. He began moving his army westward on 21 November, and the first elements arrived in New Orleans on 2 December. The final leg of the British voyage that began in England left Jamaica on 26 November to cross the Gulf of Mexico toward New Orleans. A showdown with the British was coming.

During the year that Jackson had been engaged with the Creek, another showdown had already occurred far to the north against the British. In a response to the Massacre of the River Raisin, frontiersmen from the study area had answered that call to arms, and headed north to Canada to strike the British on their territory, and win a significant victory at the River Thames.

Chapter 6

The Americans are Coming
The Battle of the Thames

The news of the massacre at the River Raisin in January 1813 swept rapidly across the frontier bringing sadness, creating outrage, arousing passions, and renewing love of country. We had the same responses when we heard about the attacks on 11 September 2001, and understand the feelings of the frontiersmen of that day. The major differences were that in 1813 there was no capability to disseminate information in great detail, accompany it with vivid images, and transmit it in real-time. The sensory overload of our experience did not occur in 1813, but the pith of the news was there. Even without pundits to contribute their views of worst-case scenarios, the tendency would be to imagine, speculate, worry, and become angry. The frontiersmen were already "riled up" before they were called to action.

Call to Duty

The first call came from General William Henry Harrison to Governor Isaac Shelby. He asked for 2,000 Kentucky militiamen to help rebuild from the heavy losses experienced, most recently at the River Raisin. Governor Shelby wrote two letters in response on 31 July 1813, one to the colonels in the Kentucky Militia, and the other addressed to the soldiers in those units. He urged the colonels to exert their influence, as he put it, to convince their soldiers to volunteer to be part of the Harrison army. It was significant that he did not order them to do anything; he just asked. The stated purpose of the letter was to ask if they would volunteer and would provide an estimate of the number of their soldiers who they thought would volunteer. One cannot imagine a modern day governor asking rather than directing action to respond to a military need.

The second Shelby letter was to the soldiers of the Kentucky Militia. He stated that the mission was to invade Upper Canada, the name used for that part of the British Canada Territory that lay north of Lake Erie. He reviewed the need for that action, and pleaded for them to volunteer to be part of it. Most dramatically, he wrote that he would personally lead them into battle. That was persuasive coming from one who had been a leader in the Revolutionary War battle of Kings Mountain. It was also quite a promise for a sixty-three year old man to make.

> **FELLOW SOLDIERS:**
> *Your government has taken measures to act effectually against the enemy in Upper Canada. General Harrison, under the authority of the president of the United States, has called upon me for a strong 'body of troops to assist in effecting the grand objects of the campaign. The enemy in hopes to find us unprepared, has again invested fort Meigs; but he will again be mistaken; and before you can take the field he will be driven from that post.*
>
> *To comply with the requisition of general Harrison, a draft might be enforced; but believing as I do, that the ardor and patriotism of my countrymen has not abated, and that they have waited with impatience a fair opportunity of avenging the blood of their butchered friends, I have appointed the 31st day of August, next, at Newport, for a general rendezvous of Kentucky Volunteers. I will meet you there in person. I will lead you to the field of the battle, and share with you the dangers and honors of the campaign. Our services will not be required more than sixty days after we reach headquarters.*
>
> *I invite all officers and others possessing influence, to come forward with what mounted men they can raise; each shall command the men he may bring into the field. The superior officers will be appointed by myself at the place of general rendezvous, or on our arrival at headquarters: and I shall take pleasure in acknowledging to my country the merits and public spirit of those who may be useful in collecting a force for the present emergency.*

Those who have good rifles, and know how to use them, will bring them along. Those who have not, will be furnished with muskets at Newport.

FELLOWCITIZEN! Now is the time to act; and by one decisive blow, put an end to the contest in that quarter.

ISAAC SHELBY

It would have taken four or five days for the governor's letter to be delivered to the Militia regiments across the Kentucky. Another several days would have been needed to get the word to each militiaman. However it happened, the word was spread among the frontiersmen who were in the Militia. They were asked to bring their horse and their own rifle, if they had one, to Newport. One can imagine that riding a horse to Upper Canada was a more attractive option than walking would have been. The promise that their length of service would be just sixty days was also reassuring considering that the promise would get them back home before winter began.

Shelby was concerned that there would not be as many volunteers as Harrison had requested, and advised him of his concerns by letter on 8 August. He had received questions about what pay the soldiers would receive, would there be reimbursement for lost horses, and would forage for the horses be provided. He pointed out that volunteerism came at a real cost to the frontiersmen who were poor, had few assets, and could not afford out of pocket expenses. For most of them, there was not enough in the pocket to jingle. That was especially true for the frontiersmen who would have to travel up to 300 miles to the rendezvous. The cost of forage for the horses and rations for the men were not minor costs to those poor men. Shelby also questioned whether or not pay would be provided if the number of volunteers exceeded the 2,000 that Harrison had previously requested. He specifically asked for assurance of pay for at least 4,000 volunteers in case that many volunteered.[1]

The Trip North

Governor Shelby designated 31 August 1813 to be the rendezvous date at Newport, across the Ohio River from Cincinnati. Newport Barracks had been established initially as just a frontier arsenal about ten years earlier, but eventually was occupied by Army units. The militiamen converged on Newport from all areas of the state. It can be surmised that the volunteers from the Kentucky part of the study area joined their company commander Captain William Berryman in Glasgow, then together passed through their regimental headquarters town of Campbellsville, and traveled through the state capital Frankfort on the way to Newport Barracks (Figure 18). If so, they would have ridden over 200 miles by the time that they arrived.

Muskets were given to those who had not brought their own rifles as they arrived at Newport. Tomahawks were provided too. But they were mounted infantry rather than cavalry, and were not given sabers or pistols as cavalrymen would have been. They were expected to dismount and fight as infantry when engaging the enemy.

Figure 18. Newport Barracks.

Although the armament aspect of the assembly at Newport Barrack was important, it was not the most important activity. In that era, governors usually did not call an entire regiment to active duty as happens today, for example when a unit is nationalized. Rather in this case, the decision to volunteer for service was an individual decision by each Kentucky militiamen. All of those individuals who arrived in Newport had to be organized into military units. Companies, regiments, brigades, and divisions were created for the expedition and the battles that would follow.

The volunteer militiamen remained in Captain William Berryman's company when it was assigned to the 11th Regiment Kentucky Mounted Volunteers that was organized on 31 August 1813 at Newport. Colonel William Williams was designated to be the commander of the new regiment. He had lived on a farm southwest of Richmond, and was a cashier in a bank when he joined the Militia as a Private. At Newport Barracks, he was promoted from Major to Colonel, and given command of the new regiment. It was assigned to Brigadier General Caldwell's Brigade that in turn was assigned to Major General Desha's Division. That division would join other divisions under Governor Shelby.[2]

The new units with their volunteers began fording the Ohio River on 1 September to begin the trip toward Fort Meigs, near where Toledo is now located. The men were faced with riding another 320 miles or more through the thinly settled state of Ohio to reach the fort. Shelby wrote again to Harrison to tell him that he was moving northward with about 3,500 mounted men. He stated that he intended to stop at Springfield, Ohio, for ammunition, hospital, and other supplies.

Harrison's plan was to position 300,000 rations at four locations on the south shore of Lake Erie for use during the expedition into Upper Canada. Those storehouses would have 544 barrels of pork, 963 barrels of flour, 4,992 gallons of whiskey, 1,100 gallons of vinegar, 350 pounds of candy, 75 barrels of salt, and 2,000 pounds of soap. The delivery of those supplies was being completed as the frontiersmen rode north.[3] The lead elements of the army reached Springfield, picked up the additional supplies, and moved on without delay (Figure 19).

They reached Urbana on 9 September. The blockhouse there had been built early in the war to store supplies. General William Hull of the Michigan Territory had cleared a road from there to Detroit, Hull's Trace as it would be known. The route was through Indian lands, and the threat from those supporting the British increased as the army traveled northward. The road was not improved by our standards through most of its length, but a corduroy road of small logs laid crosswise across it, was constructed over some of the worst swampy areas. The transportation of provisions and ammunition slowed the movement of the long lines of heavily laden wagons. The wagons could not keep pace with the frontiersmen on horseback, and those riders became impatient with the pace. Even so, they had covered about 100 miles from

Newport to Urbana in nine days. They learned to maintain their unit integrity along the way, and were becoming accustomed to their new organization and the coordination required in maneuvers.

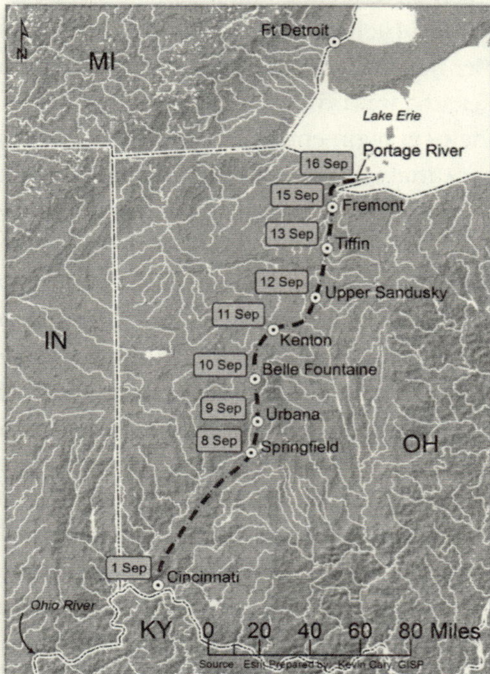

Figure 19. Route of the march from Newport to Lake Erie.

They reached Manary's blockhouse about three miles north of present day Bellefountaine on the 10th. It had been built by a settler about a year before, just a small log structure with gun portals. The soldiers were unaware that a significant victory had been achieved that very day when Commodore Perry captured the British fleet on Lake Erie. The news of that event would take several more days to reach Shelby's troops. Harrison had supported Perry's preparations by assigning 130 Kentucky riflemen from Boswell's and Johnson's regiments to him. Those sharpshooters climbed the ships' riggings and fired their long rifles down at the sailors aboard the British ships. Their accuracy hampered or curtailed movement on those ships, and was a significant factor in the eventual outcome of the battle.[4]

The march continued and they arrived and camped at Fort McArthur on the 11th. The fort was about three miles from present day Kenton. It had been built in 1812 to protect the ford across the Scioto River. A timber stockade surrounded about a half acre that had a few huts in the interior. There was not enough room inside for a few thousand men to camp.

On the 12th, Shelby's army arrived at Upper Sandusky, named because it was near the head of the Sandusky River.

They left at 8:00 a.m. on the 13th and stopped at Fort Ball near present day Tiffin. The fort was a supply depot with stockade and three blockhouses. They continued their ride to Lower Sandusky, now known as Fremont, on the 14th. Ammunition was distributed to the militiamen about midway on that ride as the potential threat from Indians increased.

On the 15th, with only fifteen miles to go before their arrival at Portage River, they received the news of Perry's victory over the British navy. The ride north over the last few miles must have been enjoyable, and their anticipation must have heightened for what was yet to come. Harrison's force would be augmented with about 1,000 mounted Kentucky volunteers commanded by Colonel Richard Johnson. Those soldiers had been provided from a previous request, and would join the volunteers who Shelby was leading northward.[5]

Perry's victory achieved two remarkable outcomes. One was that the British navy no longer posed a threat to American boats transporting supplies over the lakes to Detroit. Uninterrupted resupply to the American army as it invaded Upper Canada was thus assured. The other outcome was almost totally obverse of the first. The British had no boats or ships to transport supplies to their outposts and settlements in Upper Canada. As a result, the British army could not depend on resupply except for what could be delivered over land routes. Their options for future military actions would be severely limited.

The choice of the Portage River area as a primary forward supply point for the invasion was a fortuitous one. The location's access to Lake Erie, and the presence of Perry's ships, including the captured British ones, offered a new possibility for an invasion route. It could be made by ferrying troops across the lake and landing them on the north shore of Lake Erie in Upper Canada. Harrison and Perry chose a technique of island hopping that reminds one of General Douglas McArthur's famous amphibious invasions 130 years later in the South Pacific during World War II. Perry would use relatively small boats as ferries to hop men and supplies from Portage River to islands in the near side of the lake. The final assembly could be made on Middle Sister Island just north of the United States-Canada border. Ships would be used for the last hop of about twelve miles. The considerable effort to move men and supplies by water would still not be as great as the ride overland 100 miles westward around the swampy land and then northward to Detroit.

The new plan created one huge problem. Boats and ships did not have the capability to transport the over 4,000 horses in Harrison's army. He made the decision to send Johnson's cavalry overland around Lake Erie to Detroit, and to leave Shelby's horses behind when his troops embarked on boats. Solving that problem created another: what should be done with the 3,500 horses to be left behind? The answer lay within the Portage River area itself.

The Portage River was only forty or so miles long, but was deep and wide enough to be an obstacle to travelers. The settlers who moved westward found it necessary to portage around it, hence the name. The geography of the surrounding landscape made it an ideal staging area for the new plan for invasion using ships.

It also provided the solution for the horse problem. Inlets from Lake Erie extended southward forming a peninsula between them. The militiamen built a fence across its most narrow part, a fence about one and a half miles long. Each unit was directed to build the part of the fence line along their front. With almost 4,000 men working with hatchets, it did not take long to build. They cut poles about six to eight feet tall, and planted them in rows along the line. The treetops were piled up between the rows of poles to make an imposing barrier. The fence sealed off about 70,000 acres of grassland. That created an enormous corral into which the tired horses were released to graze and rest.

Something spooked the thousands of horses on that peninsula about four or five days later. The stampede overran a few huts that the militiamen had erected, injuring several and killing some. Some of the horses had to be extricated from the mud and sand along the riverbank. The stampede ended quickly though, and the horses grazed thereafter without incident.[6]

Roles for the troops were assigned during the preparations for the invasion. For example, all of Shelby's horses were to be left behind. Even Governor Shelby's own horse was left. Some troops would have to stay behind to guard the horses to assure that they would be available later for the ride back home. Shelby ordered each of the regiments from Kentucky to contribute one twentieth of their men for a detachment to guard and protect the horses. The regimental commanders asked for volunteers to be in that detachment.

The Kentuckians had come a long way for an opportunity to punish the British for the massacre at the River Raisin, and to meet and defeat them in combat. They did not volunteer to miss that opportunity. Some 150 Pennsylvanian militiamen had refused to cross into Canada. Kentuckians would have been greatly insulted if anyone insinuated that they too refused to be part of the invasion. So, no Kentuckians volunteered to stay behind. Each of the Kentucky regimental commanders had to assign men for that guard duty.[7] Private Ralph Williams (Chapter 11) was one of those frontiersmen from the study area who was ordered to stay behind as guards.

The Ingress

Harrison put his new plan in action. He sent Colonel Richard Johnson's 1,200 mounted militiamen back to Detroit (Figure 20). They would ford the river there on horseback into Canada and join the main invasion force that was to cross the lake by ship. Those horsemen would later play a pivotal role in the defeat of the British.

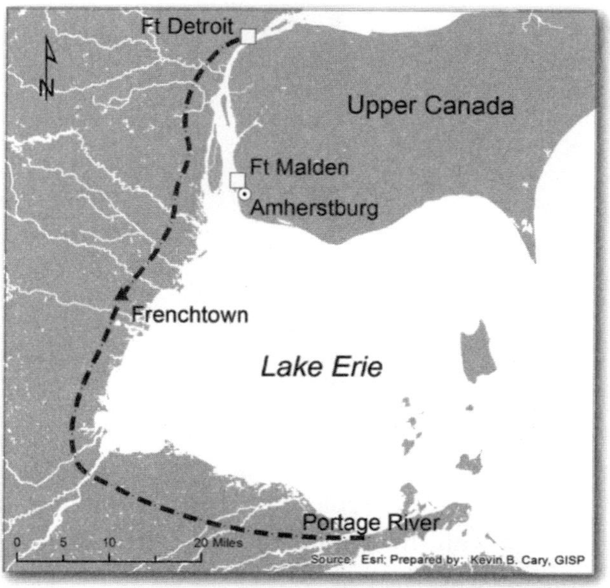

Figure 20. Mounted Kentuckians' route to Detroit.

On 20 September, Harrison embarked with his regulars, and began the island hopping. Governor Shelby sailed with part of his troops the next morning. The frontiersmen from the study area were part of General Desha's Division who were the last of the invasion force to depart. That division arrived at Middle Sister Island on 24 September, and the next two days were used to deliver and stockpile supplies. The entire invasion army and their supplies were crowded onto the tiny island, an area of only nine and a half acres of land.

On the 26th, Harrison and Perry sailed on a reconnaissance trip to choose possible landing sites, and to see the British Fort Malden. The fort was not visible from their vantage point, but they noted that a blockhouse on the shoreline had been destroyed. The question left unanswered was whether the British army was lying in wait or had already withdrawn.

The weather and winds presented near perfect conditions when Harrison ordered the embarkation of his entire force to begin on Friday morning, 27 September (Figure 21).

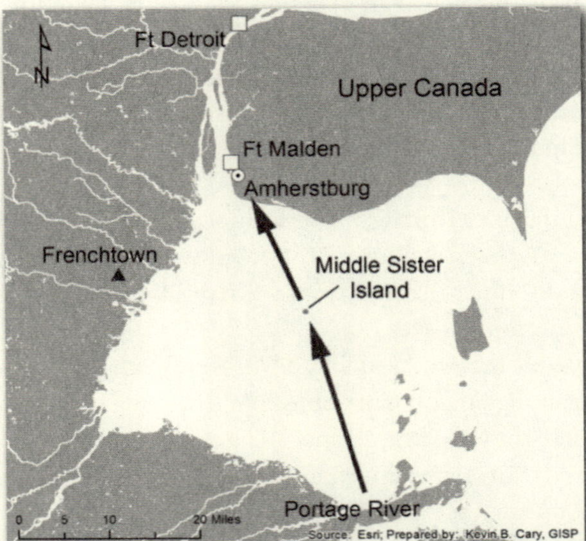

Figure 21. Ships route from Middle Sister Island to the beachhead.

It was an awesome sight. Few if any of the frontiersmen had ever seen a ship under sail. Before them were eighty sailing ships being escorted by nine gunboats. The ships were crowded with soldiers whose pulses quickened with the approach to the north shoreline of Lake Erie. The ships lined up obliquely toward the chosen landing site about four miles south of Fort Malden. When they reached shallow water near Hartley's Point, the militiamen jumped in and waded to shore. It was about four o'clock when they spread out in battle formation ready to repel any attack. But there were no enemy troops in sight.

British Colonel Proctor, he of River Raisin infamy, had withdrawn all his men, and all of the Indians led by Tecumseh. He was not outnumbered, although he may have thought that he was. He wanted to avoid the possibility that his supply route would be severed. Proctor burned the buildings at Fort Malden, and withdrew toward Sandwich, the town across the river from Detroit. Tecumseh was furious and disgusted about the retreat without a fight, without any Americans within sight, and without Proctor ever having lost a battle. Tecumseh was quoted as saying, "....if we had remained at the town ... we could have kept the enemy from landing and held our hunting grounds for our children. Now they tell me that you want to withdraw to the river Thames ....I am tired of it all. Every word you say evaporates like smoke from our pipes. Father, you are like a crawfish that does not know how to walk straight ahead." Nevertheless, even with that level of disgust, his hated of Americans was greater, and he agreed to remain with Proctor at least until they reached Moraviantown on the banks of the Thames about fifty miles east of Detroit.[8]

The abandoned Fort Malden and the town of Amherstburg were used as campsites for the Americans on their first night ashore. Harrison did not vigorously chase Proctor, but slowly moved northward awaiting Johnson's mounted infantry to come from Detroit before engaging the enemy. Harrison knew that Proctor had a large number of horses because not one could be found around the old fort and town. The following day, Harrison left a small garrison to hold the Amherstburg area, and began the march to Sandwich. His army arrived there on the 29th.

Harrison and Shelby met on 1 October, and developed a plan to pursue Proctor who was slowly moving away from them eastward along the shore of Lake St. Clair. Later that day, Johnson's mounted Kentuckians arrived in Detroit, and were urged to immediately cross the river to Sandwich that day. Harrison ordered one brigade of about 1,500 men to keep and hold Detroit and Sandwich, but prepared everyone else to be ready to move out the next morning.

The infantry began marching just after sunrise on the 2nd. Johnson's mounted men were late getting started, slowed by the need to draw provisions. After about twelve miles, the mounted men caught up, and Harrison halted his troops to allow them to pass through to the front. Harrison had about 2,700 men in tow stretched back over the three miles behind. They reached the mouth of the Thames River late that afternoon.

Perry's three gunboats and other supply boats continued the next day, shadowing the advance as they had done up to then. However, the entry into the Thames River became too dangerous. The water became too shallow in places, and there was thick vegetative growth along its steep banks that provided ideal cover for snipers. The boats stopped and a company of men was left to protect them. The remaining force pushed on.[9]

The now confident army continued to pursue on the 4th, and were challenged by the Indians near Chatham. A short exchange of fire was followed by a quick withdrawal by the Indians. Johnson's mounted men were setting the pace, and throughout the day the interval between them and the British was closing. Proctor was burning whatever he could not take with him. Somehow, his men neglected to burn all the bridges, and that accelerated the movement of the Americans. They found a still-smoldering flourmill and a distillery with 5,000 stands of arms still in flames. They camped that evening near two burning boats. It was clear that they were very close to the enemy, and they knew that there would soon be a battle.[10]

On the morning of 5 October, the Americans captured two gunboats loaded with ammunition. That was good news that indicated disorder in the British retreat. When retreat is orderly, armies do not leave ammunition behind that could be used by the enemy. Harrison continued to Arnold's Mills, a deep-water ford across the Thames. The mounted men crossed carrying infantry soldiers mounted behind them, and others men were moved across using captured boats (Figure 22).

By noon, the entire force was across to the north side. Two hours later, they came to the campsite the British had used the previous night. A captured enemy wagoner informed them that the British were waiting just ahead in battle alignment. The Americans had marched fifty-five miles in three and a half days with Tecumseh unsuccessfully trying to delay them. The army was ready for action, and their moment in history was at hand.[11]

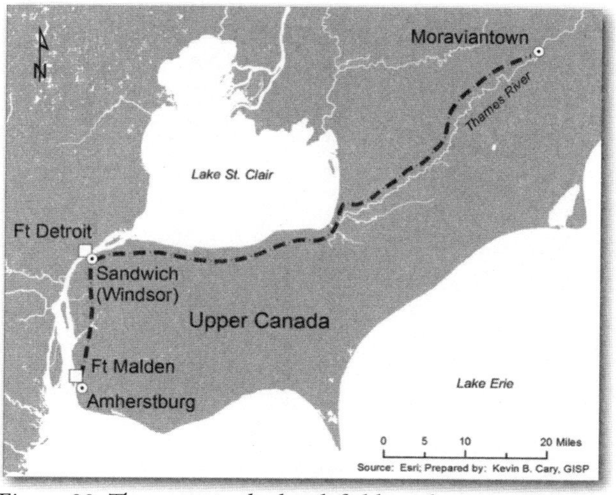

Figure 22. The route to the battlefield on the River Thames.

The Battle of the Thames

The battlefield was chosen by Proctor to provide concentrated firepower against the Americans, and limit their options to maneuver. He had his men up at six in the morning on the 6th, and placed them in their battle positions. He used the Thames River on the south side of the battlefield as one maneuver-limiting boundary. The large swamp on the north side was another similar limiting boundary, and several hundred Indians were deployed in the wooded area along its southern edge ready to open fire into the flank of any Americans who would attack on that side. A small swamp was in the center of the battlefield, and it limited the Americans to just two narrow approaches, one on either of its sides. Proctor had known that, when threatened by a superior force, choosing the place and the time of the battle offered the best opportunity for success. The battlefield was carefully chosen for the advantages it offered.

Proctor placed about 830 men facing the southern approach route. The remaining British troops and about 500 Indians were placed facing the northern approach route. The battlefield funneled toward the British lines, wider in the west and narrower to the east. The east half of the battlefield was wooded with maple, oak, and beech. No matter how the Americans approached, they would receive fire from two sides, the east and the north (Figure 23).[12]

Harrison's order of battle placed General Trotter's Brigade of 500 men in the front line with his right on the road along the river and his left extending almost to the large swamp. Trotter's men were from the counties that were home to the Kentuckians massacred at the River Raisin. King's Brigade formed a second line about 150 yards behind Trotter. The third line was Chiles' Brigade stationed behind King to be used as reserves. The frontiersmen from the study area were in Caldwell's regiment and were formed en potence, that is to say obliquely, to its adjacent front line. We would likely say that they formed a dogleg in the front line, or, perhaps, like a rotated letter L. They were in position facing Tecumseh's Indians in the large swamp to the north.

Governor Shelby, as promised, positioned himself with his aide General John Adair at the crotchet, the flex point between Caldwell and Trotter. He was in a perfect position to lead and coordinate the actions of those two as the battle developed. Harrison positioned himself near the road on the side of Trotter's front line near the river. Commodore Perry was still with him, acting as his aide-de-camp.[13]

Harrison's plan sent the few regular army men from his force, augmented by ten to twelve friendly Indians, into the thick woods on the riverbank of the Thames. Their task was to advance surreptitiously, attack, and capture the single British cannon than was covering the road along the river (Figure 23).

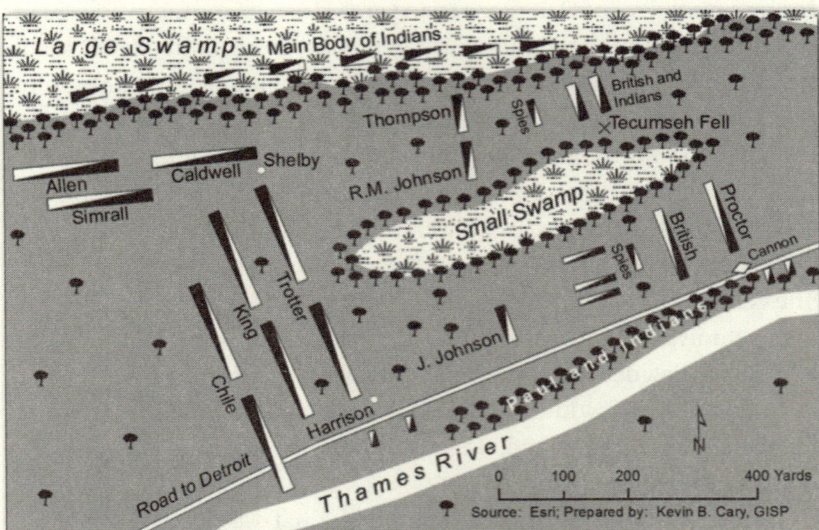

Figure 23. The Battle of the River Thames, adapted from Lossing.[14]

After looking over the battlefield, Colonel Richard Johnson saw that the British army was concentrated into two areas each with a relatively small width of 250 yards, one on the south side and one on the north side. He saw that there was insufficient maneuver room between the small swamp and the river for his entire regiment. A battalion, half of his regiment, would be about the right size to fit the space available in each approach area. He also noted that the British soldiers were posted in open order, that is to say, with intervals of three or four feet between them.

All of these factors presented a scenario for which he had previously anticipated. From May until October, Colonel Richard Johnson had given his mounted men practice maintaining a straight line while charging through a forest that had no underbrush. He had them fire blank cartridges from horseback to accustom the horses to the sounds of gunfire. He trained the men to dismount, form into battle formations, and fire blanks to simulate battle conditions. With that experience and training of both men and horses, he was confident that a cavalry charge in a frontal assault would be successful against the British open order line.[15]

The notion was that the British would not expect it because mounted infantry by tradition rode to the battlefield, carried muskets, had no sabers, and dismounted and fought as infantry. Johnson proposed his idea and Harrison approved it. Harrison later wrote, "The American backwoodsmen ride better in the woods than any other people; a musket or rifle is no impediment to them, being accustomed to carry them on horseback, from their earliest youth."[16]

Harrison approved the plan. A scout had found a path through the edge of the small swamp, and Colonel Richard Johnson led one of his battalions through it to a position on the northern approach route. That left his brother Lieutenant Colonel James Johnson's Battalion in the southern approach.

It took about an hour and a half to assemble the entire force on the battlefield, all accomplished under the watchful eyes of the British about 300 yards away. The British troops had difficulty seeing the Americans, most of whom were not uniformed. The Americans had the same difficulty because most of the British and Indians were not wearing red uniforms. Harrison noted that the British had not attacked during the time he was assembling his force. It was time for the Americans to attack before the British had a change of mind.

The plan sent a few regular Army men in his force, augmented by ten to twelve friendly Indians, into the thick woods on the riverbank. Their task was to advance surreptitiously, attack, and capture the British cannon covering the road along the river.

The advance began with Harrison ordering the bugles to sound the charge, and the British, prompted by a single gunshot from one their men, fired raggedly rather than in a massed volley. The small group of Americans, who stole through the trees along the river, attacked the only British cannon on the field. The horses spooked, fled, and carried the unfired cannon with them away from the battlefield.[17]

Between the small swamp and the river, Lieutenant Colonel James Johnson's mounted Kentuckians charged toward the British line rather than dismounting before the charge as the British expected. The British view of the charge of 500 horses charging toward them must have been awesome. Perhaps they could have stood their ground if it had been an infantry charge. But this cavalry-like charge was quite different from what they had previously faced. These horses could run over and trample them. Survival instincts caused them to side step to let the horses pass by. The British troops, tired and disheartened by the retreat from Detroit, were unprotected by any physical barriers, and stood without barricades in front of them.[18]

In a matter of a very few minutes, Johnson's men had passed through the British front line, and then through the second British line. They dismounted, turned, and attacked them from behind on foot. The redcoats were trapped between Johnson's troops and those of the advancing men from General Trotter's force. The trapped British soldiers began surrendering in groups, and the remaining British reserves facing the southern approach, along with their leader Proctor, began a disorganized withdrawal eastward. The Americans pursued, but were outdistanced by the fleeing British.[19]

Colonel Richard Johnson's smaller battalion of mounted Kentuckians charged along the northern approach between the small swamp and the large swamp. He did not fare as well as his brother did. Tecumseh's Indians held their fire until the Americans were within a few paces of them, and poured a withering fire from behind the trees along the edge of the large swamp. It became apparent that the charge could not be sustained on horseback. Johnson ordered his troops to dismount. He remained on horseback to better see the battlefield. Within the next several minutes, Johnson received wounds to his thigh, hip, and hand. His horse died of wounds on the field. However, Johnson would survive to become Vice President to President Van Buren.

The Indians confronting Johnson's men on the northern approach advanced. Fire continued from those Indians in the woods along the side of the approach. Hand to hand fighting ensued. The Indians advanced toward the crotchet between Caldwell's and Trotter's Divisions. Shelby saw that Johnson needed support. He committed Simrall's Regiment to the action in support of Thompson along the northern edge of the large swamp. Caldwell's Regiment, with the frontiersmen from the study area, had commenced a running fire with the Indians along the swamp in front of them. The fire from the large swamp continued for about a half an hour.[20]

The Indian resistance began to diminish when the sounds of battle south of the small swamp could no longer be heard. The sounds from there diminished as the British withdrawal continued, and elements of Trotter's Division chased them away from the battlefield. During the battle in the northern approach, Tecumseh was fatally shot. His death by a gunshot was credited to Colonel Richard Johnson after he had received a wound to his hand from Tecumseh.

The battle was over about fifty-five minutes after the bugles signaled the attack. Proctor continued to be pursued for about fifteen miles. However, no other battle occurred. Only about sixty of the retreating British were captured. They did not capture Proctor, but did capture his baggage, papers, and telescope.

As the evening arrived and a camp for the night was being prepared, designated soldiers searched the battlefield for the dead and wounded, wading through the grass and the underbrush. As the American dead were found, they were moved to a small hillock near the road on the east side of the battlefield where the British artillery piece was located. The British dead were also laid together near the same spot. The Indians removed all but thirty-three of their dead from the battlefield, and Tecumseh's burial site was a secret known only to them. All of the bodies were guarded through the night.

The troops dug two trenches the next morning, one for the British troops and one for the Americans. The bodies were placed in the trenches with their hands crossed over their heart, and they were covered with linsey-woolsey blankets before the trenches were filled. The names of the Americans who were buried there were carved into the bark of the beech trees that stood nearby.[21]

There were various estimates of the number of casualties. McAfee placed the American losses as seventeen men killed and thirty wounded. The British had 601 men captured, eighteen killed, and twenty-six wounded. Death is an individual statistic and its finality may be subsumed when estimates of the total battle casualties are used.

There was a sizable village of Moraviantown near the battlefield that was home to the Lenape Indians, many of whom were Christians and associated with the protestant Moravian Church. Harrison's army burned the town on the 6th to assure that the British army would not reoccupy it during the coming winter. The following day, the army began its return to Detroit.

The Egress

Most of the supplies, including those captured, were floated downstream on boats on the Thames. The wounded were transported by boat too. The remainder of the army was very tired, and the lagging men were spread over about five miles. The mounted men accompanied by Harrison arrived at Sandwich on the 9th. The infantry, including the frontiersmen from the study area and the British prisoners, began arriving the next day. A severe storm precluded passage across the river into Detroit. It was extremely cold and windy. Sleet and snow began to fall and continued all night until the storm subsided. The crossing was finally made at the mouth of the River Rouge.

The Kentuckians, who had left their horses behind before they ferried into Canada, were more than a little upset that no water transportation was waiting to take them back to their horses. They would be required to walk the hundred miles instead. Harrison assembled them to assure them that the ships were being used for important purposes, and weren't available to transport them. By the 13th, all of the Kentuckians were on their long cold walk from Fort Detroit to the Portage River area from where they had embarked across Lake Erie.[22]

The night of the 14th was wet and miserable with no tents to keep the rain away. There were several streams to cross along the way, each requiring them to wade across. The army reached the River Raisin the next day. Shelby detailed Simrall's Regiment to search the scene of the battle of Frenchtown and the massacre of the River Raisin. They were to find and bury the remains they found. They found the skeletal remains of sixty-five men, and interred them. Passing over that battlefield must have been sobering to all the men, but there must have been feelings of pride too. After all, they felt that the deaths of those men at the Battle of the Thames had been avenged.

The men had been on half rations for four days when they marched twenty-three miles on the 16th. It rained again that night, another cold and wet one, without shelter from the rain. Many men had colds or other ailments, but they had no option other than to move onward. On the morning of the 17th, a small beef was slaughtered for each regiment. That was insufficient in quantity to sate the soldiers, but they enjoyed it nonetheless. Afterward, they began to cross the Maumee River that in places was crotch deep. Bone chilling might be an adequate description for that crossing. On the 18th, they covered twenty-five miles in nine hours without stopping or resting.

The men awoke on the final day of the march, the 19th, with a heavy frost covering the ground. They persevered, covered the last twelve miles, and met the men who had been left behind with the horses. Those men had done their job well. None of the horses had escaped, and all had gained weight grazing on the abundant grass on the peninsula where they were corralled.

The Route South

The next day was snowy and blustery. Each man found a horse, and the long ride south toward home began on 21 October. A number of the sick men would die en route.[23]

The route home did not retrace their trip north. Instead, Shelby directed them to go through Upper Sandusky to Franklinton (now called Columbus). There the men deposited in the armory any arms or accouterments that they had been given at Newport Barracks on the way up (Figure 24).

From there, they traveled to Fort Bull located at Chillicothe, Ohio's state capital at that time. The 601 prisoners they had captured at the Battle of the Thames were deposited there. The prison camp already held the over 300 seaman that Commodore Perry's men had captured during the battle on Lake Erie.

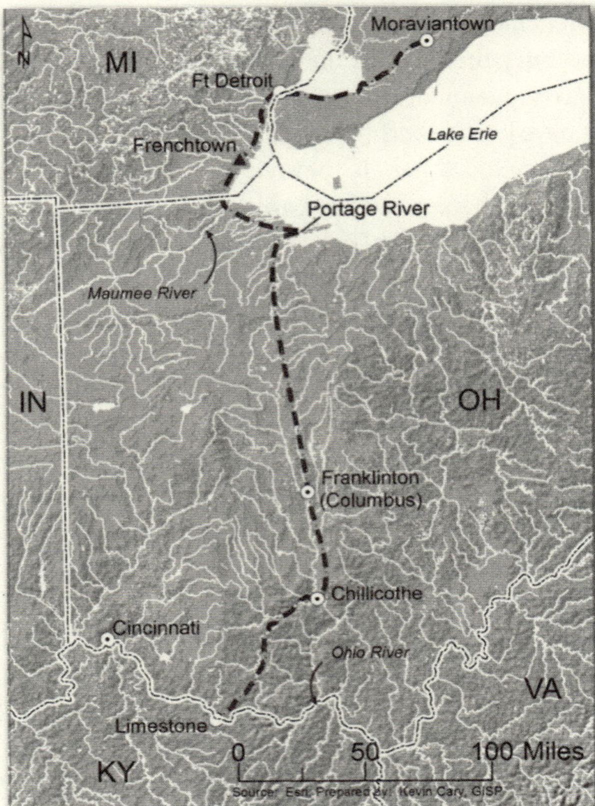

Figure 24. The route south to Limestone.

The troops continued to ride south from Chillicothe on Zanes Trace, a road that followed an old buffalo path.[24] Buffalo traces, as they were called, were obvious choices to be used as roads. The underbrush had been cleared to widen it about fifteen years earlier. The ride was good except there were no bridges. The horses would wade across or swim across where the fords were too deep. The current Ohio Route 41 generally follows Zane's Trace.

Zane's Trace passed through what is now Bainbridge and West Union to Aberdeen on the Ohio River.[25] Directly across the Ohio River was the village of Limestone (now Maysville), Kentucky (Figure 25).

Before the Ohio was altered by a series of locks and dams, it behaved like a stream rather than like a lake. As a stream, it was depositing sediment on north shore at Aberdeen producing a gently sloping sand bar. On the Limestone side, the river was cutting a deep channel next to a steep bank. The land area along the river near Limestone was narrow, hemmed in by the steep hills to the south. Limestone was a natural and logical place for the anchorage of boats. It was a port for flatboats that came downstream from Pittsburgh and other ports upstream.[26] It was another place where the horses might have to swim during the last portion of the crossing if the Ohio was not at low flow. The buffalo herds had crossed there in earlier days, so the horses could do it now.

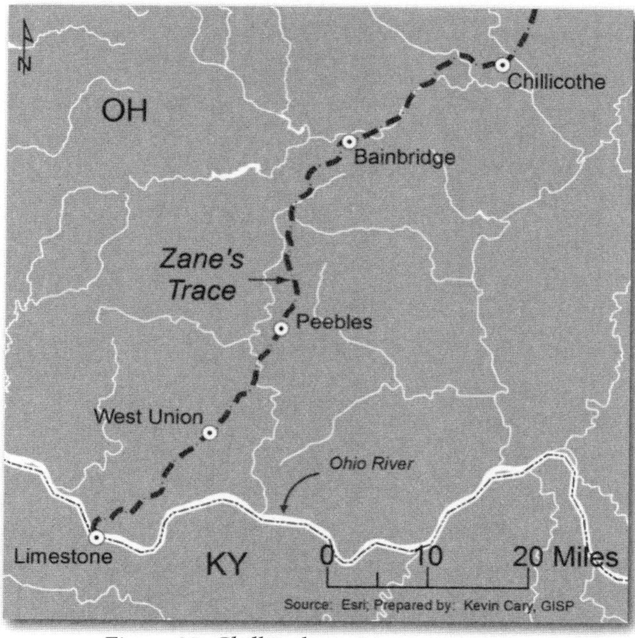

Figure 25. Chillicothe to Limestone route.

Limestone (now Maysville) was located at the confluence of the short Limestone Creek and the Ohio River. It was laid out in straight streets, and there were about 100 houses there when the frontiersmen arrived.[27]

Among the lead elements to arrive in Limestone was Private John Abshear who was there on 1 November. Most of the others arrived by 4 November when the unit was formally mustered out of service. Apparently some soldiers arrived later. Among them were Privates John Burton, James Cole, Isaiah Kerby, and others who were discharged on the 13th. Governor Shelby missed on his promise to have them serve just sixty days, but not by much. It had actually been sixty-five days when the unit was mustered out.

They were back on Kentucky soil but they were not yet home. They followed Limestone Creek that was only about four miles long. The buffalo herds had created a path along the creek to the top of the hills. The gradual grade of the path made it a good choice for the horsemen too. The buffalo trace continued at the top of the hills westward toward the salt licks that attracted them. The trace passed through Paris, Lexington, Harrodsburg, Greensburg, and Glasgow. That route would later become a stagecoach road.

The road from Limestone to Frankfort had been surveyed eighteen years earlier in 1795, and described as passing through heavy forest.[28] After that survey, the road had been the principal route for moving river borne freight from Limestone to the interior of the Bluegrass Region. It would have been a well-worn road by 1813.

The men had endured the hardships and dangers together during the past two months. They were proud of what they had accomplished together, and the nation was proud of them too. The Battle of the Thames had changed the war. Confidence had been restored in the militia and their ability to win against the British. The men had shared so much. But, now they had to say their goodbyes. Goodbyes to comrades under such circumstances are never easy, and are usually said quickly to stave off tears. No doubt they were no exceptions as they separated to find their way home.

They dispersed in all directions from Limestone, each soldier finding his way home rather than formally marching as a group. The frontiersmen from the study area had among the longest rides home. They covered well over 200 miles over that final leg home. Even if they kept a pace of twenty-five miles a day, it would have taken them about a week to get home.

The members of Captain Berryman's Company are shown in Table 5. The company was detached from its parent regiment for the expedition and assigned to the 11th Regiment Detached Kentucky Mounted Militia. The frontiersmen from the study area whose biographical sketches are in Chapter 11 are shown in bold print.[29]

There would be no bands, no parades, and no perks when they got home, just a personal satisfaction of a job well done. We find it hard to fully understand that they had traveled a total distance equal to that between their home and Albuquerque, New Mexico. They had fought and won a battle that changed the course of the war. All that was accomplished after they left home just three months before. How could their neighbors and relatives on the frontier fully appreciate what they had done in such a short time?

Staff	
William Berryman, Captain	**James Spilman, Sergeant**
Willis J. Williams, First Lieutenant	**James McCallister, Corporal**
Henry Collins, Ensign	**Jesse Kerby, Corporal**
Travers Duncan, Sergeant	Upsham Martin, Corporal
Samuel Kerby, Sergeant	Robert Duff, Corporal
Joseph Chapman, Sergeant	Barnabus Low, Musician

Privates		
Abshear, John	**Duncan, Ashley**	McKinney, Kennith
Burton, Berry	Ellison, George	Ormsby, Nicholas
Burton, John	Field, Ambrose	**Patton, William**
Carter, Charles	Foley, James	Ray, James S
Chapman, Jeremiah	**Gibson, John**	Rockburk, Benjamin
Chason, David	Gibson, Joseph	Sameboy, Adam
Davis, John	Gibson, Jacob	Thomas, Samuel
Dawson, Jonathan	**Gibson, William**	Whaley, James
Dinwiddie, James	**Hardcastle, John**	Wharton, Thomas
Dobson, James	Hardcastle, William	Wharton, Edwin
Dobson, Thomas	Hopson, Alexander	Wainscott, Robert
Dowell, David	**Kerby, Isaiah**	**Williams, Ralph**
Dowell, John	Martin, William G	Young, William

Table 5. Frontiersmen from the study area who were in the Battle of the Thames.

However, in that short time, the British had captured Washington D.C., and burned our capitol. The work of the frontiersmen was not over yet.

Chapter 7

By the Dawn's Early Light

The British Invasion

Kentucky was never attacked directly by the British during the War of 1812, but our ancestral state of Virginia was. Virginians responded to the call to duty in response to the threat of a British invasion, and then again to the invasion itself when it occurred. They defended their nation by defending their state. There were no frontiersmen from the study area involved in the military activities in Virginia. However, there were at least twelve veterans who migrated from Virginia to the frontier of Kentucky and Tennessee after the war ended. Their stories became part of this study too.

Like Kentucky, the Militias of Virginia, Maryland, and North Carolina responded to calls to duty by asking for volunteers from a particular regiment. Usually, the number of volunteers was sufficient to fulfill the request. When the number was insufficient, militiamen were drafted, that is to say selected from the ranks of the Militia, to serve.

Physically fit white men between eighteen and forty-five were enrolled into their local Militia. Neither free blacks nor slaves were permitted to become soldiers in the Virginia militia. That was true of all other state militias too. Chapter 13 explains the prohibition of their service in the army and the permission of their service in the navy.

The Virginia Militia was organized somewhat differently than Kentucky's and Tennessee's. Each county of Virginia had a numbered militia regiment and a few had more than one. Halifax County, for example, had the 69th Regiment and the 84th Regiment. All the state's regiments were under the command of the governor. He exercised that power when he directed those regiments to participate in the defense of Norfolk and Richmond, Virginia. The president of the United States had the constitutional power to call upon state militias to respond to repel invasions of other parts of our nation. For example, those two Halifax County regiments deployed to Maryland to thwart the British invasion there.[1]

In another much earlier example of a response to a national call, Virginia Militia units had been requested to augment General Harrison's force after his army had been depleted by Hull's surrender at Detroit. Virginia sent a brigade of militiamen. They crossed into Ohio in October 1812. They helped Harrison build Fort Meigs before returning home.

The British fleet arrived offshore of Hampton Roads, Virginia, in February 1813. Their objective was to blockade the entrance to Chesapeake Bay. Virginians saw the fleet as a possible prelude to invasion and an assault on Richmond.

In June 1813, the British attempted to take Craney Island near Norfolk with about 2,500 men, but were repelled by artillery that was part of the some 700 militiamen deployed there. Three days later, the British attacked, captured, and pillaged the town of Hampton.

In April 1814, a British force captured and occupied Tangier Island in Chesapeake Bay. That success spawned subsequent invasions into Accomack, Westmoreland, and Northumberland Counties of Virginia during June, July, and August. In each case, the British attacked, occupied the area for a short time, and then withdrew.

After the war against Napoleon's army had been successfully ended, seasoned troops sailed to augment the British forces engaged in the war with the United States. Those troops arrived offshore of Virginia. Tangier Island was used as the assembly point for the newly arrived British troops. For the first time, Virginia's militiamen were about to face well trained and battle tested regular army infantry.

President James Madison called a cabinet meeting on 1 July 1814 to discuss the defense of Washington, D.C. The secretary of war assured the president that the British objective was Baltimore, not Washington. The Madison administration had not altered its view of the state militias. They would pay expenses of only those specifically called to duty by the federal government. The opposition federalists' stand was that if the nation declared war, the federal government should pay for it.

Maryland Governor Winder, a federalist, asked the secretary of war in March if the United States would defray expenses of his state Militia if the federal government called them up in response to a British invasion. His view was that an invasion by the British was a national problem, not just a state problem, and should be supported by federal funds. The issue became focused when the president on 24 March authorized 500 militiamen to defend Annapolis and 2,000 to defend Baltimore. Who should pay?

There were no fortifications around Washington. Secretary of War John Armstrong, Jr., declared that their cost would empty the treasury, and thus none were built. For the same reason, he objected to calling up the militia before the need became immediate. President Madison supported that view also. Back in June, the British had advanced to within forty miles of Washington but, following the president's policy, the Militia was not called up. The president said that the call up of the Militia before ascertaining the British objective was financially wasteful.[2]

Attack on Washington D.C.

The British clearly identified their objectives when they sailed up the Patuxent River and landed 4,500 regulars at Benedict, Maryland on 19 August 1814. The British army under General Robert was going to Washington to capture it, and to demoralize the Americans with the loss of their capital.

The British were apprehensive about their invasion, and the subsequent march toward Washington. They expected resistance that would present challenges at any and every moment along the way. They also expected to be slowed by the destruction of bridges and obstruction of the roads. All their apprehensions were unrealized. They encountered no opposition, and had no difficulty in transit. There was no opposing force to deal with, and therefore no one to burn the bridges behind them to slow the British advance. One British soldier stated that it was like strolling though open fields on a summer picnic.[3]

The British army was going deep into their enemy's territory, and their supply lines would be stretched. Dangerous would be the word for their action. They only made six miles on the first day of the march, but the pace quickened a bit afterward with no opposition to slow them. They were at Nottingham on the 21st, just west of Upper Marlboro on the 22nd, and two days later arrived at Bladensburg. There, they could cross the Anacostia River to begin an approach toward Washington (Figure 26).

The call eventually went out to the District of Columbia, Maryland, and Virginia Militias. They responded. About 700 Virginians arrived in Washington on the evening of the 23rd. They went to the arsenal on the 24th to draw arms and ammunition. However, red tape existed even then, and that slowed the issue of arms and ammunition. The accounting process was too slow for the militiamen to get to Bladensburg in time.

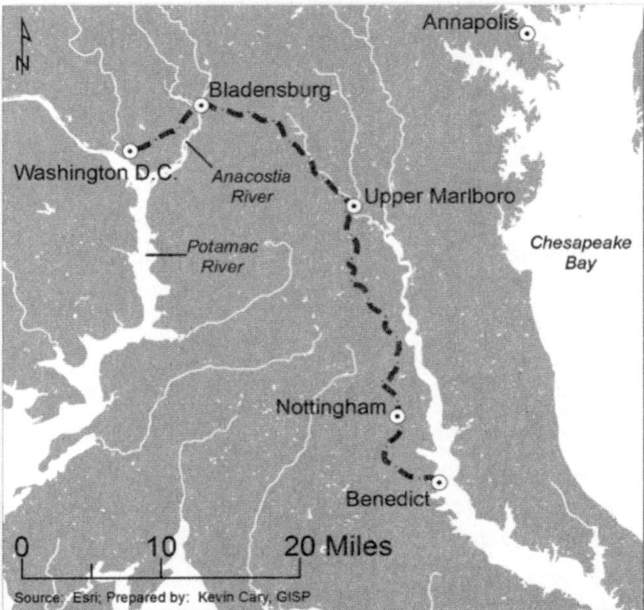

Figure 26. Attack route to Washington DC.

At Bladensburg, the Maryland commander was Brigadier General Tobias E. Stansbury. He had directed the Americans into defensive positions. Washington lay only about twelve miles away, an easy ride for the capital's politicians.

Throughout history, generals on the battlefield have received unneeded advice, instruction, or orders from politicians far removed from the scene of the battle. In 168 BC, a general said, "…if there is anyone who is confident that he can advise me about the best interest of the nation in the campaign which I am now about to conduct, let him not deny the state his services, — let him come with me to Macedonia."[4]

President James Madison, with two dueling pistols at his waist, Secretary of State and future president James Monroe, Secretary of War John Armstrong, Jr., the Secretary of the Treasury, and the Attorney General arrived on the scene at Bladensburg.[5] Without invitation, all had come to that "Macedonia." The soldiers on the field would have told all of them that war is not an appropriate spectator sport.

President Madison had served as a colonel commanding a regiment of the Virginia Militia during the Revolutionary War. His health precluded any active duty service, and he had no combat experience in that war. He was the first president to sign a declaration of war, and as Commander in Chief, had a right to be on the battlefield. Secretary of State Monroe, on the other hand, had combat experience during the Revolutionary War. He was wounded at the battle of Trenton in 1776. A bullet grazed his chest and lodged in his shoulder severing an artery along the way. The bleeding was stopped and the surgeon tried unsuccessfully to remove the bullet. Regardless of his experience, the duties of the secretary of state did not include becoming personally involved in combat operations. He did so anyway.

Without General Stansbury's knowledge, Secretary of State Monroe issued orders that moved the second line of defense. When the British assault collapsed the first line, the second could not provide support. Its new position prevented support of the first line. The valiant stand ended with a rout.[6] The observers departed "Macedonia" when it became clear that the battle was not ending quickly. The American losses were twenty-six killed and fifty-one wounded, while the British lost sixty-four killed and 185 wounded. Even so, the road to Washington was open.[7]

While Secretary of State Monroe was off to Bladensburg, one of his staff members had the foresight to gather up the Declaration of Independence, George Washington's papers, and other valuable documents. He hid them in a gristmill two miles from Georgetown.

Dolly Madison remained in the White House when President Madison went off to Bladensburg. When she heard the artillery fire coming from Bladensburg, she filled up a wagon with the mansion's silverware and other valuables and sent them to the Bank of Maryland for safekeeping. She was urged to leave, but remained until Gilbert Stuart's portrait of George Washington was removed and taken to safety. Most of the government had already fled, and she soon followed.

Ross and Cockburn's forces entered Washington about 8:00 p.m. and proceeded to the Capitol. They set about chopping up the woodwork and the furniture from the House of Representatives. The wood was used as fuel, and flames soon engulfed the building (Figure 27).

In addition to the Capitol, the first Library of Congress was burned, including the 740 books bought during Jefferson's administration. The Treasury Building was torched as well. The destruction was part of an orchestrated effort that destroyed the War Office, the National Archives, and the bridge across the Potomac. The focus of the destruction was on public buildings rather than on armories, supply depots, and arsenals. Clearly, the destruction was aimed at non-military targets to achieve the greatest interruption of the functioning government.[8]

The British fleet commander Admiral George Cockburn delighted in sitting in the presidential mansion at the dining room table that was set for forty places. He and his men drank the mansion's wine, and then carried away souvenirs. Among those were a small picture of Dolly Madison and the cushions on which Dolly sat. As they left, they lighted oil-soaked rags and tossed them into the mansion. It was soon filled with flames.

Figure 27. The burned out Capitol, source National Park Service.

The state and the war departments were burned, but the bureau of patents was spared from the torch after a passionate plea by its commissioner. The burning continued through the following day and into the night. The flames could be seen from Baltimore, thirty-four miles away.

The capital city of 6,000 residents had not been evacuated, and many of its citizens witnessed its destruction first hand. That night a violent storm struck with high winds and torrential rain. Before daylight, the British began their orderly withdrawal back toward Benedict, but stoked the fires before they left.

The British traveled away from Washington at a leisurely pace because no one was chasing them. They retraced their incursion route back to Benedict over the next three days, and began boarding their ships. [9]

Meanwhile back in Washington, President Madison called his Secretary of War Armstrong on the carpet. After any embarrassing or humiliating event, there is a demand for the formation of a "should have done" committee to identify who knew what, when they knew it, and who should be blamed for the result. Secretary of State Monroe volunteered to replace Armstrong whom he blamed for the failure of the defense of Washington. The president also blamed Armstrong, and asked him to resign. Armstrong resigned on 5 September in a letter defending his actions, and alleging that the president had kowtowed to the opinions of others. Secretary of State Monroe assumed the additional role of secretary of war. He was immediately faced with the need to borrow money from the banks to finance the nation's defense. He was finding that the "should of done" committee's work was considerably easier than that of the "what to do" committee.[10]

Attack on Baltimore

The British knockout blow was to be the capture and destruction of Baltimore. Like Washington, no fortifications had been built to defend it. The British landed 4,500 men at North Point east of Baltimore on 12 September 1814. Their commander expected to encounter resistance by regular Army soldiers, and planned to test the defenders of Baltimore.[11]

The call to duty this time resulted in a flood of militiamen who swarmed with little or no organization to meet the destroyers of our capital. The British were half way to Baltimore before they encountered the Militia. Although they outnumbered the Americans about four to three, they lost 340 killed to the American loss of 250. The first battle was fought about five miles east of Baltimore, and the next day another battle occurred at Hampstead Hill (Figure 28).

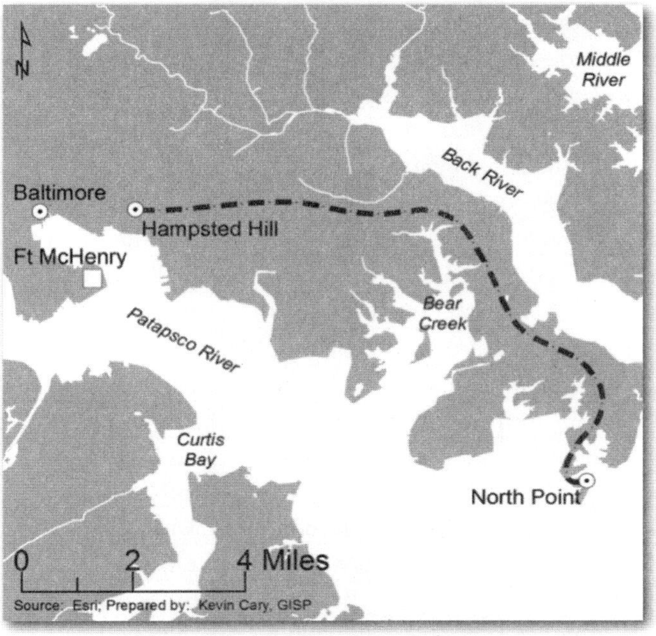

Figure 28. Attack route to Baltimore.

On the 13th, the British navy began bombardment of Fort McHenry. The next morning, a new flag was raised to replace the tattered one. From aboard a ship in the harbor, Francis Scott Key saw the flag, and wrote what would become the "Star Spangled Banner." The flag had fifteen stars and fifteen stripes, representing Kentucky's admission as the fifteenth state. That design would not be continued. New states received stars on subsequent flags, but stripes would remain at thirteen.

The British troops withdrew and embarked on ships. Their action was not over for those soldiers. The ships and the men were sent to the Gulf of Mexico where they would invade Louisiana a few weeks later and fight the battle of New Orleans.

The Militiamen

There were no residents of the study area who left Kentucky or Tennessee to serve in the campaigns of the eastern United States. However, there were a significant number of people who migrated from the east into Kentucky and Tennessee after the War of 1812 was concluded. Table 6 contains the names of twelve men who served in the Maryland, Virginia, or North Carolina areas in actions related to the British invasions. Those men are known to have subsequently moved to the frontier included in the study area. The names in italics are men who enlisted in Halifax County, Virginia, a source of several immigrants to the frontier. See Chapter 11 for the biographical sketches of the men listed in Table 6.

Soldier	Unit	Place of Service
Cooksey, Thomas	1st Reg't (Byrne) VA	Powell's Creek MD
Davasher, John C	90th Reg't (Johnson) VA	Likely around Richmond, VA
Lee, Henry	NC Drafter Reg't NC	Camp Deep Water, NC
Mitchell, Thomas	19th Reg't (Ambler) VA	Defenses of Richmond, VA
Oliver, William	1st Reg't (Stokes) NC	Likely near Norfolk, VA
Owens, Obediah	5th Reg't (Mason) VA	Craney Island, VA
Pardue, Jesse	4th Reg't (Kountz) VA	Fort Norfolk, VA
Petty, James	84th Reg't (Coleman) VA	Ellicott Mills, MD
Walker, William	Alkerson's VA Artillery	Camp Bottom Bridges, VA
Weaver, James	7th Reg't (Saunders) VA	Norfolk, VA
Weaver, William	4th Reg't (Greenhill) VA	Baltimore, MD
Wheat, Dory	5th Reg't (Mason) VA	Norfolk, VA

Table 6. Soldiers who migrated to Allen County, Kentucky, after the war.

The United States had not yet won the war but the British were now amenable to negotiating a peace treaty. The talks began in August 1814 in Ghent in the Netherlands. The draft of the treaty was not completed quickly. Agreement was not reached until six months later, but not in time to delay or stop the planned British invasion of Louisiana.

Chapter 8

The British Kept Acoming

The Battle of New Orleans

Most Americans know the story of the Battle of New Orleans, a battle that was fought before the troops involved had received word that the peace treaty had been signed weeks earlier. The contributions of the frontiersmen from the study area are less well known. Those men were involved in military actions before, during, and after that famous battle.

Andrew Jaçkson had learned of the British plan to invade Louisiana while still in Mobile after the Creek War had ended. The intelligence prompted him to leave two regiments of Georgia Militia to defend Mobile, and move the rest of his army to New Orleans. He left on 21 November 1814. Brigadier General John Coffee's Tennesseans marched overland through the wilderness, passing north of Lakes Pontchartrain, Borgne, and Maurepas, and their associated swamplands. They arrived just north of the Baton Rouge area after a tiring eleven-day trip of about 200 miles.

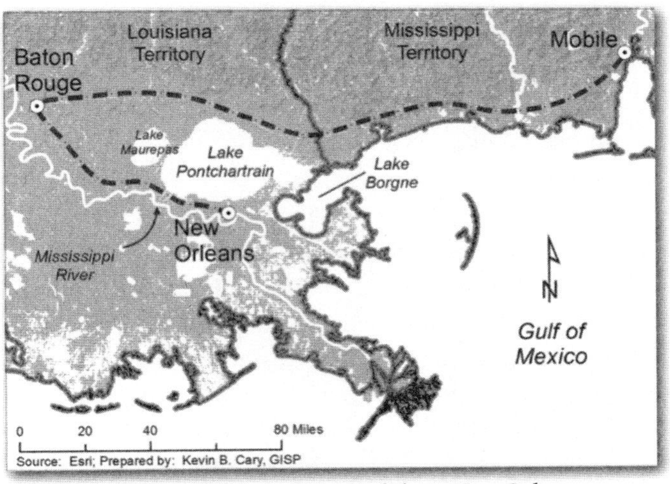

Figure 29. The route from Mobile to New Orleans.

Jackson went on to New Orleans, and his tired army followed. The frontiersmen must have been awed by the city's population of about 20,000 people. Few, if any, had seen a city of that size before. Those people were crowded into a relatively small urban area on the banks of the Mississippi River. Frequent and sometimes heavy rains coupled with poor drainage and heavy wagon traffic assured that streets were bogs of mud much of the time. The stench of open sewer ditches, and the accumulated horse dung in the streets, were memorable to say the least. To the south lay swampland with canals, drainage ditches, alligators, snakes, and mosquitoes stretching to the Gulf of Mexico. A landscape quite unlike anything the frontiersmen from Tennessee and Kentucky had ever seen or experienced before. It was winter, and they would not experience the heat and humidity of summer. Instead, they would shiver in the unexpectedly cold weather.

Preparations for the Battle

An old military adage declares that one must get ready for battle as if its exact hour and place were known. Then, no matter when and where the attack occurs, one will have already carefully examined and planned a response. Jackson's first job was to consider the possible eventualities and reactions.

Jackson began planning the defense against the anticipated British invasion. One possibility was that they would move north from the mouth of the Mississippi toward the city of New Orleans. He had little experience in being on the defensive, but he could envision it. The very next day after his arrival, he set out to remedy his defensive inexperience. During the next several days, he reconnoitered the possible approaches to the city from the south. His engineer and a senior naval officer accompanied him. The naval officer would advise on the threats of movements by boats up the river, bayous, and canals. The engineer would advise on the location and construction of fortifications. Jackson would envision how to impede or stop the advance of the British. This "what if" thinking provided Jackson with a significant advantage over the British commander wherever they would meet. The distance that the British commander could see as he advanced would be measured in yards and, without seeing, he would not be able to visualize the battlefield. He would have to rely solely upon reports from his scouts. Jackson's advantage of careful and thoughtful reconnaissance created a memory of each potential battlefield. His memory of how the battlefield looked would help balance the odds against a better trained, battle hardened, but sightless British.

He retraced back to New Orleans, and then inspected the possible approaches on the east side of the Mississippi River. The landscape there was quite different. From about four miles or so south of New Orleans, plantations lay southward one after another toward the Gulf. The cultivated strip was not very wide. The trees in the swamps to the east were visible from anywhere in it. Virtually all the land in that strip was cultivated, and extended several miles south to the swamp of the southern delta.

It was winter as Jackson investigated the defensive possibilities, and only the stubble of the sugar cane remained on the cultivated fields. He visualized a defensive line anchored at the levee along the Mississippi River on one end, to the trees visible in the swamp to the east on the other end. Parallel canals, ditches, and fences crossed the strip aligned at right angles to the river to drain away the excess water. Each one would be an obstacle to the British, and advance across them would be difficult, would slow the advance, and sap the soldiers' energy in overcoming them. In any battle, a leader tries to control what he can, and to limit the opponent's options. Jackson selected a potential battlefield site on the east side of the river. There he could make his stand, and that selection limited the options available to the British.

On 10 December, Jackson went to Lake Borgne because it was possible that the British could send troops by boats to attack New Orleans from the north. He positioned some artillery south of the lake as a precaution. He received news the next day that the British boats had been sighted on that lake. However, he decided that the northern route for a British attack was unlikely, and did not take the bait to rush troops away from the defensive lines he was readying to the south. Instead, he sent word to Coffee to hurry south from Baton Rouge as quickly as he could.[1]

All of Brigadier General John Coffee's Tennessee Militia had arrived in Baton Rouge from Mobile, and he responded immediately to Jackson's request. He rode south with 800 of his men over the 135 miles in just over three days. They camped about five miles north of New Orleans. Another 450 of his men soon followed. About 300 of his men were too sick to travel, and were left in Baton Rouge. The majority of the forces that Jackson needed and had requested were still en route. Tennesseans and Kentuckians were coming, and he anxiously awaited their arrival. They were on their way, but it was a long trip for all of them.[2]

The Trip to New Orleans

Brigadier General William Carroll's Tennessee Militia had boarded boats on the Cumberland River at Clarksville, Tennessee, and floated downstream toward the north. They arrived at the point where the Cumberland emptied into the Ohio River. There they saw the Kentucky Militia waiting on banks of the Ohio. It was clear that they were far from ready to begin their trip float trip south.

The War Department had ordered Governor Shelby of Kentucky to send 2,500 militiamen to New Orleans to respond to the expected invasion by the British. Shelby ordered three regiments into service during July and August. They were to rendezvous at different places along the Ohio River to board flatboats for the float south.

The Kentuckians expected that the federal government would provide flatboats for transportation. When they arrived at the confluence of the Cumberland and the Ohio Rivers, no boats were waiting for them. There were none coming either. The war department failed to provide the needed and expected equipment and provisions. It was similar to unfunded mandates issued by Congress in modern times. Kentucky's supply depots had been depleted because of the support given to the militiamen during the actions of 1813 that included the excursion to the Battle of the Thames. The legislature had not yet provided for replenishments of the supplies used in that campaign, and the cupboards were bare.[3]

Innovation was required. The Kentucky quartermaster borrowed money to purchase as many boats as he could find. He also bought pots and kettles, one of each to each company of eighty men. The men were put to work patching up old boats that were bought. Finally, after eight days, and with only a half supply of rations, they pushed off for the float down to New Orleans. The soldiers were without uniforms, blankets, tents, arms, and munitions. They also were without pay, and that led to a festering discontent. They began the trip with the clothes on their backs, and little else.[4]

On the other hand, the British fleet had completed their trip from England. Fifty ships armed with a 1,000 guns and carrying some 8,000 soldiers lay off the Louisiana coastline. Those soldiers had been aboard ship for almost two months with little time ashore. They were ready for dry land, room to move around, and new lands to see. They were also ready for action. The navy began rowing the troops ashore on 16 December, ferrying them to Pea Island, called Isle aux Poix by the locals. It was used as a staging point for subsequent movement of the army through Lake Borgne toward the Mississippi River.[5]

Winter officially arrived on 22 December, and right on cue, cold rain was falling. About 1,600 British soldiers disembarked. Sailors began rowing them in ten barges through the bayous toward the Mississippi. They rowed from 11:30 in the morning until midnight. They rested that night, and the next day the troops left the barges for solid ground. They began clearing a path alongside the Villeré Canal to the bank of the Mississippi. They had to cut their path through the reeds, and their advance was difficult and slow. Along the way, many bayous, streams, and ditches had to be bridged. The going became easier when they reached the northern edge of the swampy area. The thickets gave way to the cypress forest, the ground was firmer, and the path was wider. The pace quickened when they reached the strip of sugar cane fields along the east side of the Mississippi. Only the sugar cane stubble remained after the harvest at the Villeré Plantation. The British bypassed the plantation home, and made camp about a mile north on the banks of the river. They intended to wait for the remaining troops to arrive over the path they had cleared.[6]

The Battle of 23 December 1814

A Louisiana militiaman came with the news that British troops were only seven miles south of New Orleans, and were encamped on the plantation owned by Major Gabriel Villeré's father. Jackson made the decision to engage them immediately rather than waiting because assuredly the largest number of British troops were still en route. He made the unusual decision to attack at night, something rarely done in those days.

The lessons of warfare were and are passed on from generation to generation. Night warfare had long been considered to be acceptable under just a few limited circumstances: when you had an overwhelming sized army, when your enemy was in panic, when the goal was to cut through an enemy line, or when the enemy had such overwhelming numbers that a daylight attack would be doomed. Jackson knew that none of those conditions existed. However, he needed more time to prepare for the inevitable major battle. His decision was one that determined just where and when the first engagement would occur, and surprise would be a positive attribute of that decision. His objective was to delay the British advance until the Kentucky Militia arrived to maximize the number of troops under his command when the greater battle occurred.[7]

Brigadier General John Adair's Kentuckians were on the Mississippi in their makeshift flatboats. Behind them were other barges loaded with weapons and munitions also headed to New Orleans. However, the Kentuckians and the munitions were still about two weeks away.

Major General Carroll's Tennesseans had been on the Mississippi for about forty-two days when they arrived in New Orleans, just in time as it turned out. Jackson ordered them to take up positions between New Orleans and Lake Pontchartrain to thwart any assault from that direction.[8]

The combat plan was to be executed on the night of 23 December 1814. It was a bit complicated, and required coordinated maneuvers to go against about 1,500 skilled British soldiers who were encamped on the Villeré Plantation. The plan was to attack them with three prongs at once: front, left, and right (Figure 30).

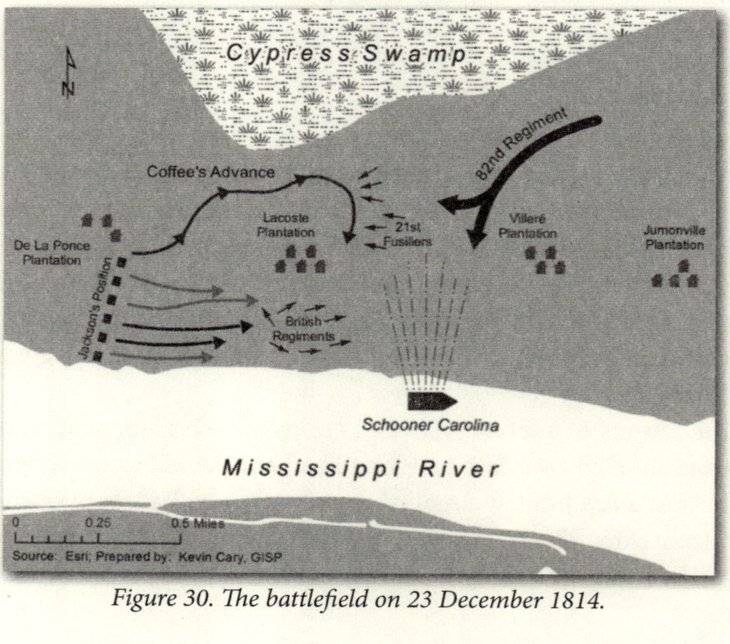

Figure 30. The battlefield on 23 December 1814.

The frontal prong was Jackson's. About 450 troops from the 7th and 44th U.S. Infantry Regiments were assigned to form the American's frontal attack. Those regular army men advanced southward along the River Road in a line perpendicular to the river. The regulars occupied the right flank next to the river. They marched toward the British southward along the east side of the Mississippi River. They would provide the frontal attack against the British.

The left side of the three-pronged attack was the responsibility of Coffee's Tennesseans. They were to advance on horseback along a road that paralleled the edge of the swamp on their left and with the British to their right. They would then dismount and turn right toward the river in a flanking move, in a position to press the British back toward the banks of the river.[9]

All maneuvers would be concealed by the darkness of the evening. Coffee had 563 soldiers. He cautioned them to maneuver quietly, and to aim carefully when the signal to fire was heard. To aim in the darkness would require them to see the enemy. They would have to be very, very close to see them.[10]

The schooner Carolina would provide the third prong, using its firepower to augment the firepower of Jackson's forces on shore. The Carolina was to move downstream on the river until it was opposite of the British bivouac site. It would fire against the encampment at an appointed time. That firing would be the signal to launch the three-sided assault.

As the Carolina quietly drifted downstream on the river, the British soldiers were building fires using rail fences as fuel, and were cooking their evening meal. Their officers sipped wine from the Villeré's cellar, and their troops huddled around the fires. They were enjoying their first night on land in a long time. They saw the Carolina approaching, yelled out to it, but heard no response. The picnic feeling of the evening was about to disappear.

Darkness fell, and the guns of the Carolina fired on the encampment at 7:30 p.m. using grapeshot. Some of the British soldiers ran to seek the shelter of the levee, but most of the disciplined troops formed picket lines ready to meet the expected American advance. The cannon fire from the ship continued, and sharpshooters on the Carolina fired at British soldiers silhouetted against the campfires.

The battle lines were ephemeral. The 7th and 44th regulars advanced along the river, contacts were made, muskets fired, bayonets used, hand-to-hand fighting followed, and undirected disengagement occurred in the darkness. Repetitions of those events happened chaotically, and both sides faced the constant danger of being cut off from their own units.[11]

Coffee's Tennesseans dismounted, left two companies of men to guard the horses, turned toward the river as planned, and came rapidly across the plantation. They pushed the pickets back almost to the levee, and pinched the British back upriver toward their encampment. That exposed them to the firing that continued from the Carolina. The fighting at each contact ended with bayonets, knives, tomahawks, and muskets used as clubs.

As the smoke of battle mixed with the fog that was forming over the battlefield, organized attacks became impossible, and the danger of engaging one's own troops increased. About 9:00 p.m., Coffee ordered his men to disengage. Jackson's troops followed suit.[12]

Coffee's men had learned from their experiences at Pensacola and their march to New Orleans. It was said that they were composed, courageous, and patient. Battles conducted at night test all of those attributes, and require strict discipline to maneuver in darkness. The members of the 44th Infantry Regiment were mentioned as being a battle tested regular army, men who held their ground when the British tried to turn their flank. Captain Baker's Company was in that regiment and was said to have shown great bravery. It included Private Israel Anderson (Chapter 11) from the study area. The entire group of Americans had performed well during this battle.

The frosty dawn brought the reports of casualties to both the British and American commanders. The British reported forty-six killed, 146 wounded, and sixty-four missing — 277 altogether. Jackson learned of twenty-four killed, 115 wounded, and seventy-four missing — 213 altogether. The battle had produced a total of 490 casualties, a portent of the severity of battles yet to come.[13]

The battle was particularly gruesome as a result of the fierce close quarter fighting. One of the British officers was quoted as saying that "wounds more disfiguring or more horrible I certainly never witnessed ...many had met their deaths from bayonet wounds, sabre cuts, or heavy blows from the butt of muskets..." That officer was clearly shaken by what he saw that following morning as the light of day revealed the carnage.[14]

The frontiersmen had met the British army, just as their friends and relatives had during the original fight for independence, and had held their own against them. The newly found confidence in their abilities gave a needed boost in their morale. The nighttime battle on the 23rd was a draw at best, but Jackson's objective was achieved. The British decided to wait until their entire force was landed before they attempted another action. Jackson had paralyzed them, at least for several days.

The battle on the 23rd confirmed Jackson's anticipation that the British would advance toward New Orleans upstream along the east side of the Mississippi River. The Americans began withdrawing from the battlefield the next morning about 5:00 a.m. The regulars of the 7th and 44th U.S. Infantry were the last to leave, and acted as the protecting rear guard in case the British pursued. There was no pursuit. The British had expected little effective actions by what they considered to be an untrained and undisciplined enemy, but they gained a new respect for the Americans. For now, they would wait.

Drawing the Lines

Jackson ordered that new positions be established along the Rodriguez Canal about two miles upstream from the site of the battle of 23 December. This new position was called Camp Jackson in the service records of the soldiers who served there. The chosen area had the shortest distance from levee to swamp, and would allow Jackson to concentrate his defensive force. The canal was four feet deep and ten feet wide, a dry ditch that ran from the river about three quarters of a mile to the swamp.

Virtually all of the Americans lay down their weapons, picked up shovels, and began digging on Christmas Eve. They dug dirt from the canal and added it to the top of the parapet along its length from the Mississippi levee to the edge of swamp. The men of Carroll and Coffee lived and slept in the mud during that cold and wet winter to guard against a surprise attack. The work continued into the New Year, and the parapet became twenty feet wide in some places. It would prove to be impenetrable to cannonballs, a significant feature in the battle that was to come.[15]

As the canal deepened, the parapet rose. Pales taken from all of the fences in the area were used to line the side of the parapet to prevent the soil from sliding down. Much of this work was done amid several days of cold and miserable heavy rain.[16]

Figure 31 shows the parapet with pales as it was reconstructed almost 200 years after the original was built.

Figure 31. Parapet along the Rodriguez Canal viewed toward the cypress swamp.

Artillery from each side each tried to silence the other during the first several days of January 1815. Harassing fire began whenever a group of soldiers came into range. The American infantrymen sought refuge in relatively safety behind the parapet whenever the British cannon fire began.

Brigadier General John Adair arrived on 2 January 1815 to assure Jackson that his volunteer Kentuckians were not far behind. He had been Governor Shelby's aide at the Battle of the Thames and was no novice to combat. About 2,250 Kentucky militiamen had arrived by 4 January and encamped at Prevost's Plantation. They were the last of the reinforcements that Jackson had requested. He was delighted by their arrival because he then had all of the forces he needed for the decisive battle.

However, as often is the case, the solution to one problem created new problems for Jackson to solve. The first was that many of the Kentuckians came without the arms that they were expecting to receive when they arrived. General Jackson wrote to the secretary of war to complain that a third of the Kentuckians were without arms, and others were armed with guns that were unfit for use. He remarked that he had never before seen a Kentuckian without his gun, a pack of cards, and a bottle of whiskey.[17]

That first problem was partially solved when Jackson gave them about 400 muskets taken from the New Orleans militiamen. He ordered a search of every home and business to find and give to them muskets, bayonets, cartridge boxes, and other needed tools.[18]

The second problem was that the Kentuckians were wearing a ragtag assortment of clothing insufficient to ward off the cold weather that was being experienced in New Orleans. They were wearing homemade clothing. Typically, frontiersmen wore thigh length homemade shirts worn hanging over their homemade pants. The pants usually had a flap as a fly that had a row of buttons on three sides. They wore moccasins that were sometimes just a leather bag over the foot that was tied around the ankle. Doeskin leggings, or perhaps laced strips of an old blanket, were common for protection during walks through bushes. They preferred slouchy wool hats, and belts of deer rawhide. There were usually a knife and a tomahawk tucked behind their belt. Their hair was long and unkempt and they had a shaggy beard. In contrast, the British soldiers were dressed in their colorful warm woolen uniforms.[19]

About $16,100 was raised locally for the purchase of blankets and woolens from which the ladies of New Orleans made 1,200 cloaks, 1,127 pairs of pantaloons, 800 shirts, and 400 pairs of shoes for the Kentuckians. The British would still derisively refer to the drab Americans soldiers as "dirty shirts," but at least they were warmer than they had been before.[20]

With the arrival of Adair's Kentuckians, Jackson army reached its full strength of 6,504 men. Of those, 2,226 were Kentuckians and 1,063 were Tennesseans. Together, they composed more than half of Jackson's army. Adair's Kentucky militiamen, who were still unarmed, formed a reserve that was placed along the Du Pré Canal on 5 January. They would arm themselves with the rifles of fallen comrades to become the second line of defense to be used if the British were successful during the battle.[21]

Jackson had previously inspected the area on the west side of the river for suitable defensive positions. He knew that the main body of British troops was on the east side of the river, but he did not want to leave the west side approach to New Orleans undefended. He assigned

400 men from Colonel Davis's Regiment of Adair's Kentucky militia to reinforce the troops already at that position on 7 January. However, 230 of those men were unarmed, and they went back to camp. Davis' remaining 170 men were armed with an assortment of muskets, and were sent out as skirmishers. They were spread over too large an area, and were separated from the 450 men of the Louisiana Militia. Their task was impossible. They encountered a much larger British force, and fled the field toward the improperly positioned American artillery. The retreating men blocked the artillery's line of fire, and the result of the chaos was that the British took the ground across the river from the where the major battle began the very next day.[22]

The next day, Jackson reviewed the alignment of his forces behind the parapet along Rodriguez Canal from the levee to the cypress swamp (Figure 32), the battlefield he had chosen.

The British activity on the west bank and the increased activity on the east bank during 6 and 7 January made clear that the moment of truth was near at hand. The movement of men and equipment was seen and the familiar sounds of assembly activity were heard. The men on the east side had fitful sleep at best on the night of 7 January.

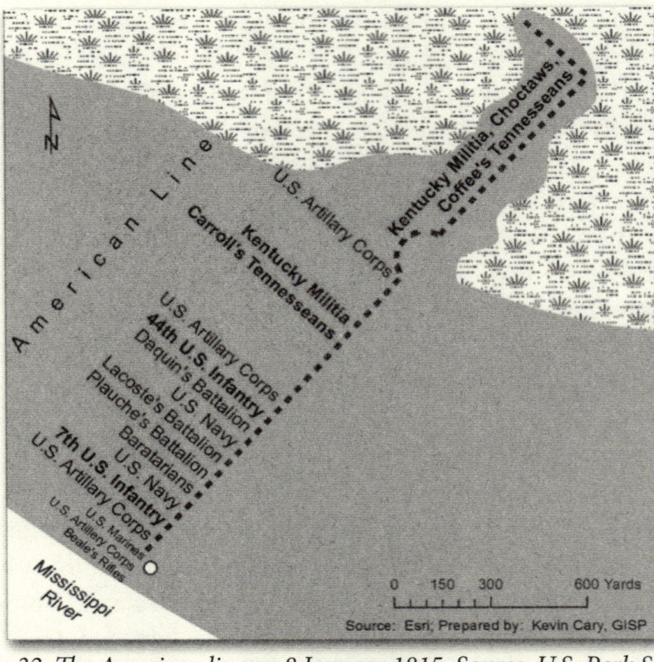

Figure 32. The American line on 8 January 1815, Source: U.S. Park Service.

The right side of the American line was anchored to the levee of the Mississippi River. Army artillery was positioned in the redoubt there to guard against an upriver movement and an advance along the river road. The 7th U.S. Infantry was between them and the battery provided by the U.S. Navy. Inland from them were two smaller units of battalion strength, and beyond them was another naval battery. The major unit between the latter battery and the Army artillery in the center of the line was the 44th U.S. Infantry Regiment with 240 men. Private Israel Anderson was the frontiersman from the study area in that unit who had survived the battle on the 23rd. He was destined to be in the center of this next battle too.

Adair's Kentuckians and Carroll's Tennesseans were next in line, about 1,600 in all. Behind Carroll's part of the line were Kentuckians held as reserves.

The night before, Adair had only 520 armed men. He went to New Orleans and pleaded with the Mayor to temporarily borrow arms that they had held to quell any insurrectionary activities. He was given the consent of the authorities, but with a promise to keep that act secret. Adair moved them after dark and thus provided arms to another 400 of his men that night.[23]

Those Kentuckians were special men. Jackson's chief engineer said that working and sleeping in mud for days had not elicited a complaint from them. He wrote, "The safety of the country was at stake, and their desire to chastise insolent invaders, operated too strongly on hearts inflamed with patriotic ardour (sic) to suffer them to perceive the uncomfortableness (sic) of their situation."[24]

To Jackson's far left, beyond an army artillery battery, was General Coffee's Tennesseans augmented by Choctaws, about 1,200 men altogether. Coffee's part of the line stretched all the way into the swamp with a dogleg left near the end. The surface on the cypress swamp side of the dogleg was a bog with mire a foot deep. That distal part of the line did not have a parapet. Instead, it had a double row of logs, laid lengthwise one over the other. The space of about two feet between the two rows of logs was filled with dirt. That would provide protection for the riflemen who would crouch behind them.

Along the entire defensive line, Jackson had the capability to place about three or four men per linear yard. That was about as many as could be accommodated during the battle. That concentration of rifle and musket fire spelled devastation for the British as they made their assault.

The Battle of New Orleans

The British began moving into assault position about 4:00 a.m. on 8 January 1815 with the intent to launch their attack at first light. The American drums awakened their own troops and they fixed a quick breakfast of bacon and cornbread. The frontiersmen finished it off with a bit of grog. They went through the early morning darkness to take their positions behind the breastworks.[25]

The British sent about 5,300 men into the battle that morning against Jackson's 4,700.[26] Although the numbers were about the same, there was not equality in circumstance. Jackson had chosen this battlefield because it provided him with two advantages. First, the Americans could fire from behind the parapets with only their heads exposed, protected from both artillery and musket fire. Second, the Americans had an unobstructed view over the rampart, and could see the British approach for about 2,000 yards across the fields of sugar cane stubble. Third, the fields were bisected with ditches and canals that would slow the British advance. The British were disadvantaged because they could not see the Americans, they would advance over a field that offered no concealment of their maneuvers, and there was no shelter from American fire.

The rising sun quickly melted the frost on the ground, and fog that had drifted in from the river partially obscured the battlefield. Jackson rode his horse along the American line giving and receiving words of encouragement. The British infantry advanced along the river road. Sounds of the opening artillery fire, drums beating cadence for the infantry, and bagpipes playing announced the assault for all to hear. The British rocket teams began launching rockets that screeched upward leaving a trail of flame and smoke. The rockets did little damage, and did not disturb the Americans on the line. As the principal direction of the assault became visible, about 1,600 of Adair's Kentuckians in two lines, moved up in close order to within fifty paces of Carroll's Tennesseans, deepening the ranks to five or six men for several hundred yards along the line.[27]

The British were in uniforms (Figure 33), approaching in a solid phalanx, shoulder to shoulder in perfect order, a beautiful sight to see albeit a somewhat daunting sight for the Americans.

The British also advanced along the river road that paralleled the river. The American artillery opened fire against them, but did not stop them. The British sustained a fixed bayonet charge. Many of them made it to and over the ditch in front of the American ramparts, and tried to spike the cannons. Fierce hand-to-hand fighting continued, and the Americans were forced to give way. The Americans recovered, pinched in behind them, blocked their retreat path, and took a sizable number of prisoners.

Figure 33. One of the British uniforms from the Battle of New Orleans.

The soldiers in the center of the American line watched the British coming toward them at double time across the field of sugar cane stubble. When the assaulting British troops were about 650 yards from the American line, a breeze began and blew the fog away thus exposing them during their advance. As they reached about 500 yards, the American artillery opened up. At about 300 yards, Jackson ordered his riflemen to fire. The white decorative bars on the chests of red uniforms on some of the advancing troops made a perfect aim point. Frontiersmen who used rifles to kill squirrels had little difficulty hitting a large target such as a man, even at long range.[28]

In minor battles, the cadence of a volley, silence, volley, silence, and volley was unnerving to an approaching enemy as they anticipated the next volley. However, that was not the primary purpose for it; rather it was the product to the technique being used. The standard practice was to have three lines of men armed with muskets. The front line fired a simultaneous volley then stepped back through the lines behind them to become the new third line. What had been the second line stepped forward, fired, and stepped back. The technique was repeated. By the time the original third line had fired, the original first line had reloaded, and was back in front ready to fire again. Proficient men could cycle through this technique about three or four times per minute. However, the stress of combat caused slowed reloading and disrupted the synchronized movements. Rather quickly, the original cadence of the volleys was lost. In the din of a major battle like New Orleans the cadence could not have been heard in any case.

The juncture between two units was considered to be a line's weakest point. The primary thrust by the British was directed at the juncture between Carroll's and Coffee's men (Figure 34).

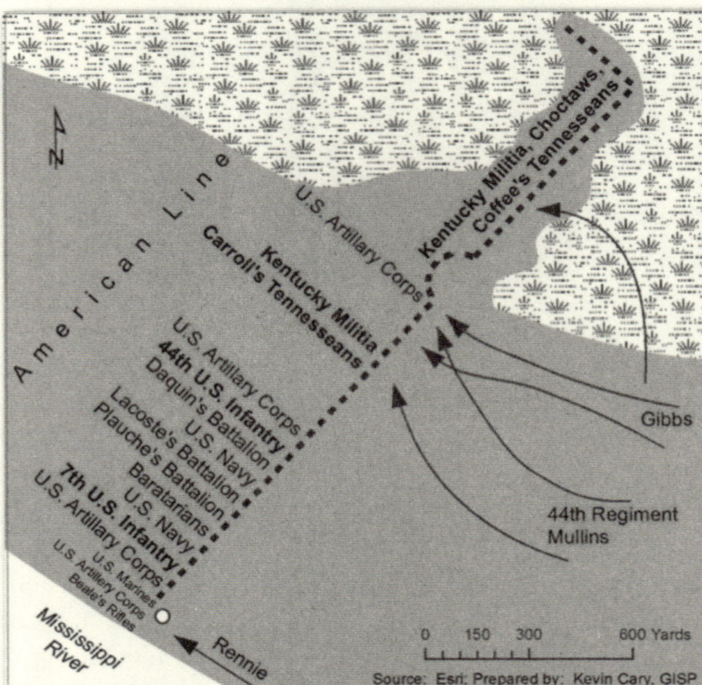

Figure 34. The British lines of attack on 8 January 1815.

The Kentucky and Tennessee riflemen held their fire until Carroll gave the order to fire. Hundreds of rifles obeyed that command, and the combined sound rolled like thunder. In the center of that line, the riflemen began firing while peering over the top of the rampart. It was crowded there as soldiers jostled to get to the front line to fire, then elbowed their way back to reload. They hurried, but each one of frontiersmen had been cautioned to take careful aim before firing.

Within minutes, the withering and deadly accurate rifle fire brought the primary assault in the center to a halt. The Americans could see the soldiers dropping on the battlefield yet the assault continued as the smoke of battle increased. The brave British made it to within 100 yards of Carroll's line.[29]

The British were attacking the part of the American line that was most heavily defended because Jackson had anticipated that would be the focal point. He had assigned his forces accordingly. The massed American rifle fire was devastating to the attacking British.

Gibbs ordered his troops forward, and they advanced in their scarlet uniforms in perfect parade ground formation. They attacked the artillery position in the center of Jackson's defensive line. Mullins' regiment was supposed to move forward at the same time, but was straggling. That allowed the American fire to be concentration on Gibbs troops. The artillery fired into those brave men, and cuts wide swaths of them down, scores with each shot. Others filled in, and the assault continued.

As the losses mounted, the attackers had to fall back. They regrouped and rallied for another assault. It became clear that they would not succeed unless they were reinforced.

About that time, Keane's 93rd Brigade that was advancing along the river was ordered to change directions to reinforce the attack on the center of the American line. After turning, their line was then moving obliquely toward the American center where the major thrust of the attack was faltering.

At the most inopportune time for the British soldiers, Jackson ordered his artillery to cease firing because the smoke had obscured the field, and the riflemen could not see their targets.

As the smoke cleared away, Keane's line of troops became visible and was an inviting target. Their diagonal approach opened their flank to fire from all along the rampart. The withering gunfire and renewed firing by the artillery cut the line to pieces. The men never got within 150 yards of the American line. The incessant rifle fire was accurate and deadly, and the bodies piled up.[30]

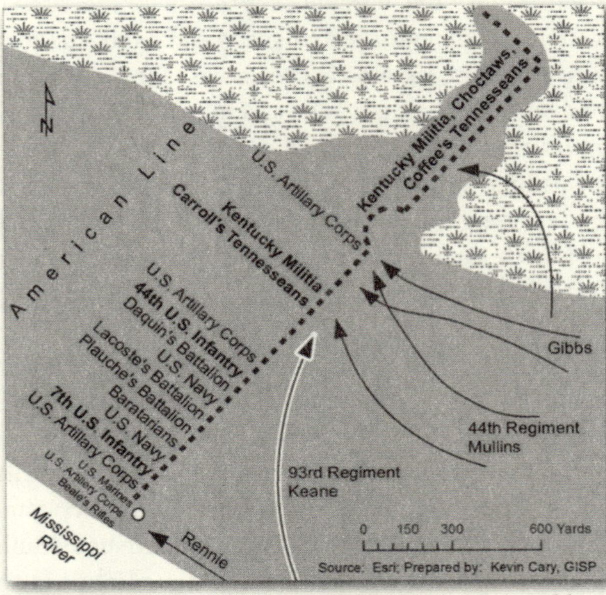

Figure 35. The oblique maneuver of the British 93rd Highlanders.

The British commander was killed early in the assault, and his replacement was appalled by the losses. Over a space perhaps 300 yards wide, the ground was covered by dead and seriously wounded soldiers and the horrendous losses made the cost of continuance too high, and at 8:30 a.m., the replacement commander gave the order to disengage, cease fire, and withdraw. The order came after about four hours of combat.

The Aftermath

The battle was over, but its effects lingered. The sounds of gun and cannon fire were replaced by the screams, shrieks, and groans of the writhing wounded British troops lying in front of the American line. There were no cheers or celebrations by the Americans. The carnage visible on the battlefield was much too sobering, and there was compassionate admiration for the bravery of those who lay there. In the ditch just beyond the rampart lay more than forty dead and up to 100 wounded. A "profound silence" fell over the Americans. Several went down on to the field to offer water from their canteens to the wounded.[31]

Later that Sunday afternoon, the Americans went onto the battlefield, and removed the wounded British soldiers. Carts were obtained from plantations in the area, and boats were collected along the river to transport them to New Orleans. Some forty carts and ten boats were involved. People in the city allowed their homes to be used for hospitals for those wounded men.[32]

The next day, the British came under a flag of truce to ask to bury the dead and retrieve the wounded. Jackson agreed to cessation until noon on 9 January. The adversaries agreed to a no man's land of about 300 yards wide between them. The bodies of the British soldiers who had died within the American side of no-man's land were carried to the British. The large number of bodies in no-man's land made the preparation of mass graves necessary.

The British removed their wounded from the field. About 300 British soldiers, who had made it across the ramparts near the river before being wounded, had previously been moved to New Orleans for treatment.[33] There was an agreement reached on 17 January to exchange prisoners. The following day, sixty-three American soldiers who were captured during the battle on 23 December were returned.

The Battle of New Orleans was over. However, the soldiers on neither side knew that. Their presumption was that the British were not permanently withdrawing. The American soldiers remained on alert for any renewed attacks, and new fortifications were being constructed. But no more attacks came.

A few days after the British left, a triumphant General Jackson rode over the battlefield to where the British camp had been. He found fourteen broken guns, and the Kentuckians picked up 3,000 cannonballs from the field. They piled them behind the ramparts they had manned during the battle.[34]

At least fifty-two frontiersmen from the study area were in units at New Orleans at the time of the call to battle. Each of them contributed in some way to victory in the most famous battle of the War of 1812. Their names are shown in Table 7.

Most of the soldiers listed in Table 7 cannot be precisely located on the day of the battle, but they were all there, and immediately available as the battle began. The histories did not routinely record the position of companies or battalions. Even the positions of regiments and brigades were rarely mentioned. Much of what is in this study comes from the service and pension records of individuals that were the primary source of biographical sketches of the frontiersmen included in Chapter 11.

Pvt Israel Anderson	Pvt Thomas Grisham	Pvt John Pulliam
Lt John Austin	Pvt Mark Hoback	Pvt James Rigsby
Pvt David Baird	Pvt John Hobdy	Pvt John Rigsby
Pvt James Brown	Pvt Hudson Howell	Pvt Asa Roark
Sgt Maj Isaac Caldwell	Cpl Matthew Johnson	Pvt James Robinson
Pvt John Calvert	Pvt Robert Johnson	Pvt John Seagraves
Pvt Alexander Chambers	Pvt Isaiah Kerby	Pvt Pleasant Seamster
Pvt David Chayson	Pvt Leonard Kerby	Pvt John Spenser
Pvt James Cowen	Sgt Terrence Kerby	Sgt Samuel Spilman
Pvt David Creek	Pvt William Lamb	Pvt Charles Stamps
Pvt Thomas Dobson	Pvt Richard Low	Pvt Drury Stovall
Pvt David Dowell	Pvt Samuel Miller	Pvt John H. Thomas
Pvt John Dowell	Pvt Thomas Mitchell	Pvt John Thompson
Pvt John Dry	Pvt Martin Moody	Pvt James Weatherspoon
Cpl Jonathan Eubank	Cpl John O'Neal	Pvt Major Weatherspoon
Pvt John Gibson	Pvt Moses Pruitt	Pvt Wiley Weatherspoon
Capt Thomas Griffin	Pvt James G Pulliam	Pvt Thomas Welch
	Pvt Benjamin Ragland	

Table 7. Frontiersmen from the study area at the Battle of New Orleans 1815.

The Trip Home

The British troops, who had arrived from Lake Borgne by boat, had to find their way back to the ships some twenty miles away. Boats were used to transport their wounded. It took nine days for the British to construct a road to Lake Borgne across the quagmire, and cover it with bundles of reeds over which the army could pass.

The British then began the total withdrawal from the delta. During that time, the American artillery continued harassment fire as they withdrew. The British soldiers were sailed by barges back to their ships when they reached the lake. They loaded onto the awaiting fleet of ships, and sailed out from Cat Island on 7 February.[35]

As the British began withdrawal from the plantations they had occupied, nearly 200 slaves followed them to freedom. The British commander, despite requests from the American slave owners, refused to send any of them back into bondage. The previous owners recorded the names, ages, occupations, and monetary values of the missing slaves, both adults and children, and sought reparations. Some of those former slaves subsequently settled in Nova Scotia and Trinidad. The Treaty of Ghent that ended the war included an agreement that both Great Britain and the United States would "use their best endeavors" to abolish slavery. Those endeavors in the United States were unsuccessful until the Civil War ended fifty years later.

The last war between the United States and Great Britain had officially ended with the signing of the Treaty of Ghent in Paris on 24 December 1814. It restored the peace, friendship, and good understanding between Britain and the United States. The only means of transmitting the treaty to the United States was by ship. As a result, the news of the treaty did not arrive in Washington until 16 February. The Senate ratified the treaty and President Madison signed in the same day. By that ratification, the War of 1812 was over on 17 February 1815 at 11:00 p.m.

The official word of the end of the war did not reach Jackson until 6 March. Until the official word arrived, the frontiersmen could not go home. While they waited, about 1,000 Kentuckians and Tennesseans died from yellow fever.[36] One of those may have been Private John Thompson (Chapter 11) who died in New Orleans on 10 March 1815. The cause was not specified, but his company commander confirmed his death, and did not report the cause as combat related. One may infer that it was by disease. In any case, he was the last frontiersman from the study area to die on while on duty during the war.

Many of the men stood muster for the last time in Louisiana on 28 February 1815. The frontiersmen's trip home could not be a trip back upstream on the rivers. They had to walk from New Orleans to Natchez, over the Natchez Trace to Tennessee, and then onward to their homes in Tennessee or Kentucky.

They began that trek on 18 March 1815. It was a long walk, more than 650 miles for most of them. They had arrived in New Orleans with inadequate clothing for the winter temperature there. The January and February temperature in New Orleans that year was very cold.

In March and April, the temperature along the Natchez Trace would have reached or neared freezing on most mornings while they were on the trail. They would have encountered frequent cold rain and, no doubt, some of the men would have developed an assortment of wintertime ailments to add to their discomfort.

They had few provisions, and had to forage for food during the trip. There were some "stands" along the Trace, houses that offered a night's lodging, for a fee of course. The soldiers probably did not have cash for such accommodations. It is likely that they stopped even if they did not use the lodging. The trace had been frequently used. An estimated 10,000 Kentucky flatboat men, on the way back to their homes from trips to New Orleans, had traveled the Trace in 1810 alone. The stands were built for their use, and the trace was well worn by travelers by the time the soldiers used it.[37]

Some suggest that the frontiersmen returning after the Battle of New Orleans were home about 1 May.[38] That seems to be an improbable presumption considering the conditions and the stamina of the men. That presumption would require them to walk an average of about fifteen miles per day for forty-four consecutive days during late winter and early spring. It seems unlikely that many of them could have sustained that pace for the entire trip. It seems more probable that it took longer for most if not all of them. Regardless of the time required, they would have arrived home fatigued, hungry, and sickly. No rest awaited them, they arrived just in time to plow and plant their food crops.

Clearly, the frontiersmen had a major role in ending the War of 1812. The long, cold, hungry walk home was not accompanied by an anticipation of a victory parade, laudatory speeches, or adulation by thankful citizens. They returned to the frontier they had left behind, and found it still to be a quiet place devoid of hustle and bustle. Not much had changed on the frontier, but the returning soldiers had been part of actions that made dramatic and lasting changes in the relationship between the United States and Great Britain.

Chapter 9

Their Service Remembered

Soldier Pensions

We have difficulty imagining a time when there were no retirement options. In reality, retirement of any sort is a relatively recent addition in our culture. There were few reasons to have a retirement plan when businesses were all family endeavors. Retirement plans provided by businesses came into vogue during the early 1900s. The Social Security system was enacted in 1935 (once referred to as Old Age Pensions) and payments of monthly benefits began in 1940.

No compensation plans at all existed for soldiers in the U.S. Army before 1800. After 1800, each man was given three months pay when he was discharged, hardly what we would recognize as a retirement plan. We know that as severance pay. The soldiers knew when they enlisted that there would be no retirement no matter how long they served. There were some incentives developed over the following years.

When the War of 1812 began, any regular Army soldier who completed a full five-year term, and was honorably discharged, was eligible for the three months severance pay and an award of 160 acres of land. If he were to be killed in service, his widow or his orphans would receive those benefits. There were only a relatively small number of regular Army soldiers, and of them, a very small number who were killed in action. Death from any other cause did not qualify for recompense. Relatively few of the soldiers in the War of 1812 enlisted in the regular Army.

Most of the soldiers in the War of 1812 served in state militias rather than the regular Army. Virtually all of them served short terms of active duty, typically three or six months rather than for five years as the regulars did. Neither severance pay nor retirements, as we know them, were an option for the militiamen who served.

The first after service pay of any sort came when Congress provided pensions for those regular Army soldiers who were disabled from while on active duty. It set the monthly rate of $8.00 for regular Army non-commissioned officers and enlisted men.[1] By a series of subsequent acts, Congress extended those benefits to disabled rangers, volunteers, and militiamen.

There were just 327 veterans, widows, or orphans who were paid benefits in 1816. The benefits were expanded during the next year to include those who died of disease while on active duty. Able-bodied veterans were not eligible under those provisions. Among those men from the study area that served in the regular Army and died of disease was Private Thomas Seagraves (Chapter 11). The 160 acres of land, that he would have received if he had lived until the end of his five-year term, was awarded to his mother in 1825. His widow, Mary, had remarried before it was awarded, and was not eligible for the land. Mary's second husband died in 1833 and, in 1858, she applied again as a widow of Thomas. She was granted the pension in 1859 when she was seventy-seven years old.

By 1829, the number of beneficiaries had grown to 596, still a very small number considering the thousands of men who had served.[2] The soldiers who survived the war without disability or indigent status initially received nothing.

Bounty Land Awards

The first significant change to after service compensation was the award of bounty land to the surviving soldiers. There were two acts of congress that provided the awards to survivors of the War of 1812. The first was in the Act of 1850, thirty-five years after the end of the war. It provided land based on the duration of the soldier's service. It ranged from 40 acres for one month's service to 160 acres for nine months or more.

The most significant provision of the Act of 1850 was that it included states' militiamen who served during the war. It did not require that an applicant had been wounded, disabled, or indigent. It represented a break with tradition in the scope of its application.

The Act of 1855 expanded that eligibility for bounty land to include all surviving soldiers, widows, and minor children. By then, the ages of most of the surviving soldiers were in the sixties or seventies.

Chapter 10 contains details of the bounty land program as implemented from those two acts. One of those who applied was Private

John Dobbs. Note that R. W. Edmund, a Justice of the Peace in Allen County, filled out the form (Figure 36). John was awarded bounty land. The applicant, like almost all soldiers of that war, was illiterate, and signed with an X as his mark.

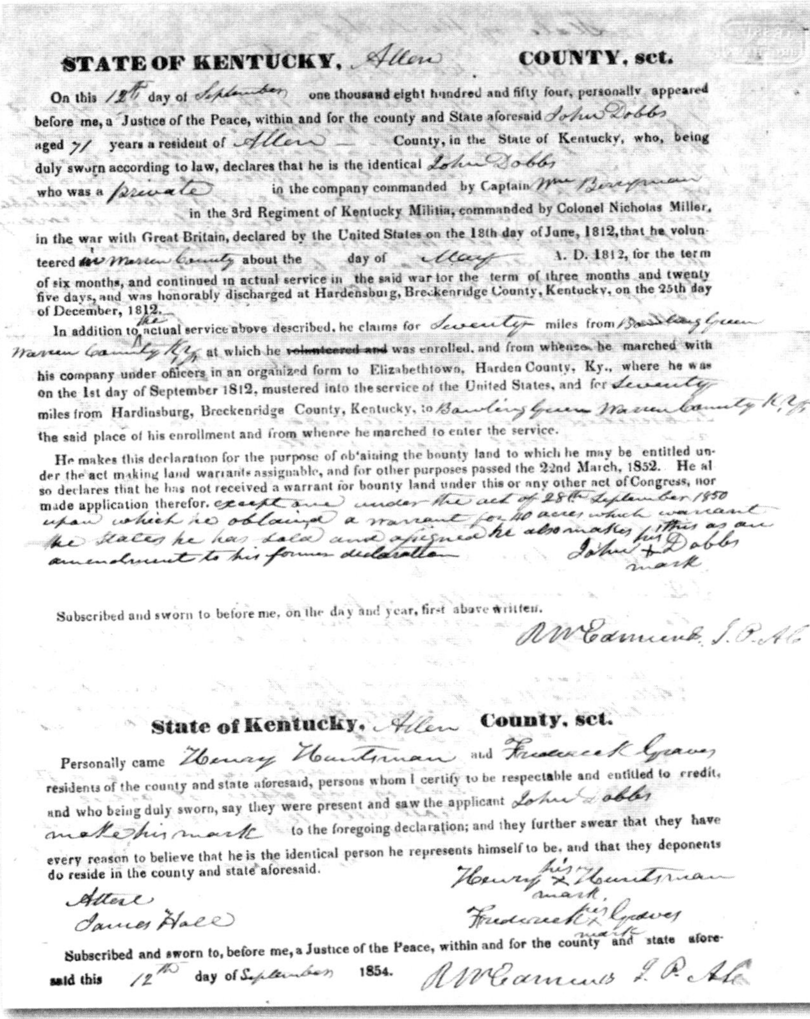

STATE OF KENTUCKY, Allen **COUNTY, sct.**

On this 12th day of September one thousand eight hundred and fifty four, personally appeared before me, a Justice of the Peace, within and for the county and State aforesaid John Dobbs aged 71 years a resident of Allen County, in the State of Kentucky, who, being duly sworn according to law, declares that he is the identical John Dobbs who was a private in the company commanded by Captain Wm Bergman in the 3rd Regiment of Kentucky Militia, commanded by Colonel Nicholas Miller, in the war with Great Britain, declared by the United States on the 18th day of June, 1812, that he volunteered in Warren County about the day of May A. D. 1812, for the term of six months, and continued in actual service in the said war for the term of three months and twenty five days, and was honorably discharged at Hardensburg, Breckenridge County, Kentucky, on the 25th day of December, 1812.

In addition to the actual service above described, he claims for Seventy miles from Bowling Green Warren County Ky at which he ~~volunteered and~~ was enrolled, and from whence he marched with his company under officers in an organized form to Elizabethtown, Harden County, Ky., where he was on the 1st day of September 1812, mustered into the service of the United States, and for Seventy miles from Hardinsburg, Breckenridge County, Kentucky, to Bowling Green Warren County Ky the said place of his enrollment and from whence he marched to enter the service.

He makes this declaration for the purpose of obtaining the bounty land to which he may be entitled under the act making land warrants assignable, and for other purposes passed the 22nd March, 1852. He also declares that he has not received a warrant for bounty land under this or any other act of Congress, nor made application therefor. except one under the act of 28th September 1850 upon which he obtained a warrant for 40 acres, which warrant he states he has sold and assigned he also makes this as an amendment to his former declaration

John his + mark Dobbs

Subscribed and sworn to before me, on the day and year, first above written.

R W Edmund J. P. A C

State of Kentucky, Allen **County, sct.**

Personally came Henry Huntsman and Frederick Graves residents of the county and state aforesaid, persons whom I certify to be respectable and entitled to credit, and who being duly sworn, say they were present and saw the applicant John Dobbs make his mark to the foregoing declaration; and they further swear that they have every reason to believe that he is the identical person he represents himself to be, and that they deponents do reside in the county and state aforesaid.

Attest
James Hall

Henry his × mark Huntsman
Frederick his × mark Graves

Subscribed and sworn to, before me, a Justice of the Peace, within and for the county and state aforesaid this 12th day of September 1854. R W Edmund J. P. A C

Figure 36. Private John Dobbs' application for bounty land.

Widows' Pensions

A series of congressional acts established pensions based on the soldier's service. However, the law came too late for many of the War of

1812 soldiers. The first of those acts was passed in 1858 and established pensions for the widows of soldiers who died while on active duty. The amount was prescribed as one half the soldier's monthly pay to be awarded for a period of up to five years. If the widow remarried, she lost her eligibility and her children who were under sixteen would receive the pay.[3]

Pensions from Act of 1871

The pensions were extended in 1871 to provide benefits to the heirs of soldiers who had been honorably discharged, and subsequently died of service related injuries or diseases contracted while in service. The half monthly pay rule still applied, but the five-year limit on receipt of benefits was extended to the life of the widow or to her remarriage.[4]

Elizabeth Dowell's husband John had served in the Tennessee militia. He died in 1844 before becoming eligible for either bounty land or a service pension. She applied for and received bounty land from the Act of 1850. In 1871, she applied for a Widow's Pension under the Act of 1871. Sadly, she died in 1872 at age seventy-eight before her application had been approved.

John Conyers lived in Allen County but was served by the post office in Gallatin, Tennessee. He served in the Tennessee Militia. His application for pension was approved without delay.

The Commissioner of Pensions administered disability pensions and established statutory rates for the disabled veteran. The rates in effect in 1872 were an example. The rate was $31.25 per month for the loss of both hands, both feet, or both eyes. It was $24.00 per month for loss or disability of one hand and one foot or the loss of a leg up to the hip joint. The rate of $18.00 applied to those who lost one hand, one foot, or an arm up to the shoulder joint. There was also $13.00 for total deafness.[5]

Years later, the Civil War caused a change in the War of 1812 pension rules. Any pensioner who took up arms against the United States or encouraged the Rebels in any manner was excluded from the pension rolls.[6] Most men in the study area joined the Union army, and were younger than the upper age limit for enrollment into the army. One would not expect that most War of 1812 veterans were too old to have joined the Confederate army. So, it was no surprise that research did not find anyone who was affected by that edict.

However, there were some delayed effects from the Civil War on some of the War of 1812 veterans. For example, Henry Brown joined the Kentucky militia from Flippin in Monroe County, Kentucky. He was on the line during the Battle of New Orleans during the War of 1812. He applied for a pension, but his initial application was rejected in 1873. He was required to provide proof that he had remained loyal to the United States during the Civil War. He was a slave owner before that war, and that may have raised concern. After providing proof, his application was approved.

Pensions from Act of 1878

The 1878 congressional act for the very first time included pay to all the survivors, as the old 1812 veterans were then called, who were honorably discharged and served fourteen days or longer. Assuming that a soldier was at the minimum enlistment age of eighteen when his service began, he would have been eighty-four when he became eligible for a pension under the 1878 law. It was statistically more likely that his widow or children would benefit from the law. It must be noted that the Act of 1878 applied to all veterans without regard to color. The African Americans who had served in the navy would directly benefit.

The bounty land applications under the earlier acts of 1850 and 1855 had required proof of service. Soldiers who applied commonly attached their discharge certificate to the application to provide that proof. Those discharge certificates were never returned to the soldiers after the bounty land warrants were approved and issued. As a result, the veterans had no proof of service when they applied for survivor pensions twenty or more years later. Their applications were initially rejected because of the lack of proof of service. The 1878 act solved that problem by legally recognizing that the award of bounty land warrants was prima facie proof of both the soldier's service and his honorable discharge. It entitled the veteran or his widow to a pension. It authorized reapplication if a pension had previously been disapproved based on the lack of pension papers.[7]

The pension office established rules for approval of pensions for widows. Those rules were administered rigidly, and documentation was required. The rules protected against the unintentional approval of a fraudulent application but the process sometimes caused widows to endure long and frustrating waits. Federal bureaucracy was inherently slow, and the postal service of that era caused any exchange of letters to take weeks.

One of the rules seemed simple and easy enough: the fact and date of death of the veteran had to be proved. The widow also was required to provide proof of marriage to the veteran. That was more difficult. Guidelines established the credibility of the various proofs and ranked them from the best to the poorest proof. Those ranking were in the following order.

1. A certified copy of the public record or church record.
2. An affidavit of the officiating clergyman or magistrate.
3. The testimony of two or more eye-witnesses of the ceremony.
4. Affidavits of children whose ages would be proof of the commencement cohabitation.
5. A copy of a family record or bible record certified by a magistrate.
6. Testimony from two or more witnesses of cohabitation presumed to be from marriage.

The law permitted the widow of a survivor to apply even when she was a second wife. One case in point was the case of Private John Dobbs (Chapter 11) of Allen County, Kentucky, whose second wife was Melvina Riggs. Widows who were married in the early 1800s were unlikely to have written proof of their marriage, and had to obtain affidavits from people who had knowledge of the marriage having occurred.

Melvina submitted an application for a Widow's Pension on 22 May 1878. The Allen County Court Clerk, John H. Collins, wrote a four-page application in longhand on ruled paper. The faint document appears to have been prepared as a form in pencil with blanks for entries that were later made with ink. The Pension Office administrators made the underlines visible on the form.

She stated that Thomas H. Lyle performed the marriage ceremony in 1848. She stated that John had previously been married to Sarah Anderson who died in 1845. She declared that John died on 7 March 1857. Her statements provide the essential information required in the rules about marriage. Figure 37 is the portion of her application that concerned her marriage.

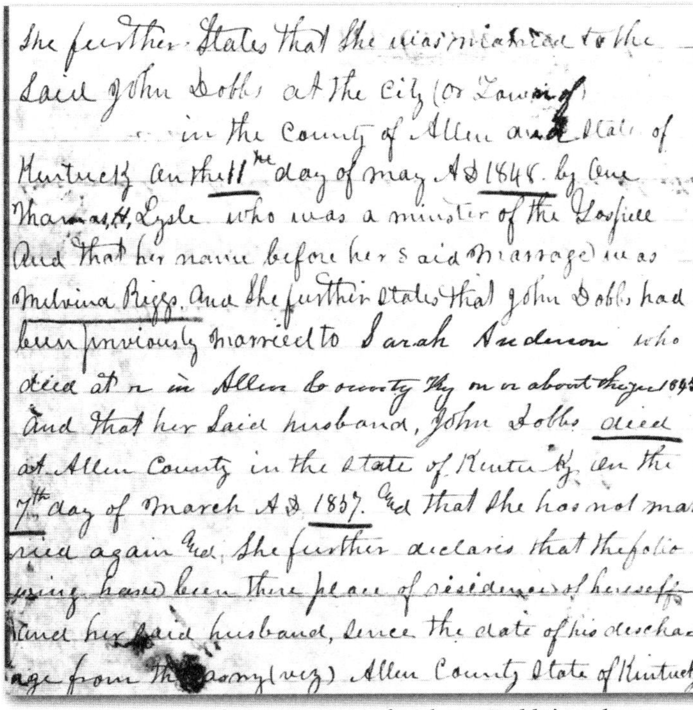

She further States that she was married to the
said John Dobbs at the City (or Town of)
in the County of Allen and State of
Kentucky on the 11th day of May AD 1848. by One
Thomas H. Lysle who was a minister of the Gospel
And that her name before her said marriage was
Melvina Riggs. And she further States that John Dobbs had
been previously married to Sarah Anderson who
died at n in Allen County Ky on or about the year 1845
And that her said husband, John Dobbs died
at Allen County in the State of Kentucky on the
7th day of March AD 1857. and that she has not mar
ried again &c. She further declares that the follo
wing have been there place of residence of herself
and her said husband, since the date of his dischar
ge from the army (viz) Allen County State of Kentucky

Figure 37. Excerpt from page two of Melvina Dobbs' application.

The pension files for John Dobbs held at the National Archives in Washington, D.C. contain thirty-seven separate items. Many of the files contain large numbers of documents. The files contain the envelopes as well as the pages that were contained within them. The application documents are excellent sources of information about John and his wife Melvina. Most of the information contained in the biographical sketches in Chapter 11 was gleaned from those records. Although the documents were not prepared for genealogical and historical reasons, they are rich sources for those researching their ancestors.

Although Melvina had provided the essential information, the best evidence for proof of a legal marriage was a marriage certificate. The County Court Clerk copied the information about her marriage from court records, and entered them onto the forms for marriage license and marriage certificate. He certified that these forms (Figure 38) were a true copy of the original records and forwarded them to the pension office.

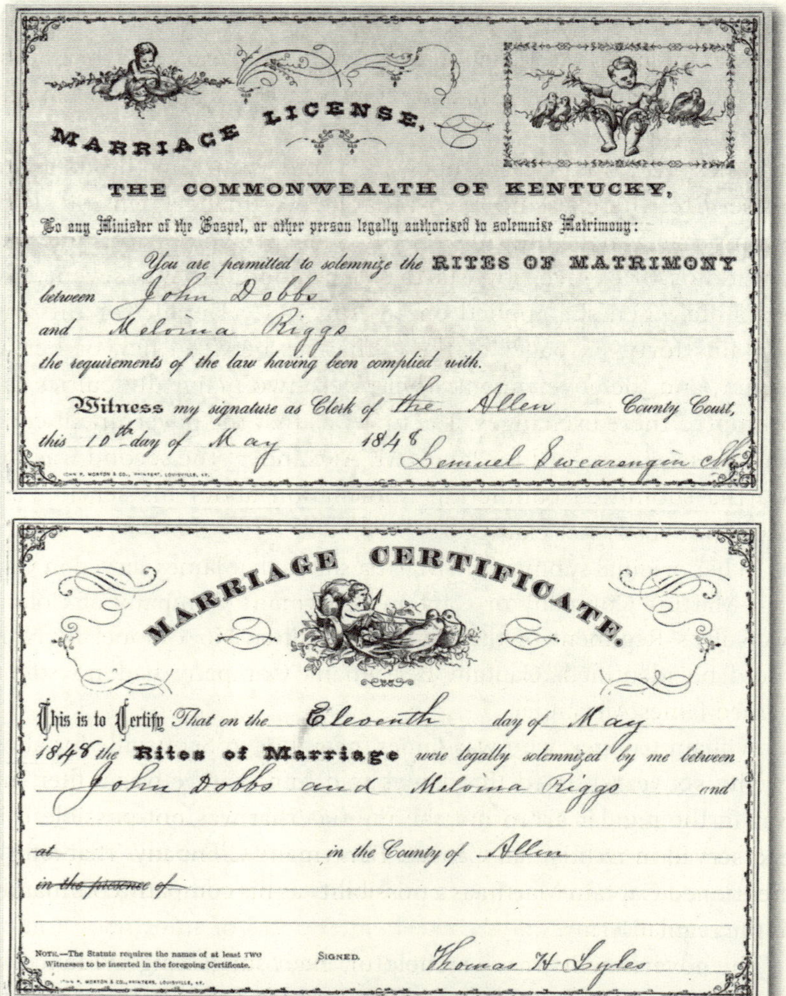

MARRIAGE LICENSE,

THE COMMONWEALTH OF KENTUCKY,

To any Minister of the Gospel, or other person legally authorised to solemnise Matrimony:

You are permitted to solemnize the RITES OF MATRIMONY between John Dobbs and Melvina Riggs the requirements of the law having been complied with.

Witness my signature as Clerk of the Allen County Court, this 10th day of May 1848 Lemuel Swearengin Clk

John P. Morton & Co., Printers, Louisville, Ky.

MARRIAGE CERTIFICATE.

This is to Certify That on the Eleventh day of May 1848 the Rites of Marriage were legally solemnized by me between John Dobbs and Melvina Riggs and

~~at~~ in the County of Allen

~~in the presence of~~

Note.—The Statute requires the names of at least two Witnesses to be inserted in the foregoing Certificate.

Signed. Thomas H. Lyles

John P. Morton & Co., Printers, Louisville, Ky.

Figure 38. John Dobbs and Melvina Riggs' marriage certification.

The pension office acted promptly when Melvina submitted the certified copy of the marriage documents. Their action was to examine the evidence of John's death. The issue was whether or not the payment should include the arrears accumulated after her original application. The decision was made that she should be authorized those arrears.

Melvina's original submission of the pension application was dated 22 May 1878 and her pension was approved on 21 February 1879. The process had taken nine months, but another two weeks were required before she at last received a Widow's Pension. Figure 39 is the approval card that authorized $8.00 per month beginning on 9 March 1879.

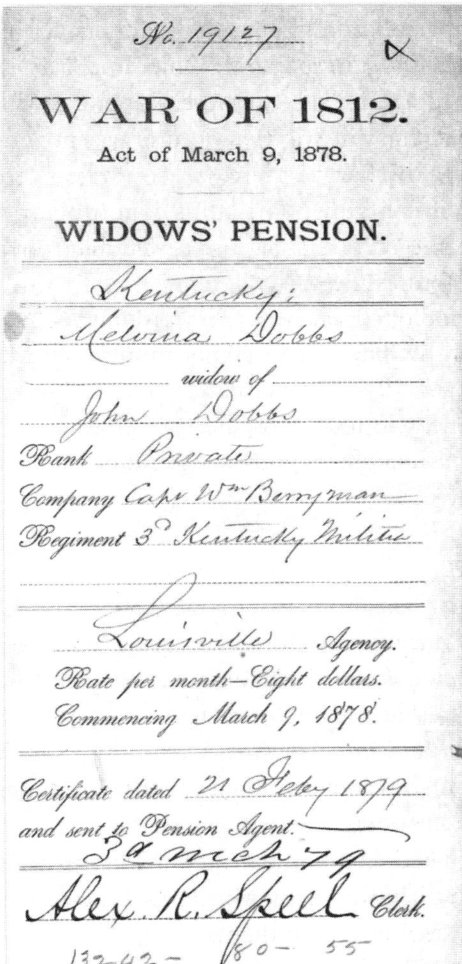
No. 19127

WAR OF 1812.

Act of March 9, 1878.

WIDOWS' PENSION.

Kentucky:

Melvina Dobbs

widow of

John Dobbs

Rank Private

Company Capt Wm Berryman

Regiment 3d Kentucky Militia

Louisville Agency.

Rate per month—Eight dollars.

Commencing March 9, 1878.

Certificate dated 21 Feby 1879

and sent to Pension Agent. 3d mch 79

Alex. R. Speel Clerk.

1342- 180- 55

Figure 39. Melvina Dobbs' pension certificate.

There was no formal retirement plan for servicemen on active duty until 1885. The eligibility requirements then were thirty years of service and an honorable discharge. The retiree received seventy-five percent of his monthly pay after discharge.[8]

A worksheet was generated during the research for this study to facilitate the accumulation of pension data discovered at the National

Archives. Additional information about the soldiers is included in the biographical sketches in Chapter 11.

Table 8 Explanation

The soldiers' names from the study area are listed alphabetically by surname in Table 8. The variant spellings of those surnames are included in the biographical sketches in Chapter 11.

Blank cells indicate that the information was not discovered or did not exist.

The wives' names are listed with the date of their marriage to the veteran. Where the soldier was married more than once, the wife's name that appeared on the pension applications was listed. The pension numbers listed are those that were assigned by the commissioner of pensions and entered on the original application of a survivor. The soldier's certificate of pension number that was assigned when the pension was approved is similarly listed. In the same way, the widow's original application is listed by its assigned number as is the widow's certificate of pension.

The pension commissioner assigned numbers to each application and certificate. Numbers that were assigned to an original application but have no associated certificate number indicate that the application was not approved. That doesn't necessarily mean that the application was disapproved. The applicant may have died in the interim, for example. In only a few instances, files at the National Archives contain the certificate of pension but the application form and its number are missing

The widows' names in Table 8 are the ones who applied for or received a pension. They may or may not be the soldier's first wife.

The marriage dates listed on the application were used except when the forms omitted that information. In that case, a search of genealogical sources was made. That date was entered on the worksheet if a marriage date was discovered.

Table 8 contains data for each of the 154 frontiersmen who served from the study area. Only eleven of them lived long enough to receive a Survivor's Pension, only about seven percent of their number. Three others applied but did not make the pension list. All the men who made the list were old before that happened. The last pensioner from in the study area to die was Private Leonard Kerby who died on 26 September 1881 at the age of eighty-seven.

There were thirty-five wives who received widow's pensions after their veteran husbands died. That small number was an indication that they too were advanced in age.

The soldiers of the War of 1812 entered the service of their country without any promise of or hope for a pension. Their motivation came from within themselves.

				Soldier		Widow	
Rank	Soldier	Wife	Married	Orig	Cert	Orig	Cert
Pvt	Abshear, John	Nancy Barnhart					
Pvt	Adcock, Tyre	Mona Holland	1816		4853		
Sgt	Alexander, James M	Martha Simmons				41456	
Pvt	Allen, Luke P	Araminta D. Perkins	5 Oct 1841			19433	9440
Pvt	Allen, William H	Sally Railey					
Pvt	Anderson, Israel	Mary Gratnet	3 Jan 1792				
Lt	Austin, John	Kitty Caruth					
Pvt	Beard, David	Nancy McClure	30 Jul 1816		25430		12355
Pvt	Barton, Berry	Barbara Graham	22 Apr 1818				
Pvt	Berry, William	Polly Moore	14 Sep 1809				
Pvt	Blackwell, William	Nancy Lyles	2 Jan 1810				
Pvt	Boucher, John	Margaret Shook					
Pvt	Brown, Henry	Ailsey Austin	15 Apr 1818	29947	14959	29947	14959
Capt	Brown, Hugh	Margaret					
Pvt	Brown, James						
Pvt	Burton, John	Anna H. Cole	14 Feb 1822	15074	16492		
Pvt	Cagle, Sampson	Fanny Smith	9 Aug 1804	1818	2067		
SgtMaj	Caldwell, Isaac	Nancy Lawrence	8 Jun 1818				
Pvt	Calvert, John	Jane Russell	1804				
Pvt	Caruth, Thomas	Edy Austin	1819				
Cpl	Chambers, Alexander	Sarah Boring	7 Nov 1819			35961	26081
Pvt	Chayson, David						
Pvt	Claiborne, Ephriam	Mary (Polly) Browning	21 Dec 1809			7647	3251
Pvt	Cole, James	Polly Moore	14 Sep 1809				
Pvt	Cole, John	Amy Mize	2 May 1825				
3Sgt	Cole, Joseph	Margaret Link	26 Nov 1806				

Table 8. Pension Information.

				Soldier		Widow	
Rank	Soldier	Wife	Married	Orig	Cert	Orig	Cert
Ens	Collins, Henry	Kitty Bruce					
Pvt	Conyers, John	Susan Spradling	Nov 1819	25259	15513		
Pvt	Cook, Sion	Winnifred Jent	10 Oct 1807				
Pvt	Cooksey, Thomas	Nancy M. Goodrum	1803				
Pvt	Cowen, James						
Pvt	Creek, David	Peggy McClure	3 Jul 1809				
Pvt	Cushenberry, Daniel	Sarah Davis					
Pvt	Davasher, John C	Elizabeth McDaniel	3 Feb 1803				
Pvt	Davis, Johathan	Catherine Hunt	6 Jan 1812				
Pvt	Dobbs, Henry S	Sarah Campbell	13 Apr 1850			35964	24478
Pvt	Dobbs, John	Melvinia Riggs	11 May 1848			24176	19127
Pvt	Dobson,Thomas						
Pvt	Dowell, David	Elizabeth Shook	13 Aug 1813				
Pvt	Dowell, John	Elizabeth				2825	
Pvt	Dry, John	Elizabeth Boone Ryals	10 May 1813	7789	4494		
Pvt	Duncan, Ashley	Rebecca	1811				
1Sgt	Duncan, Traverse	Lucinda Rogers					
Pvt	Durham, James	Lydia Gillespie	18 Jul 1820			17566	25146
Ens	Ellis, Samuel	Elizabeth Gaines	19 May 1815	14375	9354		
Cpl	Eubank, Jonathan	Stacy Reeder	9 Oct 1807			6695	2924
Pvt	Frost, Eli	Catherine Varvel	19 Apr 1828				
Pvt	Garrett, Larkin	Charlotte Short					
Pvt	Garrison, Mark	Pollly Judges	27 Nov 1891				
Pvt	Gibson, John	Susan H Cook	9 Mar 1841			38354	29654
Pvt	Gibson, William	Rachel ?					
Pvt	Goodrum, John J	Mary Cornwell	17 May 1843			27464	19532
Pvt	Graves, Frederick	Teny Black	1813			16014	10279
Pvt	Griffin, John	Nancy Spilman	27 Feb 1815				
Cpt	Griffin, Thomas	Phebe Barnhart	12 Nov1811				
Pvt	Grisham, Thomas	Lucy Foster	14Dec 1810			7141	4825
Pvt	Hardcastle, John	Margaret Willoughby	13 Feb 1811				
Pvt	Harrison, Andrew	Catherine Strader	10 Dec 1807			5540	5086
Cpl	Hatler, Michael	Sarah Bracken	6 May 1819				
Pvt	Hickman, Joseph	Martha Johnson	29 Dec 1810			4745	4496

Table 8 continued.

				Soldier		Widow	
Rank	**Soldier**	**Wife**	**Married**	**Orig**	**Cert**	**Orig**	**Cert**
Pvt	Hoback , Mark						
Pvt	Hobdy, John	Elizabeth C Hodges				29996	22544
Pvt	Hooton, Joseph						
Pvt	House, Henry	Nancy Senter (Scuter)	Jan 1858	10012	5829	18261	13818
Pvt	House, William	Polly Boyle	28 Jun 1816	6200	3450		
Pvt	Howell, Hudson						
Pvt	Huntsman, Henry	Nancy S. Mitchell	1815				
Pvt	Johnson, John	Nancy Oliver	21 Oct 1822				
Cpl	Johnson, Mathew	Elizabeth Austin					
Pvt	Johnson, Robert	Patsey Ann Goodrum	31 Aug 1808				
Pvt	Kerby, Isaiah	Sophia Kerby	18 Mar 1821		4171	10069	
Cpl	Kerby, Jesse	Prudence Dishman				23740	16495
Pvt	Kerby, Leonard	Nancy Renfro	18 Sep 1861	13129	16903	41741	32437
Pvt	Kerby, Samuel M	Nancy		13128	9126	39184	29870
2Sgt	Kirby, Tarrence						
Pvt	Lamb, William	Sarah Wheat	16 Oct 1827				
Pvt	Lee, Henry	Elizabeth Maddox	18 Sep 1807				
Pvt	Lee, Stephen	Ester				30883	18106
Pvt	Long, Benjamin	Polly	15 Jun 1811				
Pvt	Low, Richard						
Sgt	Mannon, Abel	Rebecca Pitchford	15 Apr 1818				
Pvt	Martin, Peter	Mary Dunn	28 Dec 1791			5347	
Cpl	McCallister, James						
2Cpl	McElroy, John	Elender Bright					
Pvt	Meador, Allen	Mary (Polly) Wagoner	1 Apr 1817				
Pvt	Meador,Asa						
Pvt	Meador, Eli	Sarah Turner					
Pvt	Meador, William	Mary Turner	30 Nov 1809				
Pvt	Merrifield, Samuel	Francis				5284	3569
Pvt	Miflin, Armstrong	Mary (Polly) Howard	19 Apr 1819				
Pvt	Miller, Morris	Catherine Boren	20 Aug 1811				
Pvt	Miller, Samuel	Nancy					
Pvt	Miller, William	Eliza					
Pvt	Mitchell, Thompson	Nancy Welch	27 Jun 1821				

Table 8 continued.

				Soldier		Widow	
Rank	**Soldier**	**Wife**	**Married**	**Orig**	**Cert**	**Orig**	**Cert**
Pvt	Moody, Martin	Martha Guthrie	16 Oct 1810	16613		5147	2029
Pvt	Moore, James F	Susan Oliver	28 Sep 1818				
Pvt	Morrison, James S	Susan	24 Aug 1810			36493	
Cpl	O'Neal, John	Patsey Wilson	11 Jul 1817				
Pvt	Oliver, William W	Susan Peers	21 Dec 1818	30440		39539	
Pvt	Owens, Obediah	Martha Rickman	14 Nov 1810				
Pvt	Patton, William	Letitia Spilman	2 Oct 1818				
Pvt	Pardue, Jesse	Lydia Blankenship	20 Dec 1815	15801	10055		
Pvt	Petty, James	Lucinda Williams	30 Jan 1815			30751	30378
Pvt	Pruitt, Moses	Polly Shipley	1817				
Pvt	Pulliam, James G	Susan (Sukey) Berry	1813			8937	3705
Pvt	Pulliam, John	Nancy Caldwell	29 Nov 1823				
Pvt	Ragland, Benjamin	Elizabeth Shipley	30 Apr 1808				
Pvt	Richards, Hiram	Sally Guy					
Pvt	Right, John						
Pvt	Rigsby, James	Sally Thompson					
Pvt	Rigsby, John	Elizabeth Howard	14 Apr 1804				
Pvt	Ritchie, George						
Sgt	Roark, Asa	Susan Tuder	1818				
Pvt	Robertson, Leroy	Lucy					
Pvt	Robinson, James	Hannah Adair					
Pvt	Seagraves, John	Polly Burch	11 Feb 1808				
Pvt	Seagraves, Thomas	Sally Richards Rigsby	1810				11467
Pvt	Seamster, Pleasant	Millie Nelson	10 Aug 1816				
Maj	Shacklett, Benjamin	Elizabeth Ashcraft	9 Oct 1792				
Pvt	Sherry, John	Winnifred Horton	16 Feb 1800				
Pvt	Shipley,Nathaniel	Mildred C. Prewitt	26 Dec 1802				
Adj	Smith, John	Nancy Runner					
Pvt	Spears, Ephraim	Sarah Walton	20 Nov 1799			4920	
Pvt	Spencer, John	Chloe Hill	20 Nov 1799				
Sgt	Spilman, Samuel	Nancy Burton	18 Sep 1814				
Pvt	Stamps, Charles	Margaret M. Wygall	30 May 1849			42188	33077
Pvt	Stark, Thomas	No Spouse					
Pvt	Stovall, Drury	Nancy Finney					

Table 8 continued.

				Soldier		Widow	
Rank	Soldier	Wife	Married	Orig	Cert	Orig	Cert
Pvt	Sturdy, William	Mary Crueison	14 Nov 1816				
Pvt	Swindle, Pelidge S.	Philadelphia Marsh	16 May 1856			38769	
Pvt	Taber, Henry	Patsey Taber	1 Jul 1814				
Pvt	Thompson, William						
Pvt	Thompson, John	Elizabeth W	6 Dec 1803				
Pvt	Trammel, Sampson						
Pvt	Veach, Nathan	Caroline					
Pvt	Venable, William	Sarah Pinson	1811				
Pvt	Waggle, George	Elizabeth Carrier	Feb 1814			6971	3835
Pvt	Walker, Andrew						
Pvt	Walker, William H	Sarah Richardson	6 Jul 1815	11511	6805	30997	14925
Pvt	Weatherspoon, James	Ann Coleman	29 Oct 1821		23285		25509
Pvt	Weatherspoon, Major	Jane Moody	27 Dec 1817	18837	12759	30858	22626
Pvt	Weatherspoon, Wiley	Jane Edmunds	6 Jan 1819				
Pvt	Weaver, James	Martha Crowder		20389	24312		
Pvt	Weaver, William	Elizabeth Dobson	29 Oct 1817				
Pvt	Welch, Thomas	Mary Ann Polly Martin	23 Oct 1815				
Pvt	Wheat, Dory	Mary Eubank	2 May 1811			2492	2098
Pvt	Whitney, Leommi	Jane Bush	3 Apr 1815				
Pvt	Williams, George						
Pvt	Williams, Langston	Ruth McElroy	11 Feb 1802				
Pvt	Williams, Peter						
Pvt	Williams, Ralph	Fanny McElroy	28 Sep 1818	15946	10056	23430	22204
Pvt	Willloby, Solomon	Sarah Martha Clarke	1 Jan 1785				
Cpl	Wilson, George C.	Sarah Siibles	15 Nov 1806				
Ens	Wolf, John						

Table 8 continued.

Chapter 10

Extending the Frontier Westward

1812 Soldier Bounty Land Warrants

In anticipation of war with Great Britain, Congress recognized the practical consequences of the philosophical limitations that had been placed on the size of the standing army. The state militias were organized to react to local disturbances, and extended cooperative interaction among the militias was not anticipated. The need for a larger standing army now became apparent. It also became clear that the authorized strength of the army was insufficient to assure success against the imposing British army. The remedy was also clear: the number of soldiers in the regular army had to be increased dramatically and rapidly. To accelerate the enrollment of volunteers into the regular army, Congress authorized the award of land as an enticement for enlistment in the army during the prelude to the War of 1812. The term bounty land was used to describe that form of compensation.[1]

Bounty Land Locations

Initially, bounty land surveys were to be conducted in three areas. Two million acres of arable land were to be surveyed in the Michigan Territory, two million acres in the Illinois Territory north of the Illinois River, and two million acres in the Louisiana Territory between the St. Francis and Arkansas Rivers (what is now Arkansas).

Surveys began in 1815. The surveyors reported that the lands in southeastern Michigan Territory were reported to be wet, swampy, and unsuitable for cultivation. As a result, Congress withdrew the lands of Michigan as bounty and authorized additional lands. They added one and a half million acres in the Illinois Territory and a half million acres in Missouri north of the Missouri River. Over 400 men worked on the surveys of these two areas and were to complete them by June 1817. Patents for these bounty lands became available in October 1817 in Illinois and in January 1819 in Missouri.[2]

A veteran could request one of those territories as the location of his bounty land. The actual tract of the land that each would receive in his chosen state would be determined by lot. One of the intended effects of this system was to attract a population of immigrants to the frontiers in those territories, people who were aware of or already accustomed to the rigors and dangers of frontier life. These new residents would build homes and develop their property. They would have ample reasons to desire protection of the property and their family. These immigrant men had been trained in the military and would likely be predisposed to enrolling into the local Militia as such units would be formed in the new territory. The traditional role of those new Militias in preserving the peace in the new frontiers had not been abandoned.

Bounty Land Surveys

In 1785, Congress enacted a law stating that the land in new states was to be surveyed by a grid system consisting of townships. It was to start at the intersection of a principal meridian (a north-south line) and its base line (an east-west line). These initial points were established as needed across the country. Once the original point was established and new corner points were surveyed, new land was physically referenced to the nearest corner point.[3]

The grid established in 1785 was applied to locate the bounty lands after the War of 1812. The bounty lands in Arkansas, Illinois, and Missouri used after the War of 1812, were based on either the Fourth or Fifth Principal Meridians. The Fourth Principal Meridian was established in 1815, and was the basis for the grid in the western portions of Illinois. The Fifth Principal Meridian was established to facilitate the survey of the Louisiana Purchase. It also served as the grid reference for the bounty lands in Missouri and Arkansas.

The grid was divided into six mile by six-mile squares called townships. Each township was further divided into thirty-six sections. Each was a one mile by one mile square. Each section contained 640 acres and was subdivided into aliquots, usually halves or quarters. A half section contained 320 acres, a quarter section contained 160 acres, a half quarter 80 acres, and a quarter of a quarter 40 acres.[4]

The number system was a bit peculiar. Figure 40 is an illustration of the numbering system for sections in the 1812 bounty land areas. Section numbers begin in the northeast corner.

6	5	4	3	2	1
7	8	9	10	11	12
18	17	16	15	14	13
19	20	21	22	23	24
30	29	28	27	26	25
31	32	33	34	35	36

Figure 40. Numbering system for sections used in bounty land grants.

Section quadrants can be subdivided into different sized aliquots to produce the number of acres awarded by a bounty land warrant. An aliquot is a portion contained an exact number of times within a specific larger area. There can be a variety of shapes and sizes of aliquots that could exist within a quadrant. Each aliquot is expressed as a fraction (half, quarter, eighth, etc.) of a quadrant. The number that forms the first half of the aliquot identity is its portion of the quadrant, and the number in second half of the aliquot identity reflects the quadrant of the section in which it is located. For example (Figure 41), "W ½ NW ¼" would be read as "west half of the northwest quadrant." SE ¼ SW/ ¼ would be read as "southeast quarter of the southwest quadrant."

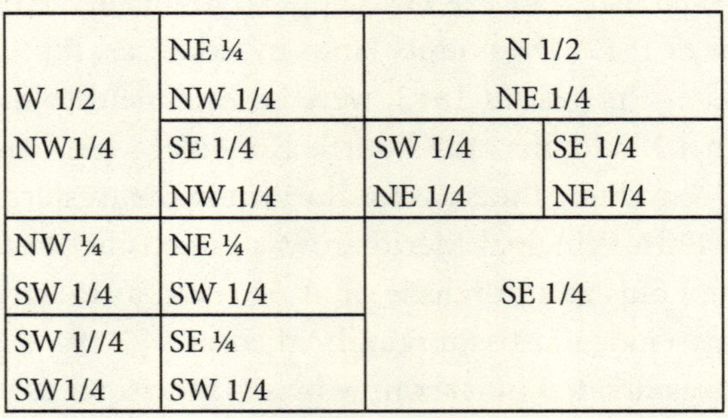

Figure 41. Examples of numbering aliquot identity within a section.

Within the system, a piece of property can be located on a map within 330 feet by words alone. It exactly and completely forms the legal description of a plat. (That is a vast improvement over the metes and bounds system, still used in Kentucky, that describes property by its perimeter and its location in respect to its neighbors. If you don't know where the neighbor's property is you don't know where the subject property is either.) When property was defined using the metes and bounds system, the result often involved a tree, a rock, or something else that two hundred years later does not exist. The section system (Figure 40) never changes over time.

Bounty Land Applications

The War of 1812 veteran or his survivors had to submit an application for the bounty lands to which they were entitled. Congress passed acts that established the procedures for filing, and the rules by which to determine eligibility. The three major acts were in 1812, 1850, and 1855. There were several other enactments to clarify or better define these acts. If the soldier's or his heir's application was approved, the individual would be issued a document called a warrant. The warrant gave the right to obtain the free bounty land.[5]

Bounty Land Act of 1812

For those non-commissioned officers or soldiers who would enlist in the regular army for a period of five years, Congress authorized payment of sixteen dollars to each volunteer upon being mustered in. After completing service, he would receive an additional three months pay and an award of 160 acres of bounty land. The law granted authority for a non-commissioned officer's or soldier's heir to apply for that bounty land in the event that the man was killed in action or died while on active duty.[6] Commissioned officers were not included in the law. They were authorized to collect two dollars for each man between the ages eighteen and forty-five that they recruited.[7] Commissioned officers were not declared eligible for the bounty land until thirty-five years after the war ended.[8]

As the need for additional military strength continued, Congress responded and authorized the call into service of 50,000 volunteers to serve for one year. The law relating to bounty lands for the regular army was expanded to include these volunteers. They too would be eligible for the 160 acres of bounty land.[9]

Collectively, the laws excluded bounty land not only for the officers[10], but also excluded the Militia, regulars who were in the army prior to 1812, and volunteers who served for six, twelve, or eighteen months. As a result of these exclusions, only five percent of the total men in the regular army, militia, and volunteers were eligible for bounty land.[11] These eligibility rules were not changed until 1850.

Example of Bounty Land Award from Act of 1812

An early form of the warrants for the War of 1812 was issued to Mary Segraves (Seagraves) of Scottsville, Kentucky, on 7 April 1826. It identified Private Thomas Segraves (Seagraves) as her son, his regular army unit as Captain Baker's Company of the 44th U.S. Infantry, and noted that the bounty land was located in Arkansas. The form (Figure 42) issued to her as warrant number 25,883.

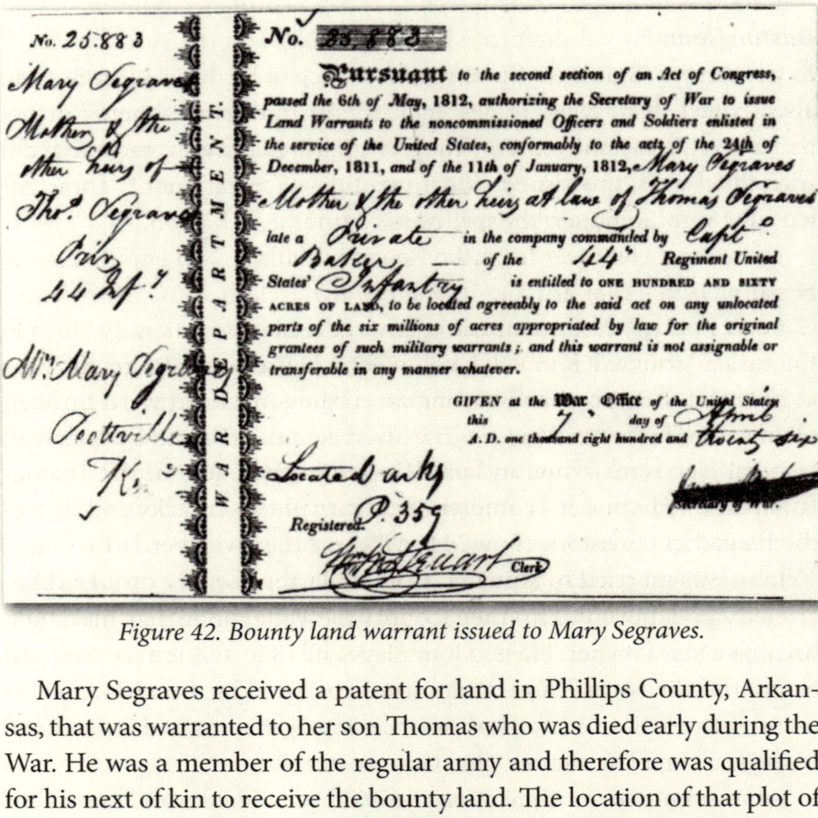
No. 25883
Mary Segraves
Mother & the other heirs of Thos. Segraves
Priv 44 Inf.
Mrs. Mary Segraves
Scottville
Ky.

WAR DEPARTMENT.

No. 25,883

Pursuant to the second section of an Act of Congress, passed the 6th of May, 1812, authorizing the Secretary of War to issue Land Warrants to the noncommissioned Officers and Soldiers enlisted in the service of the United States, conformably to the acts of the 24th of December, 1811, and of the 11th of January, 1812, Mary Segraves Mother & the other heirs at law of Thomas Segraves late a Private in the company commanded by Capt. Baker of the 44th Regiment United States' Infantry is entitled to ONE HUNDRED AND SIXTY ACRES OF LAND, to be located agreeably to the said act on any unlocated parts of the six millions of acres appropriated by law for the original grantees of such military warrants; and this warrant is not assignable or transferable in any manner whatever.

GIVEN at the War Office of the United States this 7th day of April A. D. one thousand eight hundred and twenty six

Located Arks.

[illegible] Secretary of War.

Registered. P. 359

Wm. Stewart Clerk

Figure 42. Bounty land warrant issued to Mary Segraves.

Mary Segraves received a patent for land in Phillips County, Arkansas, that was warranted to her son Thomas who was died early during the War. He was a member of the regular army and therefore was qualified for his next of kin to receive the bounty land. The location of that plot of land was described as in Township-Range 001 S 001E, in aliquot SE ¼ in Section 22. That means that as a quarter section, it contained 160 acres. That land can be seen on the plot shown in Figure 43. Note the label "Sec 22" with "640" giving the section number and its total acreage. Note also that each of the four quadrants of Section 22 had been allocated to the persons listed in each quadrant. In the southeastern one quarter are written "25,883" which is Mary's bounty land warrant number. Below that is Thomas Seagraves' name written here as "Heirs of Tho Segraves."

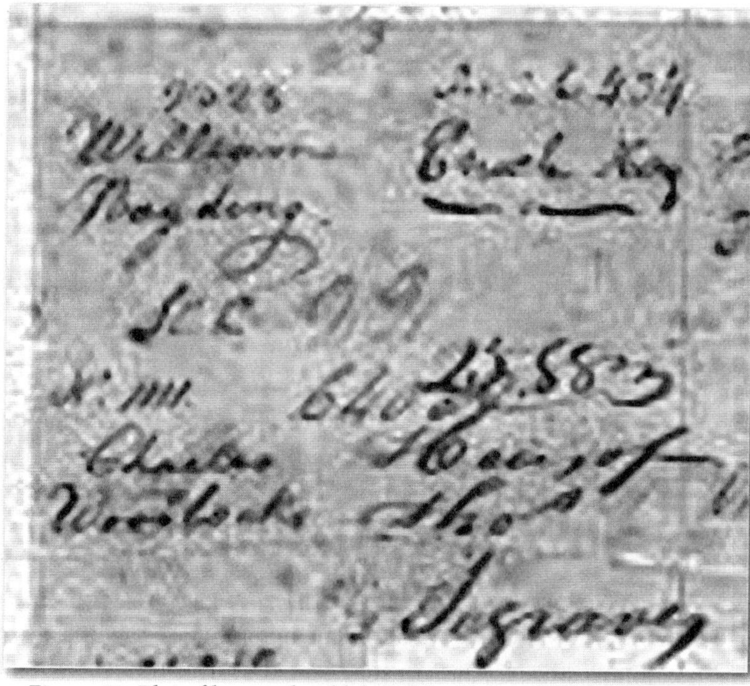

Figure 43. Plot of bounty land labeled for Heirs of Thomas Segraves.

Bounty Land Act of 1850

There were several changes in the bounty land law after it was first enacted in 1812. The first significant change was enacted on 28 September 1850. That act, and its successor in 1855, had a dramatically different intent than the one in 1812. These later two enactments, made thirty-eight and forty-three years after the end of the war, had a primary intent of rewarding the soldiers for their service. To fulfill that intent, the acts made sweeping changes to the eligibility requirements for bounty land, changes that greatly expanded the number of people who were deemed eligible.

Surviving officers became eligible and were added to the noncommissioned officers, soldiers or their widows and minor children already eligible. Eligibility was extended to all who served in any regular, volunteer, ranger, or Militia unit who served during the war. The new eligibility of militiamen encompassed most of the Kentuckians and Tennesseans who served in the war from the study area. As a result, there was a massive increase in the number of applications submitted by the soldiers.

Award of the land was based on length of service. The awards were not based on the length of service they had enlisted for but rather for the time they actually served. That caveat was necessary because enrollment into service typically preceded the actual entry by weeks or even months. Therefore, only served time would qualify. Those who actually served for nine months or longer were eligible for 160 acres, 80 acres for four months, or 40 acres for one month.

Veterans who previously had been awarded land could reapply. If they had previously received fewer than 160 acres, they would be eligible to receive an award sufficient to produce a total awarded acreage of 160. Thousands of veterans accepted the offer and submitted applications.

The heirs of soldiers, who were entitled to bounty land, also could apply. The unmarried widow of any soldier who had not previously received bounty land could receive 160 acres if her husband had been killed in action.[12]

The editions of the warrant issued were more elegant in appearance than the original 1812 one. For example, 40 acres of bounty land was awarded to Private Samuel Kirby from Allen County on 16 August 1852.[13] As one of the militiamen he had not been eligible heretofore. The warrantee form that he received is shown in Figure 44. It was still in the National Archives because he had exchanged it for the title to the land.

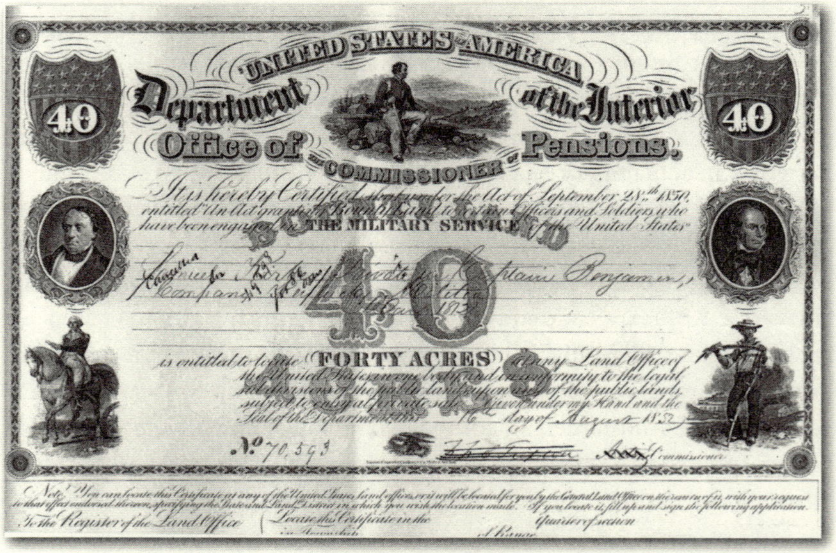
UNITED STATES OF AMERICA

40 Department of the Interior 40

Office of the Commissioner of Pensions.

THE MILITARY SERVICE

40

FORTY ACRES

No 70,593

Figure 44. Bounty Land Warrant awarded to Private Samuel Kirby.

The Bounty Land Act of 1855

The expansive act of 3 March 1855 opened eligibility for land to soldiers who were mustered in any war after 1790. For the War of 1812 soldiers, it expanded the previously approved eligibility of War of 1812 veterans to include wagon masters and teamsters not covered by previous law. All surviving soldiers, their widows, or minor children became eligible to receive 160 acres of land.

Among those who applied was Leonard Kerby, a brother to Samuel Kerby mentioned above. They lived in the Allen Springs community. After Leonard made his application, he was issued warrant number 31886 for 80 acres in Missouri. The land was in Taney County in Township Range 024N-019W, in Aliquot S ½ NE ¼, of Section 10 (Figure 45).

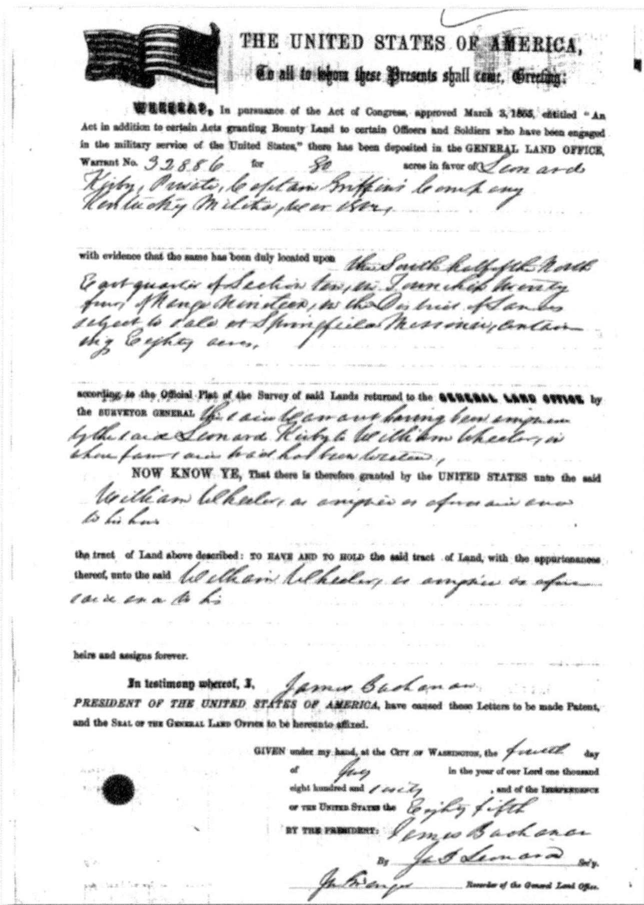

THE UNITED STATES OF AMERICA,
To all to whom these Presents shall come, Greeting:

WHEREAS, In pursuance of the Act of Congress, approved March 3, 1855, entitled "An Act in addition to certain Acts granting Bounty Land to certain Officers and Soldiers who have been engaged in the military service of the United States," there has been deposited in the GENERAL LAND OFFICE, Warrant No. 32886 for 80 acres in favor of Leonard Kirby, Private, Captain Griffin's Company Kentucky Militia, War 1812,

with evidence that the same has been duly located upon the South half of the North East quarter of Section ten, in Township twenty four, of Range nineteen, in the District of Lands subject to sale at Springfield Missouri, containing Eighty acres,

according to the Official Plat of the Survey of said Lands returned to the GENERAL LAND OFFICE by the SURVEYOR GENERAL, the said Warrant having been assigned by the said Leonard Kirby to William Wheeler, in whose favor said tract has been located,

NOW KNOW YE, That there is therefore granted by the UNITED STATES unto the said William Wheeler as assignee as aforesaid and to his heirs

the tract of Land above described: TO HAVE AND TO HOLD the said tract of Land, with the appurtenances thereof, unto the said William Wheeler as assignee as aforesaid and to his heirs and assigns forever.

In testimony whereof, I, James Buchanan, PRESIDENT OF THE UNITED STATES OF AMERICA, have caused these Letters to be made Patent, and the Seal of the General Land Office to be hereunto affixed.

GIVEN under my hand, at the City of Washington, the fourth day of July in the year of our Lord one thousand eight hundred and sixty, and of the Independence of the United States the Eighty fifth.

BY THE PRESIDENT: James Buchanan

By J. B. Leonard Sec'y.

[illegible] Recorder of the General Land Office.

Figure 45. Private Leonard Kerby's Bounty Land Warrant number 32,886.

The warrantee was granted the authority to assign the land to a patentee of his choice, a major change in the law. The warrantee was usually the soldier but if a soldier had died and left a widow, she was eligible for the bounty land award. If she had remarried, she was still eligible if she had applied before her second marriage. If the widow was deceased too and there was a minor child, that child was eligible for the land.

The land warrant had a cash value of $1.25 per acre. If the warrantee sold the land for more than its face value, the land office had to be paid the excess above $1.25 per acre. One can imagine that this circumstance did not occur frequently.

The decision to sell or retain the bounty land may have been a difficult one. It was difficult because the veterans from the study area were, by 1855, in their sixties or older. Some, perhaps most of them, owned land and had families in Kentucky or Tennessee. Some had experienced the rigors of moving to the frontier to build a homestead from the forested land. The urge to repeat that experience at their current age was likely dampened by memories of those hard times. Selling the land, that they had not seen to remain in the area they had worked hard to improve, may not have been difficult for most. The sale of the bounty land for cash was for them a good choice, particularly because cash was hard to come by in those years.

For those who did not own property or owned less desirable land, the attraction of land on a newer frontier may have been higher. After all, their ancestors had left home and families in Europe and a subsequent generation left other homes and families in Virginia to come to Kentucky. Perhaps those ancestors passed along whatever the spirit was that energized their adventurous moves.

In any case, the choice could be stated simply, either to keep the land or sell it for cash. It appears that land speculators bought much of the land at a bargain rate, perhaps 160 acres worth $200 sold for about $100 to $120 cash. A 120-acre tract brought perhaps $70 to $75. The speculators bought multiple tracks of military land. The speculative nature was the expectation that, as settlement of the areas occupied larger and larger acreage, its value would also increase.[14]

Sales of the bounty land were common but the records preserved by the Bureau of Land Management describe the transactions. These records contain information valuable to genealogists searching their families' histories.[15]

Bounty Lands in Arkansas

The Louisiana Purchase in 1803 included the smaller area that became the Arkansas Territory in 1819. Arkansas would not become a state until 15 June 1836. The tract set aside for bounty land in that territory was not the most desirable land. Because of that, the award of land there did not start until 1820. The difficulties were so great that Congress permitted the exchange of land that was unfit for cultivation for other arable land.[16] These exchanges were made by the Batesville and Little Rock land offices in the Arkansas Territory.

Bounty Lands in Illinois

The Illinois Territory was created in 1809. The first bounty lands in Illinois for the War of 1812 were awarded before it was admitted as a state. The area of land to be awarded lay between the Mississippi and Illinois Rivers south of a line ninety miles north of the Beardstown Base Line established with the Fourth Principal Meridian in 1815. This was a large area of arable land, as much as 3,500,000 acres.

The survey was conducted during 1815 and 1816 and warrants were issued to those veterans who applied. During the next two years, over 10,000 patents were issued in the Illinois tract. Many of those veterans sold their land to speculators. Subsequently, many of the speculators could not pay the increasing taxation on the property. The State of Illinois began selling the repossessed land after it became a state on 3 December 1818. The influx of settlers into the state facilitated the sales. Between 1820 and 1830, the population tripled to over 50,000. Clearly, bounty land was producing the desired migration to expand the frontier and populate it.[17]

Bounty Lands in Missouri

The Louisiana Territory was established in 1805 for part of the land acquired by the Louisiana Purchase. After Louisiana was admitted as a state, the remaining area was renamed the Missouri Territory in 1812. The area of what would become Arkansas and Oklahoma was later designated as the Arkansas Territory in 1819. Missouri became a state on 10 August 1821.

A half million acres north of the Missouri River were set aside as bounty land for soldiers of the War of 1812. The surveyors completed their work, and the first warrants were issued in January 1819.

At first, the president personally signed each warrant. As the number of warrants increased that signature workload became too much. In 1836, Congress authorized a secretary to sign the warrants instead of the president himself. After that date, the entire document was in the same handwriting.

Assignment of specific acreage in Missouri was made by lottery at the general land office. Land noted by the surveyor as being unsuited for agriculture was excluded from the lottery. The area included Carroll, Chariton, Macon, and Randolph Counties. Those tracts created less excitement because of the location. They were 175 miles from St Louis and 100 miles from the Missouri River.[18]

Records of the bounty land awards are available from the Bureau of Land Management (http://glorecords.blm.gov/search/). For example, Figure 46 is the record of the warrant issued to Elizabeth, the widow of Private William Weaver, for land in Missouri.

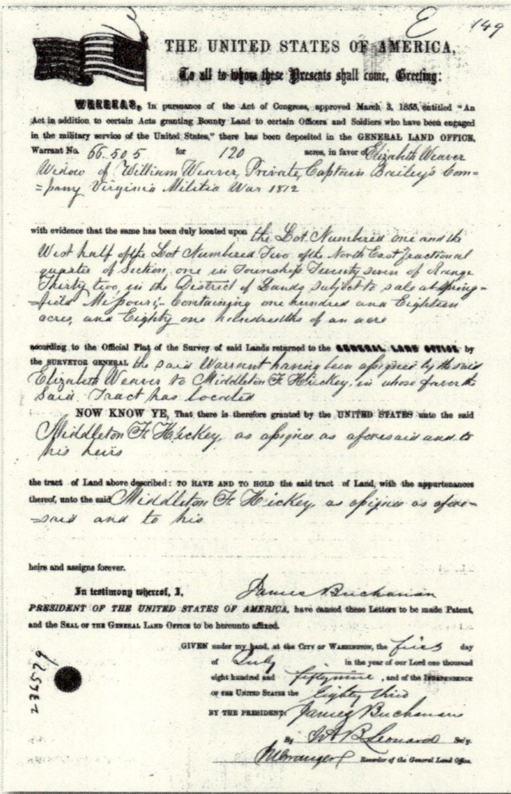

E 149

THE UNITED STATES OF AMERICA,

To all to whom these Presents shall come, Greeting:

WHEREAS, In pursuance of the Act of Congress, approved March 3, 1855, entitled "An Act in addition to certain Acts granting Bounty Land to certain Officers and Soldiers who have been engaged in the military service of the United States," there has been deposited in the GENERAL LAND OFFICE, Warrant No. 66.505 for 120 acres, in favor of Elizabeth Weaver Widow of William Weaver, Private, Captain Bailey's Company Virginia Militia War 1812

with evidence that the same has been duly located upon the Lot Numbered one and the West half of the Lot Numbered Two of the North East fractional quarter of Section one in Township Seventy seven of Range Thirty two, in the District of Lands subject to sale at Springfield Missouri; Containing one hundred and Eighteen acres, and Eighty one hundredths of an acre

according to the Official Plat of the Survey of said Lands returned to the GENERAL LAND OFFICE by the SURVEYOR GENERAL the said Warrant having been assigned by the said Elizabeth Weaver to Middleton F. Hickey, in whose favor the said Tract has located

NOW KNOW YE, That there is therefore granted by the UNITED STATES unto the said Middleton F. Hickey, as assignee as aforesaid and to his heirs

the tract of Land above described: TO HAVE AND TO HOLD the said tract of Land, with the appurtenances thereof, unto the said Middleton F. Hickey as assignee as aforesaid and to his

heirs and assigns forever.

In testimony whereof, I, James Buchanan PRESIDENT OF THE UNITED STATES OF AMERICA, have caused these Letters to be made Patent, and the SEAL OF THE GENERAL LAND OFFICE to be hereunto affixed.

GIVEN under my hand, at the CITY OF WASHINGTON, the first day of July in the year of our Lord one thousand eight hundred and fifty nine, and of the INDEPENDENCE OF THE UNITED STATES the Eighty third

BY THE PRESIDENT: James Buchanan

By W. A. B. Leonard Secy.

[illegible] Recorder of the General Land Office.

236579

Figure 46. Warrant issued to Elizabeth, widow of Private William Weaver.

Note that the bounty land was for his service in a Virginia unit before he and his wife migrated to Allen County, Kentucky.

Most of the soldiers, who applied for and received bounty land for their service from the area of this study, were militiamen. Because militiamen were not eligible until after the Acts of 1850 and 1855, most of their warrants were for land in Arkansas, Illinois, or Missouri as described above.

The frontiersmen from the study area are listed in Table 9. Variations in the spelling of the surnames are not listed. Chapter 11 contains the biographical sketches and variant surname spelling of each soldier.

Some soldiers served in more than one unit but only one is shown in the table. Refer to Chapter 11 for other regiments and companies in which they may have served.

The in and out dates of the soldiers' service are the earliest enlistment date and latest discharge date. In the case of multiple periods of service, the dates encompass all periods of service. Dates that are listed as unknown could not be verified from the service or pension records. Private Benjamin Long's record, for example, had an entry of "not stated" in the in and out spaces of the company muster roll. There was no explanation of the lack of those entries.

The bounty land columns contain the number or numbers assigned to bounty land warrants that were issued.

Rank	Name	Regiment	Company	Enrolled	Bounty Land	
Pvt	Abshear, John	11 Reg't (Williams) Mtd KY	Berryman's	30 Aug 1813		
Pvt	Adcock, Tyre	3 Reg't (Johnson) E. TN	Tunnell's	20 Sep 1814	32801	
Sgt	Alexander, James M	3 Regiment U.S. Rifles	Wyley's	8 Oct 1814	23778	
Pvt	Allen, Luke P	2 Reg't(Thomas) GA	Hendon's	12 Oct 1814	48582	27241
Pvt	Allen, William H	1 Reg't (Hall's) TN	Bledsoe's	16 Dec 1812		
Pvt	Anderson, Israel	44 Reg't (Ross) Infantry US	Baker's	2 Jun 1814	10734	
Lt	Austin, John	14 Reg't (Mitchusson) KY	Sterrett's	20 Nov 1814	21669	27744
Pvt	Baird, David	14 Reg't (Mitchusson) KY	Griffin's	20 Nov 1814	24922	
Pvt	Barton, Berry	11 Reg't (Williams) Mtd KY	Berryman's	20 Aug 1813	39415	
Pvt	Berry, William	3 Reg't (Miller) KY	Green's	1 Sep 1812	35452	102154
Pvt	Blackwell, William	Hudspeth & Brown KY	Berryman's	6 Mar 1812		
Pvt	Boucher, John	4th Reg't (Pogue) KY	Dowden's	27 Aug 1812	23726	15067

Table 9. Bounty Land Awards for frontiersmen from the study area.

Rank	Name	Regiment	Company	Enrolled	Bounty Land	
Pvt	Brown, Henry	14 Reg't (Mitchusson) KY	Sterrett's	20 Nov 1814	26457	34515
Capt	Brown, Hugh	11 Reg't (Caldwell) Mtd KY	Brown's	18 Sep 1812		
Pvt	Brown, James	14 Reg't (Mitchusson) KY	Griffin's	20 Nov 1814	2829	
Pvt	Burton, John	11 Reg't (Williams) Mtd KY	Berryman's	20 Aug 1813	44256	13768
Pvt	Cagle, Sampson	3 Reg't (Miller) Detach KY	Berryman's	1 Sep 1812	101310	70462
SgtMaj	Caldwell, Isaac	14 Reg't (Mitchusson) KY	Staff	20 Nov 1814		
Pvt	Calvert, John	14 Reg't (Mitchusson) KY	Griffin's	20 Nov 1814	39390	
Pvt	Caruth, Thomas	1 Reg't (Hall) TN	Martin's	10 Dec 1812	23644	8692
Cpl	Chambers, Alexander	14 Reg't (Mitchusson) KY	Griffin's	20 Nov 1814	2619	21918
Pvt	Chayson, David	14 Reg't (Mitchusson) KY	Griffin's	20 Nov 1814	46743	40179
Pvt	Claiborne, Ephriam	5 Reg't (Booth) E. TN	Lewis'	13 Nov 1814	44017	46356
Pvt	Cole, James	7 Reg't (Taul) Mtd KY	Gholson's	30 Aug 1813	31097	
Pvt	Cole, John	Hudspeth & Brown KY	Berryman	6 Mar 1813		
3Sgt	Cole, Joseph	1 Reg't (Allen) Mtd KY	Hamilton's	18 Sep 1812	45769	44114
Ens	Collins, Henry	11 Reg't (Caldwell) KY	Berryman's	20 Aug 1813		
Pvt	Conyers, John	2 Reg't Mt(Cannon) W.TN	Harpole's	24 Sep 1813	2833	
Pvt	Cook, Sion	11 Reg't (Caldwell) KY	Berryman's	20 Aug 1813		
Pvt	Cooksey, Thomas	1 Reg't (Byrne) Lgt Inf VA	Rice's	29 Aug 1814	28384	71196
Pvt	Cowen, James	14 Reg't (Mitchusson) KY	Griffin's	20 Nov 1814	69008	
Pvt	Creek, David	14 Reg't (Mitchusson) KY	Griffin's	20 Nov 1814	26273	40953
Pvt	Cushenberry, Daniel	Hudspeth & Brown KY	Berryman's	6 Mar 1813		
Pvt	Davasher, John C	90 Reg't (Johnson) VA	Unk	Unk		
Pvt	Davis, Johathan	7 Reg't (Pearson) NC	Krider's	1 Feb 1814	93658	
Pvt	Dobbs, Henry S	4 Reg't (Bayless) E.TN	Brock's	13 Nov 1814	11466	9138
Pvt	Dobbs, John	3 Reg't (Miller) KY	Berryman's	1 Sep 1812	46638	101594
Pvt	Dobson, Thomas	14 Reg't (Mitchusson) KY	Griffin's	20 Nov 1814	10014	39669
Pvt	Dowell, David	14 Reg't (Mitchusson) KY	Griffin's	20 Nov 1814	41662	46513
Pvt	Dowell, John	3 Reg't (Raulston) W. TN	Neale's	Nov 1814	45684	46097
Pvt	Dry, John	14 Reg't (Mitchusson) KY	Griffin's	20 Nov 1814	17909	5071
Pvt	Duncan, Ashley	11 Reg't (Williams) Mtd KY	Berryman's	20 Aug 1813		
1 Sgt	Duncan, Traverse	11 Reg't (Williams) Mtd KY	Berryman's	20 Aug 1813		
Pvt	Durham, James	39 Reg't (Walker) US Reg	Jones'	13 Dec 1813	21596	
Ens	Ellis, Samuel	1st Reg't (Wynne) W. TN	McCall's	4 Oct 1813	5966	75973

Table 9 continued.

Rank	Name	Regiment	Company	Enrolled	Bounty Land	
Cpl	Eubank, Jonathan	14 Reg't (Mitchusson) KY	Griffin's	20 Nov 1814	28919	45299
Pvt	Frost, Eli	11 Reg't (Caldwell) KY	Berryman's	Unk		
Pvt	Garrett, Larkin	1 Reg't (Hopkins) Mtd KY	Brown's	18 Sep 1812	72281	78831
Pvt	Garrison, Mark	Hudspeth & Brown KY	Berryman's	6 Mar 1813		
Pvt	Gibson, John	14 Reg't (Mitchusson) KY	Griffin's	20 Nov 1814	13153	11877
Pvt	Gibson, William	11 Reg't (Williams) KY	Berryman's	13153		
Pvt	Goodrum, John J	2 Reg't (Raulston) W. TN	Neale's	13 Nov 1814	43023	33216
Pvt	Graves, Frederick	3 Reg't (Miller) KY	Berryman's	1 Sep 1812	101653	29069
Pvt	Griffin, John	15 Reg't (Slaughter) KY	Evans	10 Nov 1814	91110	
Cpt	Griffin, Thomas	14 Reg't (Mitchusson) KY	Griffin's	20 Nov 1814		
Pvt	Grisham Thomas	14 Reg't (Mitchusson) KY	Griffin's	20 Nov 1814	20868	42343
Pvt	Hardcastle, John	11 Reg't (Williams) KY	Berryman's	30 Aug 1813	42696	64587
Pvt	Harrison, Andrew	2 Reg't (Cocke) W. TN	Crunk's	13 Nov 1814	5555	45492
Cpl	Hatler, Michael	1 Reg't (Caldwell) Mtd KY	Brown's	18 Sep 1812		
Pvt	Hickman, Joseph	24 Reg't (Bissell) US Inf	DeSha's	19 Jul 1812	11164	
Pvt	Hoback , Mark	14 Reg't (Mitchusson) KY	Griffin's	20 Nov 1814		
Pvt	Hobdy, John	US Reg't (Carroll) Rangers	Donaldson's	20 Nov 1814	3616	
Pvt	Hooton, Joseph	Hudspeth & Brown KY	Berryman's	6 Mar 1813		
Pvt	House, Henry	3 Reg't (Raulston) W. TN	Hamilton's	14 Nov 1814	18529	19411
Pvt	House, William	1 Reg't (Raulston) W. TN	Wallace's	10 Dec 1812	32497	12088
Pvt	Howell, Hudson	14 Reg't (Mitchusson) KY	Malone's	20 Nov 1814	53304	
Pvt	Huntsman, Henry	3 Reg't (Miller) KY	Berryman's	1 Sep 1812	36508	101596
Pvt	Johnson, John	14 Reg't (Mitchusson) KY	Malone's	20 Nov 1814		
Cpl	Johnson, Mathew	14 Reg't (Mitchusson) KY	Sterrett's	20 Nov 1814	21795	26495
Pvt	Johnson, Robert	14 Reg't (Mitchusson) KY	Griffin's	20 Nov 1814	53304	
Pvt	Kerby, Isaiah	14 Reg't (Mitchusson) KY	Griffin's	13 Nov 1813	8452	
Cpl	Kerby, Jesse	11 Reg't (Williams) KY	Berryman's	20 Aug 1813	10070	8553
Pvt	Kerby, Leonard	14 Reg't (Mitchusson) KY	Griffin's	20 Nov 1814	32886	16776
Pvt	Kerby, Samuel M	14 Reg't (Mitchusson) KY	Griffin's	20 Nov 1814	45907	36617
2Sgt	Kirby, Tarrence	3 Reg't (Miller) KY	Berryman's	1 Sep 1812	2489	
Pvt	Lamb, William	14 Reg't (Mitchusson) KY	Dodds'	20 Nov 1814		
Pvt	Lee, Henry	NC Drafter Militia	Boykin's	24 Jul 1813	39961	
Pvt	Lee, Stephen	KY (South) Vol Mtd Inf	Sturgus'	18 Sep 1812	19870	
Pvt	Long, Benjamin	11 Reg't (Caldwell) KY	Berryman's	Unk		
Sgt	Mannon, Abel	Hudspeth & Brown KY	Berryman's	6 Mar 1813		

Table 9 continued.

Rank	Name	Regiment	Company	Enrolled	Bounty Land	
Pvt	Martin, Peter	4 Reg't (Bayless) TN	Jones'	4 Oct 1813	22008	
Cpl	McCallister, James	11 Reg't (Williams) KY Mtd	Berryman's	31 Aug 1813		
2Cpl	McElroy, John	7 Reg't (Barbee's) KY	Burnett's	23 Aug 1812		
Pvt	Meador, Allen	3 (Raulston) W. TN	Haynie's	13 Nov 1814	15939	26020
Pvt	Meador, Asa	2 Reg't (McCrory) W. TN	Metcalf's	Unk		
Pvt	Meador, Eli	3 Reg't (Copeland) W. TN	Wilkerson's	28 Jan 1814	55678	
Pvt	Meador, William	3 Reg't (Raulston) W. TN	Haynie's	15 Nov 1814	19642	28920
Pvt	Merrifield, Samuel	3 Reg't (Miller) KY	Yeakey's	1 Sep 1812	51920	
Pvt	Miflin, Armstrong	Hudspeth & Brown KY	Berryman's	6 Mar 1813		
Pvt	Miller, Morris	Hudspeth & Brown KY	Berryman's	6 Mar 1813		
Pvt	Miller, Samuel	14 Reg't (Mitchusson) KY	Griffin's	20 Nov 1814	17757	22232
Pvt	Miller, William	14 Reg't (Mitchusson) KY	Griffin's	20 Nov 1814		
Pvt	Mitchell, Thompson	19 Reg't (Ambler's) VA	Booker's	18 Mar 1813		
Pvt	Moody, Martin	15 Reg't (Slaughter) KY Mil	Evans	10 Nov 1814	28912	49786
Pvt	Moore, James F	2 Reg't (Donald-son) Mtd KY	Menifee's	26 Aug 1813		
Pvt	Morrison, James S	11 Reg't (Caldwell) Mtd KY	Berryman's	1 Sep 1812	77139	
Cpl	O'Neal, John	14 Reg't (Mitchusson) KY	Griffin's	20 Nov 1814	37789	52014
Pvt	Oliver, William W	1 Reg't (Stokes) NC Militia	Goode's	Unk		
Pvt	Owens, Obediah	5 Reg't (Mason) VA	Moore's	5 Jul 1813	22424	
Pvt	Patton, William	11 Reg't (Caldwell) KY	Berryman's	20 Aug 1813	64186	14598
Pvt	Pardue, Jesse	4 Reg't (Kountz) VA	Pepper's	12 Sep 1813	14090	22154
Pvt	Petty, James	84 Reg't (Cole-man) VA	Royal's, J. B.	30 Aug 1814	114548	
Pvt	Pruitt, Moses	14 Reg't (Mitchusson) KY	Griffin's	20 Nov 1814	7415	
Pvt	Pulliam, James G	14 Reg't (Mitchusson) KY	Griffin's	20 Nov 1814	55186	37606
Pvt	Pulliam John	14 Reg't (Mitchusson) KY	Smith's	20 Nov 1814		
Pvt	Ragland, Benjamin	14 Reg't (Mitchusson) KY	Griffin's	20 Nov 1814	54882	20532
Pvt	Richards, Hiram	2 Reg't (Benton) TN Vols	McEwen's	10 Dec 1812	11465	28195
Pvt	Right, John	11 Reg't (Caldwell) KY Det	Berryman's	Unk		
Pvt	Rigsby, James	14 Reg't (Mitchusson) KY	Griffin's	20 Nov 1814	15765	16129
Pvt	Rigsby, John	14 Reg't (Mitchusson) KY	Griffin's	20 Nov 1814	15797	433543
Pvt	Ritchie, George	11 Reg't (Caldwell) KY	Berryman's	20 Aug 1813		
Sgt	Roark, Asa	3 Reg't (Raulston) W. TN	Haynie's	13 Nov 1814	23281	34276

Table 9 continued.

Rank	Name	Regiment	Company	Enrolled	Bounty Land	
Pvt	Robertson, Leroy	Unk	Unk	Unk		
Pvt	Robinson, James	15 Reg't (Slaughter) KY	Woods'	10 Nov 1814		
Pvt	Seagraves, John	14 Reg't (Mitchusson) KY	Griffin's	20 Nov 1814		
Pvt	Seagraves, Thomas	44 Reg't (Ross) Infantry US	Baker's	25 Apr 1813	25883	
Pvt	Seamster, Pleasant	15 Reg't (Slaughter) KY Det	Berry's	10 Nov 1814	13155	
Maj	Shacklett, Benjamin	3 Reg't (Miller) KY	Shacklett's	25 Jul 1813		
Pvt	Sherry, John	Hudspeth & Brown KY	Berryman's	6 Mar 1813		
Pvt	Shipley, Nathaniel	3 Reg't (Miller) KY	Yeakley's	1 Sep 1812		
Adj	Smith, John	14 Reg't (Mitchusson) KY	Sterrett's	13 Sep 1812		
Pvt	Spears, Ephraim	3 Reg't (Miller) KY	Berryman's	1 Sep 1812		
Pvt	Spencer, John	15 Reg't (Slaughter) KY Det	Wood's	10 Nov 1814	62379	
Sgt	Spilman, Samuel	14 Reg't (Mitchusson) KY	Griffin's	20 Nov 1814	10946	40582
Pvt	Stamps, Charles	14 Reg't (Mitchusson) KY	Griffin's	20 Nov 1814	11467	26792
Pvt	Stark, Thomas	Hudspeth & Brown KY	Berryman's	6 Mar 1813		
Pvt	Stovall, Drury	14 Reg't (Mitchusson) KY	Griffin's	20 Nov 1814	62566	
Pvt	Sturdy, William	3 Reg't (Miller) KY	Berryman's	1 Sep 1812	36294	55402
Pvt	Swindle, Pelidge S.	IL Militia	Eaton's	1812	33461	
Pvt	Taber, Henry	Hudspeth & Brown KY	Berryman's	6 Mar 1813		
Pvt	Thompson, John	14 Reg't (Mitchusson) KY	Griffin's	20 Nov 1814		
Pvt	Thompson, William	17 U.S. Infantry	Hunter's	21 Jun 1814	8276	
Pvt	Trammel, Sampson	Hudspeth & Brown KY	Berryman's	6 Mar 1813		
Pvt	Veach, Nathan	24 Reg't U.S. Infantry	Stockton's	5 Apr 1811		
Pvt	Venable, William	11 Reg't (Caldwell) KY Mil	Berryman's	Unk		

Table 9 continued.

Total Bounty Land Warrants Awarded

The precise number of bounty land warrants that were awarded, like the precise number of those eligible, is murky to say the least. Some estimates are that the original act of 1812 produced 29,186 warrants. That number compared favorably to the 16,720 warrants issued after the Revolutionary War but not when compared to the total number of men in service.

The Acts of 1850 to 1855 brought the militiamen and others into the eligibility circle. In response to those inclusions, another 464,419 warrants were issued. That raised the total number of warrants for the entire 1812 War to 627,785.[19] Within the study area, ninety-four of the 154 individuals (61%) are known to have had bounty land awards made based on their service. Considering that almost all awards were first available when many of the men or their widows were in their sixties or older, that percentage seems remarkable.

The 1855 statute was the most far reaching and accounted for most of the increases in bounty land awards. The first two parts of it are quoted below.

"10 U.S. Statutes 701-702

THIRTY-THIRD CONGRESS. Session II. 1855

CHAP. CCII. — An Act in Addition to certain Acts granting Bounty Land to certain Officers and Soldiers who have been engaged in the Military Service of the United States.

Be it enacted by the Senate and House of Representatives of the United States of America in Congress assembled, That each of the surviving commissioned and noncommissioned officers, musicians, and privates, whether of regulars, volunteers, rangers, or militia, who were regularly mustered into the service of the United States, and every officer, commissioned and non-commissioned, seaman, ordinary seaman, flotilla-man, marine, clerk, and landsman in the navy, in any of the wars in which this country has been engaged since seventeen hundred and ninety, and each of the survivors of the militia, or volunteers, or State troops of any State or Territory, called into military service, and regularly mustered therein, and whose services have been paid by the United States, shall be entitled to receive a certificate or warrant from the Department of the Interior for 160 acres of land; and where any of those who have so been mustered into service and paid shall have received a certificate or warrant, he shall be entitled to a certificate or warrant for such quantity of land as will make, in the whole, with what he may have heretofore received, 160 acres to each such person having served as aforesaid: Provided, The person so having been in service shall not receive said land warrant if it shall appear by the muster rolls of his excepted regiment or corps that he deserted, or Was dishonorably discharged from service: Provided further, That the benefits of this section shall be held to extend to wagon-masters and teamsters who may have been employed, under direction of competent authority in time of war in the transportation of military stores and supplies.

Sec. 2. And be it further enacted, That in case of the death of any person who, if living, would be entitled to a certificate or warrant as aforesaid under this act, leaving a widow, or, if no widow, a minor child or children, such widow, or, if no widow, such minor child or children, shall be entitled to receive a certificate or warrant for the same quantity of land that such deceased person would be entitled to receive under the provisions of this act, if now living: Provided, That a subsequent marriage shall not impair the right of any such widow to such warrant if she be a widow at the time of making her application: And provided, further, That those shall be considered minors who are so at the time this act shall take effect."

Chapter 11

When Duty Called

Frontiersmen Who Served in the War of 1812

Just over 200 years have elapsed since the frontiersmen from the study area marched off to the War of 1812. Their lives were disrupted by their departure to go wherever our nation would send them; they faced the uncertainties that all soldiers confront as combat looms; they worried about the families that they left behind; and yet they persevered. Their belief in our country and the principles of freedom it represents is evident in their actions. The following biographical sketches attempt to place some humanity beyond just the names of the servicemen from the study area.

It was first necessary to define and delimit the study area before the search for biographical information could begin. That definition and delimitation was somewhat arbitrary because of the place names used in military and related documents. Some documents used post offices as the location and that sometimes resulted in what we now perceive to be strange. For example, some Allen County, Kentucky, residents used post offices in other counties such as Franklin, Fountain Run, and Claypool in Kentucky or Gallatin in Tennessee. Some of the men who lived in Sumner County, Tennessee, used New Roe, Kentucky, as their post office and Warren Countians who used Allen Springs in Allen County as theirs. To keep the study area manageable, any soldier who was born in, lived in, died in, filed papers in, or used post offices in what later became Allen County, Kentucky, was included. Thus, contiguous county areas were also included in the study area. Chapter 12 presents the geographical changes in the study area that the returning soldiers encountered, for some who came home to find that they lived in a different county from the one they left.

Some veterans saw service in other states, and moved to the study area afterward. Some saw service from the study area, but subsequently moved away to other counties or states. Some widows of soldiers who served in other areas moved here later on, and other widows left the county after their husband's death. In general, whenever there was doubt about whether an individual's connection was within the study areas, they were included with the doubts explained.

Sources

The biographical sketches of the soldiers were based on two primary sources of information. All military information came from the files examined at the National Archives in Washington D.C. Copies of those documents are on file in the Allen County Historical Society's library in Scottsville, Kentucky. Those service and pension records were the source for almost all of the individual military information contained herein. Exceptions to that source are footnoted.

Genealogical information was obtained from the family history files accessible from the Allen County Historical Society's Library and from the genealogical URL Ancestry.com. It was not uncommon for genealogists to disagree about that information. So, when genealogists produced conflicting information, the information that seemed to be the most illogical was excluded. There was no attempt to verify the genealogical information that was included because that was far beyond the scope of this study. As a result, it is probable that genealogical errors were inadvertently included or reliable information was omitted. Hence, it would not be advisable to use the genealogical data herein as a reference in building anyone's family tree.

Of course, no contemporaneous records about the War of 1812 contain any mention of Allen County because it was not established until April 1815, after the war's end (see Chapter 12). Prior to that time, it was not possible to know whether the soldier lived in the western half that was in Warren or the eastern half that was in Barren. Phrases like "in what would become Allen County" or "what was then Warren County" are used herein instead of either Warren or Barren Counties when that distinction was needed. Similarly, Macon County in Tennessee was not created until many years later and the same phrases were used for that area.

There are several representatives from some military units and few for others. For example, the 14th Regiment (Mitchusson) Kentucky Detached Militia that fought at New Orleans had a large number of frontiersmen from the study area. It was assumed that a reader might not choose to read all the biographical entries for members of that unit. To make each individual sketch stand alone, repetition of some information was required and indulgence is asked from the ones who read all of them. The reader is referred to the other chapters for descriptions of the major battles, but other activities of the individuals were included in as much detail as the information allowed.

The biographical sketches that follow are unequal in detail because of the abundance of information available or the relative lack of it. That difference does not infer a diminution of the importance of an individual's contributions or in his patriotism. It is regretful that information for some of them was not discovered in hoped for detail. The amount of information about widows is unequal too, even more so than for the men. Most of the detailed information about them was gleaned from their pension papers. The amount available from the census enumerations was severely limited because only the head of household was listed by full name before 1850. All others were just identified by sex and age cohort during that time.

In every identity case, there was an attempt to match the soldier's name to a name found in other records from the study area. Some matches were relatively easy to make, but others were less obvious. One question had to be answered in each case. Was the soldier the same person as the one who appeared with that name in the census, tax, marriage, or other records? That question was often difficult. For example, there were multiple John Smiths living in just Warren and Barren Counties in 1812. Also, the use of the words Junior and Senior was uncommon in 1812. It was difficult to distinguish between John Smith and his son John Smith when both were within the ages of eighteen and forty-five that delimited service. In every case, determination of which of the potentials was the soldier had to made by circumstantial evidence when no direct evidence existed. Uncertainty in the answer was noted in the biographical sketches when significant doubt lingered about the identity.

The variations in spellings of surnames were included if encountered because almost all the soldiers could neither read nor write. The scribes recorded the names phonetically as they thought they heard them. Multiple scribes heard the name, and interpreted the spelling differently in all, but a few names. The primary spelling from the service record was arbitrarily chosen as the one used for each soldier herein. However, all the known variants from the records were also included in the sketches.

As you read these biographical sketches, remember that these frontiersmen left their homes and families on the frontier to answer their country's call to duty. The information gathered here may allow a better understanding and appreciation of the sacrifices that they, and the ones they left behind, made by answering their county's call.

Biographical Sketches

Abshear, John

This surname had various spellings in the records: Abshire, Abshere, and Absher as examples. These are good examples of how the surname spellings changed as the scribes changed. The scribe's perception of how the soldier pronounced his name determined how he wrote it.

John Abshear was a Private on the rolls of three different Kentucky Militia units. That resulted from organizational changes, not because of reassignment. First, he was a member of the Hudspeth and Brown's Regiment, followed by the 11th Regiment (Caldwell) Kentucky Militia, and finally by the 11th Regiment (Williams) Mounted Volunteer Infantry. However, he remained in Captain William Berryman's Company throughout each of those organizational changes.

He was mustered in the 11th Regiment (Williams) 30 August 1813 as a volunteer who responded to Governor Isaac Shelby's call to join General Harrison's army after the fall of Detroit. He rode his horse to the rendezvous in Newport, Kentucky. He and his company rode north to the shore of Lake Erie, left their horses and crossed the lake in boats, invaded Canada, and fought in the Battle of the Thames (see Chapter 6). After the victory there, he walked to Detroit and then southward back to Kentucky, remounting his horse en route.

He stayed at Limestone (present day Maysville, Kentucky) from 1 to 3 November 1813. He was discharged there and rode back to Allen County.

John's wife was Nancy Barnhart, but their marriage date was uncertain. He was on the Allen County tax rolls in 1826 with 200 acres of land within the Difficult Creek drainage area. No later information about them was discovered.

Adcock, Tyre

Private Tyre Adcock was born in Anson County, North Carolina. Like almost all the frontiersmen from the study area, he could neither read nor write. When a signature was required, he would make the letter X and the scribe would write "his mark" around it.

Tyre Adcock signature

He enlisted in Captain James Tunnell's Company of the 3rd Regiment (Johnson) East Tennessee Militia on 20 September 1814. Members of that unit joined from eastern Tennessee counties. He lived in Anderson County, but enlisted in Knox County. His unit marched through Chattanooga southward. They built roads and acted as wagon guards during their march (Chapter 5). They were at Camp Mandeville near Mobile in February 1814.

A letter to Governor Holmes of the Mississippi Territory described the circumstance at Camp Mandeville. There were about 2,000 men in the camp of whom 300 were sick. There was an average of one burial per day. The men were anxious about the aftermath of the Battle of New Orleans, but they expected to complete their service without having seen the British.[1]

Tyre was mustered out in Knoxville, Tennessee, on 4 May 1815 and was married to Mona (Maria) Holland in 1816. He and Mona lived in Allen County, Kentucky, during 1851-1855. They later moved to Muhlenberg County.

On 2 January 1854, he received a bounty land warrant (#32801) for his service. The eighty acres of land was in Christian County, Illinois. He assigned that land to Horatio Vandeveer in a cash sale. Vandeveer appears to have been a land speculator who bought bounty land in that area from Tyre and from several other veterans as well.

Tyre applied for a survivor's pension, as they were called, and received it by a certificate (#4853). He received $8.00 per month beginning on 14 February 1870.

Tyre died on 16 January 1878 in Muhlenberg County, Kentucky.

Alexander, James M.

Sergeant James M. Alexander was twenty-five years old when he entered into the military. He had previously moved from North Carolina to Kentucky.

James died on 24 September 1852 and with him the details of his service. There was no record that he ever made a pension claim, but his wife Martha did. Attorney E. Scott Brown of Scottsville filed a Widow's Brief given by Martha Alexander. She was seventy-five years old when she applied on 18 Aug 1881. The file for this case contains forty-six pages of the exchanges between her, or her attorney, and the government. There were two major difficulties that prompted these exchanges. The first was that the government could find no service record for James M. Alexander. The second was that Martha submitted conflicting information about his service, and could not verify her claims.

In her original submission, Martha stated that James served in Captain Martin's Company or Captain Berryman's Company of Colonel McNulty's Regiment of the Kentucky Militia. No Colonel McNulty could be identified. Captain Berryman's Company had no soldier named James Alexander.

William Cooper, who was James' neighbor in Scottsville for about twenty-six years, stated that James told him that he was a fifer, and was in the regular army, not the militia. That was not possible if he had served in militiaman Captain Berryman's Company. That left the mentioned Captain Martin as a possibility as his company commander in the regular Army.

The government was very helpful, even suggesting evidence for Martha to verify. For example, they provided information about a James M. Alexander who served in Captain Wyly Martin's Company of the 3rd U.S. Rifles, a regular Army unit. That Captain Martin matched one of the names that Martha has submitted. That James M. Alexander was a twenty-five year old laborer at the time of enlistment in October 1814. That put his birth year as 1889. He was 5' 11" inches tall, had grey eyes, dark hair, a fair complexion, and was born in Cabarrus County, North Carolina. That James had enlisted in Gallatin, Tennessee, for a term of five years, and had been discharged on 30 October 1819 at Camp Missouri when his term of service expired.

Captain Wyly Martin's service began in Tennessee when he was commissioned on 9 August 1813. He served in the 3rd U.S. Rifles beginning 17 March 1814 until he was discharged on 15 June 1815.[2]

Martha did not comment on the description that the pension commissioner's office had provided. Instead, she submitted a document that contained James' signature that she thought could be used to verify her claims. That didn't help because the fact was that the Alexander in Captain Martin's Company signed with an X used by those who could not write.

At one point in the exchange of correspondence, Martha stated that she thought that James entered service with William Wygal and George Wygal. She said that they enlisted at Thomas Burrus' mill in Warren County in the summer of 1812. But George and William Waggle served in the 3rd Regiment (Miller) Kentucky Militia that was not a regular Army unit. In addition, that regiment did not have a Captain Martin on its rolls.

Martha submitted information that James had applied for bounty land and had been awarded 80 acres of land on 1 June 1857 under a warrant (#23778) issued under the Act of 1855. However, that land was in Greene County, Missouri, and was warranted to a Sergeant John M. Alexander, not to Martha's husband James M. That land was conveyed to Joseph L. Thompson. The warrant states that this John M. Alexander entered the service in Tennessee, not Kentucky.

The cover sheet on the file containing Martha's correspondence concerning the claim contains the soldier's name as "James M. Alexander." The government clearly accepted as fact that the name was for her husband. Why she would not accept the identity provided by the Pension Office that seems so clearly to be her James, remains an inexplicable mystery.

Martha's claim was finally rejected on 16 May 1883 because James' birth date, one that she had provided, did not match any of the Alexander men whose service records were found.

Martha died before 23 April 1888 without having received a pension.

Allen, Luke P.

Some veterans of the War of 1812 came to the study area after the war. Luke P. Allen was one of those. He was born in Virginia on 1 August 1795 and reared in Georgia. He became a Private on 12 October

1814 in Captain James Henden's Company of Colonel James Thomas' Regiment of the Georgia Militia. He was discharged on 17 March 1815.

He moved to Sumner County, Tennessee, sometime after the war and was married there to Margaret Parker on 15 August 1825.

He was accepted as a Methodist minister in the Kentucky Conference in 1821 and traveled in several circuits, including Newport, Little Sandy, Goose Creek, and Greenville Circuits. His declining health caused him to be placed on the Superannuated (sic) list. It was said that he was "earnest, zealous, and useful, exemplifying in his life the religion he possessed."[3]

Luke and Margaret were still in Sumner County when the 1830 Census was taken. There were eight white persons in his household and three slaves, one male and two females. Sometime later, Margaret moved to Allen County, Kentucky, and died at her home there on 22 March 1839.

The U.S. Census of 1840 recorded Luke living in Allen County with one other male in his household. He then owned four slaves, two men and two women. The following year, Luke was married in Warren County on 5 October 1841 to Arminta D. Perkins from Logan County, Kentucky.

Luke died on 18 December 1845 and was buried in Bethpage in Sumner County, Tennessee. Arminta filed a Widow's Brief on 29 April 1878, application (#19433) as a request to be placed on the pension roles as the surviving wife of a War of 1812 veteran. Her application was approved and she received that pension by certificate (#9440) issued on 30 September 1878. She received $12.00 per month for the remaining years of her life.

Arminta made two bounty land applications. The first resulted in a warrant (#48582) for 80 acres in Vermillion County, Illinois, under the Act of 1850. She assigned that tract to Elijah Boord. She received a second warrant (#2724) for 80 acres in Woodson County, Kansas, under the Act of 1855. She conveyed that land to Thomas Sears.

Arminta drew her last pension check on 4 February 1904. It is likely that was the date of her death.

Allen, William H.

William H. Allen was the third son of Richard and Mary Allen, born in 1787 in Virginia. He was living in Tennessee when the call to duty came. He enlisted as a Private in Captain Abraham Bledsoe's Company of the 1st Regiment of Tennessee Volunteers commanded by Colonel William Hall. Bledsoe's Company was a Rifle Company in the regiment.

After a brief period of training, the regiment left in January 1813 and floated down the Cumberland, Ohio, and Mississippi Rivers to Natchez, Mississippi (Chapter 4). There, General Andrew Jackson was advised by the Secretary of War that his unit was no longer needed and the men should be discharged there. Jackson was angered by that decision and marched the army home at his own expense. Along the way, he earned the name "Old Hickory" as he led his troops back during a cold January to Tennessee.[4]

William's period of service was from 21 Nov 1812 to 22 April 1813. Initially, his monthly pay was $5.00 per month, but that was raised to $8.00 per month on 10 February 1813.

He lived in Allen County when the 1850 census was taken. His wife Sally (Railey), four daughters and two granddaughters lived with him. He died in Allen County in 1863.

Anderson, Israel

Israel Anderson was born in Orange County, North Carolina. He was married to Mary Gratner on 3 January 1792 in Washington, Virginia.[5] They traveled with two daughters to Warren County, Kentucky, in 1799 in an area that became Allen County in 1815. In 1801, he settled on 200 acres on Little Trammel Creek. By 1818, his acreage had increased to about 700 acres on Big and Little Trammel Creeks. Eventually, he had about 1,400 acres.[6]

He was designated as the substitute for Mark Garrison of the 11th Regiment (Caldwell's) Kentucky Militia, but the records do not indicate that he ever deployed with them.

Israel enlisted in the regular Army at Gallatin in Sumner County, Tennessee, in May 1814. He was a twenty-four years old farmer before he enlisted. He was described as being five foot eleven and half inches tall, with hazel eyes, brown hair, and a light complexion. Private Anderson was assigned to Captain Isaac Baker's Company of the 44th U.S. Infantry Regiment. Colonel George T. Ross, the regimental commander, reported that the regiment was being increased to 500 enlisted men by November 1814.

The real test of the 44th would be in New Orleans (Chapter 8). Waiting for battle was not something that troops enjoyed. While they waited along the Rodriguez Canal, General Jackson ordered them to exchange their rifles for shovels and dig. Digging was perhaps worse than waiting because it seemed pointless to them at first. During the next several days, they dug and piled up the dirt on the mound along the side of the canal. As the days passed, their understanding of purpose developed, and thereafter competition developed between the units to see which could build the mound quicker and higher. By Christmas Eve, the mound had grown to three feet high. That mound would be their sheltering protection when the British attack began.

As the Battle of New Orleans began on 8 January 1815, the 44th U.S. Infantry was on the line with Battery 5 of the artillery between them and Carroll's Tennessee Militia to their left. Adair's Kentuckians were farther beyond them to the left.[7] General Jackson depended on the 44th as a regular unit to anchor the line between the Mississippi River and the state militias. They did exactly that.

Immediately after the battle and the end of the war, the federal government's perceived need for a standing regular Army regiments diminished. The 44th was disbanded and its members discharged at New Orleans on 8 April 1815. Israel and the other men walked home as civilians.

On 6 November 1817, Israel received a warrant (#10734) for 160 acres of bounty land in Warren County, Illinois, as authorized by the Act of 1812 for regular Army veterans. He also was listed as the patentee, and one can infer that he too held the land rather than selling it.

Austin, John

John Austin was a North Carolinian by birth, born there in 1793. He was one of the earliest settlers in Barren County, Kentucky. He and his brothers-in-law, Thomas and Walter Caruth, purchased a large land track in the area where the town of Fountain Run would be developed later. John was involved in the location and layout of that community. It was important to have such people as the frontier was being developed.

John was about twenty-one years old when he was married to Kitty Caruth who was about fifteen years old at the time. Very soon thereafter, duty called and he was commissioned as a Lieutenant in the Kentucky Militia.

Lieutenant Austin became the second highest-ranking man in Captain Thomas Sterrett's Company of the 14th Regiment (Mitchusson) Kentucky Detached Militia. The unit was formed on 20 November 1814 in response to General Jackson's plea for help in the New Orleans campaign. John's salary was $30.00 per month.

The unit almost immediately began the boat trip down the Cumberland, Ohio, and Mississippi Rivers to New Orleans. John became ill at Camp Jackson and was admitted to the Army hospital at Camp Dupree downstream from New Orleans on 31 December 1814. The hospitalization was an extended one and he was not dismissed until 28 February 1815. His illness was not specified in his service records. His hospitalization caused him to miss participation in the Battle of New Orleans. He did not miss the long walk back to Kentucky. He was mustered out of service on 20 May 1815 in Russellville.

John applied for and received 80 acres of bounty land in Illinois by a warrant (#21669) under the Act of 1850. That tract was sold to Steven C. Wright. He also received 80 additional acres in Missouri by warrant (#27744) under Act of 1855. He sold that tract of land to William D. Jourdan.

John Austin died in 1862.

Barton, Berry

Berry Barton was born in Laurens County, South Carolina, about 1790. He moved to Warren County, Kentucky, sometime before his enrollment into the Kentucky Militia on 20 August 1813. He became a Private in Captain William Berryman's Company of the 11th Regiment (Williams) Mounted Kentucky Volunteers.

Berry traveled to Newport, Kentucky, where the regiment assembled for the ride north for the invasion of Canada. He was among those who left their horses when they began ferrying across Lake Erie. Once ashore, they joined with the other units of General Harrison to attack the British in the Battle of the Thames (Chapter 6).

After the Battle of the Thames, he marched to Detroit and to the corral on the south shore of Lake Erie. He retrieved his horse and rode back to Kentucky. He crossed the Ohio River at Limestone (now called Maysville) and was discharged on 13 November 1813.

Berry was married to Barbara Graham in Bowling Green on 22 April 1818. They moved to Graves County, Kentucky, before the 1840 census. They were living near Cuba, Kentucky, in that county when Berry died in 1850.

Beard, David H.

The Beard surname had spelling variants such as Bird and Baird. His pension application used the Beard spelling, but his service record listed Baird. David H. Beard was a North Carolinian by birth, born in the community of Salisbury in Rowan County in 1792.

David was living in what is now Allen County when he enrolled in the Kentucky Militia and was assigned to Captain Thomas Griffin's Company of Colonel Mitchusson's 14th Kentucky Detached Militia on 20 November 1814. He and the other men in the 14th began the trip by boat over the Cumberland, Ohio, and Mississippi Rivers to New Orleans. They were participants in the Battle of New Orleans (see Chapter 8).

Like his comrades, he remained in New Orleans for over two months before he began the trip home on 18 March 1815. He was mustered out on 20 May after that long walk.

David was married to Nancy McClure on 30 July 1816. They were living in Allen County when the 1820 census was taken. They raised a family there, but moved to Gasconade, Laclede County, Missouri, in 1857 where he became a farmer. Three years later on 19 July 1860, he applied for an invalid pension, application (#12355), and stated that he became diseased from exposure, and had never fully recovered from it. He did not describe the exposure but, in the cold January in New Orleans, the troops were not properly clothed for those low temperatures that were common that month. The walk back to Kentucky was made before spring and was a cold time as well. Whatever the case, his request for a pension was not approved.

David applied for and received a bounty land warrant (#24922) for 80 acres in Wright County, Missouri, on 5 October 1861 under the Act of 1855. The land was assigned to Robert Darden.

He died in Laclede County, Missouri.

Berry, William H.

General Harrison wanted an army of about 10,000 men with the intent to retake Detroit after its fall to the British. Kentucky provided many of those troops. As part of that buildup, the 3rd Regiment Kentucky Detached Militia was organized on 1 September 1812 with Lieutenant Colonel Nicholas Miller in command. Captain Liberty Green commanded the sixth of the nine companies in that regiment. Private William H. Berry was enrolled in that company on the day it was organized.

Subsequently, General Harrison decided to delay the move on Detroit and into Canada until winter froze the rivers and made the crossings easier. Private Berry's enrollment was for three months. As his period was nearing its end, he headed toward home. He arrived at Hardinsburg, Kentucky, where he was mustered out on 25 December 1812.

He would apply for and receive a bounty land warrant (#35452) under the Act of 1850 that provided 40 acres in DeWitt County, Illinois. He sold that land to E. Randolph Smith. Under the Act of 1855, he received another warrant (#102154) for 40 acres in Dubuque Count, Iowa. He sold that land to George W. Kelly.

Blackwell, William

Of course, the earliest settlers of the study area were all born elsewhere. William Blackwell was born in Virginia in 1787. The date of his immigration to Kentucky is not known, but he was married in Warren County on 2 January 1810. His bride was seventeen-year old Nancy Lyles. She had emigrated from Virginia too.

William was enrolled as a Private in the Hudspeth and Brown Regiment of the Kentucky Militia. On 1 March 1813, William was present as a member of the Captain William Berryman's Company.

Volunteer militiamen from the 11th Regiment of the Kentucky under Lieutenant Colonel Samuel Campbell were detached on 31 August 1813 to provide troops to augment General Harrison's army in preparation for the invasion of Canada. Captain Berryman and some other volunteers from his company were among those who were detached to that mission. Private David Dowell (see his biographical sketch herein) substituted for William Blackwell in that excursion and, as a result, William did not go.

After the war was over, William and Nancy were still in Allen County during the census of 1820. They owned one slave according to that census. By some genealogical accounts, they moved prior to 1830 to Morgan County, Alabama, an unusual direction if true. He was said to have died there in 1855.

Boucher, John

One of the earliest settlers in the study area was Peter Boucher who came to Warren County, Kentucky, between 1795 and 1797. He owned 2,300 acres according to the 1797 Warren County tax records. The land lay near the confluence of Bays Fork Creek and Barren River, an area that is now included in Allen County.

John Boucher was one of Peter's sons, born before his parents arrived in Kentucky from Virginia. He was about thirty years old when he became a Private in Captain John Dowden's Company, 4th Regiment of the Kentucky Volunteer Militia. The regimental commander was Lieutenant Colonel Robert Pogue when it was organized on 27 August 1812.

John received additional pay above his normal Private's pay. The amount was $1.34 for one period within his service from 1 January 1813 to 13 March 1813. One could surmise that he received that compensation because he accompanied Pogue when the regiment went to build a fort on the banks of the Auglaize River near the present town of Wapakoneta, Ohio. They built two story blockhouses in each corner of the fort. Eleven-foot log palisades connected hem to form the perimeter. Pogue gave his daughter's name to their handiwork and it became known as Fort Amanda. The Kentuckians turned the fort over to Ohio Militia in February 1813 and afterward it was used as a supply depot.[8] John's period of service was over and he was mustered out on 13 March 1813.

John Boucher received a bounty land warrant (#23726) that awarded 80 acres in Champaign County, Illinois, under the Act of 1850. That land was assigned later to James Meharry. He received a second award (#15067) on 10 September 1859 under the Act of 1855 for an additional 80 acres in Guthrie County, Iowa. He conveyed that land to James Crawford.

According to some genealogists, a John Boucher was married to Margaret Shook in September 1817 in St. Clair County, Illinois. He died in 1854 in Jones, Iowa.

Brown, Henry

Henry Brown was born in the Raleigh area of Wake County, North Carolina, on 4 February 1794. He made two very long walks in his life. The first was his trek as a young man with his family to what is now Allen County, Kentucky. That trip was well over five hundred miles and brought him to the community called Puncheon in the southeastern part of the county. He established a farm near that community.

The call came from General Andrew Jackson for Kentuckians to join him in New Orleans. Henry answered that call at Flippin in Monroe County. He volunteered as a member of the Kentucky Militia on 1 September 1814 and was mustered in at Russellville on 20 November. He was assigned to Captain Thomas Sterrett's Company of Lieutenant Colonel William Mitchusson's 14th Kentucky Detached Militia that had been formed specifically for the New Orleans campaign.

Henry made the second very long trip of his life with the rest of that unit on flatboats down the Cumberland, Ohio, and Mississippi Rivers to New Orleans. About half of the over 2,000 men who made the trip to Camp Jackson near New Orleans did not see action because of the lack of weapons. Henry apparently was among those who did participate in the Battle of New Orleans (Chapter 8). He and his company manned the "third breastworks" on the defensive line as the battle began. That seems to be reference to the breastworks at the Dupré Plantation because he was at Camp Dupree (sic) on 28 February after the battle. The breastworks were backup lines of defense manned by troops ready to go to the point of the main thrust of the British, wherever that might come. Those troops augmented the Kentuckians who were resisting the main attack as the battle developed.

During the battle, he received a wound to his knee from a tomahawk. Many of the War of 1812 soldiers carried tomahawks. The original word "tomahawk" referred to a Native American stone cutting implement. Europeans began trading iron hatchets with the Native Americans, and the word "tomahawk" grew to apply only to the small lightweight iron axes traded to them.

Several weeks after the battle, the troops walked up the Natchez Trace on their way back to Kentucky. He was discharged at Russellville on 22 April 1815. His round trip to New Orleans covered more than 1,500 miles.

Henry resumed life as a farmer in Allen County. He used the nearest Post Office that was located in Fountain Run in Monroe County. Across the border south of his farm lay Smith County, Tennessee, part of which became Macon County much later. It was in Smith County that he met twenty-year old Ailsey Austin. They were married there on

15 April 1818. According to the tax rolls of 1826, she owned 744 acres of land and five slaves with a taxable value of $2,034.00.

Henry submitted an application (#25430) for a pension, but it was rejected on 14 April 1873 because there was no proof of his loyalty to Union. He and Ailsey were slave owners until after the Civil War, and that may have aroused suspicions. The rules required him to prove that he had remained loyal to the United States during that war.

He received two bounty land grants. The first, under the Act of 1850, was a warrant (#26457) for 80 acres in Franklin County, Illinois, that was subsequently assigned to Ira Brashears. The second, warrant (#34515), under the Act of 1855, was for 91.[9] 1 acre in Clare County, Michigan, and was awarded on 10 February 1864. That tract was subsequently assigned to David Irvine.

After Henry had died on 14 October 1877, Ailsey applied (#29947) for a Widow's Pension under the Act of 9 Mar 1878. The loyalty issue had been resolved and her approved pension certificate (#14959) authorized $8.00 per month beginning on 16 January 1879. She died on 25 August 1880 in Scottsville.

Brown, Hugh

Little was discovered about Hugh Brown's early life. His record begins with the eve of the War of 1812. Recruitment of volunteers from the state militia resulted in the formation of the 11th Regiment Kentucky Mounted Volunteer Militia on 18 September 1812. The custom at that time was for the members of a company to select their officers. They elected him as the commander of the 8th Company of that regiment and he became Captain Hugh Brown. Josiah Short was elected Lieutenant and John Wolf as Ensign in the company.

Captain Brown led members of his company to deliver supplies to General Harrison's force in the Indiana Territory. He was part of the futile foray conducted by Major General Hopkins (Chapter 3). That trip covered over 300 miles. Hugh was discharged from that assignment on 30 October 1812 at Bosseron (one of several spellings of Busseron, Indiana) in the Indiana Territory. He received pay of $30.00 per month and his total was $56.00 for six weeks of duty.

Hugh was also on the rolls as a Major who was the Brown of the Hudspeth and Brown Regiment. That Militia unit was created on 3 February 1813 to serve a period not to exceed six months.

After the war, Hugh played an important role in the establishment and development of the new Allen County that was created by the Kentucky Legislature on 11 January 1815. Governor Isaac Shelby appointed seven men to be Justices of the Peace, the equivalent of the current magistrates, to be administrators in the local government. On 10 April 1815, they presented their commissions, and were sworn in at the home of Willis Mitchell about four miles north of where Scottsville would be located. Hugh Brown was one of those original seven men who were part the first governing body of the county.

Among the historic activities of those magnificent seven was the appointments they made of men needed to form the county government and become the first county officials in those capacities. They appointed the first sheriff, jailer, county court clerk, commonwealth attorney, coroner, surveyor, constables, and tax commissioners. The records of the county court have frequent references to Hugh Brown over the next several years.

The 1820 census listed Hugh as an owner of one slave. Ten years later, the census listed him with a female (presumed to be his wife), three slaves, and one freed black.

Kentucky land grants were issued to Hugh for 30 acres on a Branch of Big Barren River on 3 August 1826 and on 7 March 1816 for 250 acres on Barren River.

Brown, James

Several veterans of the War of 1812 filed affidavits with the Allen County Court attesting to their service and appointing attorneys to "ask, demand, and receive" pay they were owed for their service. James Brown filed his affidavit on 10 August 1816. He appointed Anak Dawson as his attorney. He stated that he had served as a Private in Captain Thomas Griffin's Company of the 14th Regiment (Mitchusson) of the Kentucky Detached Militia formed to go to New Orleans.

James was mustered in at Russellville, Kentucky, on 29 November 1814. The regiment went by the Cumberland, Ohio, and Mississippi Rivers to supplement the forces gathered in New Orleans by General Andrew Jackson.

On 31 December 1814, he was in Camp Jackson (Chapter 8). He remained there through the battle and until 28 February 1815 when the troops began the long walk back home. He was discharged at Russellville, Kentucky, on 20 May 1815. For his service, he was owed a salary of $8.00 per month. There was no record of whether or not he received the back pay that caused him to appoint an attorney to collect. One presumes that he did receive it at some point.

James filed for bounty land under the Act of 1850. He was warranted (#2829) 80 acres in Mason County, Illinois, on 1 November 1851. He retained possession of the land rather than selling it.

Burton, John

Charleston, South Carolina, was the place of birth for John Burton, also spelled Barton, on 31 March 1795. His father, Cuthbert Burton, had moved his family there from Virginia. The family moved again with two slaves, this time to what was then Warren County (now Allen) in 1805. Some scribes spelled his surname as Barton.

John was a volunteer from the Kentucky Militia who enrolled at the home of James McElroy on 20 August 1813. He became a Private in Captain William Berryman's Company of the 11th Regiment (Williams) Kentucky Mounted Kentucky Volunteers. He rode to the rendezvous at Newport, Kentucky, and accompanied the force northward through Ohio to the shores of Lake Erie. They were ferried across to Canada with General Harrison's army, and participated in the Battle of the Thames (Chapter 6). He, and his compatriots, returned to Kentucky and he was discharged in Limestone (now Maysville) on 13 November 1813.

John was married to Anna H. Cole in Barren County on 14 February 1822 and they lived in Allen County thereafter. John, like his father, became a slave owner. He had four slaves in 1840 and ten in 1860 just before the Civil War. Those slaves would be freed by the 13th Amendment to the U.S. Constitution in December 1865. He and Anna lived in the Carolina District of Allen County in 1870.

John submitted an application (#15074) for a Survivor's Pension for his service during the War of 1812. His certificate (#16492) was awarded on 14 February 1872 and he received a pension of $8.00 per month beginning in 1872.[11]

He also applied for and received two bounty land warrants. The first (#44256) was for 40 acres in Orange County, Indiana, under the Act of 1850. He assigned that land to John Bush. The second (#13768) was for 120 acres in Hamilton County, Iowa, under the Act of 1855. He assigned that land to James A. Lyon.

John age eighty-five, listed as a farmer, and Ann age eighty-six were on the 1880 census of Allen County, Kentucky. He died on 19 July 1883 when he was eighty-eight years old.

Cagle, Sampson

Sampson Cagle, also sometimes spelled Cagel and Kegel, was born in North Carolina on 8 June 1782. His family was said to have immigrated to Davidson County, Tennessee, about 1800. It must be that Sampson joined them later because he was married to Fanny Smith on 9 August 1804 in Montgomery County, North Carolina. The 1810 census listed him, his wife, and children in what was then Warren County, Kentucky, and he was in the Allen County tax records in 1825.

Sampson Cagle signature

Sampson was eighty-nine years old when he applied for a Survivor Pension on 14 March 1871. His declaration stated that he volunteered in May 1812 for a six-month term. He said that he was required to hold himself in readiness to march when asked to do so. He went to the rendezvous at Bowling Green on 24-25 August 1812 and became a member of Captain William Berryman's Company of Lieutenant Colonel Nicholas Miller's 3rd Regiment Detached Kentucky Militia. Twelve others from our area served in this regiment that saw action in what was called the second Battle of Tippecanoe (see Chapter 3). He stated that he first went to Louisville, Kentucky, through Vincennes, Indiana, to Fort Harrison on the Wabash River. From there, he went to Tippecanoe for the battle with the Indians and returned to Vincennes. The timing of his service excludes the possibility that he was present at the first Battle of Tippecanoe, but rather described the later battle that was fought there.

The itinerary in his statement exactly fits the action preceding and after the second Battle of Tippecanoe, also called the battle of Wild Cat Creek (see Chapter 3). The more famous first battle there was fought on 7 November 1811, about a year before Sampson's service began. The combat that he saw a year later was quite real, with several men from his regiment being killed in action. His service records show that he was mustered in on 1 September 1812 and served until he was discharged on 25 December 1812. His pension file contained thirty-four pages of documentation about his service.

He received approval for three bounty land warrants referring to his service in Captain Berryman's Company. The first warrant (#70462) was issued on 2 October 1854 under the Act of 1850 for 40 acres in Polk County, Missouri. The second (#101310) was for 40 acres under the Act of 1850 in Iowa County, Iowa. The third (#17762) was under the Act of 1855 and was for 80 acres in Waushara County, Wisconsin. Each of those was assigned to others, the first to Burton Potter, the second to Albert Cross, and the third to George Knowles.

His application for pension (#1818) was approved on 2 August 1871 (#2067) and his service was confirmed by the Pension Office and attested to by his commander Captain Berryman. He received $8.00 per month commencing on 14 February 1871.

He had been discharged at Vincennes on 25 December 1812. In conjunction with his bounty land claims, he also submitted a claim on 6 September 1854 for travel pay. He stated that he had traveled seventy miles from Bowling Green to Elizabethtown and another seventy miles for the return trip of from Hardinsburg to Bowling Green after his discharge.

Sampson died on 15 January 1874 and was buried on his farm. His wife Fanny was buried there too on 12 April 1872.

Caldwell, Isaac H.

It was very unusual for a Kentucky soldier from the frontier to have been born in Kentucky. That required the parent's arrival being very early in Kentucky's history. Isaac Caldwell was one such exception. He was born in Warren County, Kentucky, but his date of birth was listed differently in various family trees. The 1860 census listed his age as 65 and that would make this birth year about 1795. If so, he would have been older than the minimum age of eighteen for enlistment in the militia. His father Matthew was on tax rolls in Warren County in 1800.

Isaac Caldwell was the Sergeant Major on the Staff of the 14th Regiment (Mitchusson) Kentucky Detached Volunteer Militia. He was mustered in on 20 November 1814 for a period of six months. His pay was $12.00 per month. On 31 December 1814, he was at Camp Dupré, southeast of New Orleans. His unit saw action during the Battle of New Orleans (Chapter 8). He was mustered out on 2 May 1815 at Russellville, Kentucky.

Genealogical records indicate that Isaac was married to Nancy Lawrence on 8 June 1818 in Allen County. He was on the Allen County tax rolls in 1825 and 1827. He moved to Posey County, Indiana, sometime thereafter. They appeared on the 1850 census where he was a farmer near Marrs in Posey County.

No pension or bounty land records were discovered. Isaac died on 11 Oct 1865 in Posey County, Indiana.

Calvert, John

John Calvert was born in 5 January 1782 in Virginia. He and his father Francis settled on Barren River near Holland, Kentucky. He was a farmer in 1810 in what was then Barren County (now Allen).[12] John and Jane Russell were married in 1804 and lived near Long Creek.

John was one of the volunteers from the Kentucky militia being sought to help defend New Orleans. He became a Private in Thomas Sterrett's Company, 14th Kentucky Detached Volunteer Militia under Colonel Mitchusson. He was mustered in that unit on 20 November 1814 at Russellville.

On 31 December 2014, he was at Camp Jackson near New Orleans. He participated in the Battle of New Orleans (Chapter 8), and received a bullet wound to his knee. He was still at Camp Dupré below New Orleans on 28 February 1815. The walk back to Kentucky ended with a discharge at Russellville on 20 May 1815.

John's first wife Jane died in 1832. He was married to Elizabeth Fishburn on 27 June 1833 in Allen County.

The 1838 tax records show that John was a successful farmer. He was listed being taxed on his 1,007 acres of land, six slaves, and eleven horses. His total tax assessed value was $8,100.

John died in Allen County in 13 February 1856, and was buried in the Calvert Cemetery on his farm. His will gave two of his slaves to his wife, three to his son Jesse, three to his son Tolivar, three to his son John J., and three to his son James.

Elizabeth applied for bounty land for his service and received a warrant (#39390) on 10 March 1860 for eighty acres in Pine County, Minnesota, under the Act of 1855. She assigned her patent on the property to David H. Campbell.

Caruth, Thomas

Family heritage is difficult to establish for the early settlers on the frontier. Thomas Caruth was born in 1793 in Mecklenburg County, North Carolina. He probably moved with his parents to an area of Smith County, Tennessee, that became Macon County. For certain, he enrolled in the 1st Regiment Tennessee Volunteers commanded by Colonel William Hall on 21 November 1812. He was mustered in on 10 December 1812 and became a Private in Captain Brice Marin's Company.

The regiment accompanied General Andrew Jackson on an abortive mission to Natchez, Mississippi (Chapter 4). The unit returned from Natchez to Tennessee and was disbanded. He was mustered out on 22 April 1813. During his service he earned the customary $8.00 per month private's pay. In Allen County, Kentucky, Thomas appointed Moses J. Bonner as his attorney on 27 September 1816 to recover whatever unpaid benefits were due him from his service.

He, his brother Walter, and John Austin bought a sizable tract of land on 6 February 1817 near Barren River. His partner's sister, Edy Austin, became his wife in 1819.

The census of 1830 listed his household as a family of seven with three slaves in Allen. The 1838 tax records list his taxable assets as 150 acres with four slaves and six horses worth $2,566.[13] His farm was in the Puncheon area of southeast Allen County.

On 16 June 1856, he was awarded 80 acres of bounty land in Lawrence County, Missouri by warrant (#8692) under the Act of 1850. On 10 September 1959, he was given a warrant (#23644) for an additional 80 acres of bounty land in Putnam County, Missouri, authorized by the Act of 1855. Both tracts were assigned to others, the first to William M. Skelton and the second to Samuel Hall.

His wife Edy died on 5 June 1858. He and Pheriba Poe were married on 11 August 1859. Thomas died in 1867.

Chambers, Alexander

The westward migration into south central Kentucky was well underway when the War of 1812 began. As a result, census records that were taken once each decade were incomplete for those en route at the time it was taken. Alexander Chambers may be one who was missed. The census of 1850 identified his birth year as about 1792 and his birth state as North Carolina. His next historical record was that he enrolled into the army in Scottsville and was mustered in at Russellville on 20 November 1814. He became the 4th Corporal in Captain Thomas Griffin's Company of the 14th Regiment (Mitchusson) Kentucky Detached Militia.

His regiment was present at Camp Jackson near New Orleans on 31 December 1814. After the battle (Chapter 8), he and the others in his unit were still at Camp Jackson on 28 February 1815, ready and no doubt anxious to begin the walk back home. He was discharged at Scottsville about 1 April 1815, one of the earliest arrivals of the militiamen who walked from New Orleans by way of the Natchez Trace. He was officially mustered out at Russellville on 20 May 1815.

As a Corporal, Alexander had earned $10.00 per month. However, like most soldiers, he was not paid in the field. He sold rights to whatever back pay he might have been owed to a man named Porter in Scottsville and gave his discharge paper to him. The lack of his discharge papers complicated Alexander's subsequent application for a pension.

Relatively soon after his arrival back home, Alexander continued his westward migration and settled in Missouri. He was married to Sarah Boring at Dry Creek in Jefferson County, Missouri, on 7 November 1819. They were living in Franklin County, Missouri, in 1850 and 1855. He was a tavern keeper at those times. He appeared to have operated a boarding house too when the 1850 census was taken. The apparent boarders were a grocer, a lawyer, two stagecoach drivers, and a schoolteacher, all listed as living in his household.

He had received a bounty land warrant (#2619) on 1 October 1852 for 80 acres in Franklin County where he lived. He traded in his warrant for the land issued under the Act of 1850. He received the patent for that land. On 15 May 1860, he received an additional 80 acres of bounty land by a warrant (#21918) under the Act of 1855 in Washington County, Missouri. He subsequently assigned those acres to Jacob Clark.

He and Sarah were living in Springfield in Greene County, Missouri, when Alexander died in April 1862. Sarah filed for a Widow's Pension on 1 December 1871. The pension was granted (#26081) and she began receiving $8.00 each month starting on 13 July 1872. She lived in Rocheport in Boone County, Missouri, in 1879, and died about 1883.

Chason, David

Some surnames of men, who could neither read nor write, generated alternate spellings by scribes who were hooked on phonics. Private David Chason was a perfect example of such a surname. In his military records, his surname was spelled as Chayson, Clayson, Chaseen, Chasen, and Chaston. Census takers added to the spellings with Chaston and Chasen. A bounty land recorder spelled it Chason. That was the latest spelling and it is used here, but with no assurance that the choice was what David would have preferred or considered to be correct.

It was difficult to find ancestral information because of the multiple spellings and the lack of understanding of what the correct spelling of his name actually was. His military record was consistent even when the spelling was different. He was on the rolls of the 11th Regiment ((Williams) Kentucky Militia as a member of Captain William Berryman's Company. He served from 20 August 1813 and was discharged at Limestone (now Maysville), Kentucky, on 3 November 1813 after having helped win the Battle of the Thames in Canada (Chapter 6). He was paid $6.70 for his service and $10.40 for the use of his horse.

On 20 November 1814, he was mustered in for a second time, this time at Russellville. He was assigned to Captain Thomas Griffin's Company of the 14th Regiment (Mitchusson) Kentucky Detached Militia. He made the trip to New Orleans with them to augment General Jackson's force and was on duty there on 31 December 1814. His service record shows that he was still there in Camp Jackson on 28 February 1815 after the battle (Chapter 8). He was discharged on 28 May 1815 at Russellville.

David was listed in the 1820 census of Allen County with his surname spelled Chaston. In1850, the census taker in Simpson County recorded his name as D. Chasen and that he was born in North Carolina. The census listed him as a fifty-five year-old farmer with a wife N. Chasen. The slave schedule of that census showed that he owned five slaves.

The Act of 1850 made him eligible for bounty land. He received a warrant (#46743) on 1 January 1854 for 80 acres in Pulaski County, Illinois. He assigned that land to Francis D. Atherton. Under the Act of 1855, he received another bounty land warrant (#40179) on 10 May 1859 for an additional 80 acres in Henry County, Missouri. He assigned that land to William E. Adams.

Claiborne, Ephraim

This surname had several spellings: Clayborne, Clayborn, Clybourn, and Claybourn in the historical record. The spelling used in his pension paper is used herein. Ephraim Claiborne was born on 7 December 1788 in Robeson County on the coastal plains of North Carolina.

Ephraim moved to Tennessee and was married to Mary Browning on 21 December 1809 in Knox County by John McCampbell (Figure 47). He was twenty-one years old and she was seventeen.

The call to arms came as the Tennessee Militia was readying for actions against the Creek Indians (Chapter 5). He was mustered in Knoxville on 13 November 1814 as a Private in Captain John Lewis' Company of Colonel Edwin E. Booth's 5th Regiment of the East Tennessee Drafted Militia.

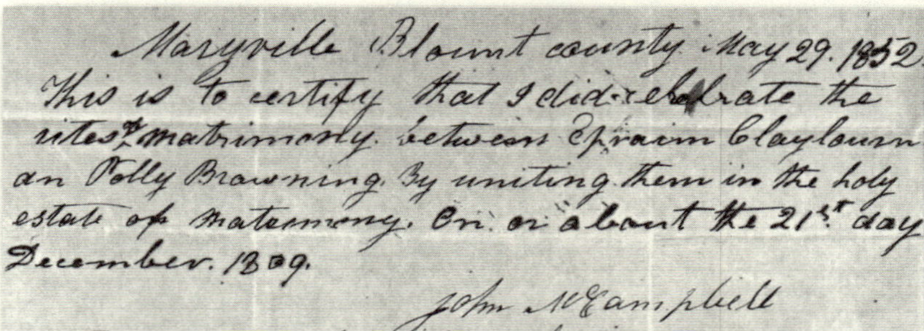

Maryville Blount county May 29. 1852
This is to certify that I did celebrate the
rites of matrimony between Ephraim Claybourn
an Polly Browning by uniting them in the holy
estate of matrimony. On or about the 21st day
December. 1809.
John McCampbell

Figure 47. Minister's certificate of marriage for Ephraim and Polly Claybourn.

The 5th Regiment, along with the 3rd and 4th Regiments, was in a division commanded by Major General William Carroll. They were sent to Mobile, in what is now Alabama, in the Mississippi Territory. They traveled through Lookout Mountain and Fort Strother along the way. At Mobile, they began the construction of a fort. Many of those men were stationed at Camp Mandeville, a military post outside of Mobile. They were to defend the area against the Creek and the British, if necessary. They were on the shore of Mobile Bay working on the fort when the news arrived that the peace treaty with Britain had been signed.

When the War of 1812 ended, there was immediate action by the U.S. government to begin disassembly of the standing Army. The unit was considered unneeded and it was dissolved and its frontiersmen returned home. Ephraim was mustered out on 13 November 1815 at

Knoxville. Soon afterward, he appointed James William Park, an attorney, to obtain whatever back pay he was due. His pay had been $8.00 per month during his service.

Ephraim was in Wilson County, Tennessee, in 1830 and in DeKalb County in 1840, according to the censuses of those years.

In 3 July 1848, Ephraim and Polly, the name she preferred, left Tennessee and bought 58 acres for $60.00 from Joseph Stinson in Allen County, Kentucky, near Puncheon Creek. A year later, Ephraim sold that farm and went to Illinois where his son William Divine Claybourn lived. A short time later, Ephraim came back to Allen County where he died on 11 May 1850.

Polly received a bounty land warrant (#44017) on 2 January 1854 under the Act of 1850. She became the patentee for 80 acres in Perry County, Illinois. Subsequently, she assigned the land to Joseph Capewell. On 10 September 1861, she received another 80 acres in Le Sueur County, Minnesota, under a warrant (#46356) by the Act of 1855. She assigned that property to Ludwig Magedan.

Polly filed a claim (#7647) for a Widow's Pension. She had the help of T. R. Hughes who was an attorney in Fountain Run in Monroe County. Her application was approved (#3251) on 13 July 1872. She received pension checks through the post office that was located in Fountain Run, the one nearest to her residence. Polly's last pension check was dated 16 December 1874. That was likely the date of her death as well.

Cole, James

Many frontiersmen who moved from their birthplace to the study area stopped along the way before reaching their final destination. That seems to be the case for James Cole who was born about 1791 in Virginia. He must have lived in Cumberland County, Kentucky, for a while. While there, he became a member of Captain James Gholson's Company of the 7th Regiment Kentucky Mounted Volunteer Militia under the command of Colonel Michael Taul. His service records showed that he was mustered in at Newport, Kentucky, on 30 August 1813.

His unit was part of the force assembled by Governor Shelby for the invasion of Canada. After the rendezvous in Newport, they rode northward and participated in the Battle of the Thames (see Chapter

6). There was a notation in his record that he was sick and left behind at Franklinton, Ohio. That settlement later became the downtown portion of the current city of Columbus. Because his muster out date of 13 November 1813 was the same as the other members of the company, it seems likely that he was left behind on the trip northward. But, it also suggests that he subsequently rejoined his unit, perhaps before the Battle of the Thames.

His entire company was paid for their travel to and from Newport according to this note on his service record. From that calculation, he was paid $19.20 for his service and travel, and $30.00 for the use of his horse.

> *"The within company, in addition to the time embraced in the within roll, is entitled for pay for 11 days for traveling from Burkesville, in Cumberland County, their place of residence, to Newport, their place of rendezvous, being 220 miles, one day being allowed for every 20 miles."*

He received a bounty land warrant (#31097) on 1 May 1860 for 160 acres in Brown County, Kansas, under the Act of 1855. He assigned that land to Milton Dickson.

James was in Allen County for the 1820 census and for the 1825 tax roll. He was taxed on one horse valued at $40.00. Perhaps that horse was the one he rode to Canada and back twelve years earlier. He and his wife E. Cole, who was born in North Carolina, were enumerated in the 1850 census with three adult children. He was a farmer. He last appeared in the 1870 census living in the household of Richard Bandy.

Cole, John

There are at least five men with the name John Cole who lived in Allen, Barren, Simpson, and Warren Counties during and soon after the War of 1812. Attempts to associate the service record with just one of those were not completely successful. In particular, the genealogical records were too difficult to unravel. For sure, John Cole was on the roll of the 11th Regiment (Caldwell) Kentucky Militia. He also appeared on the 6 March 1813 roll of the Hudspeth and Brown Regiment of the Kentucky Militia.

One John Cole was between 26 and 44 years old in the 1820 census. There was a female who was also in that age cohort and five members of that household under the age of sixteen. A John Cole was taxed by Allen County on two horses in 1825, but not taxed on any land. In the 1833 tax record, he was listed as John Cole, Sr., still taxed only on his horses. There was another John Cole, perhaps his son, who was taxed on 100 acres in the Trammel Fork Creek watershed. John Cole, Sr. does not subsequently appear on the tax rolls.

The definitive link between the soldier John Cole and a specific one of the five John Coles in the study area could not be verified.

Cole, Joseph

One phonetic variation in the spelling of the surname in this soldier's service record was Coal. Clearly, the correct spelling was Cole. Joseph Cole was born on 28 November 1786 in Washington County, Virginia. He and Margaret Link were married there on 26 November 1806.

They were living in Bourbon County, Kentucky, when Joseph was among those listed in Captain Robert Hamilton's 6th Company of Lieutenant Colonel James Allen's Mounted Volunteer Regiment of the Kentucky Militia. He was mustered in on 18 September 1812, the day the unit was first organized. He arrived in Vincennes, Indiana Territory, on 27 September (Chapter 2). He was mustered out at Busseron in the Indiana Territory on 30 October. His pay for that service included twelve travel days with twenty-five cents for each day and forty cents each day for the use of his horse. During his forty-three days of active duty, he traveled 244 miles.

His second period of service was in Captain Sterrett's Company of the 14th Regiment (Mitchusson) Detached Kentucky Militia. He was with them before, during, and after the Battle of New Orleans (Chapter 8).

By the 1830 census, he and Margaret were in Allen County. Joseph died on 9 November of the following year.

On 1 July 1854, Margaret received a bounty land warrant (#45769) under the Act of 1850 for 80 acres in Williamson County, Illinois. On 1 October 1860, she received another warrant (#44114) for eighty acres under the Act of 1855 in Tuscola County, Michigan (Figure 48). She assigned both tracts to others. The bounty land documentation proved his service.

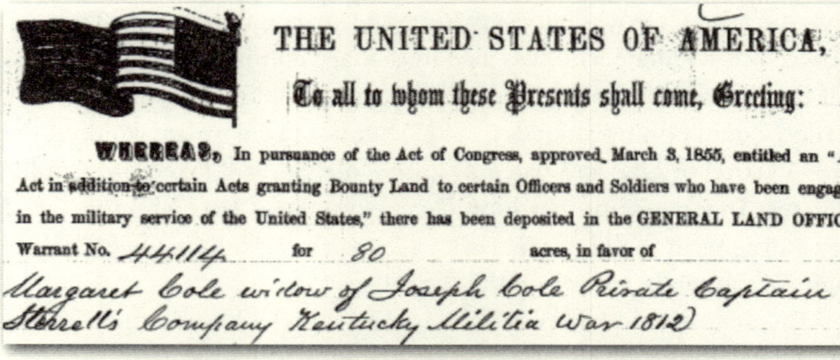

THE UNITED STATES OF AMERICA,

To all to whom these Presents shall come, Greeting:

WHEREAS, In pursuance of the Act of Congress, approved March 3, 1855, entitled an "A[n] Act in addition to certain Acts granting Bounty Land to certain Officers and Soldiers who have been engag[ed] in the military service of the United States," there has been deposited in the GENERAL LAND OFFIC[E] Warrant No. 44114 for 80 acres, in favor of Margaret Cole widow of Joseph Cole Private Captain Sterrell's Company Kentucky Militia War 1812

Figure 48. Excerpt of bounty land award to Margaret Cole.

Collins, Henry

One of the first settlers in Allen County was Henry Collins. He was born on 13 June 1772 in Spotsylvania County, Virginia. He came to what is now Allen County in the spring of 1798 where he cleared and homesteaded on two acres. He built a log cabin on that site in 1799. That qualified him for a land grant from Kentucky. He claimed 200 acres from that grant award. The acquisition of a home site was timely because he was married to Kitty Bruce on 3 August 1800.

Under the Virginia Land Law of 1779, the residents of the Kentucky District of Virginia were authorized in 1779 to purchase Certificates of Settlement and Preemption Warrants provided that they qualified under the residency requirements. If the settler had lived in Kentucky County prior to January 1, 1778, had improved the land, and planted a corn crop, he could obtain 400 acres for the land that was improved. They also became eligible to buy an additional 1,000 acres that was adjacent to the settled land.

Henry was enrolled in Captain William Berryman's Company of the 11th Mounted Kentucky on 20 August 1813. He was about forty-three years old when he enlisted. He was given the rank of Ensign, the junior of the three officer ranks in the company that was the equivalent of a Second Lieutenant in today's army.

He made the trip to the rendezvous at Newport of the force that invaded Canada and fought at the Battle of the Thames (Chapter 6). Henry was discharged in Limestone (now Maysville), Kentucky on 13 November 1813.

Henry was a charter member of Gilead Baptist Church when it was organized in 1829, and participated in the establishment of other Baptist churches in the county. He was very active in public service as well. His name appears often in the Day Book of the Allen County Court.

He was appointed in October 1831, along with four others as commissioners, to select a site for a poorhouse and to contract for it to be built. In February 1837, he was appointed with four others to determine the best route for a road from Scottsville to Bowling Green. In April 1837, he was similarly tasked to determine the route for a road between Glasgow and the Square in Scottsville.[14]

Henry lived in Allen County until his death on 24 January 1865 at the age of 92.

Conyers, John

John Conyers was born in March 1788 in North Carolina in what is now Sumner County, Tennessee. It seems likely from that date that his parents were among the very first settlers in that area.

Other soldiers from the study area served longer, but Private John Conyers saw more combat in more major battles that anyone else found in this study. His War of 1812 service was in three segments, each featuring combat. The first began when he enlisted on 24 September 1813 and became a Private in Captain John Harpole's Company on the 2nd Regiment (Cannon) of the Tennessee Militia. They were part of the first campaign into the Creek Nation. They marched from Fayetteville, through Huntsville, to Fort Strother. They fought the Creeks at Tallushatchee on 3 November and at Talladega on 9 November (Chapter 5). Virtually every company in the regiment suffered casualties in those two battles. He was discharged at Ditto's Landing on the Tennessee River on 7 January 1814.

His second stint began almost immediately in February 1814. He became a substitute for a man named White and joined Captain George W. Still's Company of Colonel Stephen Copeland's 3rd Regiment of the Tennessee Militia. They marched from Fayetteville though Fort Deposit and Fort Strother to Fort Williams. They were held in reserve during General Jackson's engagement in the Battle of Horseshoe Bend on 27 March 1814 (Chapter 5). Although initially held in reserve, the regiment must have been committed to combat because it had casualties in that battle. He was discharged in May 1814.

John's third period of service began with enrollment on 14 September 1814. He was enlisted 20 September 1814 into Captain Beverly Williams' Company of the 2nd Regiment (Williamson) West Tennessee Militia at Fayetteville, Tennessee. They marched from there to Camp Gaines, thirty miles from Fort Montgomery. They were part of General John Coffee's Brigade in General Jackson's army that took Pensacola from the Spanish on 7 November 1814. They moved to New Orleans, and were in the battle that was fought at night on 23 December (Chapter 8). John was with them in the Battle of New Orleans on 8 January (Chapter 8). In March 1815, they began the trek northward by way of the Natchez Trace back to Tennessee, a very long walk. He was discharged at Columbia in Maury County, Tennessee on 27 April 1815.

According to his pension records, John married Susannah Spradlin on 4 November 1819 in Lebanon, Wilson County, Tennessee. Their residence was recorded as being in Allen County in 1871, but using a post office in Gallatin in Sumner County.

He submitted a request for bounty land and was issued a warrant (#2833) on 10 November 1853 for 160 acres in Knox County, Missouri, under the Act of 1850. He assigned the land to Green B. Harris.

John was living with John and Mary Smith according to the 1870 census. He filed for a survivor pension from Allen County (#25259) when pensions were first authorized (Chapter 9). His pension was approved on 13 April 1872 by certificate (#15513). He began receiving $8.00 per month beginning on 14 February 1874 at age eighty-six. Sixty-one years elapsed after his first enrollment before the old hero received his first payment. It was a small reward for his participation in six fierce combat engagements at Tallushatchee, Talladega, Horseshoe Bend, Pensacola, New Orleans on 23 December, and New Orleans on 8 January. Now, two hundred years later, we are amazed by his endurance, persistence, and bravery.

Cook, Sion

Tracing an individual becomes easier when a first name is unusual. Sion Cook's first name appeared to be one of those. However, a complication arises when parents, ancestors, or descendants honor an individual by giving a child his or her name. Such seems to have been the case with this soldier.

Private Sion Cook appears on the roll taken on 6 March 1813 of Captain William Berryman's Company of the Lieutenant Colonel Hudspeth and Brown's Regiment of the Kentucky Militia. The company was to be detached from the regiment for a period of six months. He also appeared on the rolls the 11th Regiment (Caldwell's) Kentucky Militia. Private John Right substituted for him in Captain William Berryman's Company that deployed for a rendezvous in Newport, Kentucky, and subsequently was part of the invasion of Canada and the Battle of the Thames that followed.

Sion was born in Wake County, North Carolina, in 1775. He and Winniford (Winny) Gent (Jent) were married on 10 October 1807 in that county. They immigrated to Barren County, Kentucky, (in what would later become Allen County) before his enrollment into the Kentucky Militia. That means that the Sion Cook who served in the Buncombe County Regiment in North Carolina in 1812, could not have been our soldier Sion.

Sion and his family were listed in the 1810 census in Barren County in the Puncheon area of would later become Allen County. They were in Smith County, Tennessee, during the 1820 and 1830 censuses. Smith County was adjacent to Allen County, and in an area that would later become Macon County.

He was a farmer with two children who paid taxes on four horses and 75 acres of land in the Long Creek drainage basin of Allen County in 1831. Five years later, he and several other farmers in the area were assigned by the county court to widen the road to fifteen feet from Long Creek to the state line.

Sion and his family were enumerated in Allen County during the 1840 and 1850 censuses still living in the Puncheon District close to the Tennessee border. So close to the border that the changes in the location of their residence by just a few miles could have produced the appearance of major relocations.

Winny died on 28 January 1858 of the palsy. Sion Cook died six weeks later on 9 March 1858 at the age of eight-five in Allen County. According to the Kentucky death records, the cause of death was "old age." One is reminded of a poem, coincidently written the same year, about a horse drawn shay built so that no one part would wear out before any other part. The shay was demolished when all its parts wore out at the exact same moment of old age.[15]

Sion's death record also recorded his parents as Jacob and Frances Cook of North Carolina.[16] He and Winny are buried in the Puncheon Baptist Church Cemetery in Allen County.

The 1860 census of Allen County lists a Sion Cook with a wife M. J. and seven children living in the Puncheon area. That Sion was likely a namesake son of the soldier Sion who had died two years earlier.

Cooksey, Thomas

Thomas Cooksey was one of the soldiers who served in Virginia during the War of 1812 before moving to Kentucky. Thomas was born about 1775. He was thought to be the youngest of his siblings because he was the last to get married. He was married to Nancy Mason Goodrum on 13 December 1803 according to some family records.

His father, also named Thomas, deeded 100 acres to him in Greensville County, Virginia, on 13 December 1805. His father died the following year. In May 1809, Thomas used his 100 acres as collateral for a debt he owned. On 8 January 1810, his siblings sold the remainder of his father's 250-acre farm. He was still in Greensville County in the 1810 census. He appears to have been a prosperous man when his country needed his service as a soldier.

Thomas Cooksey was mustered in on 29 August 1814 as a Private in Captain John B. Rice's Company of Light Infantry, probably in Brunswick County, Virginia. His company was one of those in the 1st Regiment of the Virginia Militia commanded by Lieutenant Colonel James Byrne. Most of that service was at Camp Powell's Creek in Prince George County. He was paid $25.33 for that service. The amount included travel of sixty-three miles for his return home.

John and Nancy came to Kentucky after the death of his father's widow. They arrived in Allen County in 1820 and made their home in the Allen Springs area.

Thomas may have died before the 1830 census when the head of household was listed as Nancy. The same circumstance existed in 1840 and 1850 as well. Nancy filed as a widow for bounty land and was awarded a warrant (#28384) for 40 acres in Franklin County, Illinois, on 2 January 1854 under the Act of 1850. She assigned the land to Allen Isaacs. She applied again under the Act of 1855 and received an additional warrant (#71196) for 120 acres in Dickenson County, Kansas, on 1 May 1861. She assigned that land to Atwood Hobson.

Cowen, James

The surname Cowan generated several variant phonetic spellings and among them were Cowin, Cowan, Cowing, and Cowden. The variety made genealogy research difficult.

Private James Cowen was a member of Captain Thomas Griffin's Company, 14th Regiment (Mitchusson) Detached Kentucky Militia. He was mustered in at Russellville on 20 May 1815 and was at Jackson's Camp in New Orleans from 20 Nov 1814 to 31 Dec 1814. Captain Griffin's Company participated in the Battle of New Orleans (Chapter 8). He was listed as being in Camp Jackson on Feb 28 1815 when the trip back home to Allen County began. He was mustered out at Russellville on 20 May 1815.

He appeared in Allen County in the 1820 census and as a farmer in Monroe County in 1840. Later records were not discovered.

James received a bounty land warrant (# 69008) for 160 acres in Texas County, Missouri, on 2 May 1860 under the Act of 1855. That warrant states that the award was for his service in Captain Griffin's Company under the name of "James Patterson" during the War of 1812. The name is identified as an alias. The word "alias" was used to identify a soldier whose records existed under a different name than his own. It does not necessarily mean that the soldier had knowingly used two names. The name James Patterson and the name James Cowen both appear on the same bounty land document. There was no explanation of the alias, but it may have been just a clerical error in Washington that caused the Patterson name to be used. No other mention of James Patterson was found in other sources. James assigned his bounty land to Spencer H. Mitchell.

A search of the 1860 census, including Monroe County's, done in July 1860 failed to locate James either as a Cowan or a Patterson.

Creek, David

David Creek appeared before the Allen County Court on 7 September 1816 to appoint an attorney, Anak Dawson, to represent him in all matters pertaining to pay due him from his War of 1812 service. David was a Private in Captain Thomas Griffin's Company of the 14th Regiment (Mitchusson) Kentucky Detached Militia that mustered in on 20 November 1814 in Russellville. By 31 December, he had completed the flatboat trip down the Mississippi and was with his unit in New Orleans at Camp Jackson. His regiment was formed to defend New Orleans and was there when the battle was fought (see Chapter 8). His unit left Camp Jackson on 28 February 1815 and began the walk home and he was discharged at Russellville on 20 May 1815.

Genealogists list his marriage to Peggy McClure on 3 July 1809 in Warren County. He was counted on the 1820 census in Barren County. Family histories indicate that he moved to Jackson County, Missouri, in 1830 and was in Leavenworth County, Kansas, in 1855.

David applied for and received a warrant (#26273) for 80 acres of bounty land in Caldwell County, Missouri, on 2 June 1854 under the Act of 1850. He received another warrant (#40953) for 80 acres of bounty land on 1 August 1860 under the Act of 1855. That tract was located in Chippewa County, Wisconsin. He assigned the first tract to John Prophet and the other to Thacker Blake. No records of pension applications were discovered for either David or his wife Peggy.

Cushenberry, Daniel

Daniel Cushenberry was born in Bourbon County, Kentucky, after his father and mother moved there from Virginia. Daniel received a Kentucky Land Grant on 12 February 1812 for 200 acres on Difficult Creek in what is now Allen County. The census of 1820 recorded him living in Allen County.

He became a Private in Hudspeth and Brown's Regiment of Kentucky Militia and was in Captain William Berryman's Company appearing on its roll dated 6 March 1813. He joined for a term of six months. Subsequently, his company was assigned for duty with the 11th Regiment (Caldwell) Kentucky Militia. At about age forty-two, he was one of the oldest militiamen in the unit.

There are no records of him having received a pension or a bounty land grant. That seems to indicate that he did not see active service. Nevertheless, the militiamen were required to meet periodically much in the same way that National Guardsmen do now.

The county tax rolls credited Daniel with 200 acres of land, one adult slave, and four horses.

Daniel died in 1844 before the Acts of 1850 and 1855 that would have provided him with bounty land.

Davasher, John C.

Even with many hours of research, specific documentation of John C. Davasher's service could not be found. The surname was one difficulty: the spellings varied so widely that normal searches were unproductive. It was variously spelled Dewasse, Dewasser, DeWasser, DeWasher, Devasure, and Devassier. The second difficulty was that his service likely began in Virginia and that complicated the search. The third difficulty was that it could not be determined whether he was in the regular Army or the militia.

Even without documentation, there was a certain reference to his service in "A History of the State" by Battle, Perrin, and Kniffen, third edition, in 1886. John's history appears in a biography of his son William T. Davasher in the volume that included Allen County. John's father-in-law was John Calvert who was a War of 1812 soldier and was at the Battle of New Orleans. With that relationship, it is inconceivable that statements of John's service would have been distorted.

John came as a child to America with his father Joseph Davasher, who was a Revolutionary War patriot at a time when he was a new immigrant from Germany. Joseph was in Richmond, Virginia, when he began service with Francis Marion, according to family history. Joseph had seven years of military experience with the German army. He migrated to Maury County, Tennessee, between 1810 and 1812, and lived there until his death. The gold watch that he was given for his service in the German army is still possessed by his descendants.

John was married to Elizabeth L. McDaniel in Amherst County, Virginia, on 2 February 1803. He appears on the 1810 census of that county. Assuming that his son John lived there too, he would likely have been a member of the 90th Regiment commanded by Lieutenant Colonel Philip Johnson. That unit served in the defense of Richmond.

John received a grant for 120 acres of land in what later became Barren County, Kentucky, in the Walnut Creek watershed area. The land was surveyed on 30 September 1807. The grant spelled his name Devasure.

Family history says that John was a blacksmith by trade and served in the War of 1812. That service was said to include participation in the Battle of New Orleans. John's son, William T. Davasher, was in the U.S. Army during the Civil War. The strong patriotic feelings exhibited generation after generation makes John's service seem certain. However, no specific documentation of his service was found.

Davis, Jonathan

Jonathan Davis was a North Carolinian born in Burke County in 1791. Soon after the war began, he became a Private in Captain Henry Katts' Second Company detached from the Second Rowan Regiment, part of the North Carolina Militia. He was mustered in on 1 February 1814 to serve for six months, but it was in Captain Jacob Krider's Company of the 7th Regiment at a camp near Fort Jackson. He was sick and was left behind when that company departed on 26 March 1814. He later rejoined them at a camp near Fort Hawkins at what is now Macon, Georgia.

Jonathan Davis[17]

Colonel Jesse J. Pearson moved with a force that included Jonathan's Company from Camp Pike near Fort Hawkins during the period 16 July to 17 August. They arrived in the Creek Territory in what is now Alabama after General Jackson's Battle of Horseshoe Bend. Pearson's troops accepted the surrender of 600 Creeks at Cooleemee near the confluence of the Coosa and Tallapoosa Rivers.

He was mustered out on 4 September 1814. He was paid for his 120-mile, six day round trip travel from his home to the rendezvous with the unit in Rowan County and return. With his $8.00 per month salary, and some subsistence during the travel, he received a total of $50.32 for the six-month enlistment.

He received a Kentucky land grant on 5 November 1826 for 100 acres in the Trammel Creek watershed. It was in the part of Kentucky south of the Walker Line that became Sumner County when that line was confirmed as the state boundary (Chapter 12). On 23 May 1840, he received 50 acres in the area of the Middle Fork of Drakes Creek in Allen County.

In the 1838 tax roll, he was assessed $5,940 for 500 acres in the Trammel Fork drainage area, his twelve slaves, and his four horses. The 1850 census recorded him and his wife Katy and their family living in the Butlersville area along with eighteen slaves. He became a major slave owner in Allen County. He had owned twelve slaves in 1840 and would own twenty-six in 1860. He provided five slave houses for his slaves. He had been appointed Captain of the patrollers in his area in 1852. The patrollers were used to apprehend runaways and disrupt assemblies of slaves. His taxable land assets had grown to 1,400 acres by 1860.

Jonathan's wife Katy, whose maiden name was Hunts, died on 14 September 1854. He was married to Samantha Landers on 15 June 1858 in Allen County.

After his death, a warrant (#90658) was issued on 1 April 1861 under the Act of 1855 for 160 acres of bounty land for his service. The land was located in Wabaunsee County, Kansas. His widow, Ann Davis, was listed as the patentee. It is likely that Ann was Samantha's nickname. She assigned the land to Charles Willemsen.

Dobbs, Henry S.

Henry S. Dobbs was different from most frontiersmen because he could sign his name. He also was older than most of the members of the militia. He was a four years old boy living in Virginia when it became one of the thirteen states that ratified the U.S. constitution in 1789. Imagine the stories he must have heard as a child about the fight for independence and the ratification of that historic document. He would have brought those stories with him when he moved to Tennessee.

He was living near Tazewell in Claiborne County in northeastern Tennessee when he enrolled into the militia on 13 November 1814. His term of service was for a period of six months. He was mustered in as a Private in Knoxville and assigned to Captain John Brock's Company in 4th Regiment East Tennessee Militia commanded by Colonel Samuel E. Bayless.

Henry Dobbs signature

His regiment was placed under Major General William Carroll and was sent to the Mobile area of the Mississippi Territory (now Alabama) to defend against either Indian or British attacks. Carroll's unit manned the forts in that general area: Fort Claiborne, Fort Decatur, and Fort Montgomery among others. It was not pleasant duty. Many of the soldiers became ill and diseases spread rapidly among the troops living in the relatively confined area within a fort. Morale was low and desertion rates were high. But Henry persisted until his discharge at Mobile on 18 May 1815 at the end of his six-month enlistment.

He moved to Allen County, Kentucky, from Tennessee before the 1820 census. Amos Harris, who was a Justice of the Peace, performed the marriage of Henry and Sarah Campbell on 13 April 1850 in Allen County. They were living in the Mt. Aerial community when the 1860 census was taken.

Two bounty land grants were awarded to Henry. One warrant (#14666) was issued on 2 October 1854 for 80 acres in Johnson County, Missouri, under the Act of 1850. It was conveyed to Leonard McReynolds. The second (#9138) was awarded under the Act of 1855 on 1 March 1858 for 80 acres in Guthrie County, Iowa. That tract was assigned to Edmund H. Taylor.

Henry died on 31 December 1867 in Allen County at the age of eight-two. Sarah applied (#35964) for and received a Widow's Pension (#24478) beginning on 28 May 1879. She was living in Cumberland County, Illinois at that time. The payment of $8.00 per month was backdated to begin on 9 March 1878. Sarah died about 1886.

Dobbs, John

Stokes County is located in the piedmont region of North Carolina that borders Virginia. It was the birthplace of John Dobbs. He had moved to Allen County before the early calls came for enlistments into the Militia. He became a Private in Captain William Berryman's 9th Company of Colonel Nicholas Miller's 3rd Regiment of Kentucky Detached Militia.

The recruits for that regiment include twelve others from the study area in this unit that saw action in the second Battle of Tippecanoe, also called the Battle of Wild Cat Creek (Chapter 3). They marched to Elizabethtown where the regiment was mustered in on 1 September 1812. They went to Vincennes and continued by way of Fort Harrison to Tippecanoe. They fought a battle near there at Wildcat Creek and returned. At the end of their enlistment, they returned to Kentucky and were discharged on 25 December 1812 at Bowling Green.

John appeared on the census taken in Allen County in 1820. He raised a family and remained there for the rest of his life. He received an eleven-acre land grant from Kentucky on 22 Jun 1839. The land lay in the Big Trammel Creek watershed. His first wife, Sarah Anderson, died about 1845.

On 11 May 1848, he was married for a second time. His new bride was Melvina Riggs. Thomas H. Lyle was the minister who performed the ceremony. They lived in the Chapel Hill area of Allen County

John applied for and received two bounty land warrants. The first warrant (#46638), was issued on 1 March 1854 under the Act of 1850, was for 40 acres in Ramsey County, Minnesota. It was assigned to John H. Zollinger. The second warrant (#101594) under the Act of 1850 was issued on 15 January 1856 was for 40 acres in Delaware County, Iowa. It was assigned to John M. McDaneld. A third bounty land warrant (#13242) was issued in John's name on 1 April 1859 under the Act of 1855 and was for 80 acres in Hancock County, Iowa. It was assigned to Ezra R. Butler.

John became partially paralyzed before he died of apoplexy on 8 March 1857. Melvina received a Widow's Pension (#19127) beginning on 9 March 1878 at a rate of $8.00 per month.

Dobson, Thomas

Most early Kentucky settlers emigrated from Virginia. Two of those were recently wed. Thomas Dobson was married to Elizabeth Nichols in Halifax County on 25 March 1811. Soon thereafter, the newlyweds moved to what later would become Allen County, Kentucky. That must have been quite a honeymoon trip.

Thomas was a Private in Captain Berryman's 9th Company of the 11th Regiment (Williams) Kentucky Mounted Volunteer Militia. Soldiers from this regiment were assembled for the Thames campaign that took it to Canada. His service began on 20 August 1813 at Newport, Kentucky, and ended on 3 November 1813 at Limestone (now Maysville). In between those dates, the unit rode to Lake Erie, crossed and fought the Battle of the Thames, and returned home (Chapter 6).[18]

Thomas enrolled for another tour of duty about a year later. He traveled to Russellville and, on 20 November 1814, was mustered into Lieutenant Colonel Mitchusson's 14th Regiment Kentucky Detached Militia as a Private. After a flatboat trip to New Orleans, he was in Jackson's Camp on 31 December. He and the others in that regiment were part of Brigadier General John Adair's Brigade during the Battle of New Orleans (Chapter 8). He departed Camp Jackson on 28 February 1815 for the walk back to Kentucky. He was discharged at Russellville on 20 May 1815.

On 12 September 1816, he appointed Thomas Gatton as his attorney to draw whatever may have been due him from his service.

Thomas and his wife appeared on the first Allen County census of 1820. In 1830, they were listed with four children in their household. He was a farmer by trade.

Thomas received a bounty land warrant (#10014) for 80 acres in Miller County, Missouri, on 9 November 1854 under the Act of 1850. He assigned that land to Andrew Bilyen.

In the 1860 census, Elizabeth was living in the household of William Nichols, who may have been a relative. They were residing in Miller County in central Missouri. Two years later, Elizabeth filed as a widow, and received another bounty land warrant (#39669) on 1 October 1862 under the Act of 1855. She received 80 additional acres in Bates County, Missouri, on the Kansas border. She assigned that land to William Powers.

Dowell, David

During the War of 1812, any man could avoid service for any reason, illness or inconvenience for example. He could do so by procuring a substitute. David Dowell was procured by William Blackwell to be his substitute when the call to duty came. Kentucky law established a maximum of $100 that could be paid, and the substitute could negotiate the fee not to exceed that amount.

David was married to Elizabeth Shook in Sumner County, Tennessee, on 13 August 1813, just over a year before agreeing to become a substitute. He enlisted as a Private in Captain Thomas Griffin's Company of the 14th Regiment (Mitchusson) Kentucky Detached Militia on 20 November 1814 in Russellville. There followed the trip by river to New Orleans. He arrived there on 31 December 1814. He was in the Battle of New Orleans (Chapter 8) and began the return trip to Kentucky on 28 February 1815. He was discharged in Russellville on 20 May 1815.

David appeared on the 1820 census in Allen County, but that thread does not continue. Elizabeth appeared in the 1850 and 1860 censuses as head of household living in her home county of Sumner in Tennessee.

David received two bounty land warrants. One (#41662) was issued on 15 June 1857 for 90.28 acres in Greene County, Arkansas, under the Act of 1850. He assigned that tract to William R. Cain. The second (#46513) that was dated 1 May 1860 was for 80 acres in Montgomery County, Iowa, under the Act of 1855. That land was conveyed to James Blythe.

Dowell, John

Variant spellings of a surname may be the obscurant of the early life of some soldiers. For other individuals, this surname was spelled Doyl, Doyle, and Dawell. For whatever reason, the earliest record of John Dowell was his marriage to Elizabeth Travelstreet. One transcribed court record had the date as 2 April 1811 in Warren County, Kentucky. She could neither read nor write. However, one must believe that was a date that she would remember. She stated in her application for a Widow's Pension that the marriage was on 4 April 1810 in Kentucky by a Justice of the Peace named Ben Milton.

John Dowell was entered on the rolls of Captain Matthew Neal's Company of the 3rd Regiment West Tennessee Militia Infantry commanded by Colonel James Raulston. The unit was mustered in November 1814. Its men were from Sumner and Smith Counties among other counties that bordered Kentucky. That unit was part of Major General William Carroll's Division at the Battle of New Orleans. The unit suffered casualties on 28 December 1814 in a skirmish and also had two fatalities during the Battle of New Orleans on 8 January 1815 (Chapter

8). General Carroll mentioned Captain Neal as having the honor of receiving and repelling the attacks of the British forces.

John was fifty-one when he was enumerated by the 1840 census of Allen County with eight others in his household. He died on 19 March 1844.

Elizabeth received a bounty land warrant (#45684) on 2 October 1854 under the Act of 1850 for which John's widow was qualified. The award was for 80 acres in Livingston, Illinois. She assigned the land to Matthew Budd. On 15 August 1860, she received another warrant (#46097) for 80 acres in Pocahontas County, Iowa, under the Act of 1855. She assigned that tract to Henry C. Carter.

Elizabeth filled out a declaration (#2825) for a Widow's Pension in Gallatin, Tennessee, on 27 April 1871. She was 78 years old and, according to her Gallatin postmaster, lived about eighteen to twenty miles from Gallatin in the village of New Roe, Kentucky. He also reported to the pension office in Washington when she died on 9 May 1872 without having been awarded her pension.

Dry, John

John Dry was another veteran who could sign his name. He was born in Mercer County, Kentucky, in 1795 shortly after his parents had arrived from North Carolina.

John Dry[19]

Several of the War of 1812 soldiers were the sons of patriots who were in the Revolutionary War. John Dry was one example. His father was Jacob Dry who joined the Continental Army in Mecklenburg County, North Carolina, in 1779. Jacob was in Charleston, South Carolina, when the American troops were surrendered to the British after a lengthy siege. Jacob was later paroled, walked back to North Carolina and again joined the American army. He served until after the war ended. His applications for a pension were denied because his time in service was deemed short of the six months required. His last of many submissions was when he was 95 years old. He died the following year without a pension.

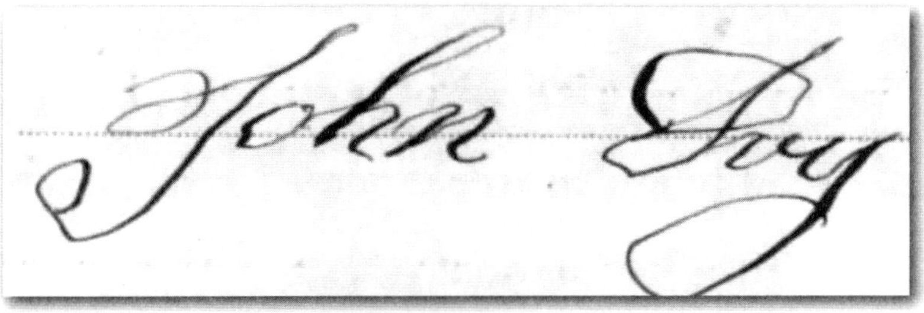

John Dry signature

Apparently, his father's experience with bureaucracy did not dissuade John from joining the fight against the British in the War of 1812. When the call to duty came, John was living in what would become Allen County, Kentucky. He was on the 6 March 1813 rolls of Hudspeth and Brown's Regiment in Captain William Berryman's Company with a term of service of six months.

He served in Captain Thomas Griffin's Company of the 14th Regiment (Mitchusson) Kentucky Detached Militia. The unit was organized on 20 November 1814 at Russellville. From there, they traveled to Jackson's camp near New Orleans arriving about 31 December 1814. They participated in the Battle of New Orleans as part of Brigadier General John Adair's Brigade (see Chapter 8). He was discharged in Russellville (Figure 49).

John was married to Elizabeth (Betsy) Ryals on 10 May 1813 in Allen County. By 1830, they had moved with their family to Randolph in Clay County, Missouri. By 1850, they were living in Monroe County, Missouri.

John received two bounty land grants for his service. His first (#5071) on 1 August 1852 was issued under the Act of 1850 and awarded 80 acres in Monroe County, Missouri. He did not sell that land, perhaps because he lived in Paris near that land. His second warrant (#17909) was for another 80 acres under Act 1855. It was issued on 1 August 1860 and located in Atchison, Kansas. He sold that land to Christian Winkler.

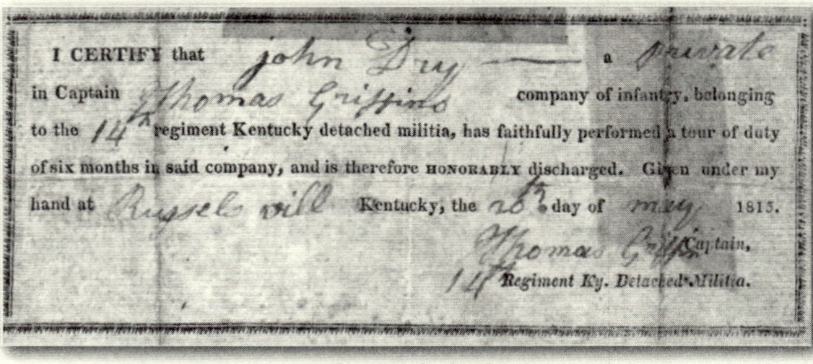

I CERTIFY that john Dry — a private in Captain Thomas Griffins company of infantry, belonging to the 14th regiment Kentucky detached militia, has faithfully performed a tour of duty of six months in said company, and is therefore HONORABLY discharged. Given under my hand at Russelsvill Kentucky, the 28 day of may 1815.

Thomas Griffin Captain,
14th Regiment Ky. Detached Militia.

Figure 49. John Dry's discharge paper.

He was living in Monroe County, Missouri, when he applied for a Survivor's Pension (#7789) and when a certificate (#4494) was given to him. He began receiving a monthly pension of $8.00 on 14 September 1871. He died there on 24 July 1873.

Duncan, Ashley

Several of the early settlers in the study area were veterans of Revolutionary War who received land grants for their service. Ashley Duncan's father was one of those who settled on such land in what was then Warren County, Kentucky.

Family histories indicate that Ashley married Rebecca about 1811, probably in Warren County.

Ashley Duncan became a Private in Captain William Berryman's Company of the 11th Regiment (Williams) Kentucky Mounted Volunteers on 31 August 1813. Ashley rode his horse to the rendezvous at Newport Barracks, Kentucky, to join in Governor Shelby's militiamen on their way to reinforce General William Henry Harrison's army in his fights with the British. That culminated in the Battle of the Thames (Chapter 6). He returned after the battle and was discharged in Limestone (now Maysville) on 3 November 1813. For his two months and twenty-four days of service, he received a total of $56.19. Of that amount, $34.00 was for the use of his horse.

In 1813, his father sold 200 acres of his military land grant property in what was then Warren County to Ashley and his wife Rebecca. The sales price was five cents, just enough to keep it from being a gift.

Ashley was in Allen County on the first census of 1820. He was on the tax rolls with the 200 acres in 1825, but he also had two other tracts by then. One was 157 acres and the other was 92 acres. All located in the Trammel Fork drainage basin. The tax list of 1838 valued his 450 acres at $2,365.00, a man of means for sure.

His will was probated on 11 May 1846. He left his assets to his wife Rebecca and nine living children.

Duncan, Traverse

An unusual first name usually makes information about that person more readily findable in public or genealogical records. Traverse Duncan is an exception. Only brief glimpses of his life were found. For example, he bought 200 acres on Bays Fork Creek from Theophillus Read for $300.00 on 3 December 1812.

He was an admired and capable individual. That is evident when he was selected to be the First Sergeant of a Kentucky militia company. He was mustered in with that rank on 31 August 1813 into Captain William Berryman's Company of the 11th Regiment (Williams) Kentucky Mounted Volunteers. He rode his horse to Newport where the unit was assembled. He rode northward with the Eleventh to Lake Erie. They crossed Lake Erie and fought the Battle of the Thames before beginning the return trip (Chapter 6).

The return trip brought him to Limestone (now Maysville) where he was discharged on 13 November 1813. He received $11.00 pay per month as First Sergeant, amounting to $30.51 for the entire excursion. In addition, he was paid $34.00 for use of his horse.

According to his service record, he "lost his horse" at Fort Ball near present day Tiffin, Ohio. He was paid $70.00 for the loss of his horse. Fort Ball was constructed as a supply depot for General Harrison's force. The supply route was followed northward by the Eleventh. About a year earlier, General Harrison had described that route as being almost impassable for wagons because that area was a swampy wilderness. It was so bad that many horses had worn down and been discharged. Perhaps, the severity of the trip had taken its toll on Traverse's horse.

On 21 May 1817, Traverse and his wife Lucy sold their 200 acres in Allen County to Theophillus Read, the previous owner, for $500. Traverse profited $200. Traverse was living in Montgomery County, Kentucky, at that time. He died in Montgomery County in 1846.

Durham, James

It was unusual for a person, who was born in Warren County, North Carolina, to move and live in Warren County, Kentucky. It was unusual for a veteran of the War of 1812 to have been in the regular army; most frontiersmen served in the militia. It was unusual for one to have lived within the disputed land south of the Walker Line because the area was relatively small (Chapter 12). It was unusual for a person to live in one state and use a post office in another. James Durham was unusual in all four of these respects.

James was born in Warren County, North Carolina, on 10 March 1786. He moved to the disputed land that Kentucky claimed was part of Warren County, Kentucky. A few years later, that area was conceded to be in Sumner County, Tennessee. James' home was described as being "just over the border" in Tennessee.

The U.S. army was recruiting in the area to form a new regiment. On 26 December 1813, he was mustered in as a Private in the 39th U.S. Infantry Regiment in Nashville. The recruiter described him as a 30-year old who was 5' 11¼" tall. He was assigned to Captain John Jones' Company. Peter Martin, another man from the study area, was in the same company.

The 39th was authorized as a regiment of the regular Army on 29 January 1813. Colonel John Williams, previously an East Tennessee Militia regimental commander, was the first commander of the 39th that was composed of recruits from Tennessee. The unit was sent south to augment General Jackson's force fighting against the Creek. It arrived at Fort Strother in what is the Alabama Territory on 6 March 1814.

Jackson was pleased to have a regular Army regiment to demonstrate discipline to the militiamen. He put the 39th to good use in the Battle of Horseshoe Bend (Chapter 5). He placed them in the middle of the assault with militia on either side. That middle position assured their exposure to fierce combat, and they absorbed heavy casualties. Sam Houston, who later became the President of the Republic of Texas, was in the battle. An arrow struck him in the thigh during the battle. Captain John Jones' Company was in the thick of it too and it lost one man killed in action and ten wounded.[20] Fortunately, James survived.

Jackson moved the 39th and his army south to Mobile. They were part of Jackson's force that attacked and drove the Spanish out of Pensacola during the period from 7 to 9 November 1814. Some regular army men had been enlisted for the duration of the war. But, James Durham had enlisted for only one year. He was discharged on 14 December 1814, most likely at Pensacola, and returned to Sumner County.

James was married to Lydia Gillespie on 18 July 1820, and by the time the 1840 census was taken, there were eight children in their household.

On 20 February 1858, James received a bounty land warrant (#21596) under the Act of 1850 for 160 acres in Williamson County in southern Illinois. He assigned that land to Harlan Abshear.

James died on 3 September 1856. Lydia applied (#17566) for a Widow's Pension and gained approval (#25146) on 24 June 1879. The start date of her monthly payments was calculated to be 8 March 1878, the date she submitted her claim. Her pension pay was sent to her nearest post office. That was at New Roe in Allen County.

Lydia died on 14 August 1880.

Ellis, Samuel

We now associate the rank of Ensign as the junior rank of naval officers, but it was once an army rank as well. During the War of 1812, an infantry company commander was usually a Captain. He was assisted by a First Lieutenant and by one or more Second Lieutenants. There was also an Ensign who was just below the Second Lieutenant in rank and was the most junior officer of the unit. The Ensign rank was eliminated from the infantry when the army was reorganized in March 1815.[21]

Samuel Ellis was the Ensign in Captain William McCall's Company of the 1st Regiment (Wynne) West Tennessee Militia. His service began with his enlistment on 4 October 1813 in Gallatin, Tennessee. He was mustered in at Fayetteville, Tennessee, and marched south to Huntsville to join General Jackson's army that was opposing the Creeks in what is now Alabama. From there, they marched to Fort Coffee, to

Fort Deposit, and finally to Fort Strother. His company fought at the Battles of Tallahatchie and Talladega against the Creek (Chapter 5), but Samuel was sick and did not participate. He was discharged at Fort Strother on 18 December 1813, and described as disabled at that time.

Samuel applied for bounty land as a resident of the New Roe community in Allen County. He had moved there before 1850 from Sumner County, Tennessee. He received two bounty land grants. The first warrant (#5966) was issued on 1 September 1853 under the Act of 1850 for 40 acres in Franklin County, Illinois. That land was conveyed to Andrew Moore. The second warrant (#75973) was awarded on 10 November 1859 under the Act of 1855 for 148 acres in Butler County, Iowa. That tract was assigned to Nathan Linn.

He lived near the post office at Temperance in Simpson County in 1870. He filed (#14375) for an invalid pension while living in the Gum community in Simpson County. He received a pension certificate (#9354) for $8.00 per month beginning on 14 February 1871.

Samuel was born in Culpeper County, Virginia,22 on 17 October 1791 and was married to Elizabeth Gaines on 19 May 1815 in Allen County. He came to the New Roe area about the same time as a French Huguenot, Allen D'Berry, and the brothers John and James Mayhew came.[23]

He was living with his son Fountain Ellis at Gum in Simpson County when he died from paralysis on 20 September 1879. He was born in North Carolina in 1785 and was eighty-eight years old when he died.[24]

He was a prominent layman in the Stony Point United Methodist Church in Allen County. His and Elizabeth's graves are in the Stony Point Cemetery at the church near the Simpson and Allen County border.

Eubank, Jonathan

The names of many of the frontiersmen who made the early treks to what became Allen County, Kentucky, appeared as soldiers in the War of 1812. One such frontiersman was Jonathan Eubank. He was among the earliest settlers in the Stony Point area of southwestern Allen County. He moved to the New Roe community in what was then Warren County from the Pendleton District of South Carolina.[25] Justice of the Peace William Melton married Jonathan and Lucy Stacy Reeder on 9 October 1807 in what is now Allen County.

He was on the 6 March 1813 rolls of the Hudspeth and Brown Regiment as having enlisted for six months in the Kentucky Militia. He was later listed in Captain William Berryman's Company of the 11th Regiment (Caldwell's) Kentucky Militia, but was not one of those militiamen who were detached for service for what became the Battle of the Thames.

Jonathan's duty began when Kentuckians responded to General Jackson's call for help in defending New Orleans. He left his wife Stacy behind when he became a 3rd Corporal in Captain Thomas Griffin's Company of the 14th Regiment (Mitchusson) Detached Kentucky Militia. He signed up in Bowling Green and was mustered in on 20 November 1814 at Russellville. He was at Jackson's Camp in New Orleans on 31 Dec 1814 and was at the Battle of New Orleans (Chapter 8). He volunteered to go to the breastworks during the battle (see Tarrance Kerby's story in this chapter). He remained in New Orleans until 28 February 1815 when the trip home began. He was discharged at Russellville on 20 May 1815. He made it home in time to be was listed in the first Allen County tax rolls of 1815.

Jonathan filed for bounty land under the Act of 1850 and received a warrant (#28919) on 2 October 1854 for 80 acres in Johnson County, Missouri. He assigned that plot to Samuel Wagoner. He was awarded a second warrant (#45299) on 1 May 1860 under the Act of 1855 for 80 acres in Shelby County, Iowa. He assigned that land to Eliab S. Lemon.

Jonathan died 17 September 1862 in the New Roe community in Allen County. His widow Stacy filed for a Widow's Pension (#6695) from the more conveniently located Gallatin post office in Sumner County. Her pension file contains documentation submitted from Simpson County too. Nevertheless, she lived in Allen County throughout the pension process. Her application was approved (#2924) and she was awarded $8.00 month beginning on 14 February 1871.

Stacy was buried alongside Jonathan in the Harrell graveyard near the Kentucky and Tennessee border.

Frost, Eli

Eli Frost was in Allen County, Kentucky, when the War of 1812 began, and was on the rolls as a Private in the Hudspeth and Brown Regiment and, later, in the 11th Regiment (Caldwell) Kentucky Militia. There were no records to indicate that he left the county with any of the detached groups that sallied forth during the war. However, Eli and all other members of the militia were required to attend periodic meetings during which time military training was accomplished.

He appeared on the 1820 census in Allen County and on its 1831 tax records with a horse valued at $40. The 1837 tax records showed him living in the Trammel Fork watershed with 88 acres of land and two horses. He did not appear on the tax records after 1837.

The 1850 census had more information than any other source. He was listed as farmer who was fifty-nine years old and who was born in North Carolina. He also appeared on the 1860 census with his wife Catherine and their four children. There is a marriage record from Sumner County, Tennessee, for Eli Frost and Katherine Varvel with a date of 19 April 1828.

Garrett, Larkin

Census records indicate that Larkin Garrett was born about 1787, making him twenty-five when he joined the militia in Allen County, Kentucky. His service records show that he served as a Private in Captain Hugh Brown's Company of the 1st Regiment Kentucky Mounted Volunteer Infantry, commanded by Samuel Hopkins.

That company was organized on 18 September 1812, and detached for duty under General Hopkins. Larkin rode to Vincennes in the Indiana Territory (Chapter 3). From there, he and his comrades rode to Fort Harrison, near to the present Terra Haute, Indiana. Subsequently, he received pay for the eleven days of travel. The pay included $2.75 for rations, $2.30 for his soldier pay, and $4.40 for use of his horse. He, and almost all of his company, was discharged at Busseron in the Indiana Territory, on 30 October 1812. He subsequently received soldier pay of $9.32 and another $17.20 for the use of his horse for the ride back home.

He appears on the first Allen County Tax Rolls in 1815. On 27 September 1816, he appeared in the Allen County Court and recorded that he had appointed Britton Holland from Barren County as his attorney to receive whatever payments for his service for which he might be eligible. His former Company Commander Captain Hugh Brown, by then a Justice of the Peace, signed as a witness.

Genealogists record his marriage to Charlotte Short in Allen County soon after his service. He was enumerated as a farmer by the census taker of 1850 as Larking Garrett with his wife Lottie living in Hardeman County, Tennessee. Both were listed as having been born in North Carolina.

Larkin Garrett received two bounty land warrants. The first warrant (#72281) was on 10 May 1854 under the Act of 1850 for 39.7 acres in Jackson County, Louisiana. He conveyed the land to Horace M. Polk. The second warrant (#78231) was under the Act of 1855 issued on 10 November 1859 for 120 acres in Marathon County, Wisconsin. He assigned that land to Joseph Crawford.

Garrison, Mark

Early settlers often followed a relative or neighbor who preceded them to the study area. One of the best known of the early settlers in Allen County, Kentucky, was Samuel W. Garrison who came in 1797 and operated a grist mill on Bays Fork Creek at the Hartsville Road ford near present day Scottsville. Two years later, his brother Mark Garrison followed. He settled on the land on both sides of Bays Fork Creek where US 231 now crosses it, just northwest of the woods that were cleared when Scottsville began as a town sixteen years later.[26]

Mark was born in Mecklenburg, North Carolina, about 1765 and moved to what was then Warren County in 1799. He married Mary (Polly) Judge on 27 November 1801 in what is now Allen County. Families grew rapidly in those days. The 1810 census counted eight children with him and his wife. That was the size of his family when he enrolled in the Militia.

Mark appeared as a Private on the rolls of the Hudspeth and Brown Regiment of the Kentucky Militia on 6 March 1813 in Captain William Berryman's Company. Israel Anderson (biographical sketch is in this Chapter) was designated to be the substitute for Mark in the 11th Regiment (Caldwell) Kentucky Militia that was detached for service in the Battle of the Thames. The records do not indicate whether either Mark or his substitute actually deployed with the regiment.

The 1820 census enumerated eleven children with Mark and Polly. By 1837, they had accumulated 350 acres of land. Soon thereafter, they moved to Parke County, Indiana, and were reported in the 1840 census there. Their son John F. was one of the first settlers in northwestern Missouri in 1835.

Mark Garrison died about 1843. No records were found of pensions or bounty land awards.

Gibson, John

Many soldiers served three-month tours, some six-months, and some had one-year enlistments. Private John Gibson had three separate periods of service, and he was a combatant in each one of them.

He first volunteered and was assigned to Captain William Berryman's Company in Colonel Nicholas Miller's regiment. Later, his wife Susan said that he was in Captain McWilliams' company. The confusion may have come from King L. Williams who was an Ensign in John's company. According to John, he was mustered in at Louisville about 25 August 1812, and served until he was discharged at the Ohio River on 25 December 1812 on his way back home. During his tour of duty, his unit was in the Battle of Wild Cat Creek, also known as the Second Battle of Tippecanoe (Chapter 3).

He volunteered for a second time in Warren County on 20 August 1813. He was mustered in with Captain Berryman's Company of the 11th Regiment (Williams) Kentucky Militia in Newport, Kentucky. He served until 3 November 1813 when he was discharged at the north bank of the Ohio River opposite Limestone (now Maysville), Kentucky. His unit fought at the Battle of the Thames (Chapter 6) during that tour of duty.

His third period of service was from 20 November 1814 to 20 May 1815. He was mustered into the 14th Regiment (Mitchusson) Kentucky Detached Militia at Russellville. He was at Camp Jackson from 31 Dec 1814 to 28 February 1815, and his unit saw action at the Battle of New Orleans (Chapter 8). He was discharged at Russellville on 20 May 1815.

John was married to Susan H. Cook in Simpson County on 9 March 1841. The 1850 census lists Georgia as John's birthplace. Susan and all the children in the household were born in Kentucky.

John was sixty-one years old and living in Simpson County when he applied for a bounty land grant on 2 November 1850 under the Act of 1850. He was awarded a warrant (#13153) for 80 acres in Clay County, Illinois, on 10 May 1854. He assigned the land to William H. Morgan.

On 2 April 1855 in Simpson County, Susan applied for a bounty land grant under the Act of 1855 as John's widow. She lived near Franklin at that time. She was given a warrant (#11877) for John's service on 10 May 1859 for an additional 80 acres. That land was located in Henry County, Missouri. She assigned it to Asa Holland.

Still living in Simpson County on 14 November 1879, Susan applied for Widow's Pension (38354) using the post office at Gallatin, Tennessee. According to Susan, John died while on a visit to east Tennessee. He died on or near the Tennessee River in Chattanooga in the latter part of December 1853 or the first part of January 1854. Susan's pension (#29654) began with pay back dated to 9 March 1878.

Gibson, William

Some soldiers' ancestries were difficult to ascertain even when their service to our country was not. William Gibson was one of those. He was a Private in Captain William Berryman's Company of the 11th Regiment (Williams) Mounted Kentucky Volunteers beginning in 20 August 1813, and he served until 26 October 1813. He was in the Battle of the Thames in Canada (Chapter 6). He was discharged at Limestone (now Maysville), Kentucky. He was paid $17.54 plus another $26.80 for the use of his horse during the excursion to Canada.

William appeared in the 1820 census of Allen County as the head of household who had seven others in his family and owned one slave. He was also listed in the Allen County tax roll for 1825 with one slave, five horses, and 200 acres of land in the Difficult Creek watershed. The assessed value of his property was $1,600.00.[27]

The Difficult Creek location of William's property supported the opinion that he was the William who was the son of John Gibson, and a brother of the John who served in the same unit. The father John was one of the early settlers in the Cedar Springs area of what would become Allen County. One of his children was listed as William Gibson. They both were listed as being in the same watershed.

William subsequently disappeared from the records. There was a Will Gibson living in the Middle Fork watershed in later years, but the connection was unverifiable. The genealogical researchers agree that William's wife was Elizabeth (Lizzie) Duncan, and that their marriage year was 1820.

Those genealogical records then radically diverge into three incompatible directions. One had his death in Missouri, another stated he died in Louisiana, and a third listed his death in Texas. Missouri was a common emigration destination from Allen County, Texas less so, and Louisiana unlikely. The truth about William after 1820 could not be factually discerned.

Goodrum, John J.

This surname was also spelled Goodram and Goodman. People who came to the frontier study area in the early 1800s sometimes took months or even years to get there. For example, genealogical information listed John J. Goodrum's birth in Greenville County, Virginia, on 25 May 1794. He was a teenager when his family moved to Tennessee about 1807. He joined the Tennessee Militia there and came to Allen County after the end of the War of 1812.

John stated that he enlisted in Captain William McCall's Company of the 1st Regiment (Wynn) West Tennessee Militia during the war against the Creek. He rendezvoused in Fayetteville, Tennessee, on 4 October 1813 for a three-month commitment. His unit fought the Creeks at the Battle of Talladega on 9 November 1813, and it had heavy casualties (Chapter 5). He was discharged at the end of his enlistment at Nashville, Tennessee, in January 1814.

He volunteered for a second time at Nashville on 13 November 1814 for a period of six months. This service was in Captain Matthew Neal's Company of the 3rd Regiment (Raulston) Tennessee Militia. This company participated in the Battle of New Orleans (Chapter 8) and was singled out for recognition. The commander General Carroll stated, "…they had the honor of receiving and repelling the attacks of the British forces." He was discharged in Nashville on 13 May 1815.

John was married three times. He first was married to Marjory Carothers on 13 November 1816 in Sumner County, Tennessee. They had five children. His second wife was Eliza Ragsdell to whom he was married in 1828 in Giles County, Tennessee. They had seven children before she died in Maury County, Tennessee, in 1842. G. O. Harris, a minister in Warren County, Kentucky, married John and Mary Cornwell on 17 May 1843. They lived there for about ten years before moving to Allen County. They had six children.[28]

John lived in Warren County when he applied for bounty land under the Act of 1850 on 10 May 1854 under the surname Goodrum. He received a warrant (#42023) for 80 acres in Jasper County, Illinois. He assigned the land to William R. Cather. His application for bounty land under Act of 1855 was dated 14 August 1855. He received an additional 80 acres by a warrant (#33216) on 5 August 1869 with his surname spelled Goodram. The land was located in Missaukee County, Michigan, and he assigned it to Lewis Miller.

John died 27 March 1865. His third wife Mary applied (#27464) for and received a Widow's Pension certificate (#19532). She listed Allen Springs as her post office and that was where she received $8.00 per month beginning on 9 March 1878.

According to the 1883 list of pensioners in Allen County, Mary was living in Halifax and owned 185 acres. This change of address may have been the result of the use of an actual location rather than one of the Post Office at Allen Springs. Mary died on 27 February 1900 in Allen County. Her pension at the time of her death was $12.00 per month.

Graves, Frederick

The War of 1812 soldiers had to live for a long time before photography became available. A soldier who was eighteen in 1812 would have been over sixty by the time tintypes were invented, even older for images on photo paper. As a result, photographs of the War of 1812 veterans were relatively rare and those that exist were images of the soldier in his old age. The image of Private Frederick Graves was one of the few of soldiers from the study area whose photographs survived.

Frederick Graves[29]

Frederick was born about 1790 in Spotsylvania County, Virginia. He was married to Christena (Teny) Black in Sumner County, Tennessee, in 1813.

Frederick volunteered in Bowling Green and was assigned to Captain William Berryman's Company of the 3rd Regiment (Miller) Kentucky Militia. He enlisted on 1 September 1812 and went to Louisville. There he remained in camp for several weeks before moving to Vincennes in the Indiana Territory. Frederick stated that he was one of the soldiers who were left behind to guard the fort while a portion of the unit was sent north. Those men were in the Battle of Wild Cat Creek. He remained at the fort until he was discharged 25 December 1812. Twelve other soldiers from the study area were in the same regiment (see Chapter 3).

In 1815, Frederick and Teny lived in Allen County about ten miles west of Scottsville. By then, they owned a large amount of land on John's Creek in the county. Their family would eventually grow to include ten children, and the family became active members of Walker's Chapel Church.

Frederick filed (#16014) for an invalid pension on 12 September 1854 declaring his service "in the war with the Indians" as he put it. He recounted his march after his discharge at Hardinsburg on the Ohio River in Breckenridge County. He traveled about seventy miles to Bowling Green where he had entered the service. His pension was approved (#10279) on 22 December 1871 for eight dollars per month.

He applied for bounty land on two occasions. He received bounty land 40 acres in Dallas County, Arkansas, by a warrant (#7506) on 2 October 1854 issued under the Act of 1850. He assigned that tract to Thomas L. Watt. He subsequently received an additional 40 acres in Adams County, Iowa, on 15 January 1856 under a second warrant (#101653) and he conveyed that land to Anthony Berry. When additional bounty land was authorized under the Act of 1855, he received a third warrant (#29069) on 1 March 1860 for 80 acres in Decatur County, Iowa. He assigned that land to Edward A. Temple.

The decadal censuses in Allen County recorded him after 1820. He died in 1871. Frederick was buried in the cemetery at Walker's Chapel Methodist Church where he had long been a member. A grave was marked in his memory by his descendants in 2000.

Griffin, John

John Griffin was on the rolls of the 11th Regiment (Caldwell) and of the Hudspeth and Brown's Regiment. In both units, he was in Captain William Berryman's Company. He attended meetings of the units, but apparently did not deploy with them away from the county.

He was born in Culpeper County Virginia, 1785. He and Nancy Spilman were married in Allen County on 27 February 1815. They had ten children.

John was on the Allen County tax rolls in 1825 with 200 acres valued at $1,100, and located in the Difficult Creek watershed. He became the administrator for his father Anthony Griffin's estate after his death in 1823. John also owned a town lot in the village of Port Oliver.

Development of a county road system had a high priority in the early years. In February 1827, the County Court appointed John and four others to "view an alteration in the old state road beginning above Mrs. Griffin's thence to the intersect of the old road near a mud hole on the top of the hill." They were to report on the "conveniences and inconveniences of each way."

The 1850 census recorded John and Nancy living with five sons and two daughters still living in their household.

John died 29 September 1854 in Allen County at the age of sixty-nine. The cause of death was listed as the flux, sometimes called the bloody flux. The term was used for what we now call dysentery.

His widow Nancy filed for bounty land based on his service after the Act of 1855 was passed. She received a warrant (#91110) on 15 August 1861 for 160 acres in Otoe County, Nebraska. She assigned the land to George W. Norton. The warrant stated that he had been a private in Captain Berryman's Company of Kentucky.

Griffin, Thomas

Thomas Griffin married Phebe Barnhart in Warren County, Kentucky, on 12 November 1811. Two years later, 20 November 1814, he was selected to be a Captain and to become one of the company commanders in the newly formed 14th Regiment (Mitchusson) Kentucky Detached Militia. He and his company rendezvoused with the Regiment for the trip to New Orleans to join General Jackson's army. Their flatboat trip was cold and long. The first recorded muster in New Orleans was on 31 December 1814. He led his company during the Battle of New Orleans[30] (Chapter 8), and he was in Camp Jackson as late as 16 March 1815 awaiting their release from their six-month enlistment. The long cold walk brought him back to Kentucky where he was mustered out in Russellville on 20 May 1815.

His total pay from 20 November 1814 to 31 March 1815 was $172.90, at a rate of $40.00 per month. He received an additional $67.10 for his service from 1 April to 20 May when he was discharged in Russellville.

Thomas appeared in front of the Allen County Court on 6 October 1816 and appointed Thomas Gatton, an attorney in Scottsville, to obtain whatever money he might be due from his service.[31]

Widow Elizabeth Wright Thompson asked Thomas to verify that her husband, Private John Thompson (see biographical sketch in this chapter), had served in his company. She needed to verify her husband's service. He did so before the Allen County Court Clerk on 1 October 1816, and certified that John Thompson's death occurred in New Orleans.

Research for other information about Thomas found no confirmed mention of his ancestry or his life after his service other than those two appearances in court. His name was mentioned in many pension claims from members of his company, but little found about his life.

Grisham, Thomas

There were multiple spellings of the Grisham surname in the records. Among those were Grissom, Grisson, Grissond, and Gresham. The pension record for Thomas used the name Grisham.

Thomas Grisham and Lucy Foster were married on 14 December 1810 in Smith County, Tennessee. Her father, Drury, lived in what was then Warren County, Kentucky. At that time, what was then Smith County, Tennessee, adjoined it to the south. Thomas was on the 1810 tax list of Warren County, Kentucky.

Private Thomas Grisham appeared on the rolls of Captain William Berryman's Company of the Hudspeth and Brown's Regiment and in the same company in the 11th Regiment (Caldwell) Kentucky Militia.

He volunteered on 20 November 1814 into Captain Thomas Griffin's Company of the 14th Regiment (Mitchusson) Kentucky Detached Militia. The 14th made the flatboat trip to New Orleans, and was in the Battle of New Orleans in January 1815 (Chapter 8). He was discharged on 20 May 1815 after the tiring walk home up the Natchez Trace. He would have learned when he arrived at his home that it was located in the new Allen County that had been formed just a few days before his arrival (Chapter 12).

He, Lucy, and their two children appeared in the Allen County census of 1820, but they moved to Giles County, Tennessee, before the 1830 census. Thomas died there on 10 March 1839.

Lucy applied for and received a bounty land warrant (20868) on 15 April 1853 under the Act of 1950. She received 80 acres in Clinton County, Iowa. She assigned the land to Mary A Milliken. On 1 May 1860, she received another bounty land warrant (#42343) under the Act of 1855. She received 80 acres from it in Montgomery County, Iowa. She assigned those acres to John Carter Brown.

Lucy applied for a Widow's Pension (#7141) from Tishomingo County, Mississippi, where she was residing at that time. She was awarded the pension on 26 February 1873 (#4825) under the Act of 1872. Her pension record revealed that Lucy had lived in Tishomingo County, Mississippi, from 1851 through 1873. Lucy died there on 23 September 1873.

Hardcastle, John

Genealogical records indicate that John Hardcastle (also spelled Hordcastle) was born in Johnston County, North Carolina, about 1791. He lived in what was then Warren County, Kentucky, when he was married to Margaret (Peggy) Wiloby (Willoughby) on 3 February 1811. She was also a native of North Carolina.

John served as a Private in Captain William Berryman's Company of the 11th Regiment (Williams) Kentucky Mounted Volunteer Militia. He accompanied them on the march to Canada, and fought in the Battle of the Thames (Chapter 6). He entered active duty on 31 August 1813 and was discharged on 13 November 1813. Like others in mounted units, his horse earned more than he did, $34.00 for the horse and only $22.19 for him.

John was mustered out of service at Limestone (now Maysville), Kentucky, on 3 November 1813. He rode back to his home where his wife and daughter awaited him.

When the 1820 census of Allen County was taken on 7 August 1820, the census taker counted John, his wife, and two children in his household. However, John Hardcastle did not appear in Kentucky in subsequent censuses. Genealogical records did not agree on where he went. Some genealogical sources state that John may have been in White County, Arkansas, when the 1840 census was taken and may have died there about 1845. Others disagree.

Margaret applied for the bounty land for which John was eligible. On 6 February 1854, she received a warrant (#42696) for 40 acres in Johnson County, Illinois, under the Act of 1850. She assigned those acres to James Gray. On 2 July 1860, she received another warrant (#64587) for 120 acres in McDonald County, Missouri, under the Act of 1855. She assigned the land to James Archer. Both awards identified Margaret as the widow of John.

Harrison, Andrew

Most of the early settlers in the frontier west of the Appalachians had already experienced moving from a known environment at their home prior to emigration to an unknown one on the frontier. They had limited knowledge about what to expect from the frontier, and what difficulties they would encounter. Andrew Harrison would be included in that group. He was born on 25 November 1786 in Lincoln County, North Carolina, and traveled to the frontier before he turned twenty.

Some dramatic changes in his life were about to occur. The first was his wedding. He went to the home of his bride-to-be, Catherine Strader, in Logan County, Kentucky, on 10 December 1807. John Hendricks conducted the marriage ceremony at Katy's father's home. Andrew and Katy would eventually have a family of nine children.

The second big change was the beginning of the War of 1812. Like all men of service age, he had been a member of the Militia, and would have expected a call to duty.

Andrew answered his call to duty during the War of 1812 on 13 November 1814. He enlisted for a six months tour as a Private in Captain Richard Crunk's Company in Colonel John Cocke's 2nd Regiment of the West Tennessee Militia. The nature of the frontier in the study area at that time was reflected in the Militia's name. West Tennessee was the term used for what we now know as Middle Tennessee. What we now know as west Tennessee was then lands claimed by the Chickasaw.

Colonel Cocke's regiment was one of three in Major General Carroll's command. All of them went down to New Orleans on flatboats by way of the Cumberland, Ohio, and Mississippi Rivers. These regiments were in the center of the American line that bore the brunt of the British attack during the Battle of New Orleans (Chapter 8). After the battle, they walked up the Natchez Trace to their homes. He was discharged 13 May 1815 (Figure 50).

Andrew and Katy were counted the censuses of 1820, 1830, 1840, and 1850 as residents of Allen County. They lived about halfway between Scottsville and Franklin.

Andrew died on 10 April 1851. For his service, Katy received a bounty land warrant (#5555) for 80 acres in Clay County, Illinois, on 1 August 1853 under the Act of 1850. The patentee for the land was James Edward Holman. Katy received another bounty land award

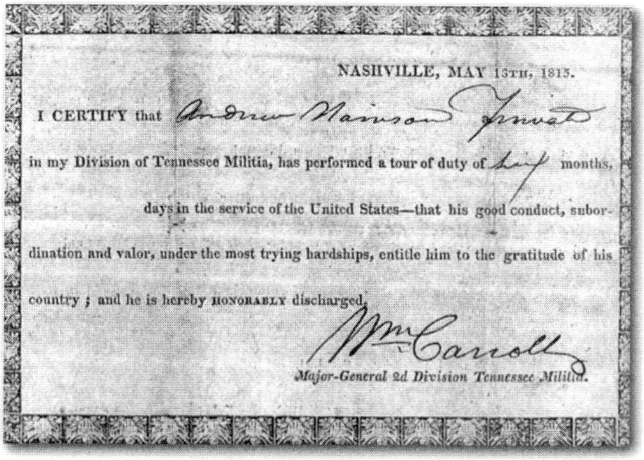

NASHVILLE, MAY 15TH, 1815.

I CERTIFY that Andrew Harrison Private in my Division of Tennessee Militia, has performed a tour of duty of six months, days in the service of the United States—that his good conduct, subordination and valor, under the most trying hardships, entitle him to the gratitude of his country; and he is hereby HONORABLY discharged.

Wm Carroll

Major-General 2d Division Tennessee Militia.

Figure 50. Andrew Harrison's discharge paper.

(#45492) under the Act of 1855. It was for an additional 80 acres in Harrison County, Missouri. She assigned that tract of land to John T. Hughes.

Katy applied for a Widow's Pension (#5086) on 19 April 1873. Her post office at the time was in Franklin, but she still resided in Allen County. She was confined at home with cancer "for years" and depended on her son for support.

There was the routine question of loyalty that was asked of all applicants after the Civil War. Her lawyer was reputed to be a confederate sympathizer. Apparently, a specific question of Katy's loyalty resulted. Mr. J. L. Stanford of Franklin in Simpson County sent a copy of her marriage record to the pension bureau and attached an unsolicited note about her loyalty. He wrote, "The person who reported Catherine Harrison as disloyal will do to watch, it would have been more honorable in him to have robbed the dead." His was a very strong statement of confidence in Katy's loyalty that seems to have been written while he was still steamed about the outrageously accusatory question.

Hatler, Michael

Few men served in both the Revolutionary War and the War of 1812 because an eighteen year old in 1778 would have been fifty-two in 1812, past the forty-five year old upper limit of the service rules. Nonetheless, Michael Hatler was one of those very few.

Michael was born near Baltimore, Maryland, on 15 July 1760. He declared in his pension application submitted in 1832 that he had enlisted as a substitute for John Norman in Culpeper County, Virginia. He served as a Private in the Virginia Militia for three months during the winter of 1778-79 in Ensign Richard Hickman's Company. During that period, he was assigned to guard prisoners held at the Albemarle Barracks. Afterward, he returned to his father's home.

He was called to duty again when his number was drawn and went back to Albemarle Barracks for another three-month tour of duty. Afterward, he went to his father's home in Abington in Washington County.

A few months later, Michael volunteered again, this time into a regiment being formed by Colonel William Campbell of Abington to go against the British at Kings Mountain, North Carolina. Fourteen days later while still en route toward Kings Mountain, Michael's horse was lost (presumably died) and, as a result, he was released from his obligation for duty. He returned again to his father's home.

For his service during the Revolutionary War, Michael received a pension (#13938) that began on 15 July 1833 after he had arrived in Allen County, Kentucky. He received $121.35 per year.

Michael's service during the War of 1812 was as a Corporal. He served in Captain Hugh Brown's Company of the 1st Regiment (Caldwell) Kentucky Mounted Volunteers. He was entered on the roll on 18 September and was discharged on 30 October 1812 at Busseron, Indiana Territory. He had traveled 230 miles for which he was paid based on a presumption of twenty miles per day. His pay was $7.33 per month, with eleven rations at $0.25, and $0.40 per day for the use of his horse. He collected a total of $27.46 for his one month and twelve days of service.

During this period of service, his group of Kentuckians was part of a force led by General Hopkins against the Indians of the Prophet. There was an engagement on 21 October during which his unit lost eighteen men either killed, wounded, or missing. It was said that many of the Kentuckians were shoeless and shirtless, having only summer clothing during the approach of winter (Chapter 3). On the 25th, they returned to Vincennes over snow-covered ground.[32]

Michael's surname was variously recorded or transcribed as Hatter, Hallin, and Hatlern.

He was in the census of 1810, and apparently lived on the eastern side of Barren County that became Allen County in 1815 (Chapter 12). He was enumerated there in 1820 and 1830.

He was married to Sarah Bracken in Allen County on 5 Jun 1819. Some genealogists record one or more subsequent marriages, and genealogists disagree on the number of children. One listed him with seventeen children. Michael died in 1843 in Allen County.

Hickman, Joseph

Enlistment into the regular Army required a commitment to a longer period of service than the usual one of the state Militias. On the other hand, there were some advantages of enlisting in a regular Army regiment instead of in one of state Militias. The regulars were provided uniforms and better weapons. For whatever reason, Joseph Hickman enlisted on 19 July 1812 in the regular Army.

He was recruited by Captain Robert Desha and assigned as a Private in his Company. After the war, Desha would be elected for two terms as a Representative to Congress from Kentucky. Desha's Company was part of Lieutenant Colonel Daniel Bissell's 24th U.S. Infantry Regiment. Joseph did not have long to wait for action. His regiment arrived at Fort Belle Fountaine on 30 November 1812. That fort was the first ever built in the Louisiana Territory area, and was located near the current city of St Louis, Missouri.

On 28 March 1813, his unit headed north to Fort Madison in what is now Iowa, a place that was in constant danger from the Blackhawk Indians. They began construction of a blockhouse on 5 July. The workers were attacked three days later and suffered two killed and one wounded. That fall, lacking a sufficient food supply, the fort was evacuated and they returned to Fort Belle Fountaine, arriving there on 25 November. They were issued new blue woolen uniforms with red cuffs and collars on the 27th.[33] Joseph was discharged on 18 January 1814 at the end of his enlistment.

Joseph was married to Martha Johnson on 29 December 1810 in Sumner County, Tennessee. James Hart, a Justice of the Peace, conducted the wedding. In 1820, they were living in Allen County with two children. Two years later, Joseph was on the tax roll, but there was no property tax was listed. After twenty-nine years of marriage, Joseph died on 5 April 1839 at his home in Allen County. It had been forty-nine years since his birth on 14 February 1790 in Rowan County, North Carolina.

Regular Army men were authorized by the Act of 1850 to receive 160 acres of bounty land. Joseph's bounty land warrant (#11164) awarded those acres in Livingston County, Illinois, to his widow Martha on 1 September 1853. She assigned the land to Atwood G. Hobson.

Martha also applied for (#4745) a Widow's Pension on 16 June 1871. She lived in the Allen Springs area at that time. She received a Widow's Pension (#4496) and received $8.00 per month beginning on 14 February 1871.

Martha was in the 1850 census of Allen County as M. A. Hickman. She was listed as being sixty years old Virginian, who lived with forty-nine year-old named Mary and a five year-old with the initials J. A.

Hoback, Mark

Little was recorded about Mark Hoback beyond his service to our country. He enlisted from what was then Warren County into Captain Thomas Griffin's Company of the 14th Regiment (Mitchusson) Kentucky Detached Militia on 20 November 1814. He made the trip to New Orleans and was in Jackson Camp from 31 December 1814 to 28 February 1815. He was listed as being one of the Kentuckians in the Battle of New Orleans (Chapter 8).[34] He was discharged as a Private at Russellville on 20 May 1815.

Mark appeared in the Allen County Court on 18 August 1816 to appoint Moses Bonner of Scottsville as his attorney. The purpose was to collect any pay due him for his service. His name could not be found in later census, tax, birth, death, marriage, court, and genealogical records.

Hobdy, John W.

John Hobdy was born in Northampton County, North Carolina, in 1790. His surname had various spellings, including Hobday, Dobdey, and Hoddey.

John's service began on 1 September 1814, according to his Widow's Pension papers, and was discharged on 1 September 1815 at the end of his one-year commitment. He served as a Private in Captain John Donaldson's Company in Colonel William Carroll's Regiment of Mounted Rangers at the Battle of New Orleans. Mounted Rangers were a special group within the regular army. Seven of these companies were authorized by Congress in January 1812 to patrol between the forts on the frontier. Kentucky was one of the four states from which the men were originally recruited. Ten more companies were authorized during the following year.[35]

Companies were typically one-tenth the size of a regiment. As a result, regiments were usually the smallest group whose actions were included in historical accounts of the War of 1812. Ranger Companies were an exception because the role they played was sometimes as important as a regiment. Such was the case when John Hobdy's company became very important in the nighttime battle near New Orleans on 23 December 1814 (Chapter 8).

The Americans launched an attack eastward against a British Camp on the bank of the Mississippi. Darkness, fog, and gun smoke made the operation difficult for John and his comrades of the Ranger Company. As they were circling inland from the river to attack from the north and toward the river, they became isolated from the other American forces. They found themselves amid a British unit whose commander demanded their surrender. "Be dammed if we do!" replied Captain Donaldson, the Ranger company commander. The ensuing skirmish produced three of the company killed and three captured, but the rest rejoined the American battle line. General Jackson called off the entire attack about 4:00 a.m.[36] John Hobdy survived both that night and the following Battle of New Orleans on 8 January 1815. He and his unit were discharged at Murfreesboro, Tennessee (Figure 51).

He returned home and was married to Nancy Cummings on 4 October 1817 in Sumner County. They had four children. He was married to a second wife Elizabeth Clay Hodges on 22 September 1835, also in Sumner County. They had eight children.

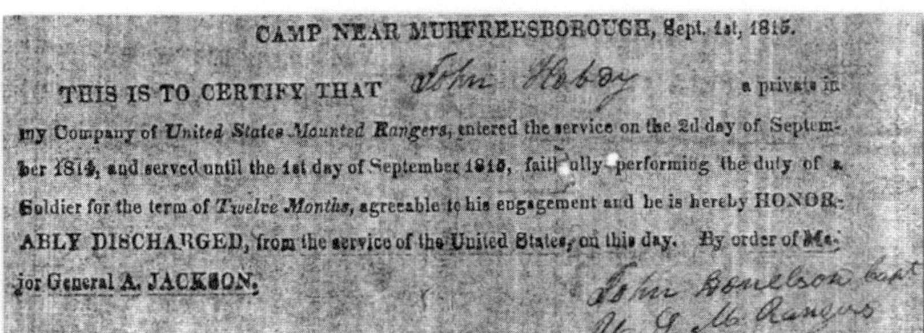
CAMP NEAR MURFREESBOROUGH, Sept. 1st, 1815.

THIS IS TO CERTIFY THAT John Hobdy a private in my Company of *United States Mounted Rangers*, entered the service on the 2d day of September 1814, and served until the 1st day of September 1815, faithfully performing the duty of a Soldier for the term of *Twelve Months*, agreeable to his engagement and he is hereby HONORABLY DISCHARGED, from the service of the United States, on this day. By order of Major General A. JACKSON.

John Donelson Capt
U. S. M. Rangers

Figure 51. John Hobdy's discharge paper paper.

John died on 22 August 1850 in Sumner County and his will was probated in January 1853.

As a regular Army member, he was entitled to 160 acres of bounty land under the Act of 1850. That land was awarded on 2 October 1854 in Cass County, Missouri, under a warrant (#3616) with his name spelled as John Hobday. The patentee for the land was Edward S. Peyton.

His widow Elizabeth (Betsy) resided in Sumner County until she moved to New Roe in Allen County in 1874. She appeared on the 1880 census there. She filed for a Widow's Pension on 18 December 1878 and was awarded $12.00 per month effective from 9 March of that year. She received that pension until she died there on 13 July 1899.

Hooton, Joseph

Joseph Hooton appeared on the Warren County census of 1810 as being between sixteen and twenty-five years old with a wife and a male child younger than ten years old. He probably lived in what became Allen County in 1815 because he appeared on the 1820 census there without his wife, but with three children in his household. His son was listed as being between ten and fifteen. There are three others in his household, two boys under ten and a girl under ten. There is a note that two of those three are "foreigners not naturalized."

Joseph was listed as a Private on the Hudspeth and Brown's Regimental roll dated 6 March 1816, and was recorded absent for that roll call. He also was listed in Captain William Berryman's Company of the 11th Regiment (Caldwell) Kentucky Militia.

The search for information about Joseph in subsequent years was unsuccessful.

House, Henry

Young men of middle Tennessee responded to the call for volunteers from General Andrew Jackson to defend Louisiana from invasion by the British. Henry House was a North Carolinian who had immigrated to Tennessee and was about nineteen years old when he became one of those who responded. He volunteered for six months service and became a Private in Captain Henry Hamilton's Company, 3rd Regiment (Raulston) Tennessee Militia on 13 November 1814 in Nashville. Many of the men in that regiment were from Sumner County, Tennessee, where he lived at the time of enlistment.

His regiment suffered casualties during a skirmish on 28 December 1814 in a swamp near New Orleans. They were in the thick of things during the Battle of New Orleans on 8 January 1815, on the line with General Carroll's Division taking the brunt of the British attack. Two of their men were among the few Americans killed during that battle (Chapter 8).

Henry made the long walk back home, and was discharged at Nashville on 13 May 1815. He married Mary Boyle on 28 June 1816 in Sumner County, and lived there as their family grew. They had seven children before Mary died.

He was awarded a warrant (#18529) under the Act of 1850 for 80 acres of bounty land in Macon County, Missouri, on 15 June 1853. Green B. Harris was listed as the patentee for that land. He received a warrant (#19411) on 10 February 1860 under the Act of 1855 for 80 acres in Jackson County, Wisconsin. The patentee for that plot was Henry N. Stanley.

Henry and Nancy Senter were married in Sumner County in January 1858. The 1870 census listed Henry and Nancy still living there.

He submitted a claim for a survivor's pension on 11 April 1871 (#10012) and a pension was granted (#5829) on 4 October 1871. He received the usual $8.00 per month for a Private until he died in Allen County on 11 July 1875.

Nancy filed for a Widow's Pension (#18261), and a certificate of pension (#13818) was approved. Her pension started on 9 June 1878, and was sent to her New Roe address. The 1883 pensioners list listed her in Allen County.

House, William

William House was Henry's brother, both of them were born in Edgecombe County, North Carolina, and both came to Sumner County, Tennessee, with their parents about 1799. Both were in the Tennessee Militia, but in different regiments.

William served as a Private in Captain John Wallace's Company, 1st Tennessee (Hall) Volunteers. He enlisted on 10 December 1812 and was mustered in 16 December 1812 in Gallatin for one year. Colonel William Hall led the regiment as part of General Jackson's expedition to Natchez (Chapter 4). General Jackson was ordered to abort the mission and the regiment eventually returned through Columbia to Nashville where they were discharged on 22 April 1813.

William applied (#6200) for a Survivor's Pension on 19 March 1871. He stated that he was a widower. He was given a pension certificate (#3450) dated 28 August 1871 with back pay beginning on 14 February 1871.

His bounty land claim was submitted under Act 1850 and a warrant (#32497) for 40 acres in Hamilton County, Illinois, was provided. The patentee for that land was Gilbert Flint. A second claim resulted in a warrant (#12088) for 80 acres under Act of 1855 in Greene County, Iowa, on 1 December 1857. He assigned that tract to Alexander Fassett. Genealogical records listed his marriage to Rachel Bowles on 28 June 1816 in Sumner County. They were still in Sumner County in the 1860 census.

Figure 52. William House's tombstone.

He spent his last days living with his son B.C. House on the Holland Road in Allen County. William was in the 1870 census, but his wife Rachel was not included. William died there on 18 February 1880, and was buried in Pleasant Hill Cemetery (Figure 52).

Howell, Hudson

Several veterans of the War of 1812 appeared in the Allen County Court records as they appointed attorneys to represent them. One of them was Hudson Howell whose surname spellings included Howel, Howl, and Hawell in other documents. He gave his power of attorney to Samuel Parker to "draw and receive from the paymaster of the 14th Regiment all and every sum or sums of money which may be due" for his service as a Private in that unit.

He had been on the rolls of 11th Regiment (Caldwell) in Captain Berryman's Company when it was called to rendezvous at Greensburg on 1 May 1813. He was listed as a substitute for John Patrick.

When the call came for troops to go to New Orleans, Hudson became a member of Captain Samuel P. Malone's Company of the 14th Regiment (Mitchusson) Kentucky Detached Militia committed to a six-month tour of duty. He was mustered in at Russellville on 20 November 1814, made the flatboat trip to New Orleans, and was at Camp Jackson near New Orleans from 31 December 1814 to 28 February 1815. He was there for the Battle of New Orleans (Chapter 8).

His service record showed that he was mustered out on 20 May 1815 at Russellville. He earned a total of $48.00 during this six-month period of service that included the Battle of New Orleans (Chapter 8).

Research to learn about Hudson's life during the subsequent years was unsuccessful.

Huntsman, Henry

Botetourt County, Virginia, was the birthplace of Henry Huntsman. He was born there about the year 1786. He and his brother immigrated to what is now Allen County in the early 1800s where they had acquired farmland.[37]

Henry was a Private in Captain William Berryman's Fifth Company of the 3rd Regiment (Malone) Kentucky Detached Militia. It was organized on 1 September 1812 by Lieutenant Colonel Nicholas Miller. Twelve others from the study area served in this unit that saw action in the Second Battle of Tippecanoe (Chapter 3). Henry's service records listed his discharge date as 25 December 1812 at Hardinsburg, Kentucky. He was on duty for three months and twenty-nine day and earned $25.33 for his service.

Henry's wife was Nancy Mitchell. Their first child was born in Allen County on 10 October 1816.

In the 1820 census, Henry's household was listed with one male over 26 (Henry), two boys under ten, one female over twenty-six (Nancy), and two girls under twenty, one of whom was listed as a foreigner not naturalized. By the 1840 census, Henry family had grown to eight children.

Henry received three bounty land grant warrants for his service. The first (#50481) was on 2 January 1854 for 40 acres in Hardin County, Illinois, under Act of 1850. The patentee for that land was Jerimiah Davis. The second (#101596) was on 15 January 1856 for 45 acres in Black Hawk County, Iowa. That land was assigned to patentee John

McDaneld, The third (#36508) was on 15 June 1860 for 80 acres in Anderson County, Kansas, and was assigned to James Warren.

Henry died in Allen County on 13 March 1859.

Johnson, John

Private John Johnson was on the Hudspeth and Brown's Regimental Rolls on 6 March 1813 in Captain William Berryman's Company. He also was on the rolls of that company in the 11th Regiment (Caldwell) Detached Militia. The latter group rendezvoused at Greensburg, Kentucky, on 1 May 1813.

He served in Captain Samuel P. Malone's Company of the 14th Regiment (Mitchusson) Kentucky Detached Militia. He enrolled on 20 November 1814 for six months. He was at Camp Jackson in Louisiana on 31 December 1814, engaged in the Battle of New Orleans, left Camp Jackson on 28 February 1815, and was mustered out at Russellville on 20 May 1815 (Chapter 8). He received a total pay of $48.00 for his service.

John Johnson died in Allen County in 1841. He never married, and his sister Patsy Hickman was listed as his next of kin when he died. Robert Johnson, Harry Mitchell, and William Blackburn knew John, and attested to his service, including his presence at the Battle of New Orleans. They stated that John had enlisted in Sumner County, Tennessee.[38]

Johnson, Matthew

Matthew Johnson's family Bible recorded his birth as 28 January 1786 in North Carolina. Matthew was married to Elizabeth Vaden Austin in North Carolina. They immigrated to what would become southeastern Allen County about 1807 on land near Barren River. By the time that duty called for the War of 1812, they had three children. The oldest was not quite six years old and Elizabeth was pregnant again when he went off to war.

Matthew answered the call to go to the aid of General Jackson in New Orleans leaving his wife and children behind. He was mustered in on 20 November 1814 in Russellville for a six-month tour. He was given the rank of Corporal in Captain Thomas Sterrett's Company of the 14th Regiment (Mitchusson) Detached Kentucky Militia. He was at Camp Dupré, just upriver from the primary battle site, from 31 December 1814 to 28 February 1815 (Chapter 8). He was mustered out at Russellville on 20 May 1815. He arrived home to see his then two-month old daughter for the first time.

He was a farmer who owned 1,000 acres in the Puncheon Creek area of Allen County by 1838. He was listed on the tax rolls with five slaves and seven horses to work the farm. The assessed tax value of his holdings was $2,920.00 that year, attesting to his affluence at that time.

On 1 November 1853, he received a warrant (#21795) for 87 acres of bounty land in Ste. Genevieve County, Missouri, under the Act of 1850. The patentee was John Shelly. He received a second award (#26495) of 80 acres on 10 October 1858 under the Act of 1855. In that award, his first name was spelled Mathew. The land was in Pine County, Minnesota, and was assigned to John Fitzpatrick as the patentee.

Matthew died 23 August 1867 and was buried in the Johnson-Downing cemetery on Bandy Road near Holland, Kentucky.

Johnson, Robert

Private Robert Johnson was in Captain Thomas Griffin's Company of the 14th Regiment (Mitchusson) Detached Militia. He was at the muster held in at Russellville on 20 November 1814, made the journey to New Orleans, was at Camp Jackson from 31 December 1814 to 28 February 1815, and was discharged at Russellville on 20 May 1815. He participated in the Battle of New Orleans (Chapter 8).

Piecing together the life of Robert was difficult because both his surname and his first name were so common. Even the combination of those names was common. There was more than one Robert Johnson living in Allen County. Marriage records from Sumner County, Tennessee, list a marriage between Robert Johnson and Patsy Ann Goodrum on 31 August 1808. She was a native of Virginia. Genealogists reported that they had at least five children. He was living in Allen County during the 1850, 1860, and 1870. The 1860 census listed him in the Carolina District, the area near Allen Springs. The 1870 census recorded his post office as Butlersville.

Under the Act of 1850, a bounty land warrant (#53304) was awarded Robert with 80 acres of land in Dade County, Missouri, on 10 April 1858. According to the land records, the patentee was his "widow" Sarah Johnson. That was confusing because Robert's wife Patsy Ann had died about three years earlier on 7 February 1855. Perhaps this Sarah was his daughter who was about twenty-nine years old at the time of the land grant. Survivor pensions often clarified confusions such as that, but there is no record that Robert ever applied for one. Lacking that, the mystery remains.

Robert Johnson died at Allen Springs in 1876 and was buried there.

Kerby, Isaiah

One patriarch of the Kerby (also spelled Kirby) family was a Revolutionary War veteran who was an early emigrant from South Carolina to Warren County, Kentucky, and the area of Plano. Several members the Kerby family served in the War of 1812. One of those was Isaiah Kerby who was born on 25 August 1794. He enlisted on 31 August 1813 as a Private in Captain William Berryman's Company of the 11th Regiment (Williams) Kentucky Mounted Volunteer Militia. That regiment would participate in the Battle of the Thames (Chapter 6) in Upper Canada.

Isaiah rode his horse from his home to join his unit at Newport, Kentucky. They rode through Ohio to the shore of Lake Erie. He specifically mentioned in his application that he participated in the capture and occupation of the British Fort Malden. The American force had crossed Lake Erie by ship and occupied the British Fort Malden. He may have been in the part of that unit that was left there to guard the supply route for those that continued northeastward. He was discharged on 13 November 1813 at Limestone (now Maysville). He was paid $22.19 for his service and $34.00 for his horse's service before his discharge (Figure 53).

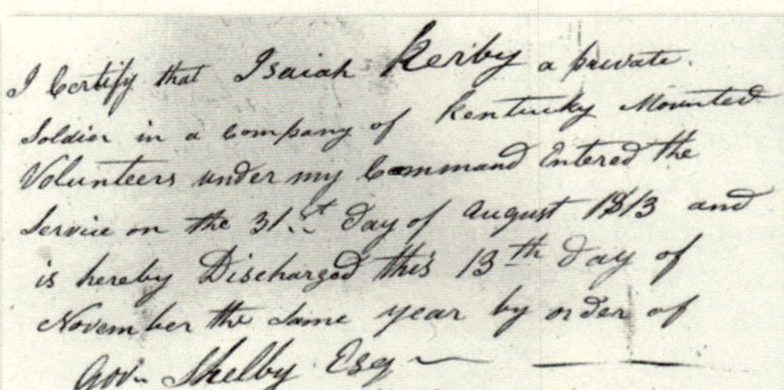

I Certify that Isaiah Kerby a private Soldier in a Company of Kentucky Mounted Volunteers under my Command Entered the Service on the 31st Day of August 1813 and is hereby Discharged this 13th Day of November the same year by order of Govr. Shelby Esqr —

Wm Berryman Capt
11th Regt Ky M.V

Figure 53. Isaiah Kerby's first discharge paper.

Isaiah enlisted a second time in Captain Thomas Griffin's Company of the 14th Regiment (Mitchusson) Kentucky Detached Militia as it was formed to augment the Americans at New Orleans. He was mustered in on 20 November 1814. His tour ended on 20 May 1815 (Figure 54) after about six months active duty that included the Battle of New Orleans (Chapter 8).

Isaiah Kerby and Sophia Kerby were married on 17 March 1821 in Warren County, and lived there for some time afterward. They were enumerated on the 1840 census.

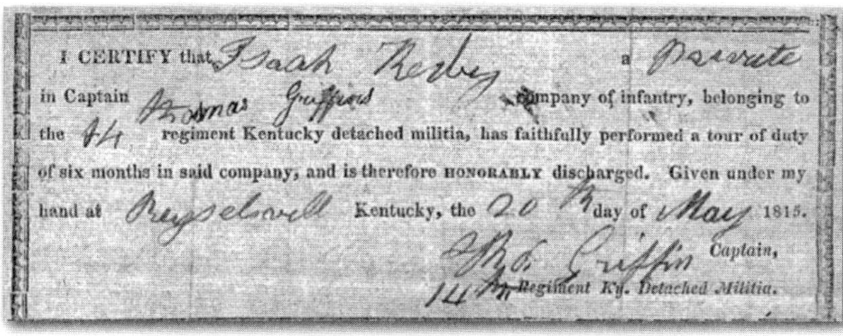
I CERTIFY that Isaah Kerby a Private in Captain Thomas Griffin's Company of infantry, belonging to the 14 regiment Kentucky detached militia, has faithfully performed a tour of duty of six months in said company, and is therefore HONORABLY discharged. Given under my hand at Russelsville Kentucky, the 20th day of May 1815.

Thos. Griffin Captain,
14th Regiment Ky. Detached Militia.

Figure 54. Isaiah Kerby's second discharge paper.

He received a bounty land warrant (#8452) for 161 acres under the Act of 1850. The total acreage indicated that both of his periods of service had been included. The land was located in Polk County, Missouri, and was awarded to him on 1 October 1852. Isaiah and Sophia moved to Polk County, Missouri, and took possession of that land. They appeared on the census there in 1870. Isaiah was listed on that census with his name spelled Isah Kirby. At seventy-four years old, he was reported to be a prosperous farmer at census time.

He submitted a claim (#10069) for a Survivor's Pension from Polk County, Missouri, on 6 April 1871. A certificate (#4171) for $8.00 month was granted on 9 September 1871 and payment commenced on 14 February 1871.

Kerby, Jesse R.

Jesse R. Kerby (also spelled Kirby) was listed in some genealogical records as Isaiah's brother. He was born in South Carolina on 6 March 1792 and probably lived with his family in what was then Warren County when the War of 1812 began.

Jesse was a Private in Captain William Berryman's Company in the 11th Regiment (Williams) Kentucky Militia. He rode with his brother Isaiah and them on the long expedition to Lake Erie, crossed by boat to Canada, engaged in the Battle of the Thames (Chapter 6), and made the return trip back home. He was discharged at Limestone (now Maysville) on 3 November 1813. He rode from there back to his home near Allen Springs.

Figure 55. Prudence Kirby's tombstone paper.

Jesse was married to Prudence Dishman on 25 November 1818 in Logan County, Kentucky. They appeared on the census of 1820 and subsequent years in Warren County. In 1850, there were ten children in his household.

Jesse was awarded a warrant (#10070) under the Act of 1850 for 83 acres in Izard County, Arkansas, on 16 June 1856. He assigned the land to patentee Robert Phillips. Under the Act of 1855, he received by warrant (#8553) for an additional 80 acres of bounty land in Olmstead County, Minnesota, on 16 July 1858. He assigned that land to patentee Foster Paige.

Jesse died on 19 November 1860, and was buried in the family cemetery. Burial in family cemeteries was still the common custom in those days. That cemetery is on Dye Ford Road in Warren County.

Prudence submitted a claim (#23740) for a Widow's Pension. That request was granted by a certificate (#16495).

The 1880 census listed Prudence as a 78 year-old widow who was the head of household with one son and two daughters living with her. Prudence died on 9 January 1883, and was buried in the Trinity Church cemetery (Figure 55). Churches had opened cemeteries by then, and those would eventually supplant the custom of family cemeteries adopted during earlier years.

Kerby, Leonard C.

Leonard Kerby (also spelled Kirby) applied for a Survivor's Pension (#16903) on 2 May 1871 and declared that his home was in Allen Springs in Allen County. He stated that he enlisted for six months as a Private into Captain Thomas Griffin's Company of the 14th Regiment (Mitchusson) Kentucky Detached Militia as a substitute for Abraham Duff.

He and his company traveled to Smithland, a small town located near the confluence of the Cumberland and the Ohio Rivers. From there, they traveled by flatboats down the Ohio and Mississippi Rivers to New Orleans. They participated in the Battle of New Orleans (Chapter 8), but he, like many of the Kentuckians who had made the trip, was without a gun. During the battle, he "jumped over the breastworks, and secured a gun from the enemy — and got back — and engaged in the fight."

Leonard stated that he was born in South Carolina, and came to Kentucky when he was fourteen. He said that there were "mighty few settlers" thereabout in those days. He lived in the Allen Spring area, sometimes in Allen and sometimes in Warren Counties, except for that trip to New Orleans. He remembered when he "offered his body as a target for English bullets." At the time of his pension application, he described himself as "mighty poorly, mighty poorly, getting old; can't get around."[39]

His pension application (#13129) was approved (#16903) on 20 May 1872, and his pay was backdated to 14 February 1871. In his pension application, he stated that he and his wife Nancy were married at her father Samuel Kerby's home in December 1817.

Leonard received three parcels of Bounty land for his service. The first was an award under a warrant (#16776) dated 1 July 1854 was for 80 acres in Montgomery County, Illinois, under the Act of 1850. That parcel was assigned to Jefferson Lynn. The second warrant (#12273) also under the Act of 1850 was issued on 2 October 1854 for 40 acres in Crawford County, Indiana. That land was assigned to William Stepro. The third award on 4 July 1860 was a warrant (#32886) under the Act of 1855 for 80 acres in Taney County, Missouri. He conveyed that land to William Wheeler.

The 1880 census counted Leonard, age eighty-four, and Nancy, age eighty-six, living in Allen County on a farm. Leonard died on 26 September 1881 at his home near Allen Springs. Nancy applied (#41741) for a Widow's Pension on 23 November 1881 at the Allen County Court. Her pension certificate (#32437) was dated 3 June 1882, and her pay began as of 27 September 1881. She was on the 1883 list of Pensioners in Allen County as a War of 1812 widow and was still living in Allen Springs.

Kerby, Samuel M.

Samuel M. Kerby (also spelled Kirby) first served in Captain William Berryman's Company of the 3rd Regiment (Miller) Kentucky Detached Militia when he was mustered in on 1 September 1812 at Louisville for a six months tour. Twelve others from the study area served in this regiment that saw action in the Second Battle of Tippecanoe, also called Battle of Wild Cat Creek (Chapter 3). He was mustered out on 25 December 1912 at Hardinsburg, Kentucky, and returned to Bowling Green.

His second tour began on 20 August and ended on 3 November 1813 when Samuel entered the 11th Regiment (Caldwell) Kentucky Detached Militia. His rank of Second Sergeant was a responsible position in a company with considerable prestige attached to it. He was the second noncommissioned officer, out ranked only by the First Sergeant.

Samuel was born in Stokes County, North Carolina, on 25 April 1788, and came to Warren County before 1812. He was thirty when he and Mary Elizabeth Martin were married on 10 April 1818 in Warren County. He was married for a second time when he was seventy-two. His second wife was Nancy Renfro, widow of Joseph E. Renfro. The ceremony was conducted at E. Smith's home in Warren County on 22 September 1861.

A certificate (#70593) that had been previously awarded to him for 40 acres was cancelled. The reason for cancellation was unclear. The certificate (Chapter 10) remained in his pension files because cancelled certificates were invalid and therefore were not returned to the Bounty Land Office.

Mary received a bounty land warrant (#36617) for 100 acres in Bates County, Missouri, on 2 October 1854. Those acres were assigned to Richard A. Broughan. She received another warrant (#45907) for 80 acres in Linn County, Kansas, on 1 April 1861 under the Act of 1855. It was unclear as to why she received the two awards rather than her husband who was still alive although she was listed as his widow. She assigned that patent to Charles Kerby.

The eighty-three year old Samuel applied (#13128) for a Survivor's Pension on 15 April 1871 soon after Congress has authorized its award. His award was approved (#9126) on 27 November 1871 for $8.00 per month backdated to commence on 14 February 1871. He died in Warren County at the age of ninety-two.

Nancy filed for a Widow's Pension with a brief (#39184) on 7 January 1880 and she was approved (#29870) on 30 June 1880 for $8.00 per month backdated to commence in December 1879, the day after Samuel's death. She changed her pension address to Pierce City, Lawrence County, Missouri, on 14 August 1880. She appeared on the 1880 census there. Nancy died on 4 August 1892.

Kirby, Tarrance

Variant surnames were common because phonetic spellings introduced the variances. Less common were variant first names because of the dominance of just a few names; John, James, Thomas, or William, for example, seldom had phonetic variances. Variances were most likely when a first name was also the surname of an ancestor. In that case, its phonetic spellings were seldom the same from document to document.

The variations in surnames, such as Kerby or Kirby, were common. Tarrance Kirby's first name was unusual, and as spelled phonetically by the scribe who was writing the document, varied wildly. Tarrant and Tarrent were examples. In successive censuses beginning in 1810, his first name was written by the census takers as Terance, Lawrance, Torrence, T., Yuence, and Laurence.

Even his genealogists had difficulty in establishing his family tree, sometimes assigning a middle name, perhaps in an attempt to "clarify" the record. In his case, the name Leonard was sometimes inserted before or after his name Tarrance without an explanation. He signed his name as Tarrance Kirby and that name was used in most of his military records. It was adopted as a convenience for use herein.

In several documents, he was called Captain Kirby, but he did not hold that rank and the title seems to have been used out of respect for him in his later years. He did not make that claim himself. He was, however, a noncommissioned officer.

Tarrance was born in South Carolina about 1793 by most genealogical accounts. For sure, he lived in Sumner County, Tennessee, when the War of 1812 began.

On 1 September 1851, he received a bounty land warrant (#2489) under the Act of 1850 for 100 acres in Pike County, Indiana, for his service with the 24th U.S. Infantry, a regular Army unit.

On 13 November 1855 at age 63, he appeared before a Justice of the Peace in Sumner County, and made a sworn statement about his service during the War of 1812. The Justice of the Peace wrote Tarrance's oral statement. The scribe wrote that Tarrance had fought against the Indians, and that he was at the Battle of Tippecanoe. But, the battle that he described was what became known as the Second Battle of Tippecanoe, also called the battle of Wild Cat Creek. The more famous battle of Tippecanoe had been fought about a year earlier than when Tarrance first joined the army.

He was a private in William Berryman's Company of Colonel Miller's 3rd Regiment during the Second Battle of Tippecanoe. Twelve others from the study area served in this unit that saw action there too (Chapter 3). Tarrance signed up for six months, and was discharged at Hardinsburg in Breckinridge County.

Afterward, he enlisted in the 24th U.S. Infantry commanded by Colonel Thomas Owens. He was in Captain Henry C. Gist (pronounced like Guess), and was promoted to 1st Corporal. He also served for a time in Captain T. L. Butler's Company. His enlistment was for one year from 28 April 1813 until he was discharged on 28 April 1814.

His unit was stationed in Fort Meigs, Ohio, (near present day Toledo) when it was under siege by the British and Indians. The heavy bombardment lasted four days during the first week of May 1813. His unit was in the battle at Fort Stephenson near Sandusky, Ohio, in August and in other actions during his tour of duty with them. He said he was at the Battle of the Thames when Tecumseh was killed on 5 October 1813. That could not be verified, but 120 regular Army men were in that battle, and he could have been one of them.

He volunteered for a third time in September 1814, and was assigned to Captain Thomas Griffin's Company of the 14th Regiment (Mitchusson) Detached Kentucky Militia. He stated that at the Battle of New Orleans on 8 January 1815, as a 2nd Sergeant, he was wounded in the right hand. The circumstances were described by him and written by the Justice of the Peace. It read in part:

> *"He was badly wounded in the thumb on the right hand by a bayonet being on the wrong side of his gun or musket which gun jerked out of the hand of a man who was sitting behind the breastwork shooting up into the air when the action commenced. He and his company were one mile from the breastworks. He then called for volunteers to follow him into battle and only 3 of his men followed him into battle. Two of whom were dead and the 3rd man Jonathan Eubanks is alive.*
>
> *For 4 or 5 weeks, the right hand and arm were greatly influenced so much so that the attending doctor thought the hand would have to be cut off. Dorris was the doctor's name, he is now dead, therefore cannot get his certificate. The hand had to be lanced some 20 or 25 times.*
>
> *It has now contracted and drawn. It has been gradually worse every since he received the wound. He is now wholely (sic) disabled from chopping or hoeing or even ploughing (sic)."*

Private Jonathan Eubank confirmed Tarrance's account of the action and the wound. He said, "...Kirby was wounded in the thumb by a bayonet splitting his thumb on the right hand from below the first joint to the end of the thumb." Eubank verified the severity of the wound, its difficulty in healing, and Dr. Dorris's anticipation of amputation. Eubank said that he himself "lanced the thumb and fingers in several places, he suffered a great deal."

There were statements by Dr. William D. Haggard and Dr. N. B. Newsom on 26 November 1855 that his hand was "much drawn" and that his wrist and thumb still showed the scars from the lancing. They judged that his disability limited his abilities by one half.

By the time he applied for a pension, he lacked living witnesses in sufficient number to verify the origin and severity of his wound as required by the rules for awarding pensions. Tarrance did not acquiesce to the inevitable rejection, and submitted a letter to the Senate and the House of Representatives in Congress.

He made his case, just as he had in the statement above, and asked them to order that "...his name placed on the roll of Invalid Pensioners, and that he be allowed to receive for life, such sum annually, as to your honorable body may deem just & proper, from all the testimony herewith presented, and as is duty bound, he will ere pray." He was, to say the least, audacious.

Thomas Barry, Tarrance's attorney wrote to U.S. Representative Charles Ready on 26 January 1856. Ready represented the Tennessee's Fifth Congressional District. The attorney attested to Tarrance's character. He stated that Tarrance had raised fourteen children, including one who died in service on the plains of Mexico.

It is somehow interesting that someone was writing to his congressman more than 150 years ago. Viewed from the current era of instant communications, writing a request for congressional intervention into a personal matter seems rather quaint. But, the 34th Congress was larger than we imagine; it had sixty-two senators and 234 representatives. Tennessee had ten representatives, five were members of the Democrat party and five were from the American (Know Nothing) party. Representative Ready was a member of the Know Nothing party. It pushed for limitations and restrictions on immigration, a major issue during that time.

Today, senators and representatives have sizable staffs to respond to individuals who ask for specific assistance. It could be that it was easier in 1856 to acquire direct access to a congressman than it is now.

In any case, Tarrance's perseverance in circumventing the bureaucratic rules paid off. Congress published the findings of a Committee on Invalid Pensions on 25 July 1856 that recommended that he be provided a pension (Figure 56).

The pension office responded on 15 June 1857 that, in compliance with a Special Act of Congress dated 3 March 1857, 2nd Sergeant Tarrance Kirby was placed on the pension rolls with half pay of a sergeant and with arrears payment to begin on 2 December 1856. Tarrance had gotten his pension at last.

However, that was not the end of the story. The pension office miscalculated the amount that he was to receive and provided for only $6.00 per month, less than the $8.50 he should have received as half if his $17.00 per month sergeant's pay. After several written exchanges, his perseverance was rewarded when the error was acknowledged (Figure 57).

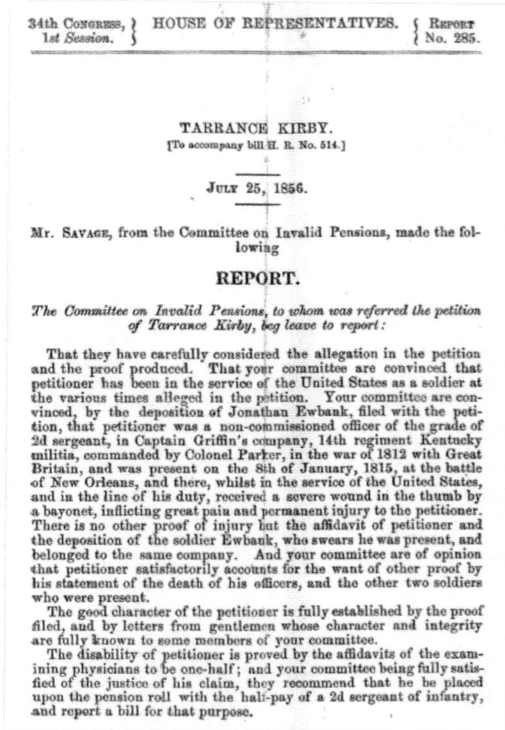

34th Congress, 1st Session. | HOUSE OF REPRESENTATIVES. | Report No. 285.

TARRANCE KIRBY.

[To accompany bill H. R. No. 514.]

July 25, 1856.

Mr. Savage, from the Committee on Invalid Pensions, made the following

REPORT.

The Committee on Invalid Pensions, to whom was referred the petition of Tarrance Kirby, beg leave to report:

That they have carefully considered the allegation in the petition and the proof produced. That your committee are convinced that petitioner has been in the service of the United States as a soldier at the various times alleged in the petition. Your committee are convinced, by the deposition of Jonathan Ewbank, filed with the petition, that petitioner was a non-commissioned officer of the grade of 2d sergeant, in Captain Griffin's company, 14th regiment Kentucky militia, commanded by Colonel Parker, in the war of 1812 with Great Britain, and was present on the 8th of January, 1815, at the battle of New Orleans, and there, whilst in the service of the United States, and in the line of his duty, received a severe wound in the thumb by a bayonet, inflicting great pain and permanent injury to the petitioner. There is no other proof of injury but the affidavit of petitioner and the deposition of the soldier Ewbank, who swears he was present, and belonged to the same company. And your committee are of opinion that petitioner satisfactorily accounts for the want of other proof by his statement of the death of his officers, and the other two soldiers who were present.

The good character of the petitioner is fully established by the proof filed, and by letters from gentlemen whose character and integrity are fully known to some members of your committee.

The disability of petitioner is proved by the affidavits of the examining physicians to be one-half; and your committee being fully satisfied of the justice of his claim, they recommend that he be placed upon the pension roll with the half-pay of a 2d sergeant of infantry, and report a bill for that purpose.

Figure 56. Congressional report on Tarrance Kirby.

He filed for an invalid pension on 26 February 1866 in Sumner County. His claim stated that he enlisted in Bowling Green in Warren County, Kentucky, on 1 September 1814 for a term of six months, that he had served in Captain Thomas Griffin's Company of the 14th Regiment (Mitchusson) Kentucky Detached Militia, and that he was in the Battle of New Orleans. He said that during that battle he had been wounded in his right hand by a bayonet and that it caused a permanent disability.

He stated that he previously had been in good circumstances, and did not need the full pension until he "lost his all" during the Civil War. He asked for payment of a pension and for the arrears. His voluminous service records grew during the next eighteen years, and his perseverance was tested again. As before, he prevailed when the issue was finally resolved in 1874. Just as he had done eighteen years earlier, he appealed to Congress. Just as it was before, Congress directed the payment of arrears (Figure 58). Once again, he had overcome the "rules is rules" type of bureaucratic delays by the personal attributes that had made him a good leader.

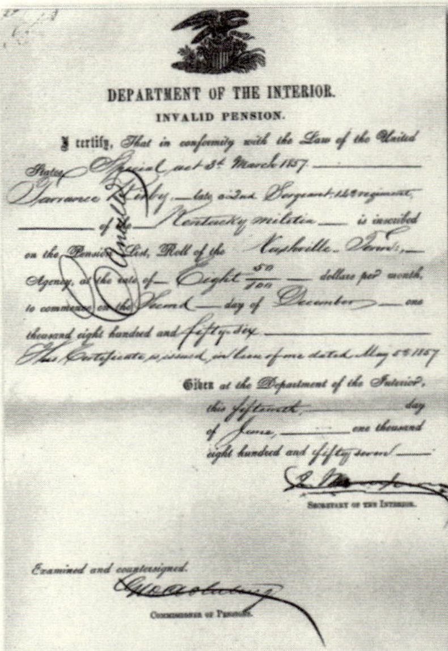

DEPARTMENT OF THE INTERIOR.

INVALID PENSION.

I certify, That in conformity with the Law of the United States Special act 3d March 1857 Tarrance Kirby late 2nd Sergeant 4th regiment of the Kentucky militia is inscribed on the Pension List, Roll of the Nashville Tenn. Agency, at the rate of Eight 50/100 dollars per month, to commence on the Second day of December one thousand eight hundred and fifty-six. This Certificate is issued in lieu of one dated May 8th 1857

Given at the Department of the Interior, this fifteenth day of June, one thousand eight hundred and fifty seven.

Secretary of the Interior.

Examined and countersigned.

Commissioner of Pensions.

Figure 57. Tarrance Kirby's invalid pension authorization.

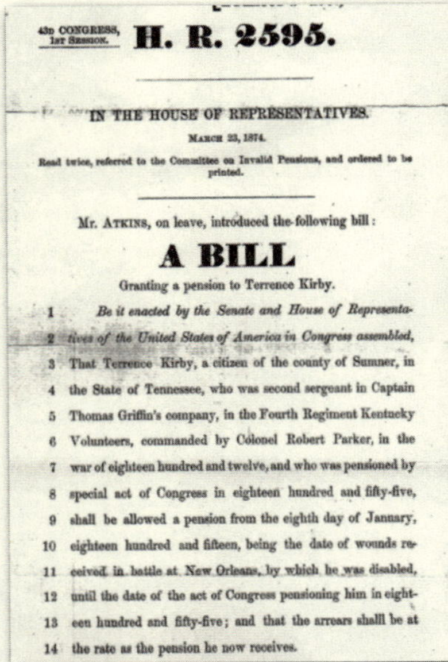

43d CONGRESS, 1st Session.

H. R. 2595.

IN THE HOUSE OF REPRESENTATIVES.

March 23, 1874.

Read twice, referred to the Committee on Invalid Pensions, and ordered to be printed.

Mr. Atkins, on leave, introduced the following bill:

A BILL

Granting a pension to Terrence Kirby.

Be it enacted by the Senate and House of Representatives of the United States of America in Congress assembled, That Terrence Kirby, a citizen of the county of Sumner, in the State of Tennessee, who was second sergeant in Captain Thomas Griffin's company, in the Fourth Regiment Kentucky Volunteers, commanded by Colonel Robert Parker, in the war of eighteen hundred and twelve, and who was pensioned by special act of Congress in eighteen hundred and fifty-five, shall be allowed a pension from the eighth day of January, eighteen hundred and fifteen, being the date of wounds received in battle at New Orleans, by which he was disabled, until the date of the act of Congress pensioning him in eighteen hundred and fifty-five; and that the arrears shalll be at the rate as the pension he now receives.

Figure 58. House of Representatives Bill 2593.

In each census from 1810 through 1860, Tarrance appears with his family in Sumner County. He is listed in the Sumner County Mortality Schedule as Larrince Kirby after he died in August 1880 of an abscess.

Lamb, William

A surprisingly large number of men answered the call to go to General Andrew Jackson's aid in New Orleans. One of those who answered was William Lamb who became a Private in Captain John C. Dodds' Company, the 14th Regiment (Mitchusson) Kentucky Detached Militia. They rendezvoused at Russellville on 20 November 1814 and made the flatboat trip down the rivers to New Orleans. His regiment was in the force that opposed the British during the Battle of New Orleans (Chapter 8) and was still in that area until 28 February. They, like hundreds of others, began the walk back to Kentucky. He was mustered out on 20 May 1815.

William was born 5 Mar 1790 in North Carolina and moved to Allen County before he enlisted in the militia. After returning from the war, he was married to Sarah Wheat in Roane County, Tennessee, on 16 October 1827.

They were in Allen County in 1837 when William and seventeen others were given a task by the County Court. They were to keep the road "in repare (sic) 15 feet wide" between the portion of the Franklin Road between Trammel Creek and the end of Defeated Branch.[40] They lived in the Butlersville community in Allen County when the census taker came by in 1850. They had seven children at that time. He died on 31 Oct 1870 in Allen at the age of eighty (Figure 59).

Figure 59. William Lamb's grave marker.[41]

Lee, Henry

Henry Lee was the only soldier from the study area who was found to have served in the artillery. He was born in North Carolina in 1789. Henry and Elizabeth Cox Maddox were married on 10 September 1807 in Rutherford, North Carolina.

He joined the North Carolina Militia as a Private in Captain Thomas Boykin's Company of Artillerists in Major Cameron's Command. He also served in Captain David L. Evans' Company of Artillerists.

He began service on 24 July 1813 for an enlistment period of six months. During that time, he was at Camp Deep Water Point from 20 November to 31 December 1813. That was where present day South Port is located. The governor of North Carolina called up the Militia to provide coastal protection against a British invasion. The militia was hampered by bad weather, shortages, inadequate shelter, and lack of medicine (Chapter 7). He was discharged on 19 January 1814 at the end of his term of enlistment.

Henry and Elizabeth moved to Barren County, Kentucky, after the war. Elizabeth died in 1850 and Henry was married to Malinda Lemons in 1852 in Allen County, Kentucky.

Henry received a bounty land award (#39961) on 2 January 1854 under the Act of 1850 for 80 acres in Jefferson County, Illinois. The patentee was Eada Lee, identified as his widow. Genealogists agree that Henry's wife Elizabeth died in 1850. The patentee's relationship was not discovered. Henry died in 1855.

Lee, Stephen

Stephen Lee was born in Virginia about 1781. He and Sarah were married in Washington County, Kentucky, on 1 September 1804. He was in Madison County when he enlisted as a Private in the militia on 18 September 1812. He was in Captain Robert A. Sturgis' Company of Lieutenant Colonel Samuel South's 5th Kentucky Mounted Volunteer Militia. He provided his horse, saddle, bridle, powder horn, tomahawk, and scalp knife (Figure 60). Scalping knives were not just for Indians. The word also referred to the knife that we would call a skinning knife.

During the research of John Burton (see an earlier entry in this Chapter), a letter was discovered that was written by an attorney in Scottsville. In a letter to the Pension Office in Washington regarding John Burton, the attorney inquired about four others who had not yet received a reply to their applications. One

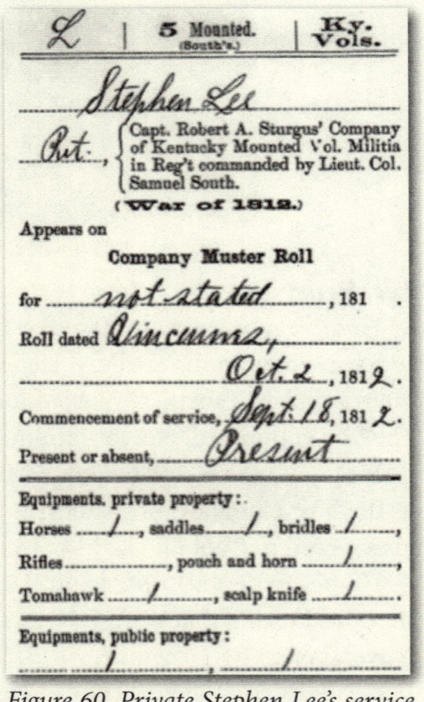
L | 5 Mounted. (South's.) | Ky. Vols.

Stephen Lee

Pvt. | Capt. Robert A. Sturgus' Company of Kentucky Mounted Vol. Militia in Reg't commanded by Lieut. Col. Samuel South.

(War of 1812.)

Appears on

Company Muster Roll

for not stated, 181 .

Roll dated Vincennes, Oct. 2, 1812.

Commencement of service, Sept. 18, 1812.

Present or absent, Present

Equipments, private property:

Horses 1, saddles 1, bridles 1,

Rifles ...., pouch and horn 1,

Tomahawk 1, scalp knife 1.

Equipments, public property:

1, 1

Figure 60. Private Stephen Lee's service record entries made on 2 October 1812.

of those mentioned was Stephen Lee, and that mention prompted research to begin on his service. So far as can be found, Stephen was not a resident of Allen County at the date of the letter. That move must have occurred later.

The 1850 census listed a Stephen Lee whose occupations were as a miller and shoemaker, still working at age sixty-nine in Allen County. His wife Sarah was listed too.

A Stephen Lee received a bounty land warrant (#19870) on 1 July 1859 for 129.88 acres in Decatur County, Iowa, under the Act of 1855. Henry Skiles was the designated patentee for that land. The association of Stephen Lee the soldier to Stephen Lee the Allen Countian is tenuous, but was included for others to decide.

Long, Benjamin

Some soldiers left meager historical records that gave only brief glimpses of their lives. One of those was Private Benjamin Long. His military record consisted of only one entry. It listed him as a substitute for Austin Baker in Captain William Berryman's Company of the 11th Regiment (Caldwell) Kentucky Militia (Figure 61).

His service record leaves the dates blank. Other soldiers' records proved that the trip to Greensburg was made just as the record indicated. It seems likely that he substituted, but was not called to active duty. Consistent with that presumption was the absence of other service records and bounty land claims.

Genealogical records

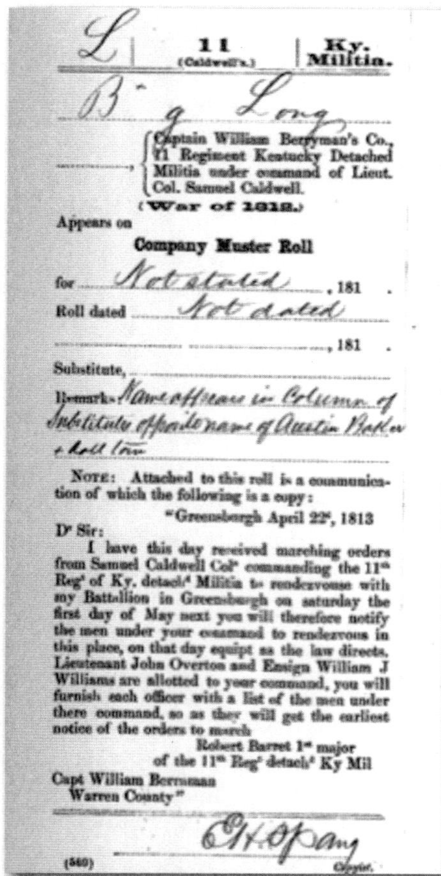

L | 11 (Caldwell's.) | Ky. Militia.

B. g Long

Captain William Berryman's Co., 11 Regiment Kentucky Detached Militia under command of Lieut. Col. Samuel Caldwell.

(War of 1812.)

Appears on

Company Muster Roll

for Not stated, 181 .

Roll dated Not dated

, 181 .

Substitute,

Remarks: Name appears in Column of Substitute opposite name of Austin Baker & roll torn

NOTE: Attached to this roll is a communication of which the following is a copy:

"Greensburgh April 22d, 1813

Dr Sir:

I have this day received marching orders from Samuel Caldwell Col. commanding the 11th Regt of Ky. detachd Militia to rendezvouse with my Battallion in Greensburgh on saturday the first day of May next you will therefore notify the men under your command to rendezvous in this place, on that day equipt as the law directs, Lieutenant John Overton and Ensign William J Williams are allotted to your command, you will furnish each officer with a list of the men under there command, so as they will get the earliest notice of the orders to march

Robert Barret 1st major of the 11th Regt detachd Ky Mil

Capt William Berrsman Warren County"

(560) Copyist.

Figure 61. Benjamin Long's service record.

showed that he was born in 1789 Culpeper County, Virginia. Those records include his marriage to Sarah (Polly) Eddins in Franklin, Kentucky, on 25 June 1811.

Benjamin was on the Allen County Tax rolls for 1815-1839 and was counted in the Allen County Census of 1820. He was mentioned in the Allen County Court's Day Book in 1830 as living near "the sulphur lick." That may have referred to what is now called Sulphur Creek located between the communities of Halifax and Settle. He and his wife were still in Allen County for the 1850 census, both at age eighty-one. His occupation was listed as a farmer. He died on 21 August 1857.

Low, Richard

No genealogical or census records were discovered for Richard Low (or Lowe) in Kentucky. Richard is included here because of an entry on his service record that stated that he substituted for Henry Lee. The Henry Lee (This Chapter) in the study area could have been that one. That connection could not be confirmed, but Richard is included here because of that possibility.

Richard was a Private in Captain John Farmer's Company of the 15th Regiment (Slaughter) Kentucky Militia. He served from 10 November 1814 through 10 May 1815. He was with them during the Battle of New Orleans in January (Chapter 8).

Mannon, Abel

Sergeant Abel Mannon's surname was spelled Mannon in his service records, but was spelled Manion in most other documents. His first name was spelled Able in some of them.

Abel was on the rolls of the Hudspeth and Brown's Regiment and on the rolls of the 11th Regiment (Caldwell) Kentucky Militia. On both of those rolls, he appeared in Captain William Berryman's Company.

Abel was born on 12 October 1894 in North Carolina. He was in what is now Allen County before 1812 in time for his entry into service. After the war, he and Rebecca Pitchford were married on 14 April 1818 in Allen County. They were recorded in the 1830 census, but apparently moved soon thereafter to Illinois.

They obtained land in Illinois in 1831, but he did not live long enough to receive a pension or bounty land. He died in Fayette County, Illinois, on 20 May 1835.

Martin, Peter

Private Peter Martin was the first of four men from the study area who died while on active duty during the War of 1812. He was born in Philadelphia, Pennsylvania, about 1768. His widow was born Mary Dunn in Middlesex County, New Jersey, on 13 June 1770. She moved with her father to Virginia about 1788 when she was about eighteen. She was married to Peter in 1791, and moved with him to Allen County about 1810.[42] The 1810 census of Warren County listed Peter, his wife, and seven children.

Peter enlisted in the 39th U.S. Infantry Regiment, a regular Army unit, on 4 October 1813 in Gallatin, Tennessee, for a term of one year. He was forty-five years old when he joined the regiment on 10 October, probably in Nashville. He was assigned to Captain John Jones' Company, a unit that included James Durham from the study area. James lived in the disputed area south of the Walker Line (Chapter 12) and that suggested that Peter might have lived in or near that area too. Unit records state that the soldiers in the 39th were recruited in Tennessee.

The 39th marched southward, and on 6 March 1814 stopped at Fort Strother in what later became Alabama. General Andrew Jackson considered regular Army soldiers to be more disciplined than the militiamen and would be more apt to stand their ground in battle. Therefore, Peter's company was placed in the middle of line as the assault began in the Battle of Horseshoe Bend (Chapter 5). His company was engaged in fierce combat that resulted in one of his comrades being killed in action and another ten being wounded.[43]

After Horseshoe Bend, the 39th marched to Mobile in what is now southern Alabama. There Peter's company joined the force General Jackson was putting together to attack and drive the Spanish out of Pensacola. Peter's enlistment was completed on 4 October, and one may presume that he was discharged on that date. Mary, his widow, reported that he had died two days later from a disease, about a month before the action at Pensacola on 7 to 9 November 1814.

Mary was listed as the head of household on the 1820 census of Allen County with seven children living in her household. She filed for a Widow's Pension from Simpson County on 22 August 1853. That application was approved and a certificate issued (#5347) according to the "old war" pension file. She drew $3.50 per month, half of Peter's monthly pay, commencing on 3 February 1853.

She was granted bounty land for Peter's service under the Act of 1850. On 10 September 1853 she received a warrant (#22008) that provided 160 acres in Edgar County, Illinois. She, as patentee, assigned the land to Hiram Sandford.

Mary managed to rear their seven children. She died in Simpson County on 27 January 1859, and was buried in Mt. Pleasant Cemetery.

McCallister, James

The service record for some soldiers was the earliest reference to them in official records. Such was the case with James McCallister; his surname was sometimes spelled McCalister or McCollister.

His service records showed that he was a 1st Corporal in William Berryman's Company of the 11th Regiment (Williams) Kentucky Mounted Volunteer Militia. He was mustered in on 31 August 1813 and served until 13 November 1813 when he was discharged at Limestone (now Maysville). He was a member of the Regiment that made the trip to Canada and fought at the Battle of the Thames (Chapter 6). He was paid $27.74 for his service and $34.00 for the use of his horse.

He appeared on the first tax rolls of Allen County in 1815, but was listed without property. He had acquired 55 acres by 1837, and had increased that holding in 1838 to 70 acres in the Difficult Creek watershed.

He and Pricilla Hood were married in Allen County on 17 April 1825. She was born in Allen County, Kentucky, in 1809.

James was an active member of the community. In 1827, the County Court appointed him and others to view the road from South Court Street to the base of the first hill on the south side of the branch flowing from the public spring. They were to recommend an alteration of the road to the west for a road to Caro. Caro may be shorthand reference to the Carolina District in the Allen Springs area.

The 1850 census listed him, his wife, and five children living in Allen County. It also listed Virginia as his state of birth, born there about 1785.

McElroy, John

John McElroy (also spelled McIlroy) was born in South Carolina in 1876, according to genealogical and census records. The next mention of him was on the militia rolls as having acquired William Bowling as his substitute on 12 September 1812. John apparently did not serve on active duty during the War of 1812.

He was listed on the 1815 tax as having 100 acres in the Trammel Fork Creek watershed.

John and Ellender Bright, also a South Carolinian, were wed in Allen County, Kentucky, on 12 July 1819. They appeared on the 1820 census there.

They next appeared on the 1840 census in Pulaski County, Missouri. He received a land certificate #1908, not a bounty grant, to 40 acres in Pulaski County, Missouri. The land was purchased on 10 April 1843, and was from Act of 24 April 1820, "An Act making further provision for the sale of Public Lands" with the land office in Springfield, Missouri.

On the 1850 census, John and Ellender were residents of Laclede, Missouri. He was appointed as the U.S. postmaster at Logan in Laclede County on 21 January 1851. He died there on 1 January 1861.

Meador, Allen

It was not unusual for brothers to join the state militias together. The Meador family had three sons who enlisted. Their surname had several phonetic variants among which were Meader, Meder, and Meadow, all rhyming phonetically. In those days, words ending with "ow " such as meadow, window, pillow, and hollow were pronounced as if they ended with "er."

Allen Meador enlisted in Captain Elijah Haynie's Company of the 3rd Regiment (Raulston) West Tennessee Militia at Nashville on 13 November 1814 for a period of six months. His brother William was in the same company and regiment. His brother Eli served in Colonel Copeland's 3rd Regiment of Tennessee Militia.

Allen, his company, and regiment went to New Orleans as part of Major General Carroll's division. They were involved in two actions. They saw combat on 28 December 1814 in a major engagement, and were in the famous battle of 8 January 1815. On that fateful day, his company was at the very focus of that British attack, and suffered two of the few American casualties that were incurred on that day (Chapter 8). He was mustered out on 13 May 1815 after the long walk home from New Orleans and was paid $48.00 for those six months of service.

Allen was about twenty-six years old when he was married to Mary (Polly) Waggoner in Allen County on 1 April 1817. They lived there when the 1820 census was taken. He appeared on the tax records as having 60 acres on Trammel Creek from 1818 through 1833.

He was awarded a bounty land warrant (#26020) on 2 January 1854 for 80 acres in Jefferson County, Illinois, under the Act of 1850. He was listed as the patentee as well. He received a second bounty land warrant (#15939) on 2 February 1863 under the Act of 1855 for an additional 80 acres located in Washington County, Missouri. The patentee for that land was recorded as Joseph W. Harfner.

Meador, Asa

John Conner, an antique dealer from Allen County, recently found a crumpled and stained newspaper clipping that described the service of Asa Meadow (sic) during the War of 1812. The newspaper and its date were not indicated, but it was valuable nonetheless because research had not discovered Asa's service.

Asa Meador, also spelled Meadow, was born on 12 August 1790 on Long Creek in what many years later became Macon County, Tennessee, but was at that time still in North Carolina.

Asa served in Captain Anthony Metcalf's Company in Colonel Thomas McCrory's 2nd Regiment of the West Tennessee Militia. He was one of the three-month enlistees who were mustered in at Franklin, Tennessee. They fought in the Battle of Talladega on 9 November 1813. After the battle, they returned to Fort Strother in what later became Alabama. Their three-month enlistment was completed and General Jackson tried to persuade them to serve until replacement troops arrived. Only one company agreed to do so. The other seven companies, including Asa's, chose not to continue, and returned.

Tennessee marriage records show Arrey (sic) Meador was married to Elizabeth Clybourn (also elsewhere spelled Clybourn and Claiborne) in Sumner County, Tennessee, on 29 December 1816. She was under age, and required her parent George Clybourn's permission.

Asa bought 60 acres of land on Long Creek on 25 June 1824, and paid twelve cents per acre to Sumner County for it. In the 1830 census, they lived in Sumner County near to several other members of the Meador family. They moved to Simpson County, Kentucky, and lived on Sinking Creek near Stevenson Church. The 1860 census listed them living there with their post office listed as Franklin and his birthplace as Virginia.

Asa received a bounty land warrant (41396) on 7 January 1862 under the Act of 1855 for 120 acres in Vernon County, Missouri, for his service.

Asa died on 27 September 1870, and Elizabeth applied for a Widow's Pension (#11049). There was no record of her receiving it before her death.

Meador, Eli

Eli became a Private in Captain Allen Wilkerson's Company of the 3rd Regiment (Copeland) of the Tennessee Militia. That was not the regiment that his brothers Allen and William were in. He was mustered in at Fayetteville, Tennessee, on 28 January 1814. He served until he was mustered out on 26 May 1814. During his service, he travelled 240 miles round trip from Smith County, Tennessee, to Fayetteville, Tennessee, and returned. He was paid a total of $33.82 for that period. Of course, he was not given travel pay for his march from Fayetteville to the Battle of Horseshoe Bend (Chapter 5) because that occurred after he had been mustered in.

His discharge paper (Figure 62), certified by his company commander Captain Allen Wilkerson, confirmed that he served in the 3rd Regiment under the command of Major General Jackson in the campaign against the Creek. Many of the men in Eli's regiment were from Smith County. Eli saw action at Horseshoe Bend and his company had casualties in that battle.

Eli was born in Bedford County, Virginia, in 1789. He moved to Smith County, Tennessee, where he and Sarah Turner were married on 31 August 1807. She was also a Virginian. They later purchased land on Drake's Creek in Sumner County.

He and his wife and three children appear in the Sumner County census of 1840. That same year, they moved to Allen County, near "Meadorville" as it was identified. It was not clear if that was the community now known as Meador or a reference to another area where a collection of the Meador family members lived.

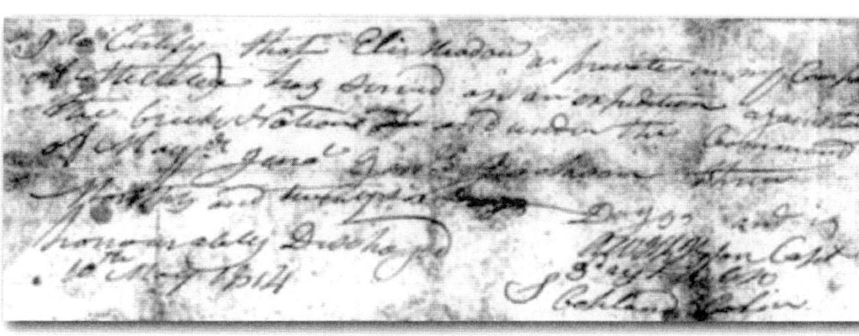

Figure 62. Eli Meador's (Meadow) discharge paper dated 10 May 1814.

Eli died in Allen County on 10 January 1847. His widow Sarah filed for a bounty land award under the Act of 1855 and it was approved (#55673) on 2 July 1869 for 162.64 acres in Douglas County, Nebraska. She assigned the land to Thomas Waller. Sarah still lived in Allen County in 1879 at the age of eighty-one.

Meador, William

The oldest of the three Meador (also spelled Meadow and Meadows) brothers who served during the War of 1812 was William. He was born on 26 April 1785 in Franklin County, Virginia.

William enlisted in Captain Elijah Haynie's Company of the 3rd Regiment (Raulston) West Tennessee Militia Infantry at Nashville on 13 November 1814, the same company as his brother Allen. His brother Eli had completed his service, and was back home by then. William must have heard the stories from Eli about his combat against the Creek. Clearly, William knew what lay ahead as he enlisted for six months. His regiment went to New Orleans and was part of Major General Carroll's Division. His company saw action on 28 December, just a few days after their arrival. On the day of the big battle, 8 January 1815, they were in the middle of the line absorbing the full pressure of the British (Chapter 8). He was mustered out on 13 May 1815.

He received a bounty land warrant (#28920) on 1 November 1853 for 80 acres under the Act of 1850 that was located in Jefferson County, Illinois. He assigned the land to patentee John W. Hall. A second warrant (#19642) was issued on 1 April 1859 under the Act of 1855. It was for an additional 80 acres located in Marathon County, Wisconsin. He eventually assigned that land to George J. Goodhue.

The genealogical records from Macon County, Tennessee, listed William Meador's wife as Mary Turner. Their marriage was on 30 November 1809 in Sumner County, Tennessee. His death date was recorded as 16 September 1856.

Merrifield, Samuel

The connection of Samuel Merrifield (also spelled Merryfield) to the study area was uncertain. He substituted for Nathanial Shipley according to his service records. How and why that came about was not discovered. Nathaniel lived in Allen County, but Samuel's location at that time could not be confirmed.

The only certain information was that Samuel Merrifield was a Private in the 3rd Regiment (Miller) Kentucky Militia in Captain Henry Yeakey's Company. Twelve others from the study area served in this regiment that saw action in the Second Battle of Tippecanoe, sometimes called the Battle of Wild Cat Creek (Chapter 3).

Samuel commenced service on 1 September 1812 and was discharged on 25 December 1812 at Hardinsburg along with the others in his regiment. He received $25.33 for his service.

Samuel's wife Frances filed (#5284) for and received (#3569) a Widow's Pension from Hardin County where they lived. They were married on 15 December 1814 in Nelson County, Kentucky.

On 15 December 1859, Samuel received a bounty land warrant (#51920) for 160 acres of land in Hickory County, Missouri under the Act of 1855. The patentee was Ludwell McKay.

Miflin, Armstrong

There were frequent interactions of people who lived in counties that were contiguous to or near their state boundaries. That was particularly true during the early days of settlement in the Kentucky-Tennessee frontier. Armstrong Miflin (also spelled Mifflin, Miflen, and Maflin) was born about 1794 in Washington County, Virginia. He became a soldier in the Kentucky militia as a Private in Captain William Berryman's Company of Hudspeth and Brown's Regiment. He was absent on 6 March 1813 when its roll was called. He appeared on the roll of the 11th Regiment (Caldwell) Kentucky Detached Militia when it rendezvoused at Greensburg on 1 May 1813.

Armstrong married Mary (Polly) Howard in Allen County on 13 April 1819 according to marriage records. She was born in Barren County that bordered Sumner County, Tennessee, in those days, perhaps in an area that later became Allen County. They lived in Sumner County in 1820, but soon moved to Gibson County.

Miller, Morris

The basic rationale for a state Militia was to enroll men who would be ready to deploy whenever the need arose. Most often, men were selected from their regimental roster to serve short periods in a detachment formed for a specific need. Private Morris Miller was an example. He was on the rolls of Hudspeth and Brown's Regiment on 6 March

1813 when its roll was called. He appeared on the roll of the 11th Regiment (Caldwell) Kentucky Detached Militia when it was ordered to rendezvous at Greensburg on Saturday, 1 May 1813. He was in Captain William Berryman's Company on each of those occasions.

When the call came to assist in the defense of New Orleans, he was detached to serve in Captain Thomas Griffin's Company of the 14th Regiment (Mitchusson) Kentucky Detached Militia. He was mustered in on 20 November 1814, was in Camp Jackson in Louisiana from 31 December to 28 February, and was mustered out at Russellville, Kentucky, on 20 May 1815. He was present at the Battle of New Orleans (Chapter 8).

Genealogists accept that he and Catherine Boren were married in Sumner County, Tennessee, on 20 August 1811. They probably lived in the New Roe area of Allen County near Borens Ford and Sulphur Fork Creek that forms the border between southwest Allen and southeast Simpson Counties.

They owned 40 acres on Sulphur Fork Creek in Allen County that was surveyed on 22 January 1819.

The census taker in 1820 recorded Armstrong living in Allen County with eleven people in his household. In 1830, he was in Simpson County. He made an unusual move afterward, at least in an unusual direction. He disappeared from Kentucky and Tennessee, and appeared in the censuses from 1840 through 1870 in Claiborne Parish, Louisiana. The 1840 census had the same distribution of ages in the family as in 1830. In 1850, he was identified as a planter living with five children ranging in age from twelve to twenty-two, each of them born in Kentucky. The consensus of genealogists accepts that he was the same Morris Miller, but there were no explanations of the reason for his move. He died in Louisiana in August 1872.

Miller, Samuel

The 1800 census of Spartanburg County, South Carolina, counted Samuel Miller as a head of household and that could mean that had been born there.

He joined as a Private in Captain Thomas Griffin's Company of the 14th Regiment (Mitchusson) Kentucky Detached Militia on 20 November 1814, was in Camp Jackson in Louisiana 31 December to 28 February, and was discharged at Russellville, Kentucky, on 20 May

1815. He was present at the Battle of New Orleans (Chapter 8), and made the long trek back home afterward.

Samuel was in Allen County, Kentucky, censuses of 1820 and 1830. In 1840, the census taker recorded him as living east of the Barren River in Barren County with just two in his household. He was in Barren County again in 1850 with his wife Nancy.

According to the Allen County Deed book B, page 105, he appointed John Wales of Allen County as his attorney to receive whatever pay was due from his service. There was no evidence of a pension application or bounty land award for that service.

He had a bounty land warrant (#17757) issued 2 January 1854 under the Act of 1850 for 86.7 acres in Hamilton County, Illinois. The patentee was Noah Boyd. He also received bounty land under the Act of 1855 that was a warrant (#22232) issued on 1 April 1859 for 80 acres in Hancock County, Iowa. The patentee for that land was Ezra R. Butler.

Miller, William

Service records show that Private William Miller was in Captain Robert Smith's Company of the 14th Regiment (Mitchusson) Kentucky Detached Militia on 20 November 1814. He deployed with his unit and was in Camp Jackson in New Orleans from 31 December to 28 February, and was mustered out at Russellville, Kentucky, on 20 May 1815. He was present during the Battle of New Orleans (Chapter 8), and walked home afterward.

There was a William Miller who was born in Virginia about 1797. He was listed in the Allen County censuses 1860. At that time, he resided with his wife Eliza in the Scottsville District. It seems likely that he was the War of 1812 soldier, but that could not be confirmed with certainty.

There was no evidence that William ever applied for a pension application or received an award of bounty land.

Mitchell, Thompson

Biographical, genealogical, and military information was limited or nonexistent for a few soldiers of the War of 1812. The book authored by Perrin, et al,[44] contained biographical history for a number of individuals from Allen County. That respected source stated that Thompson Mitchell, a native of Virginia, served in the War of 1812 as a waggoner (sic). It also stated that he died in Warren County, Kentucky. No service records, pension records, historical records, or genealogical records were found to substantiate the existence of that person with the given name Thompson in Virginia or Kentucky or of his service during the War of 1812.

Moody, Martin

Genealogical sources listed Franklin County, Virginia, as the place of Martin Moody's birth. The Reverend Henry Holstine performed the marriage ceremony for Martha Guthrie and Martin Moody on 16 October 1810. The ceremony was conducted at Elenor Guthrie's home in Botetourt County, Virginia. They subsequently moved to Kentucky before his call to duty came.

He became a Private in Captain John Evans' Company 15th Regiment (Slaughter) Kentucky Detached Militia in August 1814. His service record noted that he was a substitute for Henry Surber. He was enrolled in Somerset in Pulaski County with an enlistment for a period of six months. His service began on 10 November 1814. Gabriel Slaughter, the Regimental Commander, would find a prominent place in Kentucky's history and was elected to be Kentucky's lieutenant governor in 1816. He became governor when Governor George Madison died.

As the regiment readied for deployment to New Orleans, Lieutenant Colonel Slaughter had to raise funds to purchase the flatboats needed to transport his troops downriver. To further complicate matters, they arrived in New Orleans without arms for most of his soldiers. The citizens of the city rallied and provided guns for the men who did not have them. Martin participated in the Battle of New Orleans (Chapter 8,) and returned to Kentucky to be discharged in Somerset on 10 May 1815. He received $48.00 for his six months service.

Martin filed for a pension (#16613) on 12 February 1853 in Allen County at the age of sixty-five. He was a wheelwright at the time of his application. His was one of what are called the "Old War" records (Figure 63).

He made a bounty land claim under the Act of 1850 and was given a warrant (#49786) for 80 acres in Dodge County, Minnesota, on 1 April 1857. He assigned the land to patentee Cyrus Hethrington.

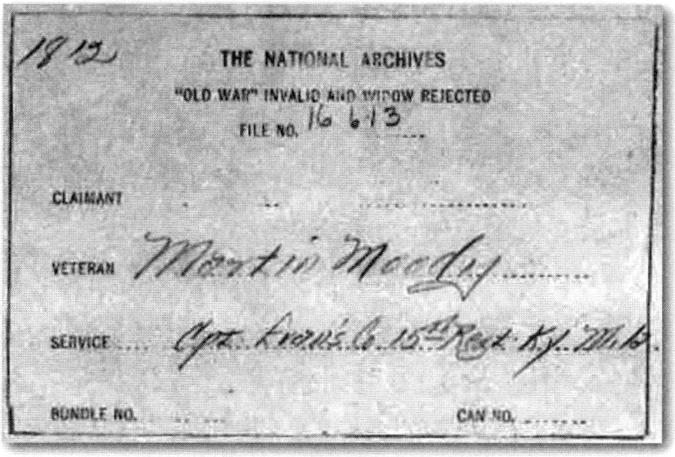
1812
THE NATIONAL ARCHIVES
"OLD WAR" INVALID AND WIDOW REJECTED
FILE NO. 16 613
CLAIMANT
VETERAN Martin Moody
SERVICE
BUNDLE NO.
CAN NO.

Figure 63. Martin Moody's Old War record.

Martin died in Allen County on 20 June 1858. He and his family were in the Allen County censuses in 1820, 1830, and 1850. They had six children. The oldest was born in Virginia in 1814, but the next five of their children were born in Allen County.

An additional bounty land warrant (#28912) for 99.76 acres in Vernon County, Missouri, was awarded on 10 December 1859 under the Act of 1855. The assigned patentee for that land was Edward O. Hawkins.

Martha filed for Widow's Pension (#5147) and received a pension certificate (#32029) dated 14 March 1872. She listed her post office as Scottsville, but noted that she lived eight miles away from there. She was 96 years old and lived with her son-in-law Enoch Buchannan at the time of the 1880 census.

Morrison, James S

The frontiersmen who lived in the study area used whichever post office was most convenient to them. There were no post offices located in what is now Allen County, Kentucky, when the War of 1812 began. Some of those who lived in what is now northwestern Allen County used the post office at Claypool that was located just over the boundary into what is now Warren County. James Sampson Morrison was one of those.

James, like most soldiers from the study area, was born elsewhere. He was born in Virginia in 1784. James S. Morrison and Susannah

Long were married in what was then Warren County, Kentucky, on 12 August 1807.

Private James Morrison was listed on the rolls of the 11th Regiment (Caldwell) Kentucky Militia as a substitute for Cater Drake. He was in Captain William Berryman's Company that rendezvoused at Greensburg on 1 May 1813. The records do not reveal that he ever entered active duty.

James Morrison was in Allen County with four children in the censuses of 1820, 1830, and 1840. In the 1850 census, he was sixty-six, Susan was sixty-three, and three children still resided with them.

James died on 8 September 1858 in Allen County. Susan and eight children carried on without him. She applied for a Widow's Pension (#36493) using Claypool as her address. In that submission, she stated that a bounty land warrant (#77139) had previously been awarded for his service. She said that the land bounty had been traded to a man in Evansville, Indiana, for a horse. That bounty land warrant had indeed been given under the Act of 1855 to James Morrison on 1 August 1860 for 160 acres in Coffee County, Kansas. That land was assigned to Renney Martindale. It appears that he was the previous owner of the horse.

In 1870, she was eighty-two, and was still using the post office located at Claypool. Susan lived to be ninety-three, but never received the pension she sought.

O'Neal, John

2nd Corporal John O'Neal was on the staff of Captain Thomas Griffin's Company in the 14th Regiment (Mitchusson) Kentucky Detached Militia when it was mustered in on 20 November 1814. He made the trip by flatboat to New Orleans, and was present when the roll was called on 31 December 1814. He was present at the Battle of New Orleans (Chapter 8), and stayed at Camp Jackson until 28 February 1815. He and the rest of the regiment were mustered out on 20 May 1815. He was about twenty years old when he was discharged. He was paid $60.00 for his six months of service

John O'Neal (also spelled O'Neale) was born in Virginia about 1795 and his parents were in Warren County in 1810. He was married to Martha (Patsey) Wilson on 11 July 1817 in Allen County Kentucky. She was a North Carolinian by birth. They were in the censuses for the years 1820 through 1840. In 1840, he was listed with a household that had a total of ten members. John and Patsey had five children counted in the 1830 and 1840 censuses.

John died about 1850 before the census was taken. In the 1860 census, Martha was living at New Roe in southwestern Allen County with three other people, enumerated only by the initials M. A., M. E., and J. R.

A bounty land warrant (#52014) was issued in his name on 1 May 1855 for 80 acres in Tama County, Iowa under the Act of 1850. The patentees were his three minor children: Lucinda, John P., and Sally Ann. A second bounty land warrant (#37789) was issued for another 80 acres in Harrison County, Missouri, on 1 Jan 1859 under the Act of 1855. That land also was assigned to his minor children Lucinda and John Patrick.

Oliver, William W

The discovery of information about each soldier in this study usually began with a name from an army unit roster, but it did not always happen that way. An example of an exception was a letter that was written by a Scottsville lawyer in behalf of John Burton, a soldier who was the intended object of research (see earlier in this Chapter). In that letter, the lawyer asked about the status of Burton's pension request. The lawyer then included one sentence that asked the U.S. Pension Office about the status of three other applications. One of those mentioned was William Oliver, an Allen Countian. It was an unexpected discovery. Research at that point had not yet discovered that he was in the War of 1812.

Private William W. Oliver was born about 1796 in Caroline County in Virginia. After the War of 1812 ended, he was married to Susan Peers (also spelled Purrs and Pierce) on 24 December 1818 in Henrico County, Virginia. They had moved to Allen County, Kentucky, before the 1820 census was taken.

He filed for a pension (#30440) based on his service in Captain Benjamin Goode's Company of the Colonel John Ambler's 2nd Virginia Regiment. That unit was first on active duty from 18 to 30 March 1813, 26 to 28 June, and 30 June to 2 July 1813. They rendezvoused at Chesterfield for a threat of British movement up the James River. They were discharged when that threat did not develop. They deployed again from 28 August to 30 November 1814 to the area near Richmond.

William Oliver resided in Allen County in 1820. He was listed as a fifty-six year old farmer in 1850 with three children, Wilson age twenty-one, Thomas Jefferson age nineteen, and C. E. (Caroline) age sixteen. He died in Allen County 1868 at age of seventy. Susan subsequently filed (#39539) for a Widow's Pension.

Owens, Obadiah

A lawyer in Scottsville was writing to the Pension Office about a pension for John Burton (see earlier this Chapter). In that letter, the lawyer asked about the status of a pension request that had been filed by Obadiah Owens. Obadiah lived in Allen County, Kentucky, and appeared on the tax rolls from 1815 to 1838. A search of the National Archives found no pension request, approval, or disapproval by that name. Neither could Obadiah Owens be precisely located in family histories or genealogical collections. However, Obadiah was in the 1810 and 1820 censuses for Warren County, and in the 1830 and 1840 censuses for Allen County.

The 1850 census was the first to record names and other information about each member of the household. It was also the first to include the individuals" birthplaces. It recorded Obediah as a farmer living in Warren County with a younger Owens couple who had two small children living in his household. Obadiah's birthplace was listed as Virginia. The National Archives had only two service records from the War of 1812 for men with the name Obadiah Owens, one from South Carolina and one from Virginia. Therefore, it was concluded that the Virginian soldier Obadiah and the Allen/Warren County Obadiah were the same man.

Obadiah began his service on 5 July 1813 as a Private in Captain Francis Moore's Company of Riflemen attached to the 5th Regiment Virginia Militia that was then commanded by Lieutenant Colonel Armistead T. Mason. That regiment was sent to defend Norfolk and his service record states that they were encamped in the rear of Fort Norfolk. He served there until 21 December when he was discharged.

On 1 August 1818, Thomas and Obey Owens appeared before the Warren County Court to petition for construction of a mill site on Buck Creek.[45] There were two brothers, Thomas and Obadiah, living in Allen County who may have been those mentioned.

Obadiah received a bounty land warrant (#22424) on 15 April 1853 for 80 acres in Martin County, Indiana, under the Act of 1850. The land was assigned to patentee Samuel Baugh.

In 1860, Obadiah was living with his son Coleman in the Carolina District of Allen County. He was working as a shingle maker at age seventy-two. That was the last mention of him in the historical records.

Patton, William

William Patton was born in Virginia on 8 June 1793 and was about twenty years old when he became a Private in the militia, left Allen County, Kentucky, and rode his horse to the rendezvous of his regiment at Newport Barracks across the river from Cincinnati. He was listed in rolls of Captain William Berryman's Company of the 11th Regiment (Williams) Kentucky Detached Militia. After the rendezvous, they rode northward to Lake Erie, went into Canada, fought the Battle of the Thames (Chapter 6), and returned home. He was mustered out at Limestone (now Maysville) on 13 November 1813. He was paid $70 for his lost horse. There was no explanation as to where, when, and why the horse was lost. It most likely that the word "lost" meant that it died. It was a long and strenuous journey that did result in horse deaths.

He and Letitia Spilman were married on 2 October 1818 in Allen County. She was born on Difficult Creek, in what was then Warren County), on 28 May 1800. They eventually had thirteen children, eleven of whom were still at home in 1850.

On 5 April 1855, William was awarded a bounty land warrant (#14598) for 40 acres in Jasper County, Missouri, under the Act of 1850. The patentee was Daniel Hunt. William received another bounty land warrant (#64186) on 10 December 1859 for 120 acres in Benton County, Missouri. Letitia became the patentee and she assigned the land to George Sutton.

William was listed as a farmer in the 1860 census. Letitia died on 16 February 1865 and William died on 14 December 1867, both in the Gainesville area of Allen County.

Pardue, Jesse

The threat from the British to the citizens of Virginia was real and increased when they declared a blockade off the coast of Virginia on 26 December 1812. Tensions remained high as they captured or sank ships attempting to reach the Virginia coastline. The threat became a reality when the British attempted to take Craney Island near Norfolk on 22 June 1813. Other military actions followed. In response, Jesse

Pardue (other spellings were Pardew, Perdue, Purdue, Pirdue, and Perdew) received the call to duty on 1 September 1813.

Jesse served as a Private in Captain William Pepper's Company of riflemen in the 4th Regiment (Kountz) Virginia Militia beginning on 16 October 1813. That unit was formed in Montgomery County, and moved to Fort Norfolk in March. His six-month tour ended on 10 March 1814. His official rank was "musician," a rank that included trumpeters, drummers, and fifers. Jesse was a fifer who relayed commands using signature musical phrases or rhythms.

He was mutilated, as he described it, in an accident during his tour, but he did not detail the specific nature of the injury. His disability papers were prepared at Norfolk, and stated that he was a "cripple" who was physically disabled and unfit for further service on 3 November 1814 (Figure 64).

Jesse and Lydia Blankenship were married at Hezekiah Blankenship's home in Franklin County, Virginia, on 20 December 1815. They and their children came to Allen County, Kentucky, and he was on the tax list of 1815 with 200 acres in the Puncheon Creek drainage area. They had seven children listed in 1830 census, and nine listed in 1840.

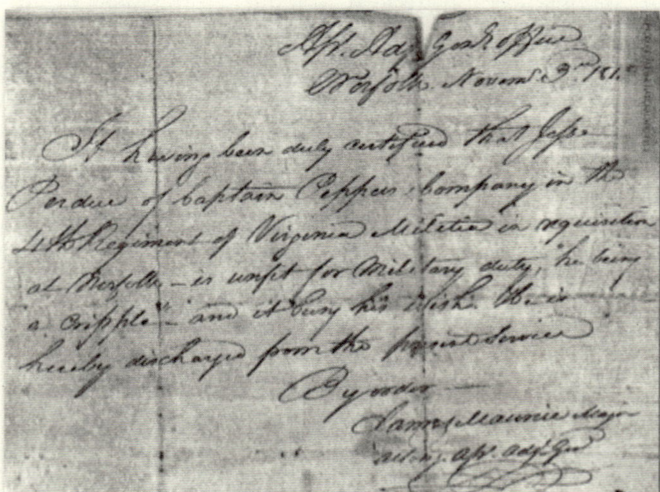

Ajt. Adj. Genl. Office
Norfolk Novem 3rd 1814

It having been duly certified that Jesse Perdue of Captain Peppers Company in the 4th Regiment of Virginia Militia in requisition at Norfolk — is unfit for Military duty, he being a Cripple — and it being his wish. He is hereby discharged from the present Service

By order —
James [illegible] Major
Actg. Ajt. Adj. Genl

Figure 64. Declaration of disability for Jesse Pardue.

He appeared before the Allen County Court on 4 February 1851 to file a claim for bounty land being provided to War of 1812 veterans. He was issued a warrant (#22154) on 15 April 1853 for 80 acres in Marion

County, Illinois under the Act of 1850. The patentee was Benjamin A. Morgan. Under the Act of 1855, he received a warrant (#14090) for an additional 80 acres in Fremont County, Iowa. The patentee for those acres was Christopher M. Johnson.

Jesse and Lydia still lived in the Puncheon area in the 1860 and 1870 censuses. Jesse used the post office at Fountain Run in Monroe County, but he actually resided in Allen County when he made his claim (#15801) on 15 May 1871 for a Survivor's Pension. He was then seventy-eight years old. He was approved for a pension by a certificate (#10055) dated 23 December 1871.

Lydia passed away before the 1880 census. In it, Jesse was listed as an eighty-six year old widower living with R.H. Pardue in Macon County, Tennessee.

Petty, James

Six foot one inch tall with a dark complexion, dark hair, and blue eyes. That was how his widow Lucinda lovingly remembered James Petty twenty-one years after he died on 25 April 1862. She submitted an application (#30751) for a Widow's Pension and included that description. Her application was not immediately successful in obtaining approval. At every turn, the process was stymied by requests for clarifications and for acquisition and substantiation of additional proofs. Her file grew to forty-eight pages of documentation by the time she finally received a pension certificate (#30378). Her pension of $8.00 per month was sent to her post office in Gainesville in Allen County in 1883.

James Petty (also spelled Pettie) was a Private in Captain John B. Royal's Company of John P. Richardson's Regiment of the Virginia Militia. The unit was formed in the area of Charlotte County, Virginia. He was discharged at Ellicott's Mills in Maryland at the same time and place as his friend William Weaver (see later this Chapter).

James and Lucinda Williams were married in Charlotte County, Virginia. She would have been about seventeen years old at that time. A minister, James Robinson, married them on 26 January 1815 (some say it was on 30 January). They lived there until the early part of 1820, moved to Halifax County until 1826 when they moved to back to Charlotte County. They left there in 1843, and moved to Allen County, Kentucky.

James died in the Raleigh precinct near the Halifax community in Allen County on 25 April 1862. Lucinda received a bounty land warrant (#114548) for James' service on 20 June 1884 for 160 acres in Luce County, Michigan, under the Act of 1855. She assigned the land to Frederick E. Driggs.

Pruitt, Moses

Moses Pruitt was in the 1790 census in Spartanburg, South Carolina. He married Rachel there. He appeared in Greenville County, South Carolina, in the 1800 census. Moses and his son Abram were both counted in Warren County, Kentucky, and listed separately as heads of households in the 1810 census. The date of Moses' arrival in the study area was not documented, but must have been between 1800 and 1810.

At first glance, Moses seemed to be too old to be in the militia. He was forty-nine in 1813. He had a son named Moses who was twenty-seven in that year, a more likely soldier one would think. The younger Moses had already left Allen County, and was living in Vanderburgh County, Indiana, during the War of 1812. Confirming that fact were the birth records of his children who were born in that county in 1810, 1812, 1813, and 1815. The latter child was born on 5 October 1815. Soldier Moses was involved in the action before, during, and after the battle of New Orleans from November 1814 through his arrival back in Kentucky in May 1815. The soldier Moses, one concludes, was not Moses' the son. It was the elder Moses who was the soldier, and still living in Allen County.

Moses was a Private in the Hudspeth and Brown's Regiment when its roll was taken on 6 March 1813. He was also present when the 11th Regiment (Caldwell) Kentucky Militia rendezvoused in Greensburg on 1 May 1813. He was in Captain William Berryman's Company on each of those occasions.

The call for men to go to the aid of General Jackson apparently aroused his spirit too. He was mustered into Captain Thomas Griffin's Company of the 14th Regiment (Mitchusson) Kentucky Detached Militia on 20 November 1814. He was recorded at Jackson's Camp in New Orleans on 3 December, and was there until 28 February 1815, encompassing the time of the Battle of New Orleans (Chapter 8). The regiment was mustered out at Russellville on 20 May 1815.

Moses went to the Allen County Court Clerk on 2 October 1816, and appointed John Wills of Allen County as his attorney to collect whatever pay was due him for his service. He had earned $48.00 for his six-month service.

On 10 November 1851, a bounty land warrant (#7415) under Act of 1850 was issued for 80 acres in Montgomery County Illinois for his service in Captain Griffin's Company. The patentee was identified as his widow, Mary Pruitt, but that relationship seems unlikely. Some of the genealogy records showed his oldest daughter with the name Polly. Polly was a common and affectionate diminutive nickname for the given name Mary. She would seem to be the most likely Mary who was the beneficiary of his bounty land. In any case, the consensus of genealogists record the year of Moses' death as 1820 in Allen County.

There were several variations of Moses' surname that appeared in the historical documents, including Pruett, Prewitt, Prewit, and Pruet. And, to keep things interesting, there were several individuals who carried the name Moses Pruitt giving rise to inconsistencies in the genealogical record.

Pulliam, James G.

Genealogical information about the War of 1812 soldiers usually raised the level of understanding about their lives. But, that was not always the case. The information about James Graves Pulliam was frustratingly conflicting. There were many such conflicts within the first twenty results from a search of the public family trees at Ancestry.com. His birth date was listed as 18 January 1797, 18 January 1799, about 1792, about 1795, and about 1797. His marriage date was listed as 1 April 1813, 18 April 1816, and 29 March 1813. His death date was listed as unknown, before 1850, and 16 January 1868. Incorrect data are worse than no data at all.

Fortunately, the military service records for James and the pension files for his wife Sukey tell quite a story that the genealogists either failed to find or disregarded.

On 6 March 1813, Private James G. Pulliam appeared on the muster roll in Captain William Berryman's Company of Lieutenant Colonel George Hudspeth and Major Hugh Brown's Regiment of the Kentucky Militia, detached for six months service.

Rev. Jacob Lock, who was a Baptist minister in Barren County, performed the marriage of James G. Pulliam and Sukey Berry. Her name was actually a common affectionate nickname for her given name Sarah. The marriage ceremony was in her father's house on 1 April 1813, less than a month after James became a member of the Militia. On 22 April, the newlywed husband was called to rendezvous at Greensburg with the 11th Regiment (Caldwell) Kentucky Militia. He served from 27 April until 8 May during that episode.

James' next call was to become a member of Captain Thomas Griffin's Company of the 14th Regiment (Mitchusson) Kentucky Detached Militia. That time he was assigned with the rank of musician and duty as a drummer. The company commander communicated with his troop through his musician, James. The musician relayed the orders using patterned drumbeats. His unit was mustered in on 20 November 1814, and shortly thereafter loaded onto flatboats for the trip down the Cumberland, Ohio, and Mississippi Rivers to New Orleans. He was in New Orleans by 31 December, participated in the Battle of New Orleans (Chapter 8), and departed for home on 28 February 1815. He received $55.00 for his six months of duty.

James was in the Hart County, Kentucky, alone in the 1830 census, and Sukey was there in 1850 with three people named Pulliam of ages indicating that they were their children.

As a widow, Sukey received a bounty land warrant (#55186) for 80 acres in Brown County, Indiana, on 20 February 1857, under the Act of 1850. She assigned that land to Samuel Lotshar. She received a second bounty land warrant (#37606) under the Act of 1855 for 101 acres in Worth County, Missouri, on 1 November 1858. Susan was the patentee, and she assigned the land to Silas T. Green.

On 19 June 1872, Richard Griffin wrote an affidavit from Allen County that stated that he knew Sukey until she left Allen County about 1822. She used his statement when she filed a claim (#8937) for a Widow's Pension. She lived in Lafayette County, Missouri, when she filed her claim on 19 August 1872. She properly stated the details of James' military service in that application, and also stated that James died on 27 April 1838. The pension was approved (#3795) on 27 August 1872.

Her last contact with the pension office was in June 1883. She died on 27 August 1883 in Bluff City in Sumner County, Kansas. Sukey was ninety-four years old.

Pulliam, John

Private John Pulliam served in Captain Samuel Malone's Company with Privates Hudson Howell and John Johnson from the study area. They were in the 14th Regiment (Mitchusson) Kentucky Detached Militia that served from 20 November 1814 to 20 May 1815, and were at the Battle of New Orleans (Chapter 8). That much is fact, but other details are less certain.

The spelling of the surname was Pulliam in the record of his service, but difficulty arose from other documentation where it was also spelled Pullum, Pullam, Pullom, Pulham, and Poolam. For example, there was a John Pullom in the 14th Regiment serving in Captain Robert Smith's Company. He was in New Orleans when he died on 29 December 1814 at Camp Jackson. Genealogists have mistakenly attributed that Camp Jackson to the Fort Jackson in South Carolina of recent history, and further obfuscated the family trees by interchanging these two individuals and other John Pulliam's in the records.

According to some genealogical sources, John Pulliam was the brother of James G. Pulliam and was first married to Nancy Roundtree on 1 January 1807 in what was then Barren County. John's second wife was Elizabeth Blackwell to whom he was married on 27 November 1810 in Franklin County, Kentucky. He and his third wife, Nancy Caldwell, were married in Allen County on 29 November 1823. There were conflicting genealogical data about each of those marriages in almost every detail. It appeared as if the lives of two or three different men named John Pulliam were being combined in various permutations.

A John Pulliam was listed as the head of household in the Allen County censuses of 1820 and 1830. He died on 3 September 1840. The circumstantial evidence indicated that he probably was the War of 1812 soldier in Captain Malone's Company, although no incontrovertible evidence of that could be found.

Ragland, Benjamin

The frontier that became Allen County, Kentucky, was sparsely populated in the earliest days, and finding a minister or magistrate nearby was unlikely. However, love always finds a way. Benjamin Ragland (also spelled Raglin) and Elizabeth (Betsy) Shipley were married on 30 April 1808 in what was then Barren County. Benjamin was born in

1785 in Greene County, North Carolina, and Betsy was likely born in Barren County, Kentucky, about 1790.

Genealogical records say that they lived in Allen County in 1820 and moved to Stewart County, Tennessee, before 1850. He was living in the household of John Melton in Stewart County in that census.

There is no uncertainty in the military records that showed him as a Private in Captain Thomas Griffin's Company of the 14th Regiment (Mitchusson) Kentucky Detached Militia. He was mustered in on 20 November 1814, was in New Orleans on 31 December, was present at the Battle of New Orleans (Chapter 8), left there on 28 February 1815, and was mustered out on 20 May.

Benjamin received two bounty land warrants for that service. The first warrant (#54882) dated 1 April 1858 was under the Act of 1850, and was for 80 acres in Cedar County, Missouri. The land was assigned to patentee Clifton H. Moore. The second warrant (#20532) was issued on 1 July 1859 under Act of 1855 and was for 80 acres in Taylor County, Iowa. That patentee was John Fry.

Richards, Hiram

Most of the men from the study area who fought the Creek Indians (Chapter 5) during the War of 1812 were Tennesseans, but a few men from our local area also joined that effort. Hiram Richards was one of those. He was born on 23 April 1790 in Virginia, but was on the 1810 census of what was then Warren County. Beginning in 1820, he was listed in Allen County, and lived and farmed in the Butlersville community. It is likely that he lived there when he joined the militia.

Hiram became a Private for a one-year tour in Captain James McEwen's Company of the 2nd Regiment (Benton) Tennessee Volunteer Infantry on 10 December 1812. The men in that unit were mostly from middle Tennessee counties. They were assigned as part of General Jackson's army that marched to Natchez on a mission that was soon aborted (Chapter 4). Many of the men from that army reenlisted in September, and became part of Colonel William Pillow's command. Hiram was one of those.

The 2nd Regiment under Colonel Pillow marched from Fayetteville, Tennessee, to Huntsville and Fort Strother in the Alabama Territory, and participated in the first of Jackson's campaigns against the Creeks (Chapter 5). Hiram fought at Battle of Talladega on 9 November 1813, and returned to Fort Strother. Hiram served until he was discharged on 20 April 1814. As with other privates, he earned pay of $8.00 per month.

Hiram was born about 1791 in Virginia and his wife Sarah (Sally) Guy was a South Carolinian. They owned 100 acres of land in 1828 in the Trammel Fork Creek watershed. The acreage increased to 185 acres in 1838, and was valued for tax purposes at $1,060.00. The 1860 census reported them living in the Butlersville area.

He was awarded a bounty land warrant (#28195) under the Act of 1855 on 10 November 1859 with his surname spelled Richard. That award was for 80 acres in Butler County, Iowa. He assigned that land to John Organ. He was given a bounty land warrant (#11465) under the Act of 1850 for 80 acres in Mercer County, Illinois, on 1 September 1863. The patentee was Charles B. Waite.

Hiram died at his home in the Butlersville community on 17 November 1869 from dropsy, a heart disease.

Right, John

Private John Right was a listed as a substitute for Sion Cook on the roll of the 11th Regiment (Caldwell) Kentucky Militia. No service records were found and no indication that he served on what we would call active duty.

The name John Right was in the census of Allen County of l820 with a household of thirteen. He was assessed $1,000.00 for tax on 300 acres in the Middle Fork Creek watershed in 1828. No other information on a John Right was found.

The surname Right may have been a phonetic version of Wright. In all the other early tax records before and after 1828, the surname was entered as Wright. The name Wright was found in the Allen County Court's Day Book for example.

Rigsby, James

James Rigsby was born on 15 February 1793 in Wake County, North Carolina. He joined the Militia on 20 November 1814 from Allen County. He became a Private in Captain Thomas Griffin's Company of the 14th Regiment (Mitchusson) Kentucky Detached Militia.

He was mustered in on 20 Nov 1814 at Camp Hynes. That location was not specifically defined, but was sometimes mentioned as being near Nashville. It seems most likely that it was a rendezvous point on the Cumberland River for the trip to New Orleans. James was in New Orleans from 31 December 1814 to 28 February 1815, a period that includes the Battle of New Orleans (Chapter 8). He was mustered out on 20 May 1815.

On 14 December 1816, James appeared before the Allen County Court Clerk and appointed Anak Dawson of Allen County as his attorney to obtain whatever pay was due him from his service.

He married Sarah (Sally) Thompson on 27 October 1817 in Allen County, and they were in the 1820 census. Sometime later, they moved to Iowa, and appeared on the Davis County census of 1850 with James, Sarah, and their five children. From their ages and birthplaces, there must have been an extended stay in Missouri along the way to Iowa. None of the children were born in Kentucky. The four oldest were born in Missouri between 1832 and 1838, and the youngest was born in Iowa in 1841.

The stop in Missouri may have been related to bounty land that James received. The first was a warrant (#15765) issued on 9 January 1854 for 80 acres in Schuyler County, Missouri. There was no indication that he disposed of this property. The second warrant (#16129) on 1 May 1860 was under the Act of 1855 and for 80 acres in Fremont County, Iowa. The patentee was Patrick Rigsby.

Rigsby, John

Genealogists wrote that John Rigsby (also spelled Regsby and Regsbey) was born about 1787 in Wake County North Carolina, and he appeared there in the 1800 census.

John was Private in Captain Thomas Griffin's Company of the 14th Regiment (Mitchusson) Kentucky Detached Militia that was formed to support General Jackson in New Orleans. Muster was on 20 November 1814 followed by the trip down the Cumberland, Ohio, and Mississippi Rivers. He was at the Battle of New Orleans (Chapter 8), and made it home to muster out on 20 May 1815.

He was in Allen County in 1820 with a household of eight individuals. Only two of those were over 25 years old. It also counted three children. They were all designated as foreigners, the census way of describing those foreign born who had not been naturalized. He appeared on the l825 tax list with two tracts, one of 60 acres and another of 107 acres, both in the Bays Fork Creek Watershed.

John twice received bounty land for his service. The first was a warrant (#15979) on 9 January 1854 under the Act of 1850 for 80 acres in Putnam/Schuyler Counties, Missouri. The patentee was Perrin Bryant. The second warrant (#43543), under the Act of 1855, was issued on 1 August 1860. It was for 69.27 acres in Lyon County, Kansas. The patentee assigned for that land was James W. Eubank.

Ritchie, George

George Ritchie (also spelled Ritchey) was the owner of four lots in the Plat Map of the new town of Scottsville as of 22 January 1816.[46] One was the second lot on the east side of North Court Street north of East Cherry Street, the second was about where the park is now on East Main beside the US Bank, the third was on the southwest corner North 2nd and East Cherry Streets, and the fourth was the entire block between East Maple and East Locust that lies West of Holland Road.

George was a Private on the roll of the Hudspeth and Brown Regiment detached for service on 6 March 1813. He was also on the 11th Regiment (Caldwell) Kentucky Militia. No records were discovered that would suggest that he served on active duty.

Genealogical data were not helpful in learning more about him. That seemed strange because his property purchases make him seem like a prominent man in the community.

Roark, Asa

Asa Roark was born in North Carolina about 1787. He and Susan Tudor were married in 1806 according to genealogical records. The first of fourteen children was born in what is now Macon County, Tennessee, in 1808. Two other children were born before Asa heard and answered his country's call to duty.

He became a 2nd Sergeant in Captain Elijah Haynie's Company, 3rd Regiment (Raulston) West Tennessee Militia on 13 November 1813 for a six-month tour. He mustered in at Nashville and went to New Orleans with General Carroll's Division. His company was almost dead center of the defensive line at the point of attack by the British during the Battle of New Orleans (Chapter 8). His regiment had casualties on 28 December 1814 and two more during the battle on 8 January 1815. The General singled out Captain Haynie's and one other company for special mention of their heroism. He stated that they "had the honor of receiving and repelling the attacks of the British Forces." That was a compliment indeed considering the fire directed at them.

Asa mustered out in Nashville on 13 May 1815 and was paid $66.00 for his period of service.

Asa and Susan lived in Smith County, Tennessee, when the 1820-1830 censuses were taken. He was living in Kentucky when the December session of the Allen County Court met on 12 December 1836. It appointed Asa and six other men to keep the Puncheon Camp road in repair in accordance with the law. He was enumerated with four children in 1840 by the census taker in Allen County. His was married to his second wife, Jane Holland, in 1845 in Allen County. They had four children. They lived in Simpson County at the time of the 1850 census.

Two bounty land warrants were issued to Asa for his service. The first (#23281) was for 80 acres in Jefferson County, Illinois, on 5 January 1854 under the act of 1850. The patentee was George W. Sturdevant. The second warrant (#34276) was issued under the Act of 1855 on 15 December 1859 for 80 acres in Bates County, Missouri. The patentee for that land was George A Cooksey.

Asa died in 1862.

Robertson, Leroy

An Allen County attorney's letter to the United States Pension Office concerning John Burton's pension (see earlier in this Chapter) also inquired as to the status of a service claim that had been submitted by Leroy Robertson. That was the beginning of a mystery.

The tax records of 1815 listed a Leroy Robertson with 100 acres of land in the Bays Fork Creek drainage area. The Allen County census of 1820 listed him with a household having one male over forty-five, one female over forty-five, one female between sixteen and twenty-five, and five children. Three of the people in his household were foreigners, that is to say, not naturalized. That Leroy was in the 1850 census when he was ninety-three years old and living with his wife Mary who was ninety-four. Lucy Robertson, age thirty-eight, lived with them.

The mystery remained unsolved because no service, pension, or bounty land records were found for a Leroy Robertson. Neither Leroy nor Lucy could be found in the genealogical records. Therefore, his service records were not discovered and no connection to the study area could be proven.

Robinson, James

James Robinson's service was mentioned, like Leroy Robertson's, in the same attorney's letter to the pension office concerning John Burton's pension. No service and pension papers were discovered.

A James Robinson is buried in Little Hope Cemetery in Barren County, who was born in 1777, and died 14 January 1858 with a note that he was a soldier in the War of 1812. He was born in Buckingham County, Virginia, and died in Edmonson County. His wife was Hannah Adair. That James may be the one that the attorney asked about.

Soldiers named James Robinson were in both the 14th and 15th Kentucky Militia Regiments. However, no positive identification was made and no service or pension papers discovered. As a result, James' contribution to the War of 1812 and his connection to the study area could not be resolved.

Seagraves, John

Service records had four different spellings of his surname, including Seagrave, Segraves, and Seagreaves. The most interesting one was an excellent example of a scribe writing what he thought he heard. That scribe wrote the name as John C. Graves, exactly what he heard. Other variant spellings occur in the genealogical records too.

Private John Seagraves was enrolled on the roster of the 14th Regiment (Mitchusson) Kentucky Detached Militia beginning 20 November 1814. He was assigned to Thomas Griffin's Company. He went with his unit on the flatboat trip to New Orleans, and was there by 31 December 1814 at Camp Jackson. His unit participated in the Battle of New Orleans on 8 January 1815 (Chapter 8), and departed for home on 28 February. He was mustered out on 20 May.

He was due a total of $48.00 for his six months service. Like many 1812 soldiers, paydays did not always occur during the service, but were paid after the service had ended. So it was that he appeared before the Allen County Court Clerk on 1 November 1816, and appointed Thomas Gatton as his attorney to collect any and all pay due for his service.

He appeared on the 1815 tax roll in Allen County, but with no taxable property. He had acquired 176 acres by 1816. He and his wife Polly (an affectionate nickname for Mary) bought 78 acres on November 1816 and recorded the transaction at the courthouse.

The Pettis County, Missouri, probate records report a John Seagraves' estate sale, and state that he died intestate on 29 June 1844. His legatees were his widow Mary, children Marshal, Betsy Hook, and Lydia Beardsley.

Seagraves, Thomas

Thomas Seagraves, listed also as Thomas C. Graves in one document and Segraves or Seegraves in others, was born in Botetourt County, Virginia. The odds of dying while on active duty during the War of 1812 were relatively low. Only four from the study area are known to have died while on active duty. The actual length of service was typically short, frequently ninety days and, less frequently, six months. Therefore, the chance of dying of a disease while on active duty was low because the service time was relatively short.

Private Thomas Seagraves was a member of the 44th U. S. Army Regiment of the regular Army in a company commanded by Captain Isaac L. Baker. The company had recruited him in Columbia, Tennessee, and about three hundred fifty other troops in middle Tennessee. He signed up on 20 April 1814 for five years or the duration of the war. They left Nashville on 15 July 1814 and marched southward. They arrived at Fort Jackson, near present day Montgomery, Alabama, on 8 August. On the 11th, they began traveling by boats downstream on the Alabama River.

On 19 August, Captain Baker wrote in his journal, "Resumed our voyage, halted for the night on the right bank of the river a little below old Fort Mims. About midnight two of my soldiers, Thomas Seagraves and Lewis Couch, died."[47] There was no comment about the cause but, lacking a comment about a skirmish, one must conclude that it was a disease of some sort. It was summer, and malaria was one possibility.

Thomas had been married to Mary (Sally) Richards about 1810 in what is now Allen County, Kentucky. After his death, she remarried, this time to Daniel Rigsby. They lived in Maury County, Tennessee.

Mary Seagraves Rigsby was still married when bounty land became available, but was not eligible for the award as the widow. Remarriage had excluded her as a next of kin of Thomas. Instead, it was his mother who became his next of kin. Thomas' mother was also named Mary, and she, not his wife, was awarded bounty land as the result of his death (Figure 65).

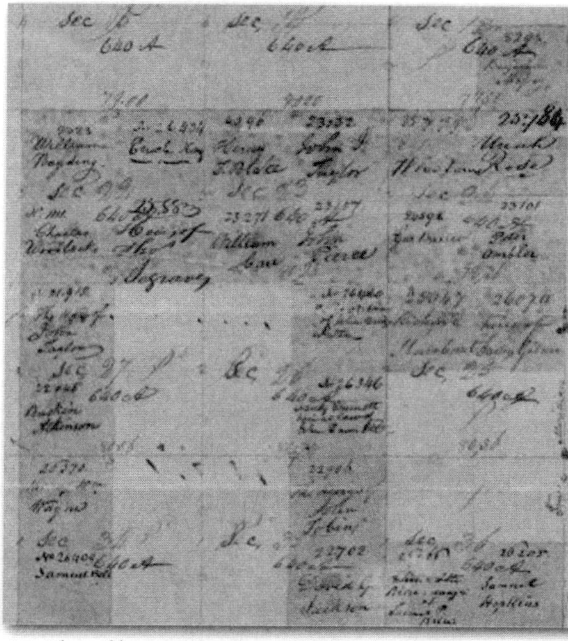

Figure 65. Plat of bounty land awarded to heirs of Thomas Seagraves.

On 7 April 1825, she was certified as being entitled by a warrant (#25883) for bounty land in his name. The form used for Thomas' mother is shown in Figure 40 of Chapter 10. The bounty land warrant for 160 acres that was located in Phillips County, Arkansas, was awarded to his mother on 5 June 1826. Figure 65 shows the location of that property.

Thomas' wife Mary filed for a Widow's Pension (#11149) on 30 June 1858 in Davidson County, Tennessee, several years after her second husband's death on 24 July 1833. Her pension (#6715) was approved on the basis of her being Thomas' first wife. Because her second husband had died, she was unmarried at the time of her application. That made her legally eligible to receive the pension. Her pension of $3.50 per month began on 21 September 1859. She was seventy-seven years old at that time.

Seamster, Pleasant

One answer to Governor Shelby's call for volunteers to join General Jackson's defenses of New Orleans came from Colonel Gabriel Slaughter. He would himself become a governor of Kentucky soon after the end of the war. Slaughter formed a regiment to go to aid Jackson. Private Pleasant Seamster (also spelled Seamser) was one of the eighty-seven men in Captain Edward Berry's Company of the 15th Regiment (Slaughter) Kentucky Detached Militia. The men were mustered in on 10 November 1814 for a six-month tour of duty.

The regiment encountered difficulties from its beginning. The federal government did not provide the needed support of boats and supplies. Colonel Slaughter had to procure private funds to acquire flatboats for the trip downriver to New Orleans. Not all the men had rifles, and the people of New Orleans did their best to provide arms to them after they arrived.

Pleasant's service records showed that he was in New Orleans at Camp Jackson on 31 December. His regiment was on the line during the Battle of New Orleans, occupying the point of the British attack (Chapter 8). He stayed in New Orleans until 28 February 1815 after which the walk back to Kentucky began. He was mustered out on 10 May 1815.

Pleasant was born about 1785 in Virginia. He was in Washington County, Kentucky, when he and Millie Nelson were married on 10 August 1816. He may have entered active duty from there. They still lived there in 1830. They had moved to Jeffersonville in Clark County, Indiana, by the 1850 census. He received a bounty land warrant (#13155) for 161 acres in Jefferson County, Indiana, on 15 April 1853 under Act of 1850. The patentee for the granted land was John D. Shryer.

Genealogists agree that he died in Allen County, Kentucky, but no documentation or dates of death were given to support those statements. It was not possible to determine which genealogist first declared that Allen County was the place of his death. It is certain that once that information was inserted, subsequent genealogists accepted it and repeated it as fact.

There were several Seamsters listed in Allen County records, but Pleasant's presence in the study area could not be verified.

Shacklett, Benjamin

The highest ranking soldier with ties to the study area was Major Benjamin Shacklett. His story was uncommon because of his birth state. He was born on 21 January 1774 in Fayette County, Pennsylvania. He migrated down the Ohio River to the falls at Louisville in 1792 and settled in what is now Meade County, Kentucky. He came with his wife Elizabeth Ashcraft; they were married on 9 October 1792 before they left Pennsylvania.

As a Major, Benjamin was second in command to Lieutenant Colonel Nicholas Miller of the 3rd Regiment (Miller) Kentucky Mounted Detached Militia. He was commissioned and entered active duty on 1 September 1812 with the expectation of serving until 25 December 1813. Twelve other frontiersmen from the study area were in his regiment. The 3rd saw action in the Second Battle of Tippecanoe, also called the Battle of Wild Cat Creek (Chapter 3). He was discharged on 25 December 1812. He earned $190.00 for that period.

Benjamin next appeared as a company commander in Colonel William Russell's Kentucky Mounted Volunteer Detached Militia. In the published record, his name was spelled Shackett. He and his company served from 24 June 1813 to 25 July 1813. During that time, Colonel Russell moved on 1 July 1813 with 573 men in a sweep through the central part of Indiana to the Mississinewa Indian villages. They rode about 500 miles over a period of a month. They found no Indians and saw no combat, but burned abandoned villages along the way.[48] He was paid $42.58 for that service.

He, like some other ranking officers, turned to politics after the war was over. He was elected to the Kentucky House of Representatives in 1815, 1817, and again in 1830. He was the first sheriff in Meade County too.

Some genealogical documents state that he was buried in Meadville Cemetery in Fountain Run, Kentucky. In fact, his grave was marked with a military headstone in the Meadville Cemetery located in Meade County, Kentucky, at was is now called Hill Grove Church. That was the church attended by the Shacklett family. Nothing was found to tie him to Fountain Run, Kentucky.

Sherry, John

John Sherry was born in Rowan County, North Carolina, in 1770 and was married to Winifred (Winnie) Horton in Rutherford County, North Carolina, on 10 February 1800.

He answered the call to become one of the Kentucky militiamen soon after his arrival. He was enrolled as a Private, and was present in Captain William Berryman's Company of Hudspeth and Brown's Regiment when the roll was called on 6 March 1813. He also was in Captain Berryman's Company in the 11th Regiment (Caldwell) Detached Kentucky Militia when it rendezvoused in Greensburg on 1 May 1813. There was no indication that he was called for other active duty service.

He and his family of seven were counted in the Allen County censuses of 1820 and 1830. Kentucky death records record John's death date as 17 July 1852 at the age seventy-three. He died in the Middle Fork community of Allen County. Winnie died at the age of eighty-seven in 1858. The cause of her death was listed as "old age."

Shipley, Nathaniel

Eligibility for service in the militia included age requirements. The upper limit was forty-five and Nathaniel Shipley was thirty-eight, approaching that limit. He was on the Militia rolls of the 3rd Regiment (Miller) Kentucky Detached Militia when it was being formed. He acquired Samuel Merryfield (Merrifield) as his substitute in Captain Henry Yeakey's Company on 1 September 1812. As a result, he did not enter active duty, and no service records were generated.

Nathaniel was born in Virginia in 1774. He married Mildred C. (Milly) Prewitt in Shelby County, Kentucky, on 26 December 1802. The census takers of 1800 and 1810 listed the name of the head of household only and Nathaniel did not appear on those records. However, he was counted in Scottsville in the 1820 census as Nat Shipley with ten individuals in his household, including one adult male slave. There were three others in his household who were designated as foreigners, not naturalized.

He lived in Barren County during the 1830 census, and lived again in the Allen County in 1850. He died in Allen County in 1858.

Smith, John

There were 819 John Smiths who served during the War of 1812. Fifty-two of them served in the Kentucky Militia. The 1820 census counted four John Smiths as head of household in Warren County, three in Barren County, one in Simpson County, and one in Allen County. Which needle in the haystack was the question to be answered?

Charles Mitchell married Nancy Runner to one of those John Smiths on 4 March 1810. Sixty-one years later on 10 June 1871, she filed for a Widow's Pension (#4920) based on his service during the War of 1812.

She lived in Warren County at that time. She stated that her John was drafted in Bowling Green in 1811. Assuming that date to be correct, he would have been in the Militia for a long time before the militiamen were detached for active duty. There was a John Smith who fit that description, one who was enrolled in Hudspeth and Brown's Regiment, and later in 11th Regiment (Caldwell) Kentucky Militia.

The pension office rigidly enforced the requirement that Widow's Pension requests had proof of the spouse's service. The widows found that proof was not easily obtained. She had none of his service records, and John had died on 31 December 1839, thirty-two years earlier. His contemporaries were old or dead, and could not provide statements of John's service. She was left with her memory. As a result, it contained what were no doubt unintentional errors. For example, she identified his regimental commander as Colonel Sterrett, but the only likely officer by than name was actually Captain Thomas Sterrett who was a company commander in the 14th Regiment (Mitchusson) Kentucky Detached Militia. The problem was that there was no record of a John Smith in his company. The bigger problem was that there were just too many John Smith's in the Army to find her John.

Her claim was rejected because she could provide no proof of her John's service. The reason for rejection was then as it is now — rules are rules! Nancy died on 31 December 1874 without having received a pension. The research for this study was constrained by the lack of specific information that would allow the soldier John Smith to be identified. Perhaps Nancy incorrectly believed that his enrollment in the Hudspeth and Brown's Regiment qualified him and her for a pension. If so, he was the needle that was being sought.

Spears, Ephraim

It was common for entire families to immigrate to the frontier. Two generations of the Spears family (also spelled Spear or Speer) came to what would become Allen County from Albemarle County, Virginia. Father William Spears, Sr. and his son Ephraim were examples. They settled in the southern part of the county where the father was on the first tax rolls for Allen County with 200 acres of land in the Trammel Creek watershed. Ephraim lived on land adjacent to his father's land.

Ephraim was married to Sarah (Sally) Walton on 23 November 1802 in Albemarle County, Virginia. They had two children born there before their move to what became Allen County, Kentucky.

He became a Private in Captain William Berryman's Company of the 3rd Regiment (Miller) Detached Kentucky Militia when it was organized on 1 September 1812. Twelve others from the study area served in that unit, and saw action in the Second Battle of Tippecanoe (Chapter 3). They served until 25 December 1812, and were discharged at Hardinsburg as they returned home. He earned $25.33 for his three months of duty.

Ephraim was included on the 1820 census, the first after Allen became a county. It showed Ephraim and an adult woman (Sarah) and ten children under sixteen years old. Of those children, three were reported to be foreigners, that is to say, who had not been naturalized. The Allen County tax list of 1829 recorded Ephraim with five children, and 250 acres of land in the Trammel Fork Creek area.

He was about 61 years old when he died in 1836. His will was probated in December of that year.

Spencer, John

One of the earlier settlers in what was then Barren County, Kentucky, was John Spencer (also spelled Spenser). He was born on 3 November 1773 in Charlotte County, Virginia, and moved to Kentucky 1797. He and Chloe Hill were married two years later on 20 November 1799 in what was then Warren County. They had three children by the time the 1810 census was taken.

No service or pension papers were found for John. He was named on the roll of Captain Henry Yeakey's Company of the 3rd Regiment (Miller) Kentucky Detached Militia. The mention did not include the muster information.

John died on 9 February 1846 in Allen County. His widow Chloe appeared as the head of household in 1850. She was listed in the household of Preston Ritchey in the Gainesville area when she made a claim for bounty land for John's service. She received a bounty land warrant (#62379) on 1 August 1860 under the Act of 1855 for 160 acres in Linn County, Kansas. The award was based on his service in Captain Yeakey's Company, and Chloe was listed as the patentee. She was seventy-four years old when she assigned the land to Henry T. Lambuth.

Spilman, Samuel

Among the early families to settle in what was then Warren County were the Spilmans, Thomas and Mary. They settled on 200 acres of land on the east fork of Difficult Creek. Birth records of their children indicate that they departed Virginia in 1791. One of those making the trip was Samuel Spilman who was born in 1791 in Culpeper County, the last of their children to be born in Virginia. Samuel grew up in Kentucky, and was married to Nancy Burton on 15 September 1814 in what was then Barren County.[49] Samuel's call to serve his country came just two months later. Samuel and Nancy lived in the Gainesville area and eventually had seven children.

He became the 2nd Sergeant in Captain Thomas Griffin's Company in the 14th Regiment (Mitchusson) Kentucky Detached Militia on 20 November 1814. The regiment was transported by flatboat down the Cumberland, Ohio, and Mississippi Rivers to New Orleans. They were participants in the Battle of New Orleans (Chapter 8), and left there on 28 February 1815 for the long walk home. They were mustered out on 20 May 2015.

He was provided a bounty land warrant (#10946) for 80 acres in Polk County, Missouri. The award was made on 2 October 1854 under the Act of 1850. The patentee for that land was William F. Spilman. He received another bounty land warrant (#40582) on 1 April 1861 under the Act 1855 for 80 acres in Cass County, Nebraska. Samuel was listed as the patentee for that land.

Almost all genealogists asserted that he died in Allen County on 14 July 1860. If so, that was an incredulous coincidence. It seems improbable because the census taker came by his home on that exact day. Samuel was alive when he arrived that Saturday. The census taker listed Samuel as living alone next door to R. M. Spilman and as having a post office address of Cedar Springs.

Stamps, Charles

Almost everyone in the study area was an immigrant from another state. Charles Stamps was born 1797 in Pendleton District in South Carolina. The family moved before 1805 to what became Allen County, Kentucky. He and Hannah Belcher were married on 24 December 1816 in Morgan County, Georgia. They had nine children before Hannah died in Allen County on 10 Nov 1848. He and Margaret M. Wygall were married on 30 May 1849 in Allen County, and they had four children.

Charles served as Private in Captain Thomas Griffin's Company of the 14th Regiment (Mitchusson) Kentucky Detached Militia from 20 November 1814 to 20 May 1815. He was paid $48.00 for his service that included participation in the Battle of New Orleans (Chapter 8).

The 1838 Allen County tax list showed him with 260 acres in the Bays Fork Creek watershed.

He was issued a bounty land warrant (#11467) on 15 April 1853 under the Act of 1850 for 80 acres in Marion County, Illinois. The patentee was Carrick N. Wilkins. Charles also received a bounty land warrant (#26792) on 10 September 1860 for 80 acres in Sac County, Iowa, under the Act of 1855. The patentee for that tract was James L. McGoodwin.

He and Margaret had a home in the New Roe area of Allen County when he died on 13 July 1860. He was buried in the Old Buck Creek Cemetery. Margaret moved to Simpson County after his death.

She filed for a Widow's Pension (#42188) that was approved by a certificate (#33077) for $8.00 per month beginning on 9 March 1878. Her pension continued until her death on 25 August 1885.

Stark, Thomas

The man with the most slaves in the study area was Jeremiah Stark who owned thirty-three African Americans in 1810.[50] He had moved from Virginia to Gainesville, Kentucky, in what is now Allen County about 1800.[51] He was living there with his nine children when the War of 1812 began. His youngest son Thomas became a member of Captain William Berryman's Company in both the Hudspeth and Brown's Regiment and the 11th Regiment (Caldwell) Kentucky Detached Militia.

No record of any active duty service by Thomas was discovered. He was apparently selected for duty when a detachment of Lieutenant Colonel Caldwell's regiment was ordered to rendezvous at Greensburg on 1 May 1813. However, he procured William Thompson as his substitute for that duty. The hiring of a substitute was perfectly legal, and was not an uncommon practice.

Thomas appeared in the 1820 census with four slaves. Thomas died sometime between that census and the publication of the 1825 tax roll. On the 1825 tax roll and for several subsequent tax years, James Stark was listed as the guardian for Thomas Stark heirs. Genealogists have concluded that he was never married. If true, the heirs may have been minor inheritors of his siblings. His taxable assets in 1825 were 200 acres in the Difficult Creek area and, of course, his slaves.

Stovall, Drury

Of the large number of men who served from the study area, only four are known to have died while on active duty. One of those was Private Drury (also spelled Drewry) Stovall who died at or near New Orleans in 1815 after the famous battle.

Drury was on the Warren County, Kentucky, tax list of 1800. He was married to Nancy Finney prior to the 1810 census of what was then Warren County. He was listed as having a family consisting of a wife and four children, three sons and one daughter.

On 14 July 1818, Nancy appeared before the Allen County Court and declared that she was a widow of Drury Stovall who was deceased. She stated that he had been a soldier in Captain Thomas Griffin's Company of Kentucky's militia that was detached from Warren County to go to New Orleans under the command of Major General John Thomas. Drury's service records confirm his service in that unit. That service included being in the Battle of New Orleans (Chapter 8).

Nancy stated that Drury died at or near New Orleans. Drury was born in 1779 in Halifax County, Virginia, and was about thirty-six years old when he died. She appointed Thomas Gatton, an attorney in Allen County, to receive any pay due her husband at the time of his death.

The 1820 census taker of Allen County counted Nancy Stovall as the head of household with her four children. That affirmed her statement about her husband being deceased. That was important because Drury's service records did not include any indications of his death. Rather, those records indicated that he, like all other members of his company, was administratively mustered out at Russellville on 20 May 1815. Nevertheless, Nancy persisted, even after she remarried.

Nancy was married to George Anderson in Allen County on 12 March 1823.[52] Her second marriage did not dissuade her from pursuing the availability of bounty lands under the Act of 1855. Her efforts were successful and resulted in a land warrant (#62566) for one 160 acres in Douglas County, Nebraska, on 1 May 1860 in Drury's name.

She was listed as the patentee for the land as Nancy Anderson, her name after she had remarried. That award states that Nancy Anderson was "formerly widow of Drury Stovall, Private [in] Captain Griffin's Company, Kentucky Militia, War of 1812." Nancy had proved her claim and substantiated Drury's service.

Sturdy, William

William Sturdy was born about 1792 in North Carolina. It is unclear as to when he arrived in Kentucky, but his call to duty must have come soon after he arrived. The service records of the Kentucky Militia showed that William Sturdy was a Private in Captain Berryman's Company in the 3rd Regiment (Miller) Kentucky Detached Militia. Twelve others from the study area served in this unit that saw action in the Second Battle of Tippecanoe (Chapter 3).

He enlisted from what was then Warren County on 16 September 1812. His service records list him as being on furlough, but it also recorded him having three months and twenty-five days of service. The furlough may have been prior to his departure. His pay was $6.66 per month, and totaled $25.33 for his tour of duty. He was discharged at Hardinsburg on 16 December 1812.

After his discharge, he and Elizabeth Mingus were married in the new county of Allen on 14 November 1816. They eventually had eleven children. They moved to Madison in Barry County, Missouri, before 1840, and were still there in 1850 when the census listed him as a farmer.

Several years later, William applied for bounty land. A warrant (#55402) for 40 acres in Barry County, Missouri, issued to him on 2 October 1854 under Act of 1850. He was listed as both the warrantee and the patentee. William received a bounty land warrant (#36294) for another 120 acres in Barry County, Missouri, on 10 July 1858. William was again listed as both the warrantee and the patentee. It seems improbable that the awards of land in his home county were purely fortuitous or providential. However, no contrary evidence was found.

Elizabeth and her younger children were still there in the 1860 census, but William was not listed.

Swindle, Pelige Spencer

For a War of 1812 soldier to have lived until photography was perfected required that he enlist young and live long. Such a man was

Pelige Swindle. According to his wife, he enlisted when he was about fifteen years old to become a Private in the Illinois Militia in Captain Eaton's Company. She declared that he had a fourteen-month tour that seems to have been in the Indiana Territory because she stated that he was discharged at Vincennes.

Pelige Swindle[53]

According to genealogists, Pelige (also spelled Pelidge) Swindle (also spelled Swingle, Swendel, and Swindell) was born in Hyde County, North Carolina, on 19 February 1798. He was married to Nancy Hickman on 18 March 1821 in Wilson County, Tennessee. They had eleven children.

His second marriage was to Philadelphia East Horn on 16 May 1856. Justice of the Peace Kirby married them in Macon County, Tennessee. They had ten children. They lived in Macon County at the times of the 1850 and 1870 censuses.

Pelige died on 25 March 1879 at about eighty-one years old, and was buried in the Johnson Cemetery in southern Allen County.

Philadelphia filed for a Widow's Pension authorized by the Act of 9 March 1878. She filed the application (#36769) in Fountain Run, in Monroe County, Kentucky, where she lived at that time. She stated that Pelige was 5' 5" tall with blue eyes and light hair. The Pension Bureau rejected her application on 26 May 1880 because she did not provide proof of his service. That was a common problem among widows of that era.

She also stated that Pelige had received a bounty land warrant (#33461). It was common that soldiers sent their discharge papers attached to their bounty land application. That would explain the absence of service proof that plagued Philadelphia when she applied for a pension. However, research did not confirm that there was such a land warrant. There were such recipients listed for that number, but none had his name in any of its many variations.

Neither could confirmation be made that a Captain named Eaton existed in either the Militia or the regular Army in the Illinois Territory. No soldier with either the names Pelege or Swindle, with any of the variations in spelling, were found in the Illinois, Kentucky, or Tennessee militias. Philadelphia must have heard the details of Pelige's service from him in his later years. It seems likely that Pelige's memory may have inadvertently altered the details enough to make substantiation of his service impossible to verify.

Taber, Henry

The family name Taber was also spelled as Tabor and with the old English spelling Tabour. One of the earliest families to settle in what would become Allen County, Kentucky, was that of Isaac Tabor. His son Henry was on the roll call of the Hudspeth and Brown Regiment as a Private at their meeting on 6 March 1813. He was also on rolls of the 11th Regiment (Caldwell) Detached Kentucky Militia in Captain William Berryman's Company. That unit received marching orders to rendezvous with members of a battalion of the 11th on 1 May 1813 in Greensburg. His service records do not mention other military activities.

Patsey Tabor was born in 1797, and Henry Tabor was born about 1794, both in North Carolina. Patsey was married to her first cousin Henry on 1 July 1814 in Warren County, Kentucky. Henry was listed in the Allen County census of 1820 as being under twenty-six years old with a wife and two children. He was recorded in the 1830 census too, but without children. He was not in later decadal censuses.

He was on the Allen County tax roll in 1825 with 50 acres on Difficult Creek. On the 1829 tax roll, he had two plots of land, both in the Bays Fork Creek drainage area. One plot was 50 acres, and the other was 60 acres. In addition, he owned one town lot in Scottsville.

Thompson, John

Service records were by nature very terse, and that attribute was further accentuated when the original records were copied to preserve the information. For example, Private John Thompson was in Captain Thomas Griffin's Company of the 14th Regiment (Mitchusson) Kentucky Detached Militia. He served for six months, but during that entire service, only four entries were made in his service records. The first recorded his muster in on 20 November 1814 and his arrival on 31 December at "Jackson's Camp" in New Orleans. The second affirmed his service from 31 December 1814 to 28 February 1815 at Camp Jackson. The third reported the period from 28 February to 20 May 1815 that ended with his muster out at Russellville. The fourth recorded his pay for the entire period, $48.00 for six months at $8.00 per month of duty. There were no remarks except the word "present" to mark his activities. In particular there was nothing in his service records that would indicate that he had died while on active duty.

John was married to Elizabeth Wright in Adair County, Kentucky, on 6 December 1803. They appeared on the 1810 census with two young children living in what was then Warren County.

Elizabeth Wright Thompson came before the Allen County Court Clerk on 1 October 1816 in an effort to claim whatever pay for which her husband was entitled. She appointed attorney William Strait from Allen County to represent her in that matter. She declared that her husband had died in service at New Orleans. It was apparent that she believed that her word alone would not be considered as sufficient proof because she had John's Company Commander, Captain Thomas Griffin, to appear on the same day. He came, and made a substantiating statement that affirmed that John had in fact died on active duty (Figure 66).

Captain Griffin's statement verified that Elizabeth was John's wife and that John had served in his company during its deployment to New Orleans. He declared that John "demeaned himself well" during the period that included the battle. He concluded by saying that "his death happened in the town of Orleans aforesaid as well as I recollect about the tenth day of March 1815."[54] Those statements made clear that John Thompson was the last of the four men from the study area to die while on active duty in the War of 1812.

John Thompson lived in what was then Warren County during the 1810 census with a wife and three children. The 1820 census for Warren did not have John, of course, but listed Elizabeth Thompson as the head of a household that included five children. There also were a man and woman over the age of forty-five living in the household. That woman was too old to be Elizabeth.

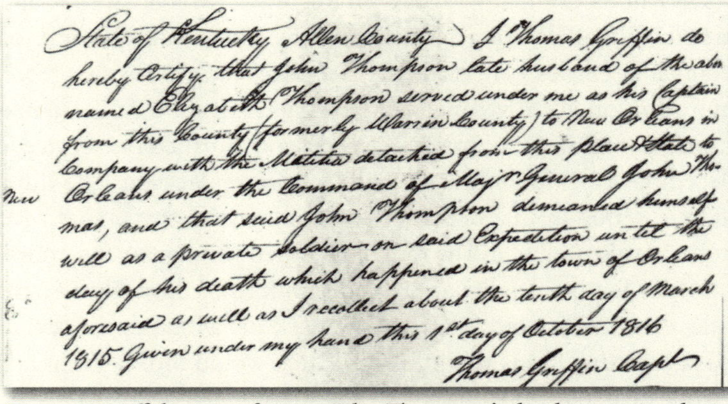
State of Kentucky Allen County } I Thomas Griffin do
hereby Certify that John Thompson late husband of the abo
named Elizabeth Thompson served under me as his Captain
from this County (formerly Warren County) to New Orleans in
Company with the Militia detached from this place & State to
New Orleans under the Command of Major General John Tho-
mas, and that said John Thompson demeaned himself
well as a private Soldier on said Expedition until the
day of his death which happened in the town of Orleans
aforesaid as well as I recollect about the tenth day of March
1815. Given under my hand this 1st day of October 1816
Thomas Griffin Capt

Figure 66. Affidavit confirming John Thompson's death on active duty.

No record was found of applications for either a pension or bounty land grants. In short, the records have not shown that Elizabeth received any recompense for John's service.

Thompson, William

Private William Thompson was on the rolls of Captain William Berryman's Company of the 11th Regiment (Caldwell) Kentucky Detached Militia when it rendezvoused in Greensburg on 1 May 1813. He was listed as a substitute for Thomas Stark. No other service records were found for William's Kentucky militia experience. He resided with a wife and ten children in Warren County, Kentucky during the 1820 census.

He was a veteran of the 17th U.S. Infantry Regiment, was a 5' 11", and twenty-eight years old when he enlisted on 17 February 1814 in Lexington, Kentucky. He began active duty on 21 June 1814, and was still serving as a Private in Captain James Hunter's Company on 17 May 1815. The record also showed that he was born in Virginia.[55] The 17th was a regular Army unit that was sent to occupy Detroit during the summer of 1814. A portion of the regiment was sent to recapture Fort Mackinaw. They were unsuccessful and returned to Detroit.

William received a bounty land warrant (#8276) on 4 January 1819 under the Act of 1812 for 160 acres in Carroll County, Missouri, for his service in the U.S. regular army.

He appeared in Missouri land records as a veteran who served with the 17th Regiment from Allen County. His bounty land was sold to John Bright on 25 August 1819 with the transaction recorded in the Logan County, Kentucky, records.[56] Genealogical records were unhelpful in learning more details about William or his family.

Trammel, Sampson

Private Sampson Trammel was present on 6 March 1813 at the roll call of Hudspeth & Brown's Regiment of Kentucky Militia. He was also on the roll of the 11th Regiment (Caldwell) Kentucky Militia when they were readying for rendezvous. He obtained the services of Elias Highsmith to be his substitute for that latter call.

Some individuals were mentioned frequently in the early records of Allen County only to have the record abruptly end. In June 1817, the Allen County Court ordered that John Trammel (Sampson's father perhaps?) be appointed surveyor of the precinct road leading from Scottsville to the head of Long Creek terminating at Samson Trammel's home and from there to the Tennessee state line.

Sampson Trammel appeared in the 1820 and 1830 censuses. In the latter, he was listed with a wife and one child. He was also on the tax rolls of 1829 with 240 acres of land in the Trammel Fork Creek watershed. He was also assessed tax on his one horse.

In March 1834, the Allen County Court noted that Sampson was infirm and incapable of labor for his own support. The biographical trail ends with that entry.

Veach, Nathan

Retirement or Social Security income for most people these days begins when the individual's age reaches the early to middle sixties. Neither of those options was available for veterans of the War of 1812. An exception was possible if a soldier could prove that he was an invalid, but there was nothing available if he was healthy. Congress eventually remedied that by authorizing a Survivor's Pension, the name of which described any veteran who had survived all those years during and after the war. So it was that on 6 May 1871, eighty-four year old Nathan Veach filed

(#15906) for a Survivor's Pension, fifty-six years after his discharge from the army.

Most if not all of pension applicants employed an attorney to prepare the necessary forms, obtain supporting documents, and elicit sworn affidavits to support the claim. Nathan chose Fountain Run attorney H.C. Franklin to represent him, a choice convenient for him because they both used the post office at Fountain Run as their address. The application process was rendered complicated by a fire in 1823 that had burned Nathan's home and its furniture. His discharge papers were among the losses in that fire. Without papers to prove his service, Nathan recounted his service, and his attorney wrote his statements. There were witnesses who swore that they saw him make his mark at the bottom of the page, the letter X made by those who could not write their name.

Nathan declared that he joined the regular Army in Burkesville, Kentucky, on 5 April 1813 and became a Private in Captain G. Stockton's Company of the U.S. 24th Infantry Regiment, a regular Army unit. He stated that he had served at Fort Ball, Fort Seneca, Fort Meigs, and in the retaking of Detroit. His memory proved to be quite good. Each of these places was vital to the war effort in the area around Lake Erie in an area occupied by the allied Indian nations of Seneca, Wyndot, Delaware, Shawnee, and Miami.

Each of the forts mentioned by Nathan was an important link on the supply route that was being constructed. Roads had been cut by the Ohio Militia to connect the forts, but they were routinely impassable much of the time because of the deep mud. General Harrison ordered the acquisition of 100 ox wagons because horses were not able to pull loaded wagons through the mire.

Fort Ball was a supply depot in what is now the town of Tiffin in northern Ohio. It was constructed in July 1813 with three blockhouses on the side facing the Sandusky River. There was a palisade of twelve-inch pickets surrounding the interior area behind the blockhouses and, in the middle, and a spring for water. It could accommodate about 500 men. Among them was Nathan.

Fort Seneca was another supply depot located on the Sandusky River about six miles north of Fort Ball. It was a few miles south of the current day community of Fort Seneca. It was depicted as having a blockhouse at each corner of the enclosed area. Nathan stated that he was at this fort too.

General Harrison's forces constructed Fort Meigs on the banks of the Maumee River in February 1813 as the principal fort in the area. When the British began their siege of the fort in May of 1813, 1,200 men were within its walls. The British were unsuccessful, although the bombardment lasted four days before they withdrew. Nathan Veach and the 24th Infantry arrived in Franklinton (now called Columbus), Ohio on 7 June 1813. They were in the fort when the British and Indians began a second siege in July, and withstood the attack.

A portion of the 24th Infantry went to occupy the liberated Fort Detroit and Nathan stated that he had been part of that effort. He was still in Detroit when his enlistment ended as his unit was dissolved on 6 April 1815.

In the 1850 census, Nathan, Caroline, and six children were listed in his household in Allen County. The census recorded his birth state as Tennessee, but the children's birthplaces as Kentucky. He was listed as a shoemaker. In 1860, the census recorded his age as seventy-nine and Caroline's as forty-five.

Nathan's application for a Survivor Pension was approved (#10281) and he began receiving $8.00 per month on 14 February 1874.

Venable, William

Biographical information was meager for some of the soldiers who served in the War of 1812. One of those was Private William Venable. He was on the rolls of 11th Regiment (Caldwell) Kentucky Militia as a substitute for Joel Callahan in Captain William Berryman's Company. No other service records or pension records were found for William.

Some genealogical work reported that a William Venable was born in Spartanburg, South Carolina, in 1775, appeared on the Warren County census of 1810, and was married to Sarah Pinson in Allen County in 1811. However, those biographical facts could not be incontrovertibly linked to William the soldier.

Waggle, George

This soldier's surname was spelled Wygle or Wygal in some documents, but the service records spelled it Waggle, a phonetic spelling perhaps. George Waggle was born in 1793 in Pulaski County, Virginia. He was in Kentucky when he joined the 3rd Regiment (Miller) Kentucky Militia, and served as a Private in Captain William Berryman's Company.

His enlistment date was 1 September 1812. Twelve others from the study area served in this unit that saw action in the second battle of Tippecanoe that was sometimes called the Battle of Wild Cat Creek (Chapter 3).

His service records showed that he served until 25 December 1812, at which time he was detached for duty with Major David Hardin. Hardin's Detachment was stationed at Fort Knox at Vincennes, the capital of the Indiana Territory. That fort had been built in 1803 about three miles north of Vincennes. George served there from 1 January to 20 January 1813 when he was discharged. The fort was subsequently dismantled, its logs floated downstream, and the fort rebuilt in the town of Vincennes later in 1813 to assure better protection for its citizens.

George and Elizabeth (Betsy) Carrier were married in February of 1814, and they lived in Allen County, Kentucky, when the 1820 census was taken. He appeared in each following census until 1860 when he was listed as living in Simpson County.

George received a bounty land warrant (#11635) for 40 acres under the Act of 1850 in Monroe County, Arkansas. He assigned that land to patentee John McCullah. He also received an additional 120 acres in Benton County, Missouri, from a warrant (#87892) under Act of 1855. The patentee for that land was Lucius Lamkin.

George died in Allen County on 13 March 1863. Eight years later on 31 July 1871, his wife Elizabeth filed for a Widow's Pension (#6971). She was then 77 years old, and lived eight miles east of Franklin in Simpson County. Her pension was granted (#3835) on 13 July 1872, and she received pay backdated to 14 February 1871.

Walker, Andrew

Andrew Walker's service record says he was the trumpeter in Captain Hugh Brown's Company of Kentucky Mounted Volunteer Militia. A trumpeter was a member of the company staff, called a bugler in some instances. He, like a drummer, was a musician who relayed orders by the musical phrase played. Everyone knows the musical order for a charge, for instance.

He enlisted on 18 September 1812, made the march to the Vincennes area, and was discharged on 30 October 1812 at Busseron in the Indiana Territory (Chapter 3).

On 25 August 1816 in Scottsville, Kentucky, he appointed James Stewart as his true and lawful attorney to procure whatever wages were due him. The biographical trail went cold after that. He was not in the 1820 census, was not on the tax rolls, and did not file for a pension or bounty land.

Walker, William H.

Some who answered the call to arms during the War of 1812 were Virginians who came to Kentucky after the war was over. William H. Walker was one of those. He was born in New Kent County, Virginia, on 29 November 1891. He was twenty-three years old when he enlisted as a Private in Captain David Glass's Company of the Virginia Militia. His company of artillery was part of Lieutenant Colonel William Trueheart's 1st Virginia Regiment. That regiment occupied Camp Bottom Bridges. He served from 25 August 1814 until 16 November 1814 in that defense of Richmond (Chapter 7). He was discharged at Camp Bottoms Bridge on the Chickahominy River in New Kent County, Virginia.

He and Sarah Richardson were married in New Kent County on 6 July 1815. They left their home in Virginia on 3 January 1816 accompanied by their four slaves, and arrived in Allen County, Kentucky, on 25 February 1816. They built a two-story house on the Old Buck Creek Road. In 1848, they bought 1,600 acres of land on which they built another two-story log house. They were generous people, and donated land for what became Walker's Chapel Methodist Church.[57] The 1838 tax record showed that he was taxed on 405 five acres of land, seven slaves, and three horses.

In the 1850 census, he was described as a farmer. Sarah would later describe him as being 6' 2 or 3" with black hair, blue eyes, and a fair complexion.

William was awarded a bounty land warrant (#7646) for land in Adair County, Iowa, on 1 October 1857 under the Act of 1855. Those 160 acres were assigned to patentee Frederick A. Tritle.

William filed (#11511) for a Survivor's Pension for his service, and received a certificate (#6805) that authorized pay beginning on 18 October 1871. He died on 29 March 1874, and was buried at Walker's Chapel Church cemetery.

Sarah filed (#30997) for a Widow's Pension that was approved. She received the certificate (#14925), and received $8.00 per month commencing on 9 March 1879.

Weatherspoon, James

James Weatherspoon (also spelled Wetherspoon and Witherspoon), and his brothers, Major and Wiley, were soldiers in the War of 1812. James was born in Wake County, North Carolina, on 15 October 1790. He moved with his parents and siblings to what is now Allen County, Kentucky.

James joined the Militia in August 1814, originally in Captain Sterrett's Company, but ended up as a Private in Captain Thomas Griffin's Company of the 14th Regiment (Mitchusson) Kentucky Detached Militia. He mustered in on 20 November 1814 and made the voyage by flatboat to New Orleans, participated in the Battle of New Orleans (Chapter 8), walked back, and was mustered out on 20 May 1815. He received $48.00 pay for his service.

James was married to Ann Coleman on 29 October 1821. She was born in Virginia about 1795. They moved to Calloway County, Kentucky, before the 1830 census. James was a farmer, and died there on 2 December 1853.

For his service, James was given a bounty land warrant (#47292) on 2 October 1854 for 80 acres in Washington County, Iowa, under the Act of 1850. The patentee was Horace B. Sisson. Ann received James' bounty land warrant (#46782) on 1 July 1861 for an additional 80 acres in Dunklin County, Missouri, under the Act of 1855. She assigned that land to John Cross.

Ann filed for a Widow's Pension (#23385) on 9 May 1878 at Murray in Calloway County, Kentucky. About a year later, she was living in New Providence in Calloway County, a few miles southeast of Murray. She still had not yet received a response to her claim.

On 5 June 1879, more than a year after she submitted the request for a Widow's Pension, she personally wrote a letter (Figure 67) to "Mr. Auditor," as she addressed the commissioner of pensions. Her impatience was evident. This quote, just as she wrote it, indicated her fiery exasperation with bureaucratic lethargy, "I think it has bin long a nuf and if ther is any back pay dew me I want you to send it also." Her letter worked. Just a month later, her pension was certified (#25509), and on 15 July 1879 her pension began with arrears paid back to 9 March 1878.

One must not overlook her ability to write, to write legibly, and to edit what she wrote. Her spelling was phonetic, but her passionate intent was conveyed. Her words still stir our hearts even now, two hundred years later.

June 5 1879
New Providence Calloway Co Ky
Mr Auditor
Sir I have
Bin Tring for a Pansion now for
one year and over and have not got
it yett I have heard it is before you
for a gestment I want to now
whether you want any mor prufe or not
if so pleas send me the nessary Blanks
I want to now what is the Reason
that it is not bin sent for I think
it has bin their long a nuf and
if their is any Back pay due me
me I want you to send it allso
and if ther is a land warent due
me I want it al so I Receive a 80 acre
acre land warent I think in 1858 or 9
and I heard that ther was and other due
me if so pleas send it; I sent my
papers to Mr George E. Lemon over
1 one year a go and he has not sent me
my Pension yet & I want to hear
from you soon
Send all of my Bisness in the care
of W. M. Witherspoon to New Providence
Calloway Co Ky
yours Ann. Witherspoon

Figure 67. Ann Weatherspoon's letter regarding her pension application.

Weatherspoon, Major

Oral histories of families, passed on from generation to generation, present many opportunities for misinterpretations. One such case occurred when a given name was the same as a word used as a military rank. Major Weatherspoon (also spelled Wetherspoon, and Witherspoon) was an example. Major was his name, not his rank. Some genealogical records use Simpson Lemuel as his given names, but all the military and census records use the given name Major. He was born in Wake County, North Carolina, in 1798, and moved with his parents and siblings to the study area before the war.

He, along with his brothers James and Wiley, joined the Kentucky Militia from what is now Allen County. They all were in Captain Thomas Griffin's Company of the 14th Regiment (Mitchusson) Kentucky Detached Militia. They mustered in on 20 November 1814, made the trip down the Cumberland, Ohio, and Mississippi Rivers to New Orleans. They were in the Battle of New Orleans (Chapter 8). Their unit was mustered out in Russellville on 20 May 1815.

Major's two brothers moved westward after the war, but the 1820 and subsequent censuses showed that Major remained in Allen County. So did the tax rolls. In 1838, he was assessed tax on 250 acres of land in the Bays Fork watershed and on five horses. The total assessment was $1,400, a sizable sum for that period.

Major filed for and received two bounty land warrants. The first (#74305) was issued on 9 February 1855 under the Act of 1850 for 81 acres in Fayette County, Iowa. The patentee for that land was Henry H. Opdycke. The second (#24486) was a warrant for 80 acres in Pettis County, Missouri, under the Act of 1855. It was issued on 1 April 1959. The patentee was that land was David McConkey.

Major and Lucinda, his third wife (surname not noted), were in the 1870 census in Allen County with Allen Springs as their post office.

Major had submitted for a Survivor's Pension (#18837), and received an award certificate (#12759) before his death in August 1876. His widow Lucinda, who was born about 1822 in Kentucky, filed (#30858) for a Widow's Pension. She received a certificate (#22626) that authorized monthly payments.

The National Archives has records of those awards that they were, in fact, made, but none of those documents on are now on file. Archivists there voiced a supposition that those records were removed from the files without documentation prior to their transfer from storage to the National Archives over fifty years ago. Although the documents may still exist, those originals may have been misfiled and could not be located.

Weatherspoon, Wiley

Wiley Weatherspoon (also spelled Wetherspoon and Witherspoon) served in the Kentucky Militia with his brothers James and Major. He was born in North Carolina in 1796 and came to what was then Warren County with his parents and siblings about 1810.

Service records showed that he and his brothers were members of Captain Thomas Griffin's Company, 14th Regiment (Mitchusson) Kentucky Detached Militia. He was mustered in 20 November 1814, made the trip to New Orleans, was in the battle there (Chapter 8), and was mustered out on 20 May 1815 in Russellville.

He and Jane Edmunds were married on 6 January 1819, and lived in Allen County for the 1820 census. About 1829, most of the Weatherspoon families (except Major's) moved to Calloway County, Kentucky.

Eventually, Wiley and Jane sold their property in Calloway County and headed farther west with their four daughters and four slaves, and arrived in Lamar County, Texas, on 23 October 1834 to settle on their 4,605 acres of land.

In 1847, they began to dispose of that land, deeding their property to their children, but holding the right to live on the home place until their deaths. Subsequently, Wiley disappeared from the historical records. Perhaps the early disposition of their property may have indicated that his death was anticipated.

Weaver, James

James Weaver (sometimes spelled Wever) heard stories about combat against the British during the Revolutionary War from his father John who was in the 1st Virginia Dragoons. John's unit of the Continental Army fought several battles, including the famous one at Guilford Courthouse. Those stories may have influenced James to join the Militia and his enlistment may have influenced his younger brother William to join just three weeks later.

James was born in 1790 in Halifax County, Virginia. He was described as 5' 10" tall, with sandy hair, gray eyes, and fair complexion. He was married to Elizabeth Durham on 10 September 1812 before he became a Private in Captain John Jennings' Company, 7th Regiment Virginia Infantry. Colonel David Saunders and his 7th Regiment operated from August 1814 to February 1815 when it was placed under the 4th Virginia Militia Regiment. During that period, its troops were stationed in Norfolk to defend it from potential British attack. That potential and expected attack did not materialize (Chapter 7).

James was discharged on 4 October 1814 at Norfolk, and made his way back to Halifax County. He recorded that he, his father John, mother Patsey, and siblings immigrated to Allen County, Kentucky, in 1816 to a community that was also named Halifax. In 1854, he was married to his second wife Martha Crowder at Ann Crowder's residence in Allen County.

James filed two claims for bounty land. One warrant (#27175) was awarded on 1 May 1855 for 80 acres in Hardin County, Iowa, under

Act of 1850. The other bounty land warrant (#44503) was issued on 1 October 1860 for an additional 80 acres in Anderson County, Kansas, under the Act of 1855.

James submitted an application (#20389) from Scottsville for a Survivor's Pension under the Act of 1871. That application was rejected on 15 July 1872 because he had not submitted proof of his service. His discharge paper had been filed with his bounty land claim some twenty years earlier, and had never been returned to him (Chapter 10). His pension certificate (#24312) was approved on 26 September 1878 and he began to receive $8.00 per month.

James died 14 February 1881 at the age of ninety-one.

Weaver, William

No British troops ever entered Kentucky during the War of 1812, and they never directly threatened families living there. That was not the case in Virginia where the British and American troops were actively engaged in February 1813. Over forty more such encounters occurred there before the end of the war. The motivation for service in the Virginia militia was clear; it was to defend against an immediate and present threat posed to their homeland and families by the British army.

William Weaver (sometimes spelled Wever) lived in Halifax County, Virginia, when his call to duty came. Like his brother James, he responded. He was about sixteen years old when he rendezvoused with his company at Terrysville (believed to have been in Mecklenburg County) on 30 August 1814. He was in Captain William Bailey's Company that was organized with members from Halifax County, Virginia. Lieutenant Colonel William C. Greenhill became the commander of the 4th Regiment Virginia Militia on 1 September 1814.

They were stationed at Fort Mims near Richmond before leaving on 6 October to march to Baltimore. The British had burned our Capitol about six weeks earlier, landed on the coast of Maryland about three weeks earlier, and attacked Baltimore (Chapter 7). They arrived too late to participate in those actions. They went to Camp Snowden, Maryland, on 27 October to defend against any future attempts by the British.

They moved to Camp Eichtenberger in Ann Arundel County on 3 November and then to Camp Crossroads at Ellicott's Mills, a flourmill, on 9 November. They were still there when their term of service was completed on 1 December 1814. Afterward, they returned to their homes in Halifax County. For three month and eighteen days of service and his travel of 300 miles, William received $28.64 (Figure 68).

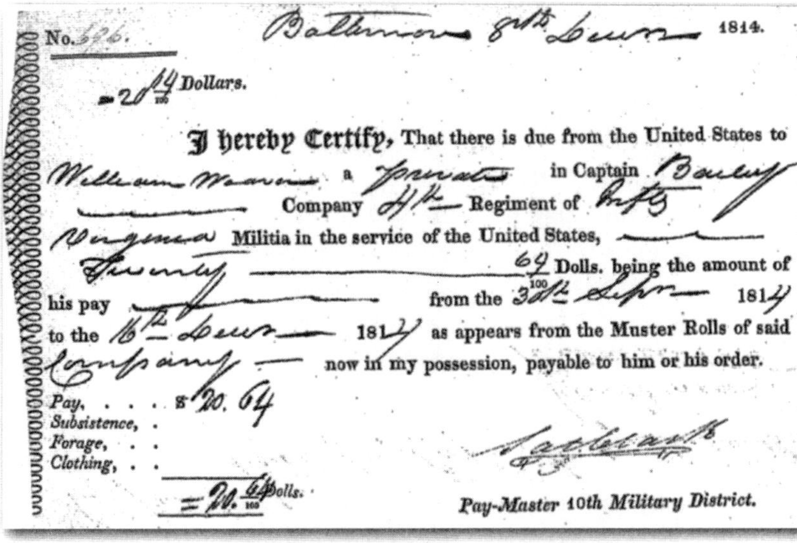

No. 526. Baltimore 8th Decr 1814.

= 20 64/100 Dollars.

I hereby Certify, That there is due from the United States to William Weaver a Private in Captain Bailey's Company 4th Regiment of Infty Virginia Militia in the service of the United States, Twenty 64/100 Dolls. being the amount of his pay from the 30th Sepr 1814 to the 16th Decr 1814 as appears from the Muster Rolls of said Company now in my possession, payable to him or his order.

Pay, . . . $20.64
Subsistence, .
Forage, . .
Clothing, . .

= 20 64/100 Dolls.

Pay-Master 10th Military District.

Figure 68. William Weaver's pay record.

According to his brother James, their father John moved his family to Allen County, Kentucky, in November 1816. It was there that William was married to Elizabeth Dobson on 29 October 1817. The Allen County census of 1820 noted him, his wife, and three children. They would eventually have eight more children.

William and Elizabeth first lived on 130 acres in the Little Difficult Creek drainage basin in the northern part of the county. He died on 9 November 1846 at the age of forty-eight and was buried in the Weaver Family Cemetery near Halifax where his father John was interred.

Thirteen years later, a bounty land warrant (#66505) was given on 1 July 1859 under the Act of 1855 for William's service. It awarded 118.81 acres in Jasper County, Missouri. His widow Elizabeth received the land as the Patentee. She assigned the land to Middleton F. Hickey.

Elizabeth was buried alongside William in the family cemetery when she died in 1880 at the age of eighty-three.

Welch, Thomas

Substitutes were solicited if a militiaman who was called to duty could not or chose not to answer the call. It was quite legal for that individual to obtain a substitute. Jeremiah Holcomb was one of those who made that choice and obtained Thomas Welch (also spelled Welsh and Walsh) to be his substitute. So it was that Thomas became a Private in Captain William Berryman's Company of the 11th Regiment (Caldwell) Kentucky Militia and was on the roll for its rendezvous at Greensburg on 1 May 1813.

Thomas was not a substitute when he joined Captain Thomas Griffin's Company of the 14th Regiment (Mitchusson) Kentucky Detached Militia. He was mustered in on 20 November 1814, was in the deployment by flat boats to New Orleans, participated in the Battle of New Orleans (Chapter 8), and walked home for discharge on 20 May 1815.

There was a marriage between Thomas Welch and Polly (an affectionate nickname for Mary) Martin in Allen County, Kentucky, on 20 November 1815. Genealogists identify her as Mary Ann (Polly) Martin.

Genealogists record that Thomas died in 1830, and supported that view by noting that the census of that year listed Mary as a head of household.

Wheat, Dory

The 1850 census taker in Barren County entered the name of Theodore Wheat on the tabulation form. That was the only use found of that given name. His wife stated that his name was Dora, likely his nickname, when she applied for a pension. That name that would have been pronounced as Dory, and it was spelled that way on most documents.

Dory was born in Prince George's County, Maryland, in 1783. He was in Albemarle County, Virginia, when Rev. Martin Dawson, Sr. performed his marriage to Polly Eubanks. She remembered the date to be 2 May 1811.

He served as a Private in Captain John C. Cole's Company of Colonel Asa Young's 5th Regiment Light Infantry of the Virginia Militia. That unit was formed in Albemarle County. His company was sent to Norfolk on 28 February 1814, and remained there until he was discharged on 9 June 1814.

He also served in Captain Triplett T. Estes' Company of the Virginia Militia. Estes kept the Stone Tavern on the square in Charlottesville, and was designated commander of troops from the district immediately south of town.[59] Dory served from 1 January 1815 to 19 January with that company.

Under the Act of 1850, he received a bounty land warrant (#28356) for 80 acres in Washington County, Iowa, on 20 July 1853. He assigned the land to patentee Elijah Albin. He received a second bounty land warrant (#6147) on 1 September 1857 under the Act of 1855 for 80 acres in Taylor County, Iowa. He assigned that land to patentee Valentine Reece. To obtain the land warrants, he had to submit his discharge papers. They were never returned to him.

Dory died in Allen County 5 February 1871. The absence of his discharge papers presented a problem to his widow Polly when she filed a Widow's Pension claim (#2492) on 24 April 1871. According to her statements, her post office was Fountain Run in Monroe County, but she lived in Allen County. She had to obtain sworn statements from people who knew her and Dory as husband and wife. She finally received her Widow's Pension (#2098) on 20 March 1872 for $8.00 per month. She was seventy-seven years old by then.

Whitney, Leommi

Variant spellings of surnames were common among the illiterate soldiers of the War of 1812. Less common were variant spellings of a given name, perhaps because of the overuse of more common names like John, James, or William. Leommi Whitney's given name elicited several variants. All appear to be phonetic variations of his uncommon name. The variations included Laomi, Loamma, and Leanmmi.

Leommi was born on 4 September 1790 in South Carolina, the seventh of ten siblings. His father, John Whitney, Sr. was a Sergeant in the Revolutionary War who moved his family to what is now Allen County, Kentucky, in 1794. John was taxed in 1825 on 375 acres of land in southeastern part of the county.

Leommi, like his father before him, answered the call to duty. He became a Private on the rolls of Captain William Berryman's Company of the Hudspeth and Brown's Regiment at its roll call on 6 March 1813. There were no indications that he was ever called to active duty.

He was married to Jane Jenny Bush on 3 April 1815 in Barren County. They were counted in the 1850 census with seven children.

Leommi died on 24 July 1886, and was buried at Austin in Barren County.

Williams, George

George Williams became a Private in the Hudspeth and Brown's Regiment, and later was in the 11th Regiment (Caldwell) Kentucky Militia. He was in Captain Hugh Brown's Company. There was no record of him having been called to active duty with any of the detached units that went off to war.

A bounty land warrant (#39842) correctly identified George as a Private in Captain Brown's Company of Kentucky Militia. He was awarded 160 acres of land in Vernon County, Missouri, on 10 December 1859 under the Act of 1855. The land was assigned to a patentee, William L. Powers. The fact that he received the maximum authorized 160 acres of bounty land means that he had a longer service period than has been discovered.

The Act of 1850 specified that the recipients must have enlisted for at least one year, and actually served at least nine months to receive 160 acres. The specifics of that one-year service were not discovered. The federal government was very cautious in awarding bounty land. One must conclude that George fulfilled that requirement and that his extant record for unknown reasons omitted that part of his service

He appeared in the 1820 census of Allen County, Kentucky, with a total of six people in his household. The 1815 tax records listed him with 105 acres of land in the Trammel Fork watershed.

Genealogical and biographical information about George was not found either. He was not found in either court or tax records.

Williams, Langston

Private Langston Williams was in Captain William Berryman's Company in Hudspeth and Brown's Regiment for six months. He was on the rolls of the 11th Regiment (Caldwell) Kentucky Detached Militia. The detachment received marching orders on 22 April 1813 to rendezvous in Greensburg on Saturday, 1 May.

Langston was born in Spartanburg County, South Carolina, on 11 July 1772. He was the son of a Thomas Williams, a Revolutionary

War Private who served from South Carolina. There are other Allen County Williams whose ancestry traces from a Revolutionary War veteran Captain Thomas Williams from Virginia, but he is a different Thomas.

Langston came South Carolina to what was then Warren County, Kentucky, before 1797 with two land grants totaling 300 acres about four miles west of where Scottville was established eighteen years later. The land was on what is now the Franklin Road. He was said to have planted the first orchard in what became Allen County.

He was married to his first cousin Ruth McElroy in what was then Warren County on 27 December 1801. He was a farmer and built his two-roomed hewn log home on the farm. It had a cellar below it and a chimney built of rocks. That home formed the basic structure from which was expanded to become a large two-story home.

Langston died in Allen County 10 September 1840 before pensions or bounty lands were made available to the veteran militiamen. His widow survived until 30 September 1870.

Williams, Peter

Peter Williams was in the Hudspeth and Brown's Regiment in Captain William Berryman's Company on its roll call on 6 March 1813. He was also in the 11th Regiment (Caldwell) Kentucky Militia.

He was listed in Simpson County in the 1820, 1820, and 1840 censuses. He was recorded as being between 50-59 years old in 1830 and 60-70 years old in 1840 census. No genealogical information was discovered and neither were pension nor additional service records.

Williams, Ralph

Few of the widows had actual marriage certificates to submit and would have to obtain affidavits from neighbors attesting that they knew the couple had been married. Fanny Williams was an exception and presented her actual marriage certificate when she made a claim for a Widow's Pension. Most widows submitted county court clerk's affirmation of the existence of a record of the wedding. Frances (Fanny) McElroy was married to Ralph Williams on 28 September 1818 by John Howard, a "minister of the gospel." The marriage was performed in her father James McElroy's home in Allen County, Kentucky (Figure 69).

About three years earlier, Ralph Williams had become a Private in Captain William Berryman's Company, 11th Regiment (Caldwell) Kentucky Militia. He enlisted on 20 August 1813. When he was seventy-seven years old, he applied (#15946) for a Survivor's Pension. His application stated that he had served in "Shelby's campaign against the British and Indian, on the southern border of Lake Erie as a private of mounted militia guarding military posts and vessels capture by Commodore Perry." The reference was to Governor Isaac Shelby who personally led Kentuckians to and during the Battle of the Thames in Canada.

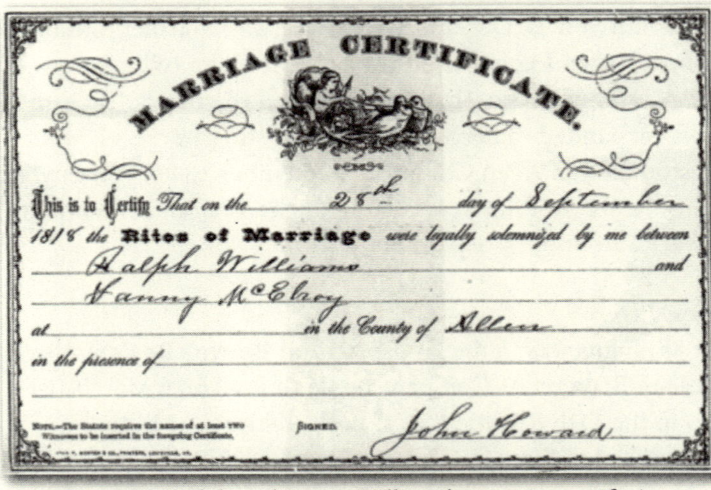

MARRIAGE CERTIFICATE.

This is to Certify That on the 28th day of September 1818 the Rites of Marriage were legally solemnized by me between Ralph Williams and Fanny McElroy at in the County of Allen in the presence of

Signed John Howard

Figure 69. Ralph and Fanny Williams' marriage certificate.

Ralph did not cross Lake Erie with that force, but fulfilled the important duty of guarding the British ships that Commodore Perry captured and brought to Put In Bay on the Ohio shore of Lake Erie. The fear was that the British, whose entire naval fleet had been captured during that famous battle, would try to recapture them. His detachment also guarded the horses left behind when the army crossed the lake (Chapter 6). After the battle, the Kentuckians came home, and Ralph was discharged at Limestone (now Maysville) on 13 November 1813. His pension was based on that service and was approved (#10056) on 19 December 1871.

After the war, Ralph moved from Allen County to Missouri. In 1817, with his war service still fresh on his mind, Ralph had a scribe write a letter for him to his brother John. The letter stated that he had been on two campaigns (sic), one to Canada [his military one] and one to the lead mines at Boon's Lick [those mines were in Missouri]. He spent one year and six months "on the water" [perhaps on ore boats] up the rivers [Lamine and Missouri Rivers in Missouri, down the Mississippi River and up the Ohio River] to the Falls of the Ohio River at Louisville, to New Orleans, and to Nashville. He concluded his letter (Figure 70) by "assigning myself your(s) till death." The scribe added that Ralph asked to hear about John's family.

Figure 70. Ralph Williams' letter written by a scribe.

Ralph subsequently returned to Allen County where he was a farmer and a blacksmith. He and Fanny lived with their children about ten miles west of Scottsville in the Butlersville community.

He submitted a claim for bounty land for his service, and was given a warrant (#35382) on 1 Nov 1853 for 80 acres in Wayne County, Illinois, under the Act of 1850. He assigned the land to patentee John Edwards. He also was given a second warrant (#39428) under the Act of 1855 on 10 September 1860 for 40 acres in Chase County, Kansas. He assigned that land to patentee Charles Medberry.

Ralph was born on 3 Nov 1793 in Spartanburg County, South Carolina, and was eighty years old when he died on 27 August 1873. He was buried in Harmony Baptist Church's cemetery in Allen County.

Fanny entered a claim (#23430) for a Widow's Pension. In her application, she admiringly remembered Ralph as a 6' 2" redhead with black eyes and a fair complexion. Her application was approved on 4 April 1879 (#22204), and she began receiving $8.00 per month thereafter delivered to the Chapel Hill Post Office. Fanny was still listed as a pensioner in 1883.

Willoughby, Solomon

Willoby was the spelling of the surname on the service record of Private Solomon Willoughby, the later spelling. Solomon was born about 1775, and became one of the early settlers in what would become Allen County, Kentucky. He arrived from North Carolina before 1799, and lived in the Trammel community of what was then Warren County. He was listed there in the 1810 census and in what had become Allen County in the 1820 census. In 1825, he was assessed tax on 150 acres in the Trammel Fork watershed, on his four horses, and on four slaves.

Solomon was a Private on the rolls of Hudspeth and Brown's Regiment of the Kentucky Militia, but was absent when they met on 6 March 1813. He was also listed on the rolls of 11th Regiment (Campbell) Kentucky Militia in Captain William Berryman's Company. There were no additional service records or any mention of a pension application. According to some genealogy records, he moved away from Kentucky sometime after the war.

Wilson, George C.

Service records showed that George C. Wilson was a Corporal in Captain Liberty Green's Company of the 3rd Regiment (Miller) Kentucky Detached Militia. Twelve others from the study area served in this regiment that saw action in the Second Battle of Tippecanoe, also called the Battle of Wild Cat Creek (Chapter 3). He was discharged at Hardinsburg, Kentucky, on 25 December 1812 and was paid $27.89 at $7.33 per month. It also noted that he was furloughed because of sickness.

George was in Allen County in the 1820 census, but no biographical or genealogical information was discovered.

Wolf, John

On 14 July 1817, John Wolf declared to the Allen County Court Clerk that he had served as an Ensign in Captain Hugh Brown's 8th Company. His rank was the equivalent of the current day Second Lieutenant. His company was in the 1st Rifle Regiment (Allen) Kentucky Mounted Volunteer Militia in a force commanded by Major General Hopkins (Chapter 3). His service records showed that he enrolled on 18 September 1812.

The uniform, such as it was, that John Wolf may have worn as a member of the 1st Regiment was described for members of another company of the regiment. It consisted of a shirt made of linsey-woolsey with slight fringe borders, and dyed either blue from indigo or a pale yellow from hickory bark. Homemade jeans and either shoes or moccasins completed the clothing. The soldiers wore a leather belt with a tomahawk stuck behind it, a strap over the shoulder to support a powder horn, a pouch for bullets also carried by a shoulder strap, and a butcher knife. Their knapsack carried other clothing and a tin cup.[60]

John applied for reimbursement for transporting three hundred pounds of baggage from the red banks of the Kentucky to the Illinois River in Indiana Territory during his deployment with Major General Hopkins. He said that the round trip was 620 miles and, at $2.00 per hundredweight for every 100 miles, he claimed $37.20. Captain Hugh Brown confirmed his service, and stated that the claim was for marching with the army and not for just a momentary incursion into enemy country.

The expiration of John' term was on 30 October 1812 at Busseron, Indiana Territory. Busseron was a settlement on the Wabash in Indiana. A Quaker Society called West Union settled there about 1800 or 1810.[61] His service record also showed that he had traveled 230 miles and returned. For that, he received $4.40 for the use of his horse and $11.69 for his pay.

John was in the Barren County census of 1810. Other details of his life could not be verified. His genealogical record was murky to say the least.

Chapter 12

Traipsing Home

Homecoming from War of 1812

Many of the frontiersmen from the Kentucky portion of the study area came back from New Orleans to a county in the study area that was not the same as the one they left. While they were gone, the new county of Allen had been created by the state legislature on 11 January 1815, just three days after the Battle of New Orleans. Its area was carved out of Warren and Barren Counties. The new county's officials appointed by the governor eventually chose a location for the county seat in a wooded area near the middle of the county. There was not even a village at that location, but the planning for one began. Things were changing.

At least, some things were changing, but the rural environment had seen little change during the soldier's absence. That study area environment was still much like what the earliest explorers and settlers found when they arrived. Most of the land was still covered with old growth deciduous forest with some small patches of tall grass prairie of bluestem, Indian grass, and tall tickseed. Oak, American chestnut, hickory, beech, and poplar were among the large trees that dominated the forest. The largest of these trees stood 100 or more feet tall forming a closed canopy that shaded the forest floor. The trees were straight with few if any limbs below thirty feet or so. Some dogwood, holly, pawpaw, or other understory trees grew in some areas beneath the canopy. The forest had little undergrowth that would impede either walking or riding.[1] The frontiersmen developed quite a skill for riding at a gallop through the forest. They became well known and admired for that most useful attribute when they went off to the war.

The earliest settlers came to the study area in the late 1700s. Their first task was to find their plot of land, and select a relatively small patch within that forest. That would become the place to plant food crops to produce sustenance for the coming year, and space in which to build a small cabin for shelter. Choosing an area without huge trees and undergrowth made the initial clearing process easier and quicker. The trees that they chose to cut could be used later to build a cabin if the logs were small. Size mattered because of the limited number of adults available to lift and move the logs.

Our mental image of that clearing is probably distorted because the initial chosen patch of forest would not have been totally cleared. When trees were cut, the area was unusable until the downed tree tops were removed, another time consuming task. Even with the downed tops removed, the stumps would remain because there was no efficient way to remove them. We have seen a forest area after the trees have been cut for lumber, and can imagine getting that area ready for planting without the aid of machines to cut or remove the tops and stumps.

There was one alternative that was used for those first few crop years. The trees could be deadened by girdling the trunk with an axed notch deep enough to sever the cambium layer. That stopped the movement of sap between the roots and canopy and killed the tree. The foliage then died and was shed. Thus the shaded area was eliminated or drastically reduced to allow sunshine to reach the planted crop. The crops were planted around and between the dead trees that were left standing.

It is probable that the farming was mostly done with a hoe at that first stage, and that the plot was a garden of sorts. It was planted using seeds of food crops that were easily transported by the settlers. The objective was to produce food, of course, but it needed to be food that would not perish quickly. It needed to be something that could be stored for use throughout the long winter, and could be replanted in the spring. Corn was one food source that best fit the requirement. Its production during the first year was critical for survival. Beans, turnips, and grains were other food options.

When the corn emerged, the settlers had to defend it from the deer, raccoons, and squirrels. The squirrels in particular were frustratingly stealthy in raiding the corn patches. There are stories about settlers who joined forces in communal hunts in a futile effort to diminish the squirrel population. The defense of the corn crop was critical for the settlers' survival, particularly during the first winter.

The establishment of a homestead was important. Henry Collins, one of the earliest settlers in Allen County, built a cabin in 1799, and tended two acres of corn for two years. That qualified him for a homestead award of 200 acres. The incentive was there to fulfill their dream of land ownership.

The dead trees were removed from the crop areas as time and effort allowed. Regardless, the size of those clear cuts increased through the years as the increased number of children in the families produced a demand for more food. That increased demand expanded even further when farm animals were introduced to the area. Farm animals introduced the need for pasture and hay. That, in turn, required more clearing of the forest.

Extensive clear cutting expanded as more and more settlers immigrated. Many of them brought slaves whose labor would have expedited the cutting.[2] The arrival of sawmills dramatically increased lumber productivity and the rate of deforestation. William and Thomas Burris built a sawmill on Trammel Creek in Allen County in 1803. Soon after, Thomas Oliver, Edward Chambers, and Frederick Carpenter each built a sawmill near creeks' mouths.[3] But, in 1812 as the war began, the cutting of trees had only just begun to take its full toll.

The population was increasing though, mostly by immigration. For example, the total population of Allen County reached 5,327 in the 1820 census. As a comparison, the population in 2010 was 19,956. The density in 1820 was about fifteen persons per square mile. The density is about fifty-seven per square mile now.

The number of households is a better statistical measurement with which to visualize just how sparsely settled the area was during and just after the war. In 1820, there were just 517 households, or 1.46 households per square mile in Allen County. It was a long way between homes and the small clearings that they occupied in the forest. In contrast, there were 7,980 households with 22.60 of them per square mile in 2010.

By the end of the nineteenth century, little remained of Kentucky's and Tennessee's old growth forests. In fact, only two small areas have escaped the saw and axe in Kentucky. Those are the 454 acre Lilley Cornett Woods with 252 acres of old growth forest southeast of Hazard, and the 2,300 acre Blanton Forest near Harlan. These two treasures contain stands of old growth trees, and give us the opportunity to see the magnificent forest just as our ancestors saw it the study area before the cutting began, and the environment was forever changed.[4]

With those two exceptions, the old growth forest is gone, and even huge individual trees are uncommon. So uncommon in fact that photographs and descriptions of many of them in Allen County were included in a recent book published by the Allen County Historical Society.[5] Large tall trees are rare now, but were very common back then.

Place Names

Place names are necessary in human activities, and are the most useful of any geographic references. Place names are included in conversations to identify the location of an area or point. Such use is common. Fishermen use names for the riffles and pools of streams. Farmers have given names to each field on their farm. These examples of place names are seldom formalized on maps, but other place names are. Most importantly, some place names persists long after the origin of the name has faded from human and historical memory.

The names given to some creeks record a bit of our history. Trammel and Drake Creeks were named for two men killed near the confluence of the two creeks during the early years of exploration. Bays Fork Creek was named for a lame bay mare left as the surveyors went home to Virginia for the winter. The following spring, she was found standing by a creek that now bears her name. Other creeks spur our imagination by their uncertain historical origin. Difficult, Long Hungry, and Pinchgut Creeks, for example, are dramatic names that may have been adopted as descriptive of an event or events. However, each of those names also existed previously in Virginia, and could have been transplanted to the frontier as a reminder of their previous homeland.

The toponymy of place names for communities is a special case worthy of our notice. Communities were established across the study area as the population increased. Many of the public schools and churches that were built decades later inherited those early names.

Community names often identified a person who was first associated with the place. The first house built by William Holland became associated with the community that developed near that location. That name Holland was later permanently preserved as the name given to a school, a post office, and a church. Gainesville was named for the storekeeper Samuel B. Gaines. Post offices formalized the names of many communities.[6] Alonzo probably got its name from Alonzo D.

Brashear who was the postmaster about 1886, and Asberry P. Meador manned the Meador post office.

Early settlers brought some community names into the area. For example, several immigrants from Halifax County, Virginia, settled in Allen County, Kentucky, and named their new community Halifax. Another example was New Roe, named for a town in Virginia.

Not much was written about the changes of the physical character of the county but there are some indications of the extent and nature of the changes in the landscape that occurred after the earliest settlers arrived. The progression of those changes was not documented. However, one can interpret what the long-term changes were using the circumstantial evidence that place names provide as surrogate documentation.

Precise attribution for the origin of some community names cannot be made. Some of them provide clues to the historical landscape at their locations. One would guess that, as the original forest was cleared away, some of those names would reflect the visual changes in the landscape that had occurred before the community or its school was named.

Oak Forest, Flat Woods, and similar names generate mental images of a forest environment. One cannot imagine those names being given to a community located in a landscape with few trees. The name must be an inference that it originated as a description of its environment.

The original forest was called a climax forest. There were smaller areas within it that were dominated by a single species most preferred by the immigrants. For example, settlers frequently preserved areas dominated by beech because the beech mast was a valuable feed source for pigs. Beech Grove would be a natural name for a community established in such an area after the surrounding forest was cut. Other names like Maple Grove, Shady Grove, and Hickory Grove leave an impression that only a small patch of woods was left from the original forest in that locale. Hickory Hill, Chestnut Point, and Walnut Hill may also indicate that they were very small forest remnants.

Mulberry and White Oak are singular names that produce images of mostly open land, but with only a prominent tree or a small cluster of one specie remaining.

Briarfield, Edgefield, Pleasant Field, Pleasant Hill, and White Plains are names that seem unlikely if a forest landscape still existed when they were named. One would surmise that the forest had been cleared in each of those areas and replaced by open fields. Cedar Hill fits into this group because cedars prefer open areas and were not found amid a forest.

Nevertheless, the truth is that most of the forest still existed when the men came home from the War of 1812. Many, perhaps most, of the current community names probably originated long after the war ended.

Transportation

The early settlers used the Wilderness Road to travel the 200 or so miles from Virginia and North Carolina through Cumberland Gap to the Bluegrass Region of Kentucky. That original road was an unimproved trail for people on foot or on horseback. It was too rough, narrow, and hilly for other means of transportation such as wagons. By 1785, the number of those emigrants leaving Virginia for the interior of Kentucky was so great that Virginia's government became alarmed at their loss of population.[7] The road was widened, and once the flow had become rapid, it would neither be slowed nor stopped. Kentucky's population growth rate was then assured. Tennessee was experiencing similar growth during that period.

Paths and trails through the forest connected the homesteads of the earliest settlers. The network of farm to market roads, as we call them, had not yet evolved. The early paths and trails became the basis for the subsequent development of that road network. Road development was a frequent topic of the county courts during the early years. The earliest efforts were to determine the route that the roads would take. Commissioners and surveyors were appointed by the county court to choose the routes. In Allen County, for example, Willis Mitchell, Sr., Bryant Hood, Samuel Willoby, and James Travis were appointed on 17 July 1826 to "view the nearest and best way of a road from Scottsville to Bowling Green" that would intersect the route being viewed by the Warren County Court from Bowling Green to the Allen County boundary. Note that this occurred eleven years after the War of 1812 ended. The commissioners were to be allowed $1.00 per day, chain carriers $0.75 per day, and the surveyor $2.50 per day. The October session of the Allen County Court accepted the report of those commissioners, appointed John Pierson to be overseer of the road to be cut.

They ordered that all the hands within two miles of the road assist the overseer in clearing and keeping the road in good repair. Those people were also required to provide the implements and equipment that were needed. In another action, the Court appointed commissioners to view a road connecting Scottsville with the Russellville Road.[8] That inferred that the destination town for that road was Russellville with no consequential town between.

The commissioners worked with the surveyors to select and designate the specific route the roads would take. The commissioners themselves did not "survey" in the modern use of the term but they were called surveyors in some documents.

One can imagine that each settler would have wanted a road to be located nearby to reap the most benefit. There can be little doubt that arbitration was a frequent role of the Commissioners. Once a route was selected, trees were cleared to allow paths at least twenty feet wide to be used as roads that would facilitate Allen County commerce. The original dirt roads were not artificially surfaced. That improvement would not occur until many years later with some dirt roads still in use in the study area after World War II.

The scale of an 1828 map of Kentucky precluded showing all but the major arteries of the counties. The map showed the villages at the ends of the roads with a smooth curved line between them. The line is purely representational. There was no attempt, indeed no capability, to show the actual meandering of the roads. This map, in today's map language, might be considered to be a cartogram (Figure 71). Cartograms show routes as straight or smoothly curved lines even though the actual routes were not straight.[9]

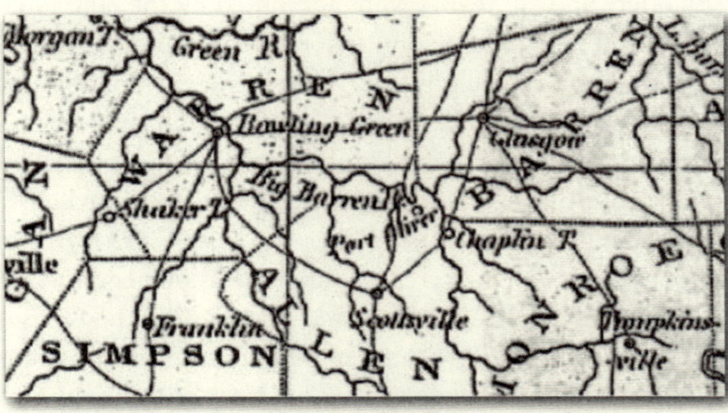

Figure 71. Adapted from Young and Dellerer Map of Kentucky 1828.

Even as a cartogram, the map shows the major routes out from Scottsville in directions that one would expect. One road led southward from Scottsville generally following the present US 231. Another road led northward crossing Barren River near Chaplin Town in Barren County. That village was where the old road crossed Peters Creek, a route similar to the current US 31E route toward Glasgow. There was a road leading northward to near Port Oliver and another northwestward toward Bowling Green that passed near Allen Springs. That road was described in January 1873 as being nothing but mud.[10]

Continuing actions by the county courts eventually produced an extensive farm to market road network in the study area counties. The creation of Macon County in Tennessee in 1842, and its county seat of Lafayette, accelerated the construction of roads in that rural area. But it took a long time everywhere and most of it after the War of 1812.

Settlements

Few settlements had been established in the study area before the War of 1812 began. Port Oliver and New Roe were the tiny Kentucky villages that existed when the soldiers marched off to war. Port Oliver was located at a ford across Barren River at a point then called Cow's Ford, named for the tracks of buffalo where they came for salt. Few roads existed throughout the study area because few villages existed to be connected. Development of villages in northern Sumner County occurred later. Macon County was not formed until 1842 with Lafayette created as its county seat.

When the last battle of the war ended in January 1815, the plans for creating the county seat of Scottsville had not yet been presented to the newly formed Allen County Court. Those plans to create a town in the midst of the forested center of the county were presented to the new court in April 1815, three months after the Battle of New Orleans.[11]

Beginning in early April 1815, the soldiers began traipsing up the trace toward home. They began arriving in May. Some arrived in a new county of Allen, but they would not have a county seat until 22 January 1816 when property was bought from John and Catherine Brown for a new town.[12] The sale of the town lots provided money for the construction of a log courthouse in the middle of the planned city of Scottsville.

Communication

During the War of 1812, Allen County had no rapid means of communicating, neither internally nor externally. Virtually all news and information had to be passed by word of mouth, a slow and often undependable way to spreading the word as the parlor game called "Gossip" dramatically illustrates. In that game, the first person is given a written paragraph to commit to memory. The information is whispered to the next person in line. Each of the persons in turn repeats the process by repeating what they have been told to the next person inline. The last person in the line then speaks the story, and the original information is read aloud. The comparison of the two reveals that the story has been unintentionally, but significantly altered as it was repeated. The same results appear even when it is not a game, but a retelling of the news that reached the frontier.

Immigrants were coming into the county more frequently, and in greater numbers with each passing year. Each brought news of events learned en route or at their previous home location. One can imagine that they were warmly welcomed, and that their audience was attentive and interested. Among the news they brought would have been information about the actions of Great Britain, and the reactions of the United States.

There had been postal service long before our independence as a nation, and our Constitution explicitly authorized a postal service for our new nation. Article I, Section 8, Clause 7 of the United States Constitution, known as the postal clause or the postal power, empowered Congress "to establish Post Offices and post Roads." When the War of 1812 began, post offices in Kentucky and Tennessee were few in number, and widely dispersed. The nearest post offices to the study area had been established in Bowling Green in 1802, and in Glasgow and Gallatin in 1803. Scottsville did not have one because the town did not yet exist. Macon County's first post office was in 1842 when it was carved out of Smith County. Carthage, after 1807, was one of the nearest post offices to that area. Most frontiersmen were illiterate, and probably were not greatly impacted by the lack of postal service. That would change when the veterans became eligible for bounty land and pensions for their War of 1812 service.

Soldiers returning from the War of 1812 had to use one of those post offices for at least a year after the Battle of New Orleans. On 13

January 1816, Daniel M. Jones was appointed as the first postmaster in Scottville (note the spelling), becoming the first in the entire Allen County as well. One can imagine that one primary qualification for the postmasters was the ability to read and write.

Just nine days later, he signed as a witness to the deed from John and Catherine Brown to the trustees conveying the 100 acres of land on which Scottville would be built. On 10 February 1816, Jones bought six lots in the newly laid out town plat for the intended town of Scottville for $100.75.[13] His lots were located on what is now Cemetery Street, three blocks north of Main Street. His Post Office was listed as Allen Court House or Scottsville. The spelling of the post office's name with an "s" in the middle of it persisted thereafter as the town's official name.[14] Jones became the director of the Allen Seminary that was incorporated on 31 January 1817 in Scottsville. He subsequently became a member of the Kentucky House of Representatives.[15]

Boundaries

One of the most important people in the first government of the United States was Thomas Hutchins. He was appointed Geographer of the United States in May 1781. His first and most important responsibility was for surveying the State boundaries, and from that, to calculate the land area of the United States and its Western Territories.[16] Among his many contributions to cartography was a map he drew on 18 June 1766 of the Falls of the Ohio where Louisville is located now.[17] Using rivers such as the Ohio was a preferred way to identify boundaries between two states or two counties. In those cases, rivers made the boundaries visible to all travelers and settlers. On the other hand, invisible boundaries have the potential for creating problems for both travelers and residents.

One such invisible boundary presented problems during the research of the study area in the frontier during the War of 1812. It was a boundary that was in dispute between Kentucky and Tennessee. The state line followed 36° 30' north latitude as had been decreed in charter by King Charles II on 30 June 1655. That boundary had existed throughout colonial days to mark the southern border of the Virginia. The line continued in use when Virginia and North Carolina joined the United States as new states. In 1779, those two states agreed to extend and mark that boundary westward to the Tennessee River.

Virginia and North Carolina each appointed surveyors to a team in 1799 to survey their border, mark it, and extend it to the Tennessee River. The area north of that extended line was part of Virginia. The area south of that line was part of North Carolina. Virginian Thomas Walker headed the combined team and was assisted by William B. Smith from North Carolina. The line that was surveyed became known as the Walker Line.

The newly surveyed boundary line was intended to visibly mark 36° 30' north latitude without altering it. However, it did not turn out to do that. Instead, as the survey teams worked their way westward from the beginning point, their surveyed line continually deflected toward the north, and was about nine miles north of the 36° 30' parallel where it crossed the Cumberland River.[18] The cause of an erratic, but continual error in the survey has not been explained. The deflection was similar to what would have resulted if magnetic north had been used instead of true north. For example, the magnetic declination in 1800 at a point on the state line due south of Bowling Green was about 6° 5'.[19] That declination would vary little from that number, but the error would have been consistent, not erratic, as the survey moved westward. Therefore, that seems not to have been the cause, but the actual cause is unknown.

Whatever the cause of the surveying error, everyone agreed that the Walker line had angled north of where it should have been. A serious dispute developed about what to do about the land between the intended boundary line of 36° 30' and the Walker line.

Kentucky wanted the disputed land to be returned to Kentucky because that was the original intent. It declared that it would be illogical to change the intent rather than to correct the error. Kentucky demanded that the 36° 30' line be used. Kentucky argued that King James of Great Britain had prescribed that line on 23 May 1609 before King Charles used it in a charter in 1655. After being used for almost two hundred years, it should not be changed to accommodate an admitted surveying error. The intended line had been legally reaffirmed several times over the intervening years. Kentucky asked that, if the error had accumulated southward instead of northward, would Tennessee have consented to abide with it? It asserted that the intended line could only be changed by an agreement between the two states involved, Kentucky and Tennessee. Specifically, it could not be resolved by the ancestral states of Virginia and North Carolina.

Tennessee agreed that the Walker Line was the result of surveying errors, but insisted it did not matter that the line was in error. It was the legal, recognized, and marked boundary and had been such for years. In Tennessee's view, any change to it would unnecessarily disrupt the lives of the citizens of that area.

Residents of the disputed area had accepted the line as surveyed by Walker to identify the state in which they were located. That had been the case after Kentucky became a state in 1792 and Tennessee in 1796. There was no reason for the residents, either Kentuckians or the Tennesseans, to question the validity of the survey, and they had lived with the surveyed boundary for at least fifteen years. They were, by then, accustomed to its location, and saw little reason to change it.

Indeed, no decision was made until after the War of 1812, but the problems remained. When a volunteer from the disputed territory wanted to enroll in a state militia, in which state's militia did he join? When he filed for a pension, was he a Kentucky pensioner or a Tennessee one? When the soldier's postal address was New Roe, Kentucky, could he have been living in the disputed area? Which state has court records? Where did the citizens vote? When genealogists find a birth record from the disputed area, which state do they choose?

It is apparent that the citizens of the area of disputation were not confused about where they lived, but it is still confusing when a researcher looks back from two hundred years later. The disputed area is shown in Figure 72 as being bounded by the current state line (dashed line) and the original state line (solid line). Oak Grove, Westmoreland, and Lafayette were in the disputed area.

Kentucky and Tennessee compromised in 1820, five years after the end of the War of 1812. The Walker Line was accepted and affirmed, but the 36° 30' line would be retained as the southern boundary of the Jackson Purchase.[20] The states' issues were settled by a legal agreement.

The disputed area remains as a potential problem for historians and genealogists in another way. That is true because of a second group of boundary changes that occurred, those of the boundaries between counties within each of the two states. Changes that occurred in those boundaries were not the result of surveying errors of disputed territories nor did they result from some nefarious intent of politicians. Rather, as the settlement of the frontier continued and the population increased and dispersed, the size of the counties was altered to accommodate the growth. As the population increased, the size of the counties decreased to make travel to the county seats more convenient.

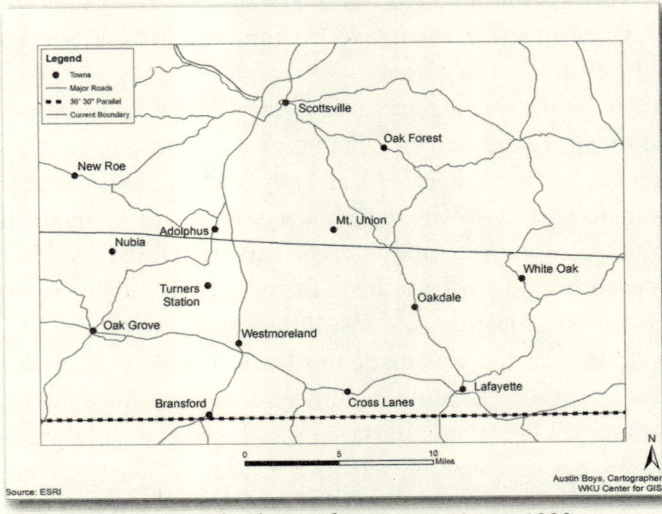

Figure 72. The disputed territory prior to 1820.

County boundaries had changed several times over the years. At the end of the Revolutionary War, Kentucky County, Virginia, encompassed all of the current state of Kentucky except for the Chickasaw Lands that were later added as the Jackson Purchase.

By 1780, Jefferson, Fayette, and Lincoln Counties had replaced Kentucky County. The south central area of what became the state of Kentucky in 1792 was in Lincoln County. Lincoln was subsequently divided into Logan and Green in 1792, and those, in turn, were subdivided into the counties of Warren in 1796 and Barren in 1798. Allen County was not formed until 1815, shortly after the War of 1812 ended. Therefore, soldiers from what is now Allen County appeared as residents of either Warren or Barren Counties during the war. Simpson County was created in 1819, and Monroe County was added in 1820.

Washington County, North Carolina, encompassed most of Tennessee at the close of the Revolutionary War. From it, Davidson County and two others were formed in 1783. Sumner County was formed from the eastern portion of Davidson by 1786, and the eastern portion of it became Smith County in 1799. Jackson County was subtracted from Smith County in 1801. Macon County was not formed until 1842, long after the War of 1812 ended. Therefore, soldiers from what is now Macon County appeared in the records as residents of Sumner, Smith, or Jackson Counties.

By 1812, the border counties used in this study were Barren and Warren in Kentucky, and Sumner, Smith, and Jackson in Tennessee. The southern parts of those Kentucky counties and the northern parts of those Tennessee counties were in the disputed area south of the Walker Line in the study area.

Historians and genealogists are still faced with problems because of the uncertainty as to which of the county governments an individual would use to record deeds, probate wills, pay taxes, or enlist in the militia. The safest assumption is that the residents of the disputed area would probably have believed that Tennessee was their home state. The Kentucky and Tennessee counties, and the disputed area as they appeared in 1812, are shown in Figure 73.

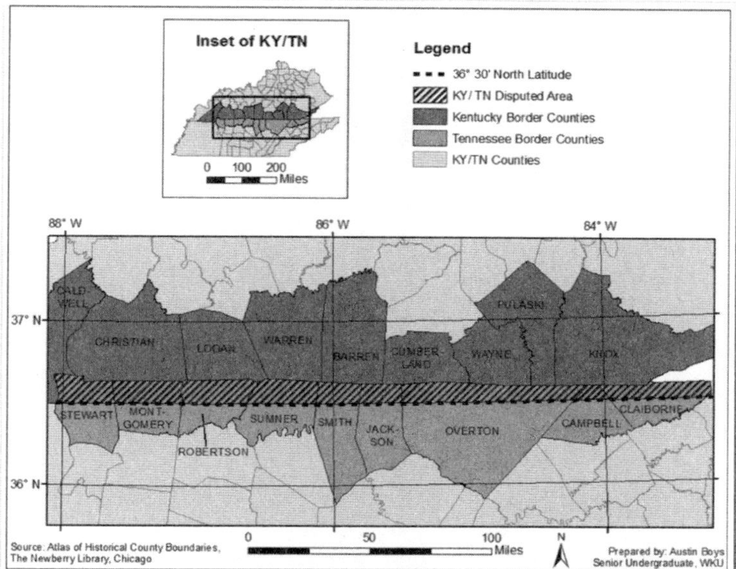

Figure 73. Kentucky and Tennessee counties in 1812.

The second boundary problem resulted from the formation of new counties after the War of 1812 ended. For example, Allen County, Kentucky, was created in April 1815. It was carved out of Warren and Barren Counties. The question that researchers confront was which areas of the new Allen County had been in Warren County and which in Barren County? No maps were available to answer that question.

The answer was found in the legislation that created Barren County from Warren and Green Counties. The southern portion of the new Barren County subsequently was taken to form Allen County. The boundary between Warren and Barren Counties was described as running due south from the junction of Skegg's Creek and Big Barren River to the Tennessee state line.

That north-south line was plotted on a current map of Allen County as a solid vertical line (Figure 74). The area east of that line was ancestral Barren County and the area west was ancestral Warren County. It also shows the subsequent boundaries with Monroe and Simpson Counties.

Figure 74 also depicts the streams in Allen County, none of which had bridges in 1812. Instead, there were fords, places where a stream was shallow enough to allow crossing with wagons. As bridges replaced fords, the names of dozens of them were lost. Essentially, wherever there is now a bridge, there once was a nearby ford that attracted the early roads. Travel was not easy on the frontier before bridges.

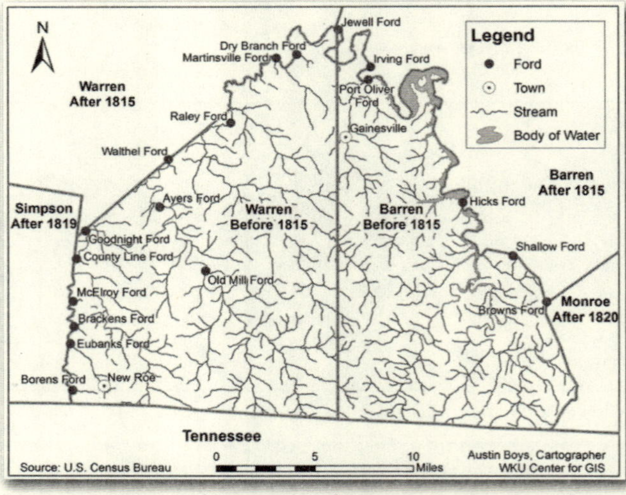

Figure 74. Ancestral Warren and Barren County Boundaries.

The Tennessee county boundaries within the study area changed for the last time when Macon County was formed. The streams in the Tennessee areas did not have bridges either during the War of 1812. The fords in those counties controlled the location of the roads, and the existing roads controlled the location of the bridges.

Chapter 13

A Matter of Color

Frontiersmen Remembered

It is probable that a mental image of an 1812 frontiersman is of a white man. That image is accurate if it was a frontiersman who became a soldier from the study area during that war. However, it is not accurate if the color of all frontiersmen is considered. For example, about thirteen percent of the frontiersmen were enslaved African Americans in the 1820 census of Allen County, Kentucky, a common proportion within the study area. Only two of those African American men were freedmen of service age. Wilson Bass had been their owner before they were freed.[1] However, their status as legally emancipated freedmen did not permit them to become soldiers because federal law prohibited all African Americans from serving in either the United States army or in any state militia, including Kentucky's. That prohibition persisted until 1863 when President Abraham Lincoln authorized the enlistment of African Americans into the armed forces of our country.

The prohibition against African American enlistment began on 8 May 1792 when the U.S. congress passed the Militia Act of 1792. The first section of the law stated the eligibility to serve in the army or militia.

> *That each and every free able-bodied white male citizen of the respective States, resident therein, who is or shall be of age of eighteen years, and under the age of forty-five years ... shall severally and respectively be enrolled in the militia ...within twelve months after the passing of this Act.*

The law specifically restricted enrollments to white and free men only, thereby excluding African Americans from service in any of the state militias.[2]

That exclusion affected a very large portion of Americans. In 1812, about one of every five Americans was a slave. The very existence of such proportion explained the attitude of whites toward them. In particular, slavery was not voluntary, and slave owners had to forcibly restrain slaves who sought to gain even a modicum of free will. The enrollment of slaves into the army would have removed the slave from his owner, moved him to a distant place, armed him, and provided him with an opportunity to taste freedom. Not only would they have learned how and why whites treasured freedom, they would have been taught how to fight for it. They would have learned that, in combat, whites and blacks were equals, and had to be so to assure success. For all those reasons, equality was an abhorrent thought to pro-slavery people.

Slave owners considered slaves to be property. As such, they were bought, traded, and sold at the whim of the white owner. Unlike other properties, these would escape if given the opportunity, and evade capture for as long as they could. Many fled to nearby states that recognized runaway African Americans as freedmen. To the slave owner, those freedmen were property, and should be returned to the legal owner. To avoid recapture and involuntary removal back to the slave owner, some runaway slaves assumed the identity of a freedman even if they had not been legally granted that status.

The specter of a large number of armed slaves returning after the war was frightening to the citizens of states with large slave populations. The fear was that the returning soldiers would foment trouble and start major insurrections among those still enslaved. That fear was probably most intense in counties were slaves far outnumbered white citizens. Also, part of that fear was that those veterans might return as freedmen, and present an economic challenge as well.

The precedence for the exclusion of African Americans from the army was established during the Revolutionary War. In the beginning of that war, freedmen had a significant role in the military actions. British soldiers in Boston in 1770 killed five men who became recognized as the first men to die in the fight for independence. Crispus Attucks, a runaway slave, was one of them.[3] Hundreds of freedmen joined after the minutemen who were organized to become the American Army, The numbers increased when 100 acres of land was proffered for enlistment to freedmen who had little hope to own land otherwise. African American minutemen were at the first battle at Lexington, and subsequently fought at Bunker Hill too.[4] Among the soldiers who fought valiantly at Bunker Hill was Salem Poor, an African American. He had earned enough money to buy his own freedom from his owner in 1769. He became famous for his bravery and his actions under fire during that battle.

On 10 July 1775, General George Washington issued orders prohibiting African Americans from serving in the Continental Army. Historians have not reached a consensus on his reason for that decision. On 31 December 1775, he partially reversed that decision for reasons still unclear, and authorized the retention of those already serving in the state militias.[5] It may have been just too complicated to construct an order that would expel men already in service without destroying the integrity of the units in which they served. The prohibition of new enlistees was left unclear.

Presidents Washington, Jefferson, Madison, and Monroe owned slaves with the first two owning large numbers of slaves. John Adams was the exception among our first five presidents. He had no slaves. Indeed, he spoke powerfully in opposition to slavery, and was one of a minority to do so. If the commander in chief was a slave owner, one could hardly have expected a drive for equality in the army. That was the case for most of the years before the War of 1812.

Some states took the stand that the federal government did not have the authority to dictate the makeup of state militias. Rhode Island, as an example, passed a law that allowed "... every able-bodied Negro, Mulatto, or Indian man slave in this State, may enlist..." and that upon enlistment be immediately "... absolutely FREE, as though he had never been encumbered with any kind of servitude or slavery."[6]

Southern congressmen objected to African Americans serving in the army. On 26 September 1775, Edward Rutledge of South Carolina moved in the Colonial Congress that all Negroes be discharged from the army. His proposal was voted down. But in October there was a meeting, with General Washington present, that discussed the issue and the committee agreed that Negroes should not be enlisted. Washington wrote his view.

> *It has been represented to me that the free Negroes who have served in this army are very much dissatisfied at being discarded. As it is to be apprehended that they may see employment in the Ministerial Army I have presumed to depart from the resolution*

respecting them and have given license for their being enlisted. If this disapproved by Congress, I will put a stop to it.

Congress responded by passing a resolution "That free negroes, who had served faithfully in the army at Cambridge, may be re-enlisted therein, but no other." In effect, those already enlisted could stay but no more could be enlisted.[7] In 1792, Congress formalized the continued prohibition of enlistment of African Americans from enlisting in the army.

There had never been a prohibition of enlistments of African Americans into the navy and congress did not expand the prohibition to apply to them. Freedmen and slaves benefited from that oversight and joined the navy. They had manned any and all types of jobs in the navy without restrictions before the War of 1812 began. The navy was small in the number of ships, and there were a disproportionately high number of African American sailors. Commodore Isaac Chauncey wrote to Oliver Hazard Perry about them.

> *I have yet to learn that the color of the skin, or the cut and trimmings of the coast, can effect a man's qualifications or usefulness. I have nearly fifty blacks on board this ship, and many of them are among my best men…attentive and obedient, and, as far as I can judge, many of them excellent seamen…*

African Americans enlisted in the navy and eventually accounted for about ten to twenty percent of American ships' crews.[8] African Americans were also recognized as excellent sailors on the privateer ships during the war.

At least 130 white Kentuckians served alongside the African American sailors who served on Perry's fleet of ships. Those Kentucky riflemen were sharpshooters assigned by General Harrison to serve with Perry to add a new dimension to Perry's options.[9] Perry sent them climbing up the ships' riggings to a vantage point that looked down on the decks of the British warships. During the battle that ensued on Lake Erie, they carefully picked off British soldiers who attempted to fire the ship's guns. Their accuracy was so good that the gunners on those ships were reluctant to try to reach their guns. The Kentuckians won the admiration of Perry, and one could surmise that the African

American sailors also won the admiration of the Kentuckians. There was ample opportunity for each to see the bravery of the other during that intense, bloody, and victorious battle.

There was one outrageous event in 1807 that led ultimately and directly to the declaration of war in 1812. One of the major confrontational issues between Britain and the United States was the continued capture and impressment of American sailors to serve on British ships. The British stopped the USS *Chesapeake* and demanded that they be allowed to board the ship and search for deserters. The American captain refused this ruse used to impress sailors into service aboard British ships, and to assert their dominance over the seas. After a short battle, the British boarded the ship and carried off three of the Chesapeake's sailors claiming that they were escaped British sailors. All three were African Americans. The United States was outraged by the incident and deplored the imprisonment of its citizens. The term "citizens" used in the complaint recognized the African Americans as equal to other citizens. But, equality was not applied to the men in the army and the militia.

Most of the states read the 1792 law as banning the enrollment of African Americans in state militias. Peculiarly, there were three exceptions, and all three were in the south. Georgia and South Carolina enrolled them as laborers or musicians. North Carolina enrolled them to bear arms. The US Army and Marine Corps held to the prohibition line. The US Navy did not because they found it difficult to get volunteers for shipboard duty with its long cruises, corporal discipline, dangerous work, and bad food. They enrolled native-born free African Americans to serve in naval ships or in privateers.[10]

African Americans served our country well in the Navy, in the militias that allowed them, and in Jackson's army at New Orleans. Their service was not rewarded with opportunities to serve in the military after the war was over. In 1820, the War Department affirmed that no Negro or Mulatto would be admitted into the service.[11]

James Madison's view was expressed in 1780, long before he became president, that enrollment was acceptable if it was done with white officers and a majority of white soldiers. There were no African American officers during the War of 1812, but Andrew Jackson made a small concession in choosing sergeants to the New Orleans Militia Battalion of Free Men of Color. "On enrolling yourselves in companies the Major-General commanding will select officers for your government from your white fellow-citizens. Your non-commissioned officers will be appointed from yourself."[12] This attitude for the necessity of white officers persisted even during the Civil War when over 185,000 African Americans, of which 23,703 were black Kentuckians, served in the Army of the United States. Their appointed officers were white.

President Harry S. Truman signed Executive Order #9981 that totally abolished racial segregation in the armed services on 26 July 1948. He directed that there would be guaranteed equal treatment and opportunity for all armed forces personnel without regard to race, color, religion or national origin.[13] As Commander in Chief, he did not need the approval of Congress, the state governments, or the military itself to do what was right. With his signature at the bottom of a page, he ended the inequality that had legally existed in the American military for over 170 years, their entire history in fact.

The integration of the military forces was orderly and systematic, done in defined increments, and fully completed before the Korean War began in 1950. During the next fourteen years, hundreds of thousands of men and women served in fully integrated units where people who were created as equals were treated equally. Integration was accomplished without the need for sit-ins, demonstrations, marches, or rancor. The veterans left service with personal experience, and certain knowledge that skin color did not matter.

EXECUTIVE ORDER 9981

Establishing the President's Committee on Equality of Treatment and Opportunity In the Armed Forces.

WHEREAS *it is essential that there be maintained in the armed services of the United States the highest standards of democracy, with equality of treatment and opportunity for all those who serve in our country's defense:*

NOW THEREFORE*, by virtue of the authority vested in me as President of the United States, by the Constitution and the statutes of the United States, and as Commander in Chief of the armed services, it is hereby ordered as follows:*

1. It is hereby declared to be the policy of the President that there shall be equality of treatment and opportunity for all persons in the armed services without regard to race, color, religion or national origin. This policy shall be put into effect as rapidly as possible, having due regard to the time required to effectuate any necessary changes without impairing efficiency or morale.

2. There shall be created in the National Military Establishment an advisory committee to be known as the President's Committee on Equality of Treatment and Opportunity in the Armed Services, which shall be composed of seven members to be designated by the President.

3. The Committee is authorized on behalf of the President to examine into the rules, procedures and practices of the Armed Services in order to determine in what respect such rules, procedures and practices may be altered or improved with a view to carrying out the policy of this order. The Committee shall confer and advise the Secretary of Defense, the Secretary of the Army, the Secretary of the Navy, and the Secretary of the Air Force, and shall make such recommendations to the President and to said Secretaries as in the judgment of the Committee will effectuate the policy hereof.

4. All executive departments and agencies of the Federal Government are authorized and directed to cooperate with the Committee in its work, and to furnish the Committee such information or the services of such persons as the Committee may require in the performance of its duties.

5. When requested by the Committee to do so, persons in the armed services or in any of the executive departments and agencies of the Federal Government shall testify before the Committee and shall make available for use of the Committee such documents and other information as the Committee may require.

6. The Committee shall continue to exist until such time as the President shall terminate its existence by Executive order.

Harry Truman
The White House July 26, 1948

The Civil Rights Act of 1964 decreed equality for civilians as President Truman did for the military sixteen years earlier. President Truman and the military had shown the way.

Chapter 14

The Afterglow

Frontiersmen Remembered

Virtually every Kentuckian and Tennessean between the ages of eighteen and forty-five was a member of their state's militia in 1812. There were 25,010 Kentuckians[1] and comparable number of Tennesseans who served on active duty during the war. The frontiersmen brought home a trove of personal stories about their service. Most of the details of those stories were ephemeral, and have not survived through the subsequent years. Nonetheless, I am left with a deep appreciation for their selfless acts that began when they left the frontier at the behest by our country to assert our rights as an independent nation.

It is clear that there was widespread public support for the war for a time after the war ended. That is evident in the naming of nineteen Kentucky counties after soldiers who served in the War of 1812. Those soldiers were John Adair, John Allen, Bland Ballard, Green Clay, John Edmonson, Benjamin Franklin Graves, Nathaniel G. S. Hart, Paschal Hickman, Samuel Hopkins, Andrew Jackson, Richard M. Johnson, Virgil McCracken, Alney McLean, James Meade, Thomas Metcalfe, Oliver Hazard Perry, Zebulon M. Pike, Isaac Shelby, and John Simpson.

In Tennessee, there are eighteen counties with names from War of 1812 veterans: Edward Bradley, David Benton, Newton Cannon, William Carroll, Robert I. Chester, William Cocke, John Coffee, Stephen Decatur, Robert Henry Dyer, John H. Gibson, Thomas Jones Hardeman, James Henderson, Andrew Jackson, James Lauderdale, William Moore, Oliver Hazard Perry, Winfield Scott, and Isaac Shelby.

It is interesting that both states have counties named for Jackson, Perry, and Shelby. It is even more interesting that the War of 1812 is now largely forgotten in the two states that between them have thirty-seven counties with soldiers' names.

The Romans learned in ancient times that the best way to prevent war was to be ready for one. That required a sizable standing army, trained and combat ready, for a war that was not imminent. It would seem that the total of over a half million men who served in the war compared to the roughly 6,000 men who were in the army in 1811, made that case for the need for a larger standing Army. But, it had not. The Army did not maintain its strength and the state militias soon lost much of their mission, manning, and training.

The disassembly of the standing armed forces began as soon as the War of 1812 ended just as it had at the end of the Revolutionary War. The army had only 11,000 in the regular army when Jefferson Davis became Secretary of War of the United States in 1853. He recognized that number was too small, and gained authority to increase it to 15,000. After he was sworn in as President of the Confederate States of America, he faced the standing army of the United States with a total of about 16,000 men, an army of his own making. To put that very small number into proper perspective, the Union army later had 23,055 casualties in the Battle of Gettysburg alone.

Before the Civil War was over, over two million men had served in the Union Army, less than one percent of them were regular Army men when the war began. There were 364,511 Union soldiers killed in that war, eighteen percent of the two million who served. Apparently, the relationship between those two percentages was either unrecognized or ignored. The disassembly of the standing armed forces began again as soon as the Civil War ended just as it had after the War of 1812. That has been repeated after each war since. Most notably, World War I and II began with a dire need for a rapid buildup of men and equipment.

There was a disassembly of the army after the Korean War truce in 1953. In 1964, as the deployment of armed forces to Vietnam began early in that war, I saw a sign there that paraphrased Winston Churchill's famous Battle of Britain quote. It read, "We have done so much with so little for so long, we now can do everything with nothing." Soldiers at the beginning of each of our wars may have agreed with that scalding sarcasm, each war began with an undermanned and inadequately equipped Army. Some lessons are not learned well.

Still, Americans admired the men who served in the War of 1812. A Tennessean, Andrew Jackson of the Battle of New Orleans fame, was elected president. A Kentuckian, Richard Johnson of the Battle of the Thames fame, was elected vice-president to Martin Van Buren. Many others found political success at state and local levels. Most of the frontiersmen did not become politicians, but meld back into the population to resume their lives of struggle to make a home on the frontier.

Why do we know so little about the War of 1812, beyond a vague knowledge of the Battle of New Orleans? Perhaps the Civil War that came forty-six years later was so horrific that the War of 1812 paled in comparison, and thus replaced it in our memories. We all remember General Sherman's quote that "War is Hell," an apt description. Fewer remember what Andrew Jackson said just before the Battle of New Orleans, "When our intellect fails us, we have to become heroes."[2] Our frontiersmen had to become heroes in what some now call the forgotten war.

To each of the soldiers in this study, war with its hell was very personal even though their activities were collectively experienced with their comrades. The individual did not yearn to become a hero, but wanted beyond all else to perform well. His comrades and his country depended on him. The war was real and personal to each individual soldier. His decisions and actions under fire had immediate consequences. He knew the correctness or error of a decision within minutes or hours after making it. He remembered each challenge that he and his comrades faced, and took pride in what they accomplished.

When a soldier recalls a war, his memories are a collection of specific and detailed experiences. Each is accompanied with vivid images of individuals, sights, and sounds. Veterans infrequently talk of their experiences because their recall is of specific details. It is very difficult for them to subdue the emotion of that recall, and to discuss battles or the war in general and dispassionate terms.

Civilians, on the other hand, can discuss a war in abstract, academic, or philosophic terms without being diverted by specific detailed memories. They can develop generalized opinions about the nature of a war, and gradually adjust them as that opinion reshapes and evolves. Those opinions are honed to perfection during each discussion or argument until they can be asserted with an absolute certainty that is comparable to divined truth. They can then become a true believer, as Eric Hoffer defined them in 1951.[3] They can join with others who accept that truth to form mass movements that try to convince non-believers to alter their views of the perceived truth.

Conversations between soldier and civilian are not usually matters of right or wrong, although both may assert that belief. Rather, both are about opinions formed from almost totally opposite viewpoints: the soldier's specific recall and the civilian's general knowledge.

The collective actions of the soldiers identified in this study are summarized and generalized to tell their history. In the generalization process, history obfuscates the experiences of an individual — his hardships, deprivations, fears, and worries. From that unraveling of specifics, generalizations can be formulated.

I have come to know each of the individuals mentioned in this study. They have become my friends. I am so proud of their service, their individual achievements, and patriotism. The War of 1812 in general may again fade in our memory, but I hope the memory of these frontiersmen may include some specifics of their service.

Endnotes

Chapter 1

[1]Hickey, Donald R. 2012. *The War of 1812, A Forgotten Conflict*. Urbana IL. University of Illinois Press.

[2]Herring, James and James B. Longacre. 1836. *National Portrait Gallery of Distinguished Americans.* New York. Vol. III, American Academy of Fine Arts. Hermon Bancroft.

[3]*Federalist No. 46*. 1937. New York. Modern Library.

[4]Hart, Gary. 2005. *James Monroe: The American Presidents Series, The 5th President, 1817-1825.* New York. Times Books, Henry Holt and Company.

[5]Cusick, James G. 2007. *The Other War of 1812: The Patriot War and the American Invasion of Spanish East Florida.* Athens, GA. University of Georgia Press.

[6]Hickey, Donald R. 2012. *The War of 1812, A Forgotten Conflict.* Urbana, IL. University of Illinois Press.

[7]Lindegren, Alina M. 1922. "*A History Of The Land Bonus Of The War Of 1812.*" M.A. thesis. University of Wisconsin, Madison.

[8]*Militia Act of 2 May 1792.* United States Statutes at Large, Volume 1, United States Congress, Public Acts of the Second Congress, 1st Session, Chapter 28.

[9]Heider, David A. 2010. *Henry Clay: The Essential American.* Random House.

[10]*Militia Act of 8 May 1792.* United States Statutes at Large, Volume 1, United States Congress, Public Acts of the Second Congress, 1st Session, Chapter 33.

[11]Ibid.

[12]Clift, G. Glenn. 1957. *The "Corn Stalk" Militia Of Kentucky, 1792-1811.* Frankfort, KY. Kentucky Historical Society.

[13]Buchanan, John, 2001. *Jackson's Way: Andrew Jackson And The People Of The Western Waters.* New York John Wiley and Sons.

[14]See note 7.

Chapter 2

[1]Edmunds, R. David. 1983. *The Shawnee Prophet.* Lincoln, NE. University of Nebraska Press.

[2]Gilpin, Alec R., 2012. *The War of 1812 in the Old Northwest.* East Lansing, MI. Michigan State University Press.

[3]Hickey, Donald R. 2012. *The War of 1812, a Conflict Forgotten.* Urbana, IL. University of Illinois Press.

[4]Library of Congress. Prints & Photographs Division, (LOCIDIgitalID=3a0008079u).

[5]Bird, Harrison. 1971. *War for the West, 1790-1813.* New York. Oxford University Press.

[6]Ibid.

[7]Drake, Benjamin. 1852. *Life of Tecumseh and His Brother the Prophet: with a Historical Sketch of the Showanoe Indians.* Cincinnati, OH. Appelgate & Company.

[8]See note 2.

[9]See note 3.

[10]Tipton, John. 1811. *John Tipton's Tippecanoe Journal.* Published in the Indiana Magazine of History 2, No. 4, December 1906.

[11]Niles, William O. 1840. *The Tippecanoe Text-book.* Baltimore, MD. Cushing & Brother.

[12]Beard Reed. 1911. *The Battle of Tippecanoe.* Chicago. W. B. Conkey Company.

[13]See note 2.

[14]Hammack Jr., James W. 1976. *Kentucky & the Second American Revolution the War of 1812.* Lexington, KY. The University Press of Kentucky.

[15]See note 3.

[16]Reilly, Robin, 1974. *The British at the Gates.* New York. G. F. Putnam's Sons.

Chapter 3

[1]Gilpin, Alec R. 2012. *The War of 1812 in the Old Northwest.* East Lansing, MI. Michigan State University Press.

[2]Beirne, Francis F. 1945. *The War of 1812.* New York. E. C. Dutton and Company.

[3]Berton, Pierre. 1988. *Flames Across the Border 1813-1814.* Ontario, Canada. Penguin Books.

[4]Ibid.

[5]Clarke, Samuel C. 1893. *Memoir of General William Hull.* David Clap & Son, Boston.

[6]Bird, Harrison. 1971. War for the West, 1790-1813. Oxford University Press, New York.

[7]Clarke, Samuel C. 1893. *Memoir of General William Hull.* Boston. David Clap & Sons.

[8]Hammack Jr., James W. 1976. *Kentucky & the Second American Revolution: The War of 1812.* Lexington, KY. University Press of Kentucky.

[9]Bird, Harrison. 1971. *War for the West, 1790-1813.* New York. Oxford University Press.

[10]McAfee, Robert B. 1816. *History of the Late War in the Western Country.* Bowling Green, OH. Historical Publishing Company.

[11]See note 8.

[12]See note 2.

[13]Philpott, Don. 2012. *The U.S. Navy Pictorial History of the War of 1812.* Lanham, MD. Rowman & Littlefield.

[14]Horton, Louise. 1975. *In the Hills of the Pennyroyal.* Austin, TX. Capital Printing Company.

[15]Lossing, Benson J. 1868. *Pictorial Field Book of the War of 1812.* New York. Harper & Brothers.

[16]Allison, Harold. 1986. The Tragic Saga of the Indiana Indians. Paducah, KY. Turner Publishing Company.

[17]Attributed to Pierre La Plante of Vincennes, see note 15.

[18]Hickey, Donald R. 2012. *The War of 1812, a Conflict Forgotten.* Urbana, IL. University of Illinois Press.

[19]See note 6.

[20]Young, Henderson Y. 1903. *The Battle of the Thames, in which Kentuckians Defeated the British, French, and Indians, October 5, 1813.* Louisville, KY. J. P. Morton and Company, Filson Club. Reprinted by General Books, Memphis, Tennessee, 2010.

[21]See note 1.

[22]Mahon, John K. 1972. *The War of 1812.* Gainesville, FL. University of Florida Press.

[23]Skeen, C. Edward. 1999. *Citizen soldiers in the War of 1812.* Lexington, KY. University Press of Kentucky.

[24]See note 8.

[25]See note 10.

[26]Hitsman, J. Mackay. 1965. *The Incredible War of 1812*. Toronto. University of Toronto Press.

[27]See note 18.

[28]See note 8.

[29]Indiana Historical Commission, 1922. *Governors, Messages and Letters*. Indianapolis, IN. Logan Esarey, Editor. W. M. Buford for State Printing and Binding.

[30]See note 10.

Chapter 4

[1]Sumner, William G. 1980. *Andrew Jackson*. New York. Chelsea House.

[2]Remini, Robert V. 1966. *Andrew Jackson*. New York. Harper & Row Publishers.

[3]Gildart, Robert C. 1999. *Natchez Trace: Two Centuries of Travel*. Helena, MT. American and World Geographic Publisher.

[4]Remini, Robert V. 1969. *Andrew Jackson*. New York. Harper & Row Publishers.

[5]O'Brien, Sean M. 2005. *In Bitterness and in Tears: Andrew Jackson's Destruction of the Creeks and Seminoles*. Guilford, CT. Lyons Press.

[6]Davis, William C. 1995. *A Way Through the Wilderness: The Natchez Trace and the Civilization of the Southern Frontier*. New York. Harper Collins.

[7]Haynes, Robert. 2010. *The Mississippi Territory and the Southwest Frontier 1795-1817*. Lexington, KY. University Press of Kentucky.

[8]Beirne, Francis F. 1945. *The War of 1812*. New York. E. F. Dutton and Company.

[9]Remini, Robert V. 2008. *Andrew Jackson*. New York. Palgrave McMillin.

[10]Rogan, Michael P. 1975. *Fathers & Children: Andrew Jackson and the Subjugation of the American Indian*. New York. Random House of Canada.

[11]Reilly, Robin. 2003. *The British at the Gates*. Toronto. Robin Brass Studio.

[12]Langguth, A. J. 2006. *Union 1812: The Americans Who Fought the Second War of Independence*. New York. Simon & Schuster.

[13]Hanning, Bud, 2012. *The War of 1812: a Complete Chronology*. Jefferson, NC. McFarland & Company.

Chapter 5

[1]Halbert, Henry S. and Timothy H. Ball. 1895. *The Creek War of 1813 -1814*. Chicago. Donohue & Henneberry.

[2]Reilly, Robin. 2003. *The British at the Gates*. Toronto. Robin Brass Studio.

[3]Remini, Robert V. 2001. *The Battle of New Orleans*. New York. Viking Penguin, Penguin Putnam, Inc.

[4]Hickey, Donald R. 2012. *The War of 1812, a Forgotten Conflict*. Urbana, IL. University of Illinois Press.

[5]Ibid.

[6]Beirne, Francis F. 1945. *The War of 1812*. New York. E. F. Dutton and Company.

[7]Southerland Jr., Henry D. and Jerry E. Brown. 1989. *The Federal Road through Georgia, the Creek Nation, and Alabama 1806-1836*. Tuscaloosa, AL. The University of Alabama Press.

[8]Love, William A. 1910. *Jackson's Military Road*. Publications of the Mississippi Historical Society, Vol. XI, by Franklin L. Riley, University Mississippi.

[9]Owsley, Frank L. Jr., 1981. *Struggle for the Gulf Borderlands: The Creek War and the battle of New Orleans, 1812-1815*. Tuscaloosa, Alabama. University Alabama Press.

[10]See note 6.

[11]See note 2.

[12]See note 4.

[13]See note 9.

[14]Halbert, H. S. and T. H. Ball. 1895. *The Creek War of 1813 and 1814*. Tuscaloosa, AL. University of Alabama Press.

[15]Etling, John R. 1988. *Trail of Tears: The Rise and fall of the Cherokee Nation*. New York. Doubleday.

[16]See note 6.

[17]See note 2.

[18]Rogin, Michael P. 1975. *Fathers and Children, Andrew Jackson and the Subjugation of the American Indian*. New York. Vintage Books, Random House.

[19]See note 2.

[20]See note 6.

[21]See note 9.

[22]Heidler, David S. 2004. *Encyclopedia of the War of 1812.* Annapolis, MD. Naval Institute Press.

[23]Remini, Robert V. 2008. *Andrew Jackson.* New York. Palgrave McMillen.

[24]See note 2.

[25]See note 4.

[26]Sumner, William G. 1980. *Andrew Jackson.* New York. Chelsea House.

[27]See note 3.

[28]See note 4.

[29]Ibid.

[30]Arrowood, C. F. 1926. *The Journal of Capt Isaac L. Baker.* Denton, TX. The Southwest Historical Quarterly, Vol. 30. Texas State Historical Association. University of North Texas.

[31]Latour, Arsene L. 1999. *Historical Memoir of the War in West Florida and Louisiana in 1814-1815.* Gainesville, FL. The Historic New Orleans Collection and the University Press of Florida. Originally published in 1816, John Conrad and Company, J. Maxwell Printer, Philadelphia.

Chapter 6

[1]Indiana Historical Commission. 1922. *Governors, Messages and Letters.* Indianapolis, IN. Logan Esarey, Editor. W. M. Buford for State Printing and Binding.

[2]Young, Bennett H., 1903. *The Battle of the Thames, in which Kentuckians Defeated the British, French, and Indians, October 5, 1813.* Louisville, KY. J. P. Morton and Company, Filson Club. Reprinted by General Books, Memphis, TN 2010.

[3]Ibid.

[4]Daugham, George C. 2011. 1812. *The Navy's War.* New York. Basic Books.

[5]Hammack Jr., James W. 1976. *Kentucky & the Second American Revolution.* Lexington, KY. The University Press of Kentucky.

[6]Ibid.

[7]McAfee, Robert B. 1816. *History of the Late War.* Bowling Green, OH. Historical Publishing Company.

[8]Berton, Pierre. 1988. *Flames Across the Border 1813-1814.* Ontario. Penguin Books.

[9]Beirne, Francis F. 1949. *The War of 1812.* New York. E. F. Dutton's Company.

[10]Hitman, J. McKay. 1965. *The Incredible War of 1812.* Toronto. University of Toronto Press.

[11]Gilpin, Alec R. 2012. *The War of 1812 in the Old Northwest.* East Lansing, MI. Michigan State University Press.

[12]Mahon, John K. 1972. *The War of 1812.* Gainesville, FL. University of Florida Press.

[13]Caselman, Alexander C. 1902. *Richardson's War of 1812.* Toronto. Historical Publishing Company.

[14]Lossing, Benson J. 1869. *Pictorial Field-book of the War of 1812.* New York. Harper & Brothers.

[15]See note 2.

[16]See note 13.

[17]See note 9.

[18]See note 12.

[19]See note 10.

[20]See note 7.

[21]See note 2.

[22]Quisenberry, Anderson C. 1969. *Kentucky in the War of 1812.* Baltimore, MD. Kentucky Historical Society. Clearfield Publisher.

[23]Sympson, James. 1813. *Diary and Memoranda of the Thames Campaign.* Included in Quisenberry's *Kentucky in the War of 1812*, Kentucky Historical Society, Clearfield Publisher, 1969, Baltimore.

[24]Howe, Henry, 1902. *Historical Collections of Ohio in Two Volumes.* Cincinnati, OH. State of Ohio, Volume. C. J. Krehbiel & Company.

[25]Evans, Nelson W. and Emmons B. Stivers. 1900. *A History of Adams County, Ohio from its Earliest Settlement to the Present Time.* West Union, OH. E. B. Stivers, publisher.

[26]Clift, G. Glen. 1979. *History of Maysville and Mason County.* Evansville, IN. Unigraphic, Inc.

[27]Ibid.

[28]Clark, Thomas D., 1979. *Historic Maps of Kentucky.* Lexington, KY. University Press of Kentucky.

[29]Quisenberry, Anderson C. 1969. *Kentucky in the War of 1812.* Baltimore, MD. Kentucky Historical Society, Clearfield Publisher.

Chapter 7

[1]Butler, Stuart. 2011. *A Guide to Virginia Militia Units in the War of 1812.* Athens, GA. New Paprys Publishing.

[2]Skeen, C. Edward. 1999. *Citizen Soldiers in the War of 1812.* Lexington, KY. University Press of Kentucky.

[3]Langguth, A. J. 2006. *Union 1812: The Americans Who Fought the Second War of Independence.* New York. Simon & Schuster.

[4]Tsouras, Peter G., 2005. *The Book of Military Quotations.* St Paul, MN. Zenith Press. Page 26.

[5]Berton, Pierre. 1988. *Flames Across the Border 1813-1814.* Ontario. Penguin Press.

[6]See note 2.

[7]See note 3.

[8]Reilly, Robin. 2003. *The British at the Gates.* Toronto. Robin Brass Studio.

[9]Ibid.

[10]Stagg, J. C. A. 2012. *The War of 1812: Conflict for a Continent.* New York. Cambridge University Press.

[11]Elting, John R. 1995. *Amateur, to Arms! A Military History of the War of 1812.* New York. Da Capo Press.

Chapter 8

[1]Reilly, Robin. 2003. *The British at the Gates.* Toronto. Robin Brass Studio.

[2]Brooks, Charles B. 1961. *The Siege of New Orleans.* Seattle, WA. University of Washington Press.

[3]Hammack Jr., James W. 1976. *Kentucky & the Second American Revolution.* Lexington, KY. The University Press of Kentucky.

[4]Quisenberry, Anderson C. 1915. *Kentucky in the War of 1812.* Frankfort, KY. Kentucky State Historical Society.

[5]Cable, George W. 2000. *The Creoles of Louisiana.* Gretna, LA. Pelican.

[6]Remini, Robert V. 1999. *The Battle of New Orleans.* New York. Penguin Putman, Inc.

[7]Von Clausewitz, Carl. 1874. *On War.* Translated edition by Michael Howard and Peter Paret. Princeton, NJ. Princeton University Press.

[8]Owsley Jr., Frank L. 1981. *Struggle for the Gulf Borderlands, the Creek War and the Battle of New Orleans, 1812-1815.* Tuscaloosa, AL. University Alabama Press.

[9]See note 1.

[10]Latour, Arsène L. 1816. *Historical Memoir of the War in West Florida and Louisiana in 1814-15.* Expanded edition edited by Gene A. Smith, published in 1999. Gainesville, FL. University Press of Florida.

[11]Beirne, Francis F. 1945. *The War of 1812.* New York. E. F. Dutton and Company.

[12]See note 10.

[13]See note 2.

[14]Quoted in note 1.

[15]Arthur, Stanley C. 1915. *The Battle of New Orleans.* New Orleans, LA. Louisiana Historical Society.

[16]Remini, Robert V. 1966. *Andrew Jackson.* New York. Perennial Library, Harper & Row.

[17]See note 3.

[18]Skeen, C. Edward. 1999. Citizen *Soldiers in the War of 1812.* Lexington, KY. University Press of Kentucky.

[19]Gilbert, Ed. 2008. *Frontier Militiaman in the War of 1812.* New York. Osprey Publishing Ltd.

[20]See note 10.

[21]Quisenberry, Anderson C., 1969. *Kentucky in the War of 1812.* Baltimore, MD. Kentucky Historical Society, Genealogical Publishing Company.

[22]See note 8.

[23]See note 4.

[24]See note 10.

[25]See note 2.

[26]Hickey, Donald R. 2012. *The War of 1812; A Forgotten Conflict.* Urbana, IL. University of Illinois Press.

[27]See note 15.

[28]Reilly, Robin, 2003. *The British at the Gates.* Robin Brass Studio, Toronto, Ontario.

[29]Ibid.

[30]Owsley Jr., Frank L., 1981. *Struggle for the Gulf Borderlands, the Creek War and the Battle of New Orleans, 1812-1815.* University Alabama Press.

[31]See note 15.

[32]See note 2.

[33]See note 26.

[34]See note 16.

[35]Smith, Zackary F. 1904. *The Battle of New Orleans.* Louisville, KY. The Filson Club Publications No. 19. John P. Morton & Company Printers.

[36]See note 1.

[37]Gildart, Robert C. 1996. *Natchez Trace: Two Centuries of Travel.* Helena, MT. American and World Geographic Publisher.

[38]See note 21.

Chapter 9

[1]Act Apr 24, 1816, 3 Stat. L., 296, c. 67, Sec 1.

[2]Clark, Robert L., Lee A. Craig, and Jack W. Wilson. 2003. *Public Sector Pensions in the United States.* Philadelphia. University of Pennsylvania Press.

[3]Act Jun 3, 1858, 11 Stat. L., 309, Sec 1656, R. S.

[4]Act Jun 3, 1858, 11 Stat. L., 309, Sec 4725, R. S.

[5]Glasson, Henry. 1916. *Laws of the United States Governing the Granting of Army and Navy Pensions, Compiled Under the Direction of the Commissioner of Pensions.* Washington Government Printing Office.

[6]Act 4 Feb 1862, 12 Stat. L., 337.

[7]Act Mar 9 1878, 20 Stat. L., 27 and 28, Sec 1.

[8]See note 2.

Chapter 10

[1]2 U. U. Stat 669, Dec. 24, 1811.

[2]Gates, Paul W. 1968. *History of Public Land Law Development.* Washington, D.C. Public Land Law Review Commission.

[3]Linklater, Andro. 2002. *Measuring America: How the United States was Shaped by the Greatest Land Sale in History.* London. Harper Collins Publishers.

[4]Longley, Paul A., et al. 2001. *Geographic Information Systems and Science.* Chichester, NY. John Wiley & Sons.

[5]National Archives and Records Administration. 1971. *War of 1812 Military Land Warrants 1815-1858.* Washington. National Archives Microfilm Publications, General Services Administration.

[6]2 U.S. Stat. 669, 24 December 1811.

[7]2 U.S. Stat. 671, 11 January 1812.

[8]9 U.S. Stat. 520, 28 September 1850.

[9]Curtis, Frank B. and William H. Webster. 1885. *Digest of Laws of the United States: Governing the Granting of Army and Navy Pensions and Bounty-land Warrants.* Washington. Pension Bureau, U.S. Department of the Interior, Government Printing Office.

[10]2 U.S. Stat. 669, 24 December 1811.

[11]Lindegren, Alina M. 1922. *A History of the Land Bonus of the War of 1812.* Thesis (M.A.) University of Wisconsin-Madison.

[12] 9 U.S. Statutes 520-521, 28 September 1850.

[13]*Samuel Kirby Pension Files.* Washington D.C. War of 1812, U.S. National Archives and Records Administration.

[14]Morrow, Mary F. 1993. *Indian Bounty Land Applications.* College Park, MD. Prologue Vol. 25 No. 3, National Archives and Records Administration.

[15]Bureau of Land Management URL http://glorecords.blm.gov/search/default.aspx?

[16]4 U.S. Statutes 190-191, 22 May 1826.

[17]U.S. Census Bureau URL last visited 17 Oct 2012. http://www.census.gov/dmd/www/resapport/states/illinois.pdf

[18]Rose, Christine. 2011. *Military Bounty Land 1776-1855.* San Jose, CA. CR Publications. Printed by Thomson Shore Inc, Dexter, MI.

[19]Military Bounty Land at the Ancestry URL last visited 17 Oct 2012. http://www.ancestry.com/wiki/index.php?title=Military Bound Land

Chapter 11

[1]Rowland, Dunbar and H. Grady Howell. 1908. *Official and Statistical Register of the State of Mississippi.* Volume 2, Mississippi Department of Archives and History. Reprint by Reprint Company, Spartanburg SC, 1988.

[2]Heitman, Francis B. 1903. *Historical Register and Dictionary of the United States Army*. Washington. Volume 1, Government Printing Office.

[3]Smith, Jonathan K. T. 2003. *Genealogical Abstracts from Reported Deaths in the Southwestern Christian Advocate 1838-1846.* Southwestern Christian Advocate. History of Methodism in Kentucky.

[4]Pickles, Tom. 1993. *New Orleans 1815: Andrew Jackson Crushes the British*. London. Osprey.

[5]Washington County, VA. *Marriage Register 1782-1820. Virginia Colonial Abstracts*, Vol. 34.

[6]Allen County Historical Society. 2004. *Allen County Kentucky Family History*. Paducah, KY. Turner Publishing Company.

[7]Brooks, Charles B. 1961. *The Siege of New Orleans.* Seattle. University of Washington Press.

[8]Ohio Historical Society. Historical Marker 1-6. Accessed 16 November 2012 http://www.remarkableohio.org/Index.aspx

[9]Horton, Louise. 1975. *In the Hills of the Pennyroyal: A History of Allen County, Kentucky from 1815 to 1880.* Austin, TX. Capital Printing Company.

[10]The Citizen-Times. Scottsville, KY. 12 October 1972, page 7.

[11]*List of Pensioners on the Roll, January 1*, Vol 5. 1883.Washington, D.C. Government Printing Office.

[12]See note 6.

[13]Gardner, Jeanetta S. 1999. Allen County Kentucky Tax record. Colliersville, TN. Published by the author.

[14]Jackson, Martha, 1992. *Allen County Day Book, 1826 – 1837.* Scottsville, KY. Published by the author.

[15]Holmes, Oliver Wendell. 1858. *The Deacon's Masterpiece or the Wonderful One-horse Shay*. New York. Republished in 1965 by McGraw-Hill.

[16]Ancestry.com. *Kentucky, Death Records, 1852-1953* [database online]. Provo, UT, USA: Ancestry.com. Operations Inc, 2007.

[17]Ancestry.com. Accessed 27 Dec 2012. http://trees.ancestry.com/tree/12337205/person/-284757260?ssrc=

[18]Skeen, Carl E. 1999. *Citizen Soldiers in the War of 1812.* Lexington, KY. University Press of Kentucky.

[19]Ancestry.com. Accessed 31 Dec 2012. http://trees.ancestry.com/tree/23337295/person/1390390281

[20]39th Infantry Muster Roll, United States Army, May 14 1814. Accessed 3 January 2013 http://www.nps.gov/hobe/upload/39infantry.pdf

[21]Tucker, Spenser, el al. 2012. *The Encyclopedia of the War of 1812: a Political, Social, and Military History.* Santa Barbara, CA. ABC-CLIO.

[22]Connelley, William E. 1922. *History of Kentucky*. Chicago. American Historical Society.

[23]See note 9.

[24]*U.S. Federal Census Mortality Schedules.* 1850-1885, District 218, Simpson County, Kentucky. For year ending 31 May 1880.

[25]See note 9.

[26]See note 6.

[27]See note 13.

[28]See note 6.

[29]Allen County Historical Society. 2004. *Allen County Kentucky Family History*. Scottsville, KY. Photo from page 239.

[30]Smith, Zachary F. 1904. *The Battle of New Orleans*. Louisville, KY. The Filson Club, John P. Morton & Co.

[31]See note 9.

[32]Lossing, Benson J. 1869. *Pictorial Field Book of the War of 1812*. Somersworth, NH. Harper Brothers, Franklin Square. Reprinted in 1976 by New Hampshire Publishing Company.

[33]Bennett, David C. 2009. *A New Perspective on the Last Days of Fort Madison*. Journal of the War of 1812, 1201, Parts 12-1 spring, 12-2 summer, and 12-3 fall.

[34]See note 30.

[35]Urwin, Gregory J. W. 2003. *The United States Cavalry: an Illustrated History, 1776-1944*. Norman, OK. University of Oklahoma Press.

[36]See note 7.

[37]See note 6.

[38]*Allen County Wills and Settlements*. Accessed 31 Dec 2012.http://www.allencountyky.com/database/will/index.html

[39]Bowling Green Democrat, 16 January 1873. *An Old-time Letter about an Old-time Man Written Years Ago.*

[40]See note 14.

[41]Photo from URL. Accessed on 26 April 2013. http://ancestry.com/tree/12157834/person/-149648686?pgNum=1

[42]Smith, Jonathan K. T. 2003. *Genealogical Abstracts from Reported Deaths in the Southwestern Christian Advocate 1838-1846*. Nashville, TN. Page 51, 5 May 1859.

[43]See note 20.

[44]Battle, J. H., Perrin, William H., and Kniffin, G. C., 1885. *Kentucky, A History of the State*. Louisville, KY. 3rd Edition, F. A. Battey Publisher.

[45]The Kentucky Researcher. Vol. 1, No. 2, December 1962. West Jordan, UT. Allstates Research Company.

[46]Allen County Historical Society. 1985. *A Pictorial History of Allen County Kentucky*. Scottsville, KY. Gerald Printing.

[47]Arrowood, C. F. 1927. *The Journal of Capt Isaac L. Baker*. Southwestern Historical Quarterly. Volume 030, No. 4, pages 272-282.

[48]Bauer, K. Jack. 1993. *Zackary Taylor: Soldier, Planter, Statesman of the old Southwest.* Baton Rouge, LA. Louisiana State University Press.

[49]See note 6.

[50]Conner, Glen. 2010. *Til Freedom Came.* Morley, MO. Acclaim Press.

[51]See note 44.

[52]Dodd, Jordan. 1997. *Kentucky Marriages 1802-1850*, on-line database. Provo, Utah. Ancestry.com. Operations Inc.

[53]Photo fromURL. Accessed 19 January 2013. http://www.ourtennesseefamilytree.com/linked/pelidge%20spencer%20swindle.pdf

[54]*Deed Book B.* Office of the Allen County Court Clerk, Scottsville, KY. Entries dated 1 October 1816.

[55]Ancestry.com. 2004. *U.S. Army, Register of Enlistments, 1796-1914* (database on line) Provo, Utah.

[56]Rising, Marsha E. 2004. *Genealogical Gems from Early Missouri Deeds, 1815-1850.* Westminster, MD. Heritage Books.

[57]See note 6.

[58]Butler, Stuart L. 1988. *A Guide to Virginia Militia Units in the War of 1812.* Athens, GA. Iberian Publishing Company.

[59]Woods, Edgar. 1901. Albemarle County in Virginia. Charlottesville, VA. The Mitchie Company.

[60]2nd Regiment Volunteer Infantry URL. Accessed 8 March 2013. http://www.2ndkentucky1812.com/uniforms-equipment/

[61]Morrow, Josiah. 1883. *The History of Brown County Ohio.* Salem, MA. Reprinted by the Higgison Book Company.

Chapter 12

[1]Braun, E. Lucy. 1950. *Deciduous forests of eastern North America.* New York. Blakiston.

[2]Conner, Glen. 2010. *'Til Freedom Came: Slaves in Allen County Kentucky, 1815-1865.* Morley, MO. Acclaim Press.

[3]Horton, Louise. 1975. *In the Hills of the Pennyroyal.* Austin, TX. Capital Printing Company.

[4]Martin, William H. 1975. *The Lilley Cornett Woods: a Stable Mixed Mesophytic Forest in Kentucky.* Bot. Gaz. 136(2): 171-183. The University of Chicago.

[5]Reynolds, Bobby, Arles Weaver, Larry Gerald, and Glen Conner. 2008. *Big trees of Allen County, Kentucky.* Scottsville, KY. Allen County Historical Society.

[6]Rennick, Robert M. 1984. *Kentucky Place Names.* Lexington, KY. The University Press of Kentucky.

[7]Connelley, William E. and E. M. Coulter. 1922. *History of Kentucky.* Chicago. Vol. I, Chapter XXV. The American Historical Society.

[8]Jackson, Martha. 1992. *Allen County Day Book 1826 -1837.* Scottsville, KY. Published by the author.

[9]Cuff, David J. and Mark T. Mattson. 1982. *Thematic Maps their Design and Production.* New York. Methuen & Company.

[10]Bowling Green Democrat, 16 January 1873. An Old-time Letter About an Old-time Man Written Years Ago.

[11]Allen County Homemakers Association. 1992. Back home in Allen County. Published by the authors, Scottsville, Kentucky.

[12]Allen County Historical Society, 1985. Scottsville, KY. *The Beginning: a Pictorial History of Allen County, Kentucky.* Gerald Printing.

[13]Tabor, Sharon. 2002. *Abstracts, Deed Book B, 1815-1819, Allen County Court Records.* Accessed 2 Aug 2012. http://www.allencountyky.com/database/land/BookBDeedspg1-49.htm

[14]See note 12.

[15]Ibid.

[16]Guide to the National Archives of the United States. Supt of Docs No.:GS 4.6/2:N21. U.S. Government Printing Office. Washington. 1974. Page 34, Part I, Records of the Continental and Confederation Congresses (Numbered Series), 1774-89.

[17]Thomas Hutchins, Frederick Hicks, and Patrick Henry, 1778. *A topological description of Virginia, Pennsylvania, Maryland, and North Carolina.* Reprint in 1904 by the Burrows Brothers Company, Cleveland, Ohio.

[18]Sames, James W. III, 1871. *Four steps west.* Published by its author, Versailles, KY.

[19]National Geophysical Data Center, Magnetic Field Calculator. Accessed 18 Aug 2012. http://www.ngdc.noaa.gov/geomag-web/#ushistoric.

[20]The Jackson Purchase was acquired in 1818 by treaty between the Chickasaw Indians and the United States represented by Governors Isaac Shelby of Kentucky and Andrew Jackson of Tennessee.

Chapter 13

[1]Conner, Glen. 2010. *'Til Freedom Came: Slaves in Allen County, Kentucky 1815-1865.* Morley, MO. Acclaim Press.

[2]The Militia Act of 1792, passed May 8, 1792, provided federal standards for the organization of the Militia.

[3]Nell, William C. 1852. *Services of colored Americans in the Wars of 1776 and 1812*. Boston. Prentiss and Sawyer.

[4]Chadwick, Bruce. 2007. *The first American Army: the untold story of George Washington and the men behind America's first fight for freedom*. Naperville, IL. Sourcebooks.

[5]Charles, Patrick. 2005. *Washington's decision: the story of George Washington's decision to reaccept black enlistments in the Continental Army, December 31, 1775*. North Charleston, SC. Book Surge.

[6]Baird, Henry C. 1863. *General Washington and General Jackson, on negro soldiers*. Philadelphia. Henry Carey Baird.

[7]Wilson, Joseph T. 1890. *The black phalanx: African American soldiers in the War of Independence, the War of 1812, and the Civil War*. Hartford, CT. American Publishing Company.

[8]Alt, William E and Betty S. Alt, 2002. *Black soldiers, white wars: black warriors from antiquity to the present*. Westport, CT. Praeger Publishers.

[9]Draughan, George C. 2011. *1812, The navy's war*. New York. Basic Books.

[10]Nalty, Bernard C. 1986. *Strength for the fight: a history of black Americans in the military*. New York. Free Press.

[11]Clinton, Catherine, 2000. *The black soldier: 1492 to the present*. New York. Houghton Mifflin Company.

[12]Reddick, L.D. 1949. *The negro policy of the United States Army, 1775-1945*. Journal of Negro History 34:9-29.

[13]Ansel, Colonel Raymond. 1990. *From segregation to desegregation: blacks in the U.S. army 1703-1954*. Thesis, U.S. Army War College. Carlisle Barracks, PA.

Chapter 14

[1]Quisenberry, Anderson C. 1915. *Kentucky in the War of 1812*. Frankfort, KY. Kentucky Historical Society.

[2]Brooks, Charles. 1961. *The Siege of New Orleans*. Seattle WA. University of Washington Press.

[3]Hoffer, Eric, 2002. *The True Believer: Thoughts on the Nature of Mass Movements*. New York. Harper & Brothers.

About the Author

Glen Conner notes that he has had "three careers" in his lifetime. His first career was in the U.S. Air Force, which included a Vietnam tour. He retired as a Colonel after 23 years, and soon began his second career when he joined the faculty in the Department of Geography and Geology at Western Kentucky University (WKU). For the next 24 years he taught meteorology and physical geography and was the State Climatologist for Kentucky.

Following his tenure at WKU, Glen began his third career as a writer beginning with his first book, *'Til Freedom Came*, for which he received a publication award for 2011 from The Kentucky Historical Society.

He is a member of his local Historical Society, researches historical records, compiles data, and writes about what intrigues him. His interest in the War of 1812 began during his time in the U.S. Air Force.

Index

H

I

J

N

O

P

Q

R

S

T

U

V

W

Y

Z